WITH BAGS AND SWAGS

AROUND AUSTRALIA IN THE FORTIES

For Jean —

Happy memories!

Wendy

WITH BAGS AND SWAGS

AROUND AUSTRALIA IN THE FORTIES

by

WENDY LAW SUART

Wendy Suart

Maps by Peter Suart
Illustrations by Malika Favre

DINGO BOOKS

First published in the United Kingdom by Dingo Books 2008
© Wendy Law Suart

ISBN 978-0-9556038-1-5

By the same author:
The Lingering Eye - Recollections of North Borneo
Golden Morning - An Australian Childhood
A Mem's Memoirs - Colonial Swan Songs

Printed by Dragon Print, Bordon, Hampshire

To the wonderful people of Australia
with gratitude

My thanks go to my six wonderful children for their contributions and support.

I also thank the Department of Information, Australia, for the photographs taken by H Dacre Stubbs

Every effort has been made to trace all the copyright holders.
The author would be pleased to rectify any omissions.

BIBLIOGRAPHY

My Tropic Isle - E. J. Banfield
E. J. Banfield - Margaret R. Bonnin
North Queensland Lullaby - Lucille Quinlan
Leisure - W. H. Davies
Famous Australians - Faith Linton
The Scarce Australians - John Yeomans
History of Australia - Manning Clark, Meredith Hooper
The Drum - Sidney J. Baker
The Magic Pudding - Norman Lindsay

.......Bunyip Bluegum decided to leave home without more ado.

The trouble was that he couldn't make up his mind whether to be a Traveller or a Swagman. You can't go about the world being nothing, but if you are a traveller you have to carry a bag, while if you are a swagman you have to carry a swag, and the question is: 'Which is the heavier?'

The Magic Pudding ... Norman Lindsay

CONTENTS

PRE-AMBLE

It really all started with the Commonwealth Bank. Although, later on, when people asked what made us start, we used to chant glibly 'Love-of-travel-and-thirst-for-adventure'. But it was the Commonwealth Bank that settled it...for me anyway. Not that my name was among those written in the book of gold; nineteen-year-old secretaries on £3 a week don't usually become captains of industry after the manner of newsboys. But the Commonwealth Bank stood in Collins Street and in 1945 it was comparatively new and its modern form was clothed in a coat of spotless cream paint.

1945 was a restless year. The end of the war might have meant homecoming and settling down for thousands of servicemen and women but it also meant the liberation of civilians. Those of us who grew up during the war years could not remember anything but restrictions and rationing. We yearned to taste the life that our elders spoke of...the gay, amazingly cheap pre-war days when one could do anything and go where one wished. If one really wanted to travel, a passage home to England could be bought for about £50. To go abroad was what we all wanted to do of course, for what Australian does not hear the call of distant lands? But during the war overseas trips were out and even interstate journeys were impossible. Rail travel was forbidden and no one had enough petrol to go by car. (Or if he did, he was soon picked up by the border police and asked why).

Two friends and I had solved the problem by taking to bicycles and already we had combed the Dandenong and Plenty Ranges in long weekends, done a four-day trip along the Great Ocean road to Lorne, another to Phillip Island, pushed out west to the Grampians and east to the Gippsland Lakes and, becoming more ambitious with each trip, had talked our parents into letting us ride to Adelaide in our annual leave. Despite their dire predictions of disaster on the Coorong, that desolate waterless ninety-mile strip of salt marsh, the trip had been a wonderful success. We were jubilant and looked about for fresher fields. But how could we find more distant ones in the meagre fortnight of leave due to us each year?

'It's maddening!' Shirl fumed. 'To think that I slave for fifty weeks a year just so I can do what I want to for the other two.'

Shirley Duncan and I had been at school together and had both worked as laboratory assistants at the Alfred Hospital until I left to seek a more artistic environment. Although she was a little older than I, we got on well together, sharing an interest in adventure and nonconformity so I too felt rebellious. And that's where the Commonwealth Bank came in.

The office of 3KZ Broadcasting Company where I worked was situated at the back of a city building in Melbourne and my window overlooked a squalid lane leading into a courtyard where wagons came to deliver goods. The great draught horses stood patiently, jingling their harness and snuffling in their chaff bags. The air reeked of manure, beer, confectionery and the numberless other scents of the city. On wet days the rain slanted into the courtyard and ran off the grey slate roofs in a dismal stream. It all seemed strangely silent out there in that dull, grey world while inside the office there were fierce lights, bright chatter and the incessant clacking of typewriters. All the incredible hurly-burly of the world of radio.

-oOo-

In the days before television, radio was king. It was vital during the war years, our source of information and entertainment. Programmes were usually transmitted live with all the nail-biting excitement that entailed. It was hugely important for bolstering the morale of the population (Community Singing was very popular) and quiz shows, classical music recitals, the weekly Hit Parade and interviews with famous visitors filled the air waves. My boss, Norman Banks, was king of Australian radio. He was a highly intelligent and versatile man with a vibrant personality. He compèred classical music programmes but also broadcast the three-hour Saturday night dance programme. He was an able quiz master and introduced the first phone-quiz to Melbourne. He was the best football commentator and yet could conduct the religious *Hymns of Prayer and Praise* programme. He also instigated the first day-long Charity Appeal in Melbourne and really made 3KZ the Brighter Broadcasting Service. Norm's greatest achievement however was the conception of *Carols by Candlelight*, breathtaking in its simplicity, and the idea spread across Australia and then across the world. It is a fitting memorial to Norman Banks.

It was exciting working for Norm and he gave me lots of opportunities to progress. But the love of travel was always gnawing away inside me. It was bad enough being confined in the office in the blazing days of summer or the wet and windy, bone-chilling days of winter. In spring though, those incomparable days that Melbourne can stage so well, I used to become restless. To waste such peerless weather was criminal. Outside, the air was crisp and thin and golden like Ringegolde. The sky was cloudless and deep blue. Flower stalls along the street loosed heavenly breaths of boronia, violets, freesias and daphne. Lunchtime crowds idled in patches of sunshine and all colour became vibrant. Looking out of my window across the courtyard below I could see the Commonwealth Bank which soared up into the sky, cream against blue, a world apart from the grey slate roofs and stone walls surrounding it. I longed to find some country or climate where the sky was always that shimmering blue, where there were clean white buildings, warmth and colour. To me, it symbolized the tropics and already I was dream-sick for Queensland and the far north.

So on the memorable day when we heard that Japan had capitulated and the war was over, I rang Shirley and, trying to make myself heard over the pandemonium in the office and the deafening cheers outside, asked her if she were ready.

'Ready...for what?'

'The war's over Dunc. I'm handing in my resignation. What about you?'

An incredulous shriek shrilled through the earpiece.

'Do you mean it Wen?'

'Of course. It's what we've been waiting for. Europe's still in a mess but we could go to Queensland for a few months. Look...I've got a map here. Oh gosh, to think we can go anywhere.....'

'What about Sharpey, do you think she'll be in it?'

Margaret Sharpe had also been at the Alfred Hospital and had accompanied us on our earlier trips. She was now doing a Science course at the University.

'I don't know. She's sitting for her finals in January and if she gets through there'll be graduation. Anyway, there's the beloved. She's absolutely starry-eyed. No, I somehow can't see her coming away for six months.'

'Look Wen, I think we should experiment first. I mean, all our other trips have been holidays. We've saved up for them and then spent our savings. But now we've got to try and earn our way. I'm not going to ask my folk for money.'

'No fear! Anyway, think of the fun we can have doing all sorts of jobs. We can be waitresses and salesgirls and usherettes…'

'We can follow the crops with the seasonal workers…apple picking in Tasmania…'

'Shirl, that's it! Tassy of course! We'll start there. It should take only a few weeks, it's not too far from home if anything should go wrong and we can prove to our parents that we can look after ourselves. Mine won't let me go to Queensland otherwise.'

'Mine neither. But we must get together and do some solid planning. I'm so excited I can't bear to go back to work.'

'Won't be for long. Then we'll have all the time in the world. Bye!'

TASMANIA

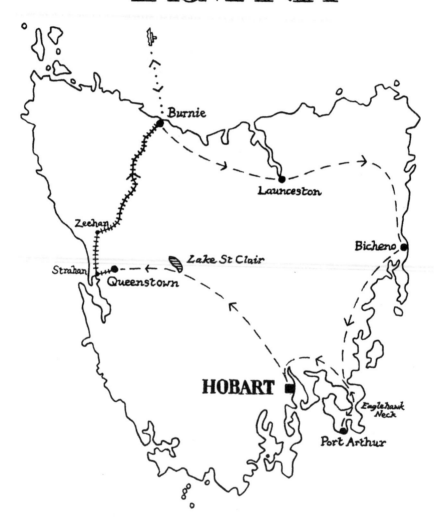

Chapter 1

ISLE OF MOUNTAINS

Monday, 28th January 1946:

'Well, that's that!' said Shirl resolutely as the last streamer snapped in her hands. She had managed to keep it intact longer than those of other passengers and the *Nairana* had already pulled out into the middle of the Yarra river and was now starting to steam downstream.

'Let's explore.'

'Wait a min Dunc.' I was still straining to keep my eyes on the members of my family clustered on the wharf. After all, who does not become sentimental about his first sea voyage, whether it be for six weeks to England or twelve hours across Bass Strait to Tasmania. But when I could no longer distinguish faces I was caught on a wonderful tide of freedom and, exhilarated, hurried after her.

We found our tiny cabin and within five minutes it was strewn with two cases (containing our glamour clothes), two haversacks which held our 'utility' or riding gear, numerous lengths of rope, bike pumps, headlamps and other impedimenta.

Perched on the top bunk, Shirl beamed ecstatically. 'Isn't this *magnificent*!'

Our cabin was not a stateroom, nor was the view through our porthole inspiring. Clustered thickly along the bank were cargo ships and tramps, long shabby warehouses, towering cranes and all the scruffy trappings of the sea. But I knew what she meant. Between its dirty banks flowed the Yarra and ahead of us was the sea itself. Admittedly it was only Port Phillip Bay but at about six o'clock we'd be through the Rip and into the rough waters of Bass Strait. The promise of adventure lay thick on the air and I doubt if Bass himself felt prouder or more intrepid on board the *Tom Thumb*.*

---

*George Bass on board the whaler *Tom Thumb* proved there was a strait (which now bears his name) between the mainland and Van Diemen's land (Tasmania).

We made our way to the tip of the foredeck and watched the prow whoosh through the waves, rising on the crests only to crash down into the troughs.

'How did your send-off go Wen?'

'Oh we had a big party in the office and all the studio mob came down. Ed Balmer and Lew Bennett made speeches and then presented me with that suitcase. They all got pretty merry and Ed was trying to warn me gently about the dangers of the road. And when I told him that I still intended to forge on, he shook his head lugubriously and said 'I think you're marvellous Wendy. I think you're doing a wonderful thing. But God! I hope my daughter doesn't grow up like you!'

Shirl laughed. 'Isn't it amazing! My friends were the same. They kept on saying 'What if you run out of money? What if you don't reach a town at night? What if you can't get any jobs?' I think that's the fun of it all – not having any plans and taking whatever comes. But every one thinks I'm mad to sling up a good steady job.'

We set off on a further exploration of the ship and on the lower deck peeped through a porthole and saw half a dozen blackened stokers having their tea. One looked up and caught us.

'Hullo!' He grinned. 'Feeling hungry? Come and have a bite.'

Within a minute of our sitting at their table, two large plates of sizzling steak and eggs, plentifully garnished with fried onions and potato chips, thumped down in front of us. Biscuits and jam followed this, whilst the stokers sat back and watched us in amazement.

'Gee, I'd rather keep you for a week than a fortnight!' one joked.

Shirl blushed and said something about not knowing where our next slap-up meal was coming from after today.

'You're not the two girls we read about in the *Herald* are you? Touring Tassy on 1/6d a day? Cripes. Y'd better take some biscuits along with you as well. If you're after experiences, y'oughta come down and have a look around below.'

We climbed down the slippery rungs of a perpendicular ladder into the engine room. A wall of heat hit us.

'115° down here,' grinned one of our guides, 'and hotter'n that in the furnace room. How'd yer like to swing a shovel in this heat?'

We joined the row of sweating men who stood in front of the gaping fires feeding them with coal. I instinctively thought of hell and was even more impressed with the idea of eternal punishment after I'd wielded my shovel five times. Shirl was panting too and her face was flushed with heat and exertion.

'I've had enough Wen. Let's get some air!'

Our hosts laughed at our discomfiture but said we were good sports and wished us luck.

-oOo

It had been a roasting January day and when we turned in at 9pm the cabin was still stifling. The porthole was small and didn't help at all. However, we lay down and managed to go to sleep. A few hours later, I began to be dimly conscious that it was cold, very cold. I huddled under one thin blanket and dejectedly thought of the snug sleeping bag strapped on my bike in the depths of the hold. I looked out the porthole and was astounded to see that the weather had changed. Huge seas pounded against the ship, sending great quantities of icy spray through the porthole and over our recumbent bodies. It has been said that if you're not sick in Bass Strait then you never will be. The *Nairana* was wallowing helplessly and already from adjacent cabins came the dire sounds of victims of seasickness. Just then Shirl's voice came out of the gloom.

'You awake Wen? Isn't this ghastly! I'm frozen stiff and the blanket's wet through.'

She was on the top bunk right under the porthole.

'Shut the porthole then, you ass.'

'It won't shut. I've been bashing it for ages.'

'Well, I'm going to unpack my groundsheet. At least it's waterproof,' and I delved into my haversack.

'I've got a better idea,' said Shirl, and swung down from her bunk. She was clad only in a singlet and panties – the necessity of carrying a light pack prevented us from indulging in such luxuries as pyjamas – 'I saw a pile of blankets down the corridor before. I'm going to pinch one.'

She peeped furtively out of the door and, the coast being clear, sped away. A minute later she reappeared at the door, shivering but triumphant, and with difficulty dragged in a large heavy object.

'They weren't blankets,' she panted. 'They were a pile of carpets folded up. But I've got one.'

And with one great heave, she shouldered the heavy rug on to the top bunk and rapidly crawled beneath it.

'Rapture!' came a blissful murmur, and then silence.

-oOo-

In Burnie, that green and pleasant archway through which Tasmania beckons, we procured some little envelope seals which publicized the town.

'*Tour Tasmania on a Tenner. Start at Burnie*' they read but within a day of our heading east to Launceston, we used to cross out the word 'tenner' and substitute 'truck'. Tasmania has been called the Isle of Mountains and no one would dispute it but for compensation it is also Land of the Truck.

What sound on earth can surpass, for sheer heart-lifting joy, the sound of a truck, a big, heavy truck, coming slowly but inexorably in low gear, up a long back-breaking hill, which one has been walking up with a bike. It must not pass us on a bend nor on the stiffest pinch of the hill for then the driver will never stop. With desperate energy we trot our bikes to a suitable place. Then, leaning wearily on the handlebars, faces scarlet with exertion, we wait. The truck sweeps grandly around the corner. We raise limp hands, the gesture has just the merest indication of the next town in it, and look piteously at the driver.

This is the critical moment. One class of driver looks at us, grins broadly, waves vigorously and disappears over the crest. Though we appreciate his friendliness, we love his truck much more. Class two roars past us but is obviously haunted by our harrowing appearance as he begins to slow down three hundred yards ahead. The third type atones for the faults of his brethren. Pulling to a halt with a grinding of brakes, he can take us not only to our destination but to another town thirty miles beyond. He swings our bikes, each laden with a sixty pound pack, onto the back of the truck and makes room for us amongst the timber or pigs or vegetables.

One meets lots of interesting people in trucks. One young man who gave us a lift over a particularly desolate stretch of country on the mainland told us that once he had found a baby emu, separated from its mother. He befriended it and reared it. It was his constant companion, always sitting in the front seat of the truck with him.

Then there was the old chap who amused us for half an hour with the story of his life. He hailed from the Old Country and had settled in Tasmania twenty years ago. Never regretted it either. Fine place this! I asked did he live by himself.

'My word, yes,' he said. 'Do everything meself. Cook me own tucker. Clean the house. Even wash and darn me own socks.'

'Wash your own socks? What happens when there's no water?' (There was a shortage when we met him.)

'Why then,' he said. 'I turn 'em and shake 'em and thank God for clean linen.'

I had an embarrassing experience the first day out of Burnie. A huge petrol tanker had stopped for us. Obviously we couldn't fit on the back, but the driver told us to hold on to the side and he'd pull us along. He was going

relatively slowly so I shut my ears to my mother's cautionary words about having tows and held on with my right hand to the left side, steering the bike with my left hand.

We bowled along merrily, revelling in the glorious sun and fresh sea breeze which whipped at our kerchiefs and made our blouses balloon like spinnakers. It wasn't till I realised the co-driver was continually poking his head out of the cabin to grin hugely at me that I discovered that the buttons of my blouse had decided to disdain the embrace of the buttonholes (which were always a bit too big) and go off on a life of their own. I must've looked particularly fetching in my singlet, my blouse still hugging my neck but blowing far behind me like a banner. Both hands fully occupied, I could do absolutely nothing to remedy the matter.

The most agonizing episode for Shirl was physical, not emotional. We had had an uneventful but delightful ride across the northern coast of Tasmania. We detoured along execrable roads to see King Solomon's Caves (the first caves I'd ever seen and which I thereafter extolled as the finest in Australia); we pleasured through charming Deloraine, a snug English-looking township painted on very green hills with lush pastures and giant rugged mountains surrounding it.

We idled through Exton, Westbury, Hagley and Hadspen, townships all suiting their English names, with very old colonial buildings, ruined churches and crumbling churchyards. It had been a perfect morning's ride. Then we hailed a truck going all the way to Launceston and the driver agreed to tow us. We each held a back corner edge, I on the right in the middle of the road, Shirl on the left at the verge. Suddenly there was a terrific crash and I saw Shirl and bike come down in the loose gravel at the side of the road and drag along the ground. I cast off and rode back.

She wasn't seriously hurt, but her left leg and arm were badly cut and of course she was suffering from shock. I whipped out my First Aid kit and dressed her wounds. Cars had been whizzing by all this time but at last a truck stopped and took her and her bike to Launceston Hospital.

I felt drained after the crisis so I ate some chocolate and set off on the remaining thirteen miles. I found Shirl at the Hospital, bandaged nearly to her eyes and looking terribly miserable.

'It's times like this that I want my mother Wen. Look, I'm ruined!'

'Just as well your mother's not here. You know how she's warned you about getting tows.'

'Gosh yes, I'm not going to tell her Wen and don't you dare mention it in your letters home.'

When we met reporters over the next few weeks, she had to pose carefully with her right side towards the camera and beg the reporter not to mention the incident.

-oOo-

Bicheno, a small cluster of houses on the East Coast, is a heavenly place for a holiday, where mountains meet the sea and long sweeps of pure white sand hem the land before plunging into deep blue water. And there are no tourists!* Three hundred yards off-shore is Diamond Island, very small and rocky and romantic. When the tide goes out one can wade across to it. We tried this several times but misjudged the tide each time and were soaked to the armpits. Such was the glorious loneliness of Bicheno, we were able to strip down to our underwear and bask in the hot sun till our clothes were dry. At last the tide receded far enough and we splashed through the shallows, feeling like the children of Israel with the waves parting before them.

We returned to the beach and met a man who was going crayfishing. He invited us to try our luck too and rushed away to find extra poles, nets and bait for us. The procedure was simple. One merely lowered into a deep rock pool a pole with a baited hook on the end of it, trailing it past promising ledges and dark crannies. Very soon a cray would come out and start to nibble the bait. Swiftly one lowered the net into the water and scooped the crayfish out. First blood went to me, then Shirl scooped out two at once. Our instructor didn't catch a thing!

At the man's cottage, his wife boiled our catch in her copper and we had an exquisite tea of delicately-flavoured crayfish sprinkled with vinegar, crisp curly lettuce, juicy tomatoes and fresh crackling bread.

At 8pm, as darkness was falling, we pushed out of Bicheno in the direction of Swansea, twenty-five miles away. We knew we couldn't hope to reach it but felt that, unless we made a start, we might be tempted to spend another day in Bicheno. There was a schoolhouse eight miles away where we hoped to shelter but after a day of activity on the rocks and beach in the golden strength-sapping sun, we were both suddenly overcome with

*There are now!

weariness. To make things worse, we were riding through a belt of burning forest. The whole range was alight, the tall gums turned into flaming torches. Tongues of flame crept quietly along the ground only to flare up in a surprise attack on a bush or undergrowth. It was an awesome spectacle seen by night; a landscape in oils, painted in crimson and black. Every now and then a great tree would crash down, sending a spray of sparks flying across the road in our path. We were worried about our tyres and picked our way carefully through the burning coals. The smoke was thick and made our eyes, already sun-dried, sting unbearably.

'Just look at that glowing log Shirl! Let's stop and make some toast.'

'Let's not. I'm almost asleep.'

We trundled on for two miles and then suddenly saw the welcoming wink of a farmhouse window. A dog rushed out, barking furiously as we approached and we paused uncertainly at the gate until someone came to the front door with a lamp. We wheeled our bikes up the long drive.

'Who is it?' called a gruff man's voice.

We answered and he called off the dog. In the light of the high-held lamp we saw the master of the house. He was about 70 years old, a typical old-timer, dressed in working clothes. We learnt later that he owned all the land for miles around. I told him we were looking for shelter for the night.

His features clouded with genuine distress. 'Girls, I'm terribly sorry, I just haven't a spare room for you.'

'A floor would do ... a verandah ...'

He shook his head.

We just couldn't have gone another inch and begged him to consider his property and think if he couldn't fit us into a barn or a milking-shed or *anything*.

He pondered for a minute, combing his moustache with the tip of one finger.

'Well ... there is a barn ... quite a good barn ... but we're in the middle of threshing and the place is stacked with sheaves of wheat. And anyway, I wouldn't feel easy letting you sleep in a barn!'

'A barn! Wheat! Oh it'd be wonderful!' I had visions of new-mown hay, (I had no knowledge of wheat), soft and fragrant, soft, soft beneath my aching body. 'Please may we see it?'

He shrugged dubiously and led us to the barn. It was a good, solid, stone building, convict-built, composed of two rooms. The first room was piled to the roof with wheat, the other had a pile of sheaves in one corner but the floor was fairly clear. The lamplight flickered on the sturdy walls and high rafters. There was a cold wind blowing outside but all was warm and snug inside.

Delighted, we assured the kindly old man that we'd be all right. He bade us goodnight, left us the lamp and pottered away. We dragged a few trusses into the middle of the floor and unrolled our sleeping bags.

Then I saw it! A patch of dark shadow moved rapidly up the wall and disappeared beyond the circle of light thrown by the lamp.

'Shirl!' I quavered. 'I've just seen a rat.'

'A RAT!' she shrieked. 'Where?'

We peered into the shadows all around us, but nothing moved.

'Well, I suppose it's only natural. Rats usually live in barns, don't they?'

'But Wen … rats *eat* people!'

Gone was the vision of sweet-smelling wheat and golden warmth. Instead we saw ourselves scarred and mutilated. But there was nowhere else to go, so we put on jumpers, gloves and headscarves, crept into our bags and blew out the lamp.

After a minute's uneasy silence, Shirl said, 'What do rats eat normally anyway?'

'They're scavengers aren't they? They always hang around rubbish dumps. But perhaps there are field rats just like field mice. These ones here must eat grain.'

On this hopeful note we relapsed into silence. Then I remembered an experience my brother Phil had once. We must have had guests because he'd been ousted from his bedroom and was to sleep on the lounge floor in his sleeping bag. Before going to sleep he read some chapters of a book entitled *Rats, Lice and History*, an account of the connection between animals and the most noteworthy plagues of the world. Then he put out the light. Some hours later he awoke to feel a warm weight on his head and something pick-picking at the balding place on his crown. Horrified, he realised it was a great rat and recalling the horrors of the book he'd been reading, he leapt out of his bag and dashed for the iodine bottle.

I recounted this morosely to Shirl and we mulled it over, talking fearfully about rats and their human-eating capabilities, then we shrouded our faces in scarves and burrowing deep within our bags, fell asleep.

Shortly afterwards I was wakened by a slight scampering sound in the wheat. On my elbow immediately, I broke out in a cold sweat and flashed my torch around the walls. Not a sign of anything. I was paralyzed with terror and the sight of Shirl's inert sleeping form filled me with self-pity. The crown of martyrdom sat snugly on my brows. What did it matter if I were haggard in the morning with nerves frayed by fear and suspense, so long as I protected my comrade from mutilation.

I felt noble but very scared. Each time I switched off my torch and settled down to sleep, ominous rustlings and scratchings and gnawings would commence. A sudden rush in the straw near my feet – and another over in the corner – and another near my HEAD! I flung out of the bag, turned on the torch and saw black shadows creeping like blots along the rafters.

'Shirl!' I screamed.

She answered immediately. 'I know. I can't stand it any longer. I haven't slept a wink. I'm roasting hot and nearly suffocating but I daren't expose even a nostril. Let's move.'

So we gathered our things and tottering outside the barn, spread our bags on the ground. It was hard and stony, but balm to my tortured mind.

We woke with the sun coming over the mountains, fiercely hot. Clouds of blowflies buzzed about us. Sleep was impossible.

'Ah Nature,' said Shirl blearily, 'is a wonderful thing. To live in the sun, wind and the rain and gambol with our furry friends and little brothers with wings ... there's nothing like it.'

'You bet there isn't!' I said drily.

-oOo-

Port Arthur was the obvious choice for a penal settlement. Geographically, it is a natural prison. The peninsula on which it stands is surrounded by sea on all sides, except for a narrow isthmus, fifty yards wide and 200 yards long, which joins it to the main body of Tasmania. Eaglehawk Neck was the only part of the island which needed guarding, and this was left to a line of chained hounds. The escaped prisoner who lacked the courage to brave the gauntlet of savage dogs fell victim to the sharks abounding in the sea. Very few Port Arthur convicts ever escaped and lived to tell of it.

I had seen plenty of photos of the Port Arthur ruins in tourist literature but I was quite unprepared for the sight which met my eyes when we topped the last rise and looked down into the valley. Straight in front of us was the Church, an empty shell, but a shell still intact, the tower still square and squat, the walls still standing firmly (convict-hewn stone, with blood and sweat for mortar, defies time). A little to the left the remains of the round powder magazine were conspicuous, its crenellated tower looking out of place in the Australian bush. There were the Penitentiary, the Governor's house, the Hospital, the garrison's quarters and the Model Prison. The latter was so named, not because it was a model building but because when the young Queen abolished whipping soon after her accession, some other form of correction had to be devised. Into the Model Prison went all the difficult prisoners and their treatment served as a model to all other rebellious convicts. Solitary confinement was the main remedy and as I walked down the cold stone passages and peered through the grilles into tiny dark cells, I wondered if perhaps whipping were not more humane.

Australia is such a young country historically speaking and has little of historical interest to show but Port Arthur opened my eyes. It was not the sense of past history which was frightening but the realization that the grim chapter was so very recent. I felt this when I looked through the small but well-stocked museum at the back of the Port Arthur General Store.

There for handling were the arrow-slashed uniforms, the prisoners' leg-irons, balls and chains, manacles, convict-made bricks stamped with the broad-arrow mark, the working tools – picks, spades and mallets and, most interesting of all, the heavy ledgers in which some long-forgotten scribe entered in a beautiful copperplate hand for posterity's horrified gaze the name, sex, age and crime of the wrongdoers. There one can see the appalling injustice which sentenced men, women and young children to transportation as punishment for such petty crimes as stealing a loaf of bread or a handkerchief or poaching a rabbit, offences as trivial as a traffic offence in our time. I wondered how many pitiable children sought escape from their unbearable confinement at Point Puer by jumping over Suicide Cliff.

But even these heartrending entries could be paralleled in similar museums all over the world. Port Arthur would be the same as any village with a gruesome past – if it weren't for the photographs!

If anyone had asked me, I should probably have said that photography was invented some time in the later years of the 19th century, yet the last convict ship arrived in 1853 and the Port Arthur Penal Settlement closed in 1877. I was shattered to see photographs of the settlement in full operation. Convicts at work, building roads or houses. Chain gangs trailing wearily back to the Penitentiary. Photographs of the layout of the village, showing the Governor's house, the Church and the Powder Magazine, those picturesque ruins which we had explored, standing in all their original permanence as part of the overall plan.

I was impressed with my heritage as never before.

-oOo-

The first thing that greeted us in Hobart was the wind. Our long-awaited entry into the capital was far from triumphal. We crossed the new bridge from Bellerive (paying threepence toll) and met a headwind so terrifically strong that we could hardly keep on our bikes. Then we saw the hilly streets, sloping down the sides of magnificent Mt. Wellington to the harbour edge, and straightaway decided that bicycles were out of the question in Hobart and trams would serve us better.

Hobart was a charming city, quiet, sunny and unhurried. It had the atmosphere of a fishing village and one could not entirely escape the spell of the sea when at every turn one was confronted with a view of the glorious harbour. In unexpected hidden corners one came across moored dinghies, barnacle-encrusted slimy stone steps creeping into the water and old retired sea captains sitting in the sun, puffing on their pipes.

Not even the city took itself seriously. Commerce had emigrated to the Mainland (as one must refer to the other Australian States) and shops and offices closed on Saturdays as well as Sundays. Housewives didn't seem to mind this 5-day shopping week and just placed a larger order on Friday. I thought it an excellent idea.

Tasmanians are wonderfully hospitable and the people of Hobart were no exception. We called at a house with a letter of introduction from a lady on the East Coast to her daughter and were promptly asked in and invited to stay as long as we liked. We slept in our bags on the lounge floor of the small flat and ate tremendous meals prepared by our friendly hostess.

In one issue of the newspaper we were very touched by a letter to the Editor reading: 'Where are the girls who paid Launceston a visit last week? Most Tasmanians could spare a cup of tea and a better place to sleep than the churchyard they had on the Northwest coast ...'

A week after our arrival the Hobart Regatta took place. We had been told that Regatta Day was the day of the year when the Spirit of Carnival walked the streets and Hobart really let down its hair. We could hardly wait to see this improbable transformation.

The day dawned bright and sunny and we made haste to the Domain. The dark blue harbour below was white with sail. Here, skimming yachts Bermuda-rigged; there, ocean-going cruisers. Small speedboats slipped in and out of the slower craft; officials' launches bright with paint and brass circled busily. Towering above everything, glorious barquentines, full-rigged, swept across the water with all the stately majesty of galleons.

As we approached the Domain, cars crawled by us like lines of orderly ants. People crowded everywhere, elbowing their way boisterously through the crush with a huge bag of fairy floss in one hand and a rubber ball on elastic in the other. Children screamed, showmen bellowed their sideshow attractions, the merry-go-round ground out a monotonous tune from under its gaily-striped canvas. Flying swings hurtled through the air. And everywhere people. More people. Fat men, sticky children, flustered mothers, loud-mouthed yachtsmen, down-at-heel touts, furtive gamblers, strolling sailors from the visiting warships, short-frocked girls with their eyes on the sailors. People. Excitement in the air and fun in plenty for all.

For all but us. After half an hour we'd had enough of the Regatta. We couldn't get near the Harbour to see the racing and we had no money to splash on sideshows or money-winning games. We hung about, looking wistfully at the posters of performing animals and the Strong Man. We peered over the shoulders of the crowds around the rifle range, the dart show and the coin games. That was where to win money or prizes but one had to have the price of a first round.

Bored and footsore we tramped in circles. The weather had turned traitor. There was an obstreperous wind whipping up clouds of fine dust which obscured the tents and made everyone bad-tempered. Once again we passed the long line of marquees. Shirl kicked at the dust with her sandal and nodded to one tent. 'Look at that poor man. No one's going to his sideshow.'

I stopped. 'You know, he needs us. Let's go and ask him if he needs any spruikers. With our bit of publicity, we might draw a crowd.'

Shirl shook her head. 'No. He hasn't a microphone. We'd have too much competition from other booths.'

We walked on but were very taken with the idea as a novel means of raising money. Then we saw another languishing sideshow and this one had a shiny microphone standing on the table in front. We approached the man who was sitting forlornly beside it. We told him that we were cycling around Tasmania trying to work our way and as we had nothing to do, would he perhaps like some help?

We were in luck. It transpired he had a dartboard to run in the afternoon and wanted to leave the sideshow in capable hands. He looked at us speculatively, then said:

'Yeh, I think I could use you. Come back at three o'clock and work till six, and you'll probably clear thirty shillings each.'

I looked at Shirl incredulously. What a windfall!

'You'd better go inside the tent and have a look while you're here.

And keep an ear open to what I'm saying. You'll soon get the hang of it.'

We stepped back and had a look at the poster. Painted in glaring colours across the front of the marquee was an outstretched human hand, on which was standing a pint-sized bull. Over it, in monumental letters, was the magical legend:

FERDINAND THE FIRST

| Pure-bred Illawarra | Height 27 inches |
| Shorthorn | Weight 72 lbs |

The smallest bull in the world.
Four years old.

We went inside.

Standing meekly in a corner of a straw-lined pen was a little bull. He may have been only a calf although he did have small horns. The poster was an exaggeration.

'Ferdie, you'd better shrink a bit. Suck in your breath or something. Business is bad!'

He looked at us disinterestedly, his jaws circling as he chewed some straw.

We left the tent in high glee, elated because we had seen one sideshow for nothing and the idea might work again.

A little further down the row we came to the Wall of Death Daredevil Motorcyclists.

'Cyclists!' breathed Shirl with a glint in her eye.

We found the boss and and asked if he'd like his spruiker to interview us on the platform outside the tent in order to draw a crowd.

'Sounds a good idea. Have you seen the show yourselves? No? Then buzz up and see it first.'

Crowing with success, we bounded up the rickety staircase to see our second show and while we watched the horrifying feats of the motorcyclists on a perpendicular wall, we could hear the spruiker outside bellowing:

'Very soon we shall be interviewing, ladies and gentlemen, two very courageous young ladies who are touring Tasmania by bicycle. They have biked all over Australia (our eyebrows shot up) and will give you their impressions of Tasmania and the Regatta.'

When the show had finished, we went outside and mounted the platform. We stood like dummies for five minutes while the man recounted the thrills of the death-defying motorcyclists. I felt I should have been wearing red satin tights, a bra-top and pill-box hat to fill the bill. Then we had a short interview and on climbing down were invited to accept a crinkly pound note for our trouble.

At three o'clock we went back to the first showman and were entrusted with money, tickets, microphone and Ferdinand.

'Right-oh girls, let's hear how you get on!'

He held out the mike to Shirl but with a look of sudden terror she passed it to me. 'You can go first Wen, ha ha,' she said, with mock courtesy.

I took the inoffensive instrument, blew into it to see if it were working and a great blast like a sirocco wheezed through the speakers. So, nervously feeling my way and using the boss's patter, I began.

'Step this way, ladies and gentlemen. Come and see Ferdinand the midget bull - the smallest bull in the world. Only two shillings for adults and elevenpence for the children. Mum and Dad, bring the kiddies in to see Ferdinand for a very special treat. They'll *love* him! He's only 27 inches high. Just imagine that! Not half as tall as this little girl in front of me. What's your name, little girl?'

I looked brightly at the beginning of an audience. She stared back stonily.

'Yes, ladies and gentlemen, he's only 27 inches high, 72 lbs in weight. What a little fella! But he's all bull! Yes, he's the genuine article, he's just the little bull that forgot to grow.'

(Hoot from Shirl behind me.)

'He's not just a young bull, ladies and gentlemen, he's four years old and fully grown. You can tell that by looking at his horns, if you know anything about cattle ….'

This indicated casually that I knew something about my subject, so I proceeded in a more technical vein.

'Ferdinand is of special interest to cattlemen. He is a pure-bred Illawarra Shorthorn (*sotto voce:* whatever that may be) and is four years old. He was specially imported from the Riverina for this Regatta, so don't miss this wonderful opportunity of seeing him. It may not occur again!'

('It won't! The farmer outside Hobart wants him back tomorrow,' piped Shirl gleefully.)

'Yes, ladies and gentlemen, he's so small, you could put him in a suitcase – but you can't take him away. Ha-ha-ha!'

No response from the circle of gaping kids, so I brought forth my *pièce de resistance.*

'Ladies and gentlemen, you've seen the rest ..... now see the best – midget at the Regatta.. You've seen the performing dogs and the midget ponies but who's ever seen a midget bull? No one here, I bet!'

('No one anywhere!' gloomed Shirl.)

I could hear the heart-warming sound of clinking coins behind me as Shirl issued tickets to a stream of curious people. One woman came up to the table and flung down a florin.

'I might as well see the confounded bull! I've heard all about it in the other tents.'

'Oh? People been telling you about it?' Shirl asked smugly.

'Heavens no! I can hear your microphone all over the blasted Regatta ground.' She stumped in to see Ferdinand.

Then Shirl started up with a new slant.

'All you people walking by, wondering what you're going to see next, you must be tired out! Come on in out of the wind and have a rest *and* see Ferdinand at the same time. Never let it be said that you'd been to the 1946 Regatta without seeing Ferdinand.'

Well! We made £3.10.0 for the owner, plus another pound which blew away in a particularly violent gust of wind. I'm sure he didn't believe that for he gave us only five shillings for all our hard work, but we didn't mind as we'd had so much fun.

Riding home through the city in the evening, we swerved to avoid a band of larrikins who, seeing us, ran after us shouting:

'Come and see Ferdinand, the midget bull!'

Worse followed. A week later, while inspecting HMAS *Bataan*, one of the visiting warships, we were having afternoon tea in the officers' mess. Dressed in our best, we were nibbling delicately at biscuits and making polite conversation. One of the stewards left the door slightly ajar on one occasion and outside we could hear hoarse whispers.

'Yeh! That's them! That's them orright!'

The ship had been overrun with small boys all afternoon and we thought some of them had recognised us as the touring cyclists. We were shattered when a tousled head thrust itself in the room and yelled, 'Come and see Ferdinand the MIDGET BULL!'

Our hosts raised courteous eyebrows. We didn't enlighten them.

-oOo-

St.David's Park in the heart of the city offers a diversion to anyone who can spare an afternoon. The site of an old cemetery was wanted for parkland and after advertisement, many relatives came forward to claim and move their ancestors' graves. The headstones of the remainder were propped up around the fence of the park and one can wander along, reading these pathetic relics of the past. The oldest ones showed the name of the town as Hobart Town. Later, it was known as Hobarton but by the 20th Century had settled down as Hobart. On the whole the stones made depressing reading, being brimful of Victorian sentimentalism. Nearly every one began, 'Weep not for me, my husband (or mother or brother) dear, I am not dead, but sleeping here.' Then there was the inscrutable type such as:

> *In the midst of life we are in death,*
> *He lived to die, he died to live.*
> *Stranger, pause! Reflect!*

But for sheer bathos I liked:

> *Dear little darling, art thou gone?*
> *Thy charms scarce to thy mother known.*
> *Removed so soon! So suddenly*
> *Snatched from my fond maternal eye.*
> *What hast thou done dear offspring! Say,*
> *So early to be snatched away.*
> *What! Gone for ever! Seen no more!*
> *For ever I thy loss deplore!*

It is a sobering thought that these effusions, composed in all sincerity and motivated by deep grief, should evoke only amusement today.

-oOo-

One of our main reasons for coming to Tasmania was to prove to our parents that we could earn our way. Up till now we hadn't had any work, unless we counted the Ferdinand episode, (to which Shirl's parents objected strongly, threatening to bring her home if there were a similar occurrence) and I had only eight shillings left. For days we trudged around Hobart, wearing a track between the Manpower Office and IXL Fruit Cannery and putting through telephone calls to orchardists in the Huon valley and hop farmers in the Derwent district. We were particularly interested in apple picking. After all, Tasmania and apples are synonymous (thanks to Bligh of the *Bounty* who was responsible for the introduction of apple cuttings into the island) and yet we hadn't seen an apple that wasn't on a fruiterer's stall.

Then it started to rain. For four days it rained and we despaired of ever getting away from Hobart. But where could we go? One afternoon at half past five the rain stopped suddenly, the sun shone through the clouds and we saw that the mists were leaving the mountain. We packed hurriedly and set off. Even at that time we stopped a truck which took us almost to Huonville. The driver suggested we enquire about picking work at a large house nearby so we wheeled our bikes along a magnificent avenue of English trees to a comfortable-looking house. The owner was Mr. Jenkins who, after hearing our request, said that he could definitely give us work. He didn't seem to mind that we were inexperienced. We were shown to a little room opening on to a back verandah. It contained a stretcher-bed and a sofa. The walls were wood-panelled and the window shuttered. It was very cosy, especially when the rain began again and beat loudly against the window pane.

It was nearly eight o'clock before we awoke. Ashamed at being late for our first day's work we hurried to the orchard with Mr. Jenkins who showed us what to do. With heavy leather pouches strapped around us, we picked green Cleopatras with a sizing ring $2\frac{1}{4}$ inches in diameter. It was a very slow business, although after a while we were able to dispense with the gauge and judge the correct size ourselves. By ten o'clock we were very hungry, having had no breakfast, and were delighted to see Mrs. Jenkins approaching, bearing hot coffee and jam sandwiches. This, apparently, was 'lunch'. Then we picked steadily till twelve, when there was an hour's break for dinner. Mrs. Jenkins invited us to partake of hot roast beef, stewed fruit, custard and cream with her, a privilege not accorded to the other pickers. Back to the orchard until three o'clock, when more 'lunch' arrived. We made the most of this snack as it was our last meal for the day.

After work finished at five we showered, ironed our frocks and rode into Huonville. It was the prettiest town I had ever seen. The beautiful broad Huon River flowed placidly through the middle of it and there was such a peaceful air that I wanted to sit on the bank, or lean over the bridge just staring at the reflections, for ever. The surrounding countryside was fresh and green with orchards. In spring, with pink and white blossom prinking the rows of trees, it must be breathtakingly lovely.

The next day we worked another section of the orchard containing Cox's Orange Pippins, a far more satisfying variety though even a Cox gives way graciously and unprotesting to the king of them all, the Australian Jonathan.

At the end of the day Mr. Jenkins told all the pickers that there would be no more picking as he had no orders on hand. He astonished us by giving us one pound each, a princely sum, particularly as he hadn't deducted anything for meals, accommodation or inefficiency. I wish I'd been able to keep that pound note for sentimental reasons. Our apple-picking was the first of a series of widely differing jobs spreading over the next few years.

The countryside throughout the Huon peninsula is the loveliest imaginable. The wide Huon estuary forms a huge Gulf which is a shade bluer than the summer sky. Along its shores march miles of orchards in orderly precision and behind them rise densely wooded mountains. As one circles the peninsula, with the waters of the D'Entrecasteaux Channel to the right, there is a delightful sequence of townships – Cygnet, Gordon and a gem called Snug. A little further and we were back in Hobart.

-oOo-

In connection with our visit to Western Tasmania, the names of two men must be mentioned. Ranger Fergusson of the Lake St. Clair Reserve (known as Fergy to thousands of people and spoken of in every book written about Tasmania), and George Nankivell of Queenstown.

We travelled north-west along the beautiful Derwent valley which is so English in character, with lanes and hedgerows bordering the hopfields with their towering vines and towns which are named to match. Claremont,

Norfolk, Ouse, Marlborough pass in dignified succession. It had started to rain again and much of the time we huddled on the back of trucks, cowering under our groundsheet capes. We reached Fergy's 'camp' on the shores of Lake St. Clair in the late afternoon. It consisted of a number of huts scattered through the bush, which were rented to visitors. We nosed about without finding anyone until our knock at a larger hut brought Fergy himself to the door. This was the Mess hut and, with a great apron tied around him, he was preparing the evening meal.

He overwhelmed us with hospitality and immediately made us sit down in front of the cooking range and down mugs of steaming cocoa and a pile of biscuits. We must have looked like wild things blown in from the storm, drenched and bedraggled.

'Now you look a bit more alive,' he said after a while. 'Bring your bikes along and I'll give you a hut.'

We followed him through the silent, dripping scrub and took possession of Hut 2. A double bed piled with blankets took up nearly all the floor space. Between the foot of the bed and the fireplace there was just room for a table and two chairs. Some wall shelves completed the furniture. Simple, but then hikers don't have much baggage and a comfortable bed, a dry roof and a warm fire are all they ask at night.

It was bitterly cold outside and still raining at intervals - and this in February! Fergy bustled about and soon had a fire blazing. Then he told us the location of his raspberry patch, some distance away in the forest.

'Eat your fill girls and bring me home two dishes full for the guests.'

So we put on our capes and hoods again and walked along a winding path to the patch. It started raining and we stood in the downpour and consumed pounds of fruit. Never have raspberries tasted so wonderful, their wild sweetness enhanced by the rain on their velvety skins. Our fingers cold, scratched and stained, we picked and picked until, remembering the object of our errand, we hastily filled our dishes and took them back to the galley. Then we shut ourselves in our hut and made stacks of piping hot toast, either soaked with butter and jam or made into toasted cheese sandwiches. Several spoonsful of condensed milk finished the meal.

Fergy had told us to come back to the kitchen so we went up for a yarn. Despite our protestations that we had already dined, he dished up two bowls of wonderfully good soup, hot roast lamb and potatoes and hot apple pie and custard! We tried to repay him by doing the washing-up.

Basking in the warmth of the kitchen was a black cat with a glorious glossy coat. When it stood up, stretched and went out of the room, I stared aghast. Its two front paws were missing and it hobbled along on the stumps.

'What *happened* to him?' I asked Fergy.

'To whom?' he said absently, scouring a pot.

'The cat. Its paws!'

'Oh, I chopped them off. He was always scratching people.'

'You WHAT!' screamed Shirl, her eyes wide with horror.

'Chopped 'em off. Can't have a bad-tempered cat about the place. People wouldn't like it.'

'How would you like it with your feet off?'

'Oh they soon get over it,' he said casually. 'I'm going to take all four off Tab here soon. He goes for all the birds in the district.'

'Naturally,' I said, staring at the wonderful, healthy tabby who lay, fat and shining, at our feet.

'Well, it's a bird and animal reserve here you know. Can't disturb the birds.'

The wash-up done, Shirl excused herself and made for the door. I followed.

'Wen,' she whispered as we walked to the hut. 'Can you imagine such fiendish cruelty!'

'I can't believe it. He's such a kind man.'

He was too. That very evening he'd arranged for a friend of his, Mr. Cole, to take us on a long boat trip to the other end of the Lake. It would be a day trip as Mr. Cole had to row all the way and would be stopping at various places to read the rain gauges.

Next morning we were called at six o'clock and after a huge bowl of Fergy's porridge, we left with Mr. Cole. He was a friendly little man, mild-mannered and shy. He pulled on the oars and we shot out onto the placid, steel-blue surface of what is acknowledged to be the most beautiful lake in the world by people who know the lakes of England, Scotland, Ireland, Italy and Switzerland. The day was perfect, cloudless and sunny, yet with a freshness in the air that was exhilarating. The water lapped softly on secluded beaches and on the shore, dense forests of myrtle-beech climbed up the steep slopes of the surrounding mountains. Here and there a gum tree tried to establish a foothold but the beeches didn't permit it and left the interloper starved and dying in their midst. I had often wondered what a mountain would look like, clothed in trees other than the eucalypts of the mainland. Here I saw it and what a glorious tree is the Tasmanian myrtle-beech!

As we cut across the lake to the opposite shore, beautiful Mt. Ida came into view, graceful and elegant. Then, as we set a course for the entrance to the Narcissus River, the Acropolis appeared, followed by Mt.Gould, the Guardians, Mounts Manfred, Cuvier and Byron and finally lordly Olympus, extending round to our left. Tasmania's mountains are magnificent and the happy marriage of them and the most beautiful lake in the world produces scenery of unparalleled loveliness. My only regret was that some of Tasmania's aboriginal names were not retained to grace the peaks. They would match the wild country much better than alien names.

Arriving at the river entrance at the far end of the lake, we paddled several hundred yards up it to the Narcissus Hut. The scenery here was quite weird and unnatural. Water lay everywhere over flat land and gaunt dead trees interspersed with living ones rose straight out of the water, making the place look like Chloe's swamp. There were no banks and no shore. We got out at a wooden jetty made of stakes driven into the ooze and Mr. Cole told us, with something approaching awe in his voice, that Fergy had built it in one day with three ribs broken. That man again! Everyone had some tale to tell of him. He had explored most of the Lake St. Clair Reserve, blazing tracks and making hiking paths throughout the many square miles of rugged mountain country. (He came for a walk with us to the Hugel Lakes the next day and I shall never forget his lithe figure as, with tireless pace, he led the way. He carried an axe in one hand and, without slackening his speed, trimmed branches which straggled across the path, cleared obstacles underfoot, checked signposts and snowpoles, at the same time giving us a running commentary on the flora and fauna about us.)

But the business about the cat still rankled. We mentioned it to Mr. Cole. He threw back his head and laughed wheezily, his shoulders shaking.

'Fergy's pulling your leg! That cat was caught in a rat trap. Why, no one loves animals like Fergy. He's got pets all over the place.'

He chuckled for a long time while Shirl and I beamed at each other.

We ate our cut lunch in the Narcissus hut then started the long ten-mile row home. It was very cold in the boat and our feet were wet all the time but Mr. Cole, fortified by several tumblers of stout, amused us immensely with his repertoire of stories as he rowed. I have said that he was a meek little man, softly-spoken, peering timidly from behind his glasses. His stories were in character. They were all pointless, weak and occasionally, surprisingly, risqué. When he told one of the latter variety, he would giggle delightedly with a look on his face which clearly said 'What a little devil I am!' then lean forward anxiously and ask 'You see it don't you? Do you see the point?'

Shirl and I were rocking with laughter because the stories were so weak and we had to force laughs and exclaim how funny they were, slapping each other on the back and guffawing loudly.

'There's another very good one,' he said, gratified by our appreciation. 'Do you know the one about the man who pulled a thorn out of an elephant's foot in the jungle and years later he went to a circus and ….'

('Oh yes,' I thought with interest, 'this is the shaggy dog parody of the old one about the circus elephant lifting his benefactor out of the 1/3d seats and putting him in the 5/- ones. Only in the new version, the elephant merely singles the man out, raises him in his trunk and dashes him to the sawdust because it is a different elephant.')

I sat forward eagerly. At last, something funny.

'… Well, the elephant walked around the ring looking at all the people and then he saw this man. The man who'd pulled the thorn out, you remember …'

'Yes, yes, go on …'

'Well, he stopped. Stopped short. And then he did a funny thing.' His eyes glistened rheumily behind his glasses. 'Do you know what he did?'

'No, no … you tell us,' I said, waiting for the elephant to hurl him.

'Well, it put out its trunk and snatched up the man and put him in the best seats.'

'Oh NO!' I reeled.

'Yes, wasn't that good. He put him in the five shilling seats.' His brow clouded. 'Oh … did I tell you … the man had been sitting in the cheapest seats. I should've said that first …'

I hung over the transom, hooting and aching.

We spent four idyllic days at Fergy's. One day we hiked along the track to Mt.Rufus in early morning sunshine. The air was fresh and sweet and mist was still lying over some of the mountains and around the lake. We passed a kangaroo sitting quietly in a patch of grass contemplating us with a peaceful 'I'm protected' look in his eyes. Reaching the ridge, we had the most superb view of all the country in every direction ….numberless mountains, lakes and creeks. Descending the other side of Mt. Rufus, we picked our way through loose boulders and rocks before coming to sandy soil and low scrub. The scenery was constantly changing – from bare mountains through pleasant green grass cropped short like a lawn, subterranean creeks and dark, moist myrtle forests. The path then led through squelchy plains, inch-deep in water, until we reached the Hugel Lakes. We were soon passing through forests. At one stage, as I was walking in front of Shirl, I heard a rustle and, looking down, beheld a large tiger snake coiled on a fallen tree at my side. It must have been asleep until disturbed by our noisy passage through the bush. It unwound and slid away just as I whispered to Shirl to 'look there!' She screamed and, pushing me on, started to dash away. I was amazed at her terror. I had never seen her frightened. Apparently she hadn't ever seen a snake before.

All Australians grow up with the probability of encountering snakes at some time and, when hiking in the Victorian bush, we always stamped loudly and called out if going off the beaten track. I knew that Australian snakes are usually timid and get out of the way of noisy humans so I wasn't frightened. Besides, we carried snake bite kits – a little wooden spindle, one end of which unscrewed to reveal a sharp pointed scalpel for scarifying the punctured skin; the other end contained a small quantity of permanganate of potash (Condy's crystals) to cover the wound. We also knew about tying ligatures to stop the venom going to the heart. We didn't see another snake.

-oOo-

The fascinating first sight of Queenstown is preceded by a curtain-raiser called Gormanston. I was absolutely stunned by the new type of scenery. Forty miles behind us lay beautiful St. Clair surrounded by mountain ranges and peaks clothed in dark, moist Walt Disney forests of myrtle-beech. The mountains encircling Gormanston were completely denuded. Fires and sulphur fumes from the Mt. Lyell copper mines had killed all vegetation – even grass. They were bare even of soil and seemed to be made up of masses of broken rock and boulders. But what rocks! They glowed with colour. Dark ochrous yellow turned to burnt orange and chocolate brown before fading to pink and mauve with shadows of grey. Along one low ridge was the row of dolls houses which formed the town. It was quite fantastic and alien, but four miles further on was Queenstown, where the same landscape was duplicated on a vaster scale. There were streets and streets of houses, for this was the capital of the West Coast, but the unearthly-looking mountains crouched on all sides, white and bare, as over the years trees had been cut down to fuel the smelters. A sprinkling of new trees was trying to establish a hold on the slopes, but the growth was so sparse that when, on approaching Queenstown, we were hurtling around dangerous bends and stopped to search for branches to use as trailing brakes, we could find nothing suitable.

We went into a café to have a malted milk and asked the proprietor if he knew of any hall or place where we could camp for the night.

'Camp!' he said incredulously. 'Not in this weather! But I know just the bloke who can help you. Hang on a tick.'

He darted through a side door and returned some minutes later with an elderly man. 'Just the bloke' was George Nankivell.

From that moment on he took charge.

'So you thought you'd come out west to have a look at Queenstown eh? Good on you … not many tourists bother to come past St. Clair. But we'll show you what we can do out here. First of all, you'd better have a slap-up meal. What'll it be?'

We were fed and given a very comfortable hotel room. We unpacked and had baths and at seven o'clock Mr. Nankivell called for us in a car and drove out a few miles to the broadcasting station where he introduced us to the people of Queenstown. We spoke about our Tasmanian journey and plans for the future then drove back to the town. As we sped along the road, I saw family groups standing at gates and front doors of houses.

'What are all these people doing?' I asked Mr. Nankivell.

'They're waiting to see you,' he said, waving to someone he knew through the window. 'They know you have to come back from the radio station along this road.'

We were greatly amused and not a little touched by this friendliness and felt we should be doing Royalty waves to each side of the street as we passed.

Mr. Nankivell took us straight to a cinema where he had arranged for us to make a stage appearance. With packs strapped to our bikes, we waited in the wings, one on each side of the stage, and after Mr. Nankivell had delivered a few introductory remarks, we wheeled our bikes nervously onto the stage.

There was a tremendous outburst of clapping, leavened with appreciative whistles. We blushed and giggled. The spotlight full on us, we could see nothing beyond the footlights. How ridiculous one feels talking to a room full of space, where one can hear rustles and murmurings but cannot see a soul.

The interview was a rollicking affair and we were fêted for the rest of our stay. Mr. Nankivell was the nerve-centre of Queenstown. He was Mayor and prime mover in several youth organisations. He'd originated the City Band, the Boys' Club and Gymnastic Club and was hailed as 'George' by everyone he met.

He told us we must ride on the ratchet railway from Queenstown to Strahan on the west coast so we spent our last shillings on a ticket. For many miles the train ran alongside the King River which, leaden and sluggish, looked like the ruffled grey curtains in my grandmother's sitting room. What must have once been a beautiful river had been polluted by the waste from the Mt. Lyell mines.

As we travelled, the opening lines of a triolet came to me, a poetic form unknown to me until I read one my sister Marj had written.

> *Only the tussocks know how sad my heart is,*
> *Wheening a plaint to the desolate wind ....*

Then the cogs engaged and clickety-clack, we started to climb. The first steep ascent lifted us 700 feet in 2¾ miles, a grade of 1 in 20. And later on there was a 1 in 6 grade for 1½ miles. Once again we were in thick forests of myrtle-beech, white-flowered leatherwood, sassafras and King Billy pines while beautiful ferns burst thick fronds through the branches, straining towards the sun, and the dark undergrowth was splashed with colourful berries, twining clematis and crimson waratah. Down again through precipitous gorges over creeks and rivers by the score until we reached Strahan on the coast. Once a busy port, it now stirred itself only for an occasional cargo ship and an influx of summer visitors.

We changed trains and travelled on north through the old mining town of Zeehan and so to Burnie. The circle was complete and the *Taroona* was waiting at the dock to take us home. We had expected to be away for only a few weeks but the trip had lasted six. It didn't matter.... our time was our own. This was freedom!

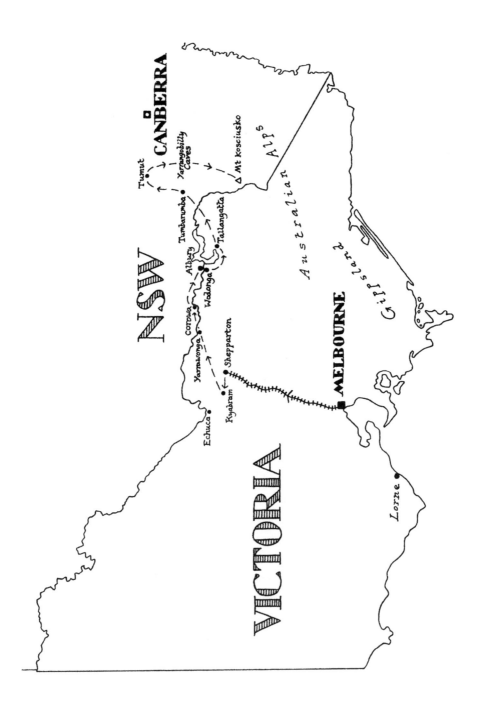

Chapter 2

FACTORY WORKERS

WANTED – Women & Girls to Can the Fruit Crop at Kyabram. Modern Factory in the heart of the Goulburn Valley. Minimum wage £2.2.0 for 5-day week of 40 hours to girls over 18 years. Piece workers can earn considerably more. Second class single fares paid and return fare paid on completion of satisfactory seasonal service.

SAVE THE FRUIT FOR BRITAIN!

Saturday, 13th April 1946:

The train pulled slowly into Shepparton station. It was 9 pm and a very cold autumn night. I peered through the windows and read the station sign under the one dim light. There was a clanking of chains, the jolt as carriage bumped carriage gently, the hiss of steam, shouts along the platform. I nudged Shirl and we dragged our haversacks down from the rack. Stumbling along the narrow corridor we dumped them on the platform. A hail came from the guard.

'Two bikes Bill! Duncan and Law.'

'Right!' we yelled and raced to rescue them as they were manhandled roughly out of the van.

A minute later, a whistle blew and the train started to move again and smoothly slid away, leaving us alone with the Station Master.

He eyed us with interest. We stood forlornly, haversacks stacked at our feet, bikes propped against the picket fence. Could we be the girls he'd read about in the *Herald*? ... it had said in the article that the first stage of their journey would be to Kyabram for the fruit canning season ...

We eyed him speculatively. It was late. We knew no one in Shepparton. It had been a very long day and we were tired. Would he be sympathetic?

'Excuse me ... do you think we might sleep the night in the ladies waiting room? We have sleeping bags and only want a floor.'

'You're the two girl cyclists aren't you? Thought you were. Yeah, I reckon you can use the waiting room. It's not very comfortable though – only got a concrete floor. Why don't you go into town and try a hotel?'

'Well, we can't afford to actually. We're trying to earn our way and if we stay at hotels every night we'll have to earn about three times as much.'

'We're quite happy,' said Shirl. 'Really. We're used to sleeping on floors. And we're terribly tired.'

'All right then. Here's the key. You'd better be out before the 8.30 comes in tomorrow'.

'We'll try. We've got to ride to Kyabram tomorrow so we'd better make an early start.'

The waiting room was small and cheerless. An empty fireplace yawned in one wall. A barred seat ran along another. There was a small door in the third wall leading to the lavatory and the door to the platform in the fourth.

'How cosy!' murmured Shirl without feeling. 'Bags the bench.'

We dragged our groundsheets and sleeping bags from our swag, and toilet bags from the top of the haversacks. Within five minutes we were in bed ... fully clothed. I had spread sheets of newspaper under me for softness and warmth but I was still miserably cold.

After a while, I heard rustlings and knew that Shirl had transferred to the floor.

'What's the matter Dunc? Lonely?'

'Grrr!' she snarled. 'I'd look like a tiger if I slept all night on that thing. No, for real comfort, give me a concrete floor any time.'

I huddled in my bag and giggled delightedly. There would be a lot of this sort of thing but it was fun.

'Gee,' said Shirl dreamily, 'to think we've really started.'

'Yes, but it was a near thing.'

-oOo-

It had been a crazy day. I had risen early to finish my packing. Mum had been at me for days to finalise things but I had been working on a fruit orchard until the last week and there was a round of farewell activities with friends and family, shopping, washing and mending and inevitably a last-minute rush. After breakfast I strapped my bulging haversack and sleeping bag on the carrier of my bike and said goodbye to Mum and Dad. 'See you in six months.' I waved gaily and disappeared through the College gates. I was to meet Shirl at Spencer Street in time to catch the 8.30 train to Kyabram.

As I wheeled my bike into the great station hall, Shirl dashed up with horror-wide eyes and shrieked:

'Wendy, the train's gone! It went at ten past eight!'

I felt slightly sick and dashed to the Man in Grey. Surely there must be another train? Yes … there would be one at 5pm to Shepparton. That would entail riding the 28 miles from Shepparton to Kyabram on Sunday, ready to start work at the Cannery on Monday.

Reaction set in and I giggled. 'How typical! Something always goes wrong with our plans. Oh well, the unexpected is always more interesting.'

'What are we going to do all day?'

'Let's go to the pictures this morning and come home to my place for lunch.'

So we idled along the streets, window-shopping until it was time for the theatres to open. After the show, we caught a tram back to the Teachers' College where my father was Principal. As we were jolting our way up Swanston Street, Shirl pointed to a man sitting next to her, who had the early edition of the *Herald*. There was a half-page spread about us with our pictures under the bold title *To Darwin on a wheel*. The reporter who had covered our story had formerly been a continuity writer at my broadcasting station and had done us proud.

'Good old Ron! But why *To Darwin on a wheel*? Sounds as though we're using those funny little one-wheeled bikes.'

'Gosh, I hope people don't recognize us. What frauds they'd think us if they saw us happily sitting in a city tram when the article clearly says that we left this morning.'

When Mum opened the door, she looked rather dazed. I think she was secretly hoping that we'd given up the whole mad idea. I prepared a tray of sandwiches, cake and fruit and we went out into the garden and spread a rug on the lawn. It was a glorious autumn day. The College gardens leapt with colour. A row of giant poplars along the Engineering School fence were torches of gold. The great round bed of dahlias flaunted flowers bigger than my head. The sun was mellow and there was a smell of fallen leaves. It was a pity to be leaving Melbourne at a time like this. Still, winter was coming. Queensland beckoned again.

We lay on the rug lazing in the sun, making extravagant plans and dreaming of the tropics when suddenly a window shot up and Mum called to us that it was half past four and we'd better hurry.

'Oh no!' I groaned, looking at Shirl in a panic.

We raced out to catch a tram. It idled gently all the way into town and we chafed with impatience. At Collins Street we changed trams and bore down on Spencer Street. I felt sick with dread and worry. At the station, with only two minutes to go, we rushed to the baggage room and begged the porter to let us have our bikes quickly. I rode after Shirl across the wide station yard, through the barrier, bundled my bike into the guard's van, searched desperately for my rail and seat reservation tickets and couldn't find them. The guard was hanging out of his van, his green flag twitching impatiently in his hands.

'Better get in miss and pity help yer if an inspector nips yer!'

I leapt on board and subsided on a seat opposite Shirl. The train started to move. I sat, completely overwhelmed and distracted and burning from the rush. As I calmed down, I realized in a disconnected way that I had left Melbourne for a very long time and that this was the Great Journey begun at last.

I settled myself more comfortably on the concrete.

'It's a funny feeling Dunc, everything – and nothing – in front of us.'

'Mmmmm,' said Shirl.

-oOo-

The ride to Kyabram was pleasant and we reached the Cannery Hostel at 4 o'clock. The Manageress, Mrs. Foster, showed us around. There was a main block containing a large dining room where meals were served cafeteria style; a recreation room with a piano, wireless and comfortable chairs grouped around an open fire and a reading and writing room. Another block contained a large room with dozens of showers, baths and hand-basins, an ironing room and telephone booth. The cannery workers slept in blocks of rooms or converted Army huts. We had a hut to ourselves.

'Now then, meal times are posted in the dining room and you've got to look sharp. You only have three quarters of an hour for lunch and breakfast. The rising bell is at 6.20 and you start work at 7.20. I think that's all you need to know. Now come and collect your bed linen and blankets.'

'Oh don't worry about that, Mrs. Foster. We're quite happy with our sleeping bags. We'll just lay them on top of the beds. It'll save laundry.'

'Rubbish! I wouldn't dream of letting you use them. You may as well have a comfortable bed as long as you're here.'

We shrugged and made up civilized beds with sheets and three blankets each.

As we were changing out of our cycling clothes, our first visitors began to call. A large round cheerful face popped around the door. It was plentifully freckled and surmounted by a mass of straight red hair, caught back with a large hairclip. The mouth was split wide in a smile of welcome.

'Can we come in? My name's Kath but they call me Blue. This here's Daph. What's your names?'

She was followed by a tall dark girl, quiet and pretty.

'I'm Wendy and this is Shirley. Sit on the bed. Turf those things on the floor. We're just settling in.'

'You've come a bit late, haven't you? We've been here since January. Daph and me follow the crops like. It's not bad. Yer see a bit of the country and the money's all right. What're you two doing?'

We told them. Blue's jaw dropped. 'Cripes! You're game aren't yer? What'd yer wanta come here for?'

'Well, we thought it'd be a novel experience to start with, and ....'

'... and they paid our fare to Kyabram! We're about a third of the way to Sydney already. That was the attraction! Otherwise we'd probably have gone by the Hume Highway or round the coast by the Prince's. But enough of that. Tell us what it's like here.'

'In the cannery? Oh, it's all right yer know. Gets a bit borin'. Daph and me do piece work stonin' the peaches. It takes a bit of practice but when you get the hang of it you can do lots of boxes a day. Yer get paid by the box.'

'Oh gosh, we'll hardly make any money at all.'

'What do you wear in the factory?' said Shirl. 'Peach juice stains doesn't it?'

'Yeah. Wear somethin' old and an apron. Anythin' you like. But wear somethin' warm. It's perishin' in there of a mornin'. Yer stand on a concrete floor and the sun doesn't get round to the winders till lunch time. My hands are that cold sometimes I can't hold me tools.'

The door opened again and another girl came in. She introduced herself as Lola and wanted to know if we were interested in going to the weekly dances at the neighbouring military and P.O.W. camps.

Lola seemed to be the hostel authority on recreation. Her appearance was not prepossessing. Her face was pale and her features weak. Her hair and clothes were untidy. Yet she spoke well and prided herself on being more refined than the other girls.

We all trooped into the canteen for tea (the evening meal) and then spent the evening talking by the recreation room fire. As we made our way to bed at half past nine, cowed by the prospect of rising at 6.20, Blue's cheerful voice pierced the night:

'Don't forget. Dress up warm! See yer tomorrer.'

-oOo-

A fearful tocsin rang out. It penetrated the innermost recesses of sleep and brought me to an immediate sitting position, blankets clasped to my chest, heart racing madly. My first thought was fire. Then I remembered everything. It couldn't be time to get up. It was still pitch dark. I heaved a shoe gently in the general direction of Shirl's bed. She moaned softly.

'Rise and shine Dunc. The factory calls.'

'I don't think I've even been asleep,' she said bitterly. 'I've never been so cold.'

'Me too. I'm going to sleep in my bag tonight. I couldn't endure another night like that. Blow Mrs. Foster and her sheets!'

We dressed rapidly, teeth chattering. After a long discussion we had decided what to wear. Trousers for warmth, our old cotton frocks, brought specially for the factory, worn outside our trousers to protect them from fruit splashes and aprons over the frocks to keep them clean.

'Add one factory net cap, garnish with rubber gloves and there you have what the well-dressed canner is wearing this season,' I said as I bundled my shoulder-length hair into the cap.

'Well, it's not for me. That looks foul, Wen. I'm just going to pin my cap on top and let my hair go free. It's too bad if any hairs fall in the peaches.'

'I think we look rather silly. I wonder what the others *do* wear.'

'Come to breakfast and you'll see. We'll have to rush, it's nearly seven.'

The canteen was already packed with girls munching determinedly with an eye on the clock. We queued for our food and took it to a long table. I was still half asleep and ate in a dream.

Then the room emptied rapidly as the girls hurried across the square to the cannery. We went back to our hut to collect our rubber gloves and the knife and peach spoon which we had been given. The latter was a sort of scoop for digging out the stone in the fruit. Feeling rather nervous and hilarious we went to the cannery. All the girls were at their benches now, poised spoon in hand, their eyes on the clock, waiting for the signal to start. The chatter stopped as we appeared in the doorway under the clock. Even the machines seemed to stop their roar. A ripple of laughter ran along the benches.

We looked around for deliverance but there was none. I shuffled my feet, greatly humiliated and tried to appear unconcerned. ('Whenever you feel awkward or embarrassed,' my sister Noel once told me, 'just tilt your nose and look superior.') But one glance at Shirl upset my feigned composure. My face crumpled and I wailed with mirth.

I was bad enough. My brown jodhpurs thrust out their fullness at my thighs and knees, giving a crinoline effect to the gaily-patterned dirndl I wore over them, but their straight tube-like legs were relatively sober. Shirley was wearing navy-blue ski-pants which ballooned out below the hem of her dress and clutched her ankles with all the frivolous abandon of harem trousers.

Our mortification was cut short by the bell. Immediately heads went down and hands started flying. Pick up a peach from a case on the left, scoop the stone out with a flick of the wrist and cast the fruit into another box. Repeat the process every two seconds and continue all day.

The forewoman, Miss Lewis, a solid woman in a dusty pink cardigan, came and snatched us up like an arrogant hen who has just found her missing chickens.

'You've come too late in the season to acquire any speed for piece work. You'd better be time workers. You'll get a flat rate of £2.2.0 a week. You,' she said to Shirl, 'can work on the peach belt. Come with me.'

We trailed along dejectedly behind her, acutely aware of the curious glances that followed our progress. A callow youth passed us, pushing a trolley laden with cases of fruit.

'Haw!' he guffawed. 'Goin' ridin'?'

We came to the peach belt. Peaches were grown at Shepparton, the centre of the stone fruit industry, and often picked by students during their vacation. The stoned peaches from the pieceworkers had been immersed in a caustic solution to remove their skins and they now came bobbing along on a moving belt, hot, steamy and oily from the bath.

'Stand here!' Shirl was thrust into a vacant position alongside the belt. 'You have to separate all the imperfect fruit. Only perfect peaches are canned whole or halved. Any that still have skin on them you put on this belt above – see – which takes them back to the caustic bath. Any that are marked you put on this belt which takes them away to the 'speckers'. After the specks have been cut off, those peaches are sliced and canned. Now, any fruit that is too badly marked or bruised, you put in these tins up on this shelf. What is left after these have been dealt with, is used for jam. Now get going. You,' to me, 'come with me.'

I cast an amused glance backwards at Shirl, who was standing, stunned and dazed, in front of the tiers of belts, one moving left, one whizzing right, and the tins above. Tentatively, she put out a hand to the moving fruit. I saw her touch her lips with the tip of her tongue and smiled. She adored tinned peaches.

'Hurry on,' came the cold, hard voice that was to haunt every waking hour. 'We'll put you here.' We had come to a row of stainless steel sinks, each attended by a girl busily wielding a knife. 'Got your gloves? Put them on. Tom!' She called to a young lad who hurried up with a kerosene tin of imperfect peaches from Shirl's top shelf.

He upended the tin and a stream of hot, mushy fruit poured into my sink. The smell was sickening.

'Now, just lop off all the bad bits and put what's left in these tins. All right?' She hurried away.

I drew on the rubber gloves, which were a good inch too long in each finger and tried to pick up a peach. It slipped through my fingers leaving a sticky coating on the glove. I tried again. This time I held one firm and made a slash at it with my sharp knife. The peach wriggled successfully out of my grasp and the knife made a neat incision in the thumb of my glove. Dipping into the sink for another peach, the liquid penetrated the slit and I felt the stickiness spread down into the palm. Ugh! I desperately snatched up another peach, cut off two-thirds of it that was rotten and nicked a finger. By now the gloves were sticking to my hand and the surplus inch of rubber at the end of each finger was adhering to itself, wall to wall.

I flapped about in the sink for an hour, occasionally producing a morsel of good peach for the jam vats, but mostly splashing and dropping and cutting myself. Then the youth ran down the row and showered another load of stinking fruit on top of my first lot.

'Hey, I haven't finished yet!' But he was gone.

I looked about me wearily. The girl next to me, Gwen, was busily cleaning out her sink. She flushed water into it, whished the last scraps of fruit down the plug-hole, wiped it around with her hand and stood back, tapping her foot and probably humming. I couldn't hear anything over the racket of the machinery.

I looked at my sink. It looked like a drowning man whose straw has just become waterlogged. The fruit underneath was now a pulpy rotten mess. I started in again and worked with a desperation born of an intimation of defeat. Grab, slice, grab, slice. I didn't pause for about half an hour and to my great joy seemed to be making some impression on the pile. Faster, faster! The level was much lower now and I fancied I could almost see the plug. Whoosh! Another tinload of peaches poured into the sink past my ears.

I looked up with a deadly calm and masterly control. The boy was retreating down the row, his cheeks blown out in what must have been a whistle. I laid down my knife, took a deep breath and with a smile of ineffable love for the world and all its wickedness, looked about me. Gwen was just coaxing the last sediment down her plug-hole. She turned off her taps, gave them a little polish with the cuff of her glove and flashed me a friendly smile.

I knew then what makes a strong man put his head on his arms and weep as a little child. I could have wept but speech was denied me. Finding I could just glimpse Shirl across the intervening benches, I lifted an eyebrow at her and headed for the Ladies. She joined me there in a minute.

'Well?' she asked in a curiously lack-lustre voice.

'Defeat is bitter on my tongue. The iron has entered deep within my soul,' I intoned flatly.

'Come and sit down and tell me all about it.'

We entered adjoining cubicles and for a minute there was no talk. Our feet were giving up joyful thanks for having our weight removed from them and the relief was delicious.

Then I told her all. She mused a minute then said ruefully:

'I don't think you're as badly off as I am. You've only had mental torment.   I've nearly been sick out there … physically sick I mean. Apparently everyone feels seasick the first day. All those belts, moving in opposite directions, with the peaches bobbing along on them … most upsetting to your semicircular canals. Yet you should see the other women there … dear old grannies with lace caps who've heard the call and come to save the fruit for Britain. There they stand, small and frail but their eyes are steady and their hands busy. And here am I, a great strong, healthy girl and I can't keep up with them. I'm a wreck already!'

I commiserated with her. 'It's the standing up. I'm exhausted too. I suppose we'll get used to it.'

'Come on then. This is the logical place for slackers to congregate. Miss Lewis probably pokes her nose in here regularly.'

'Just a minute. I'm taking off these ridiculous jodhpurs. I've never been so humiliated.'

We went back to our places and resumed work. The rest must have refreshed me for I found things much easier and fell into a rhythm. Grab, slice, grab, slice. If only my feet didn't ache so! I looked over to Shirl and found her working her arms madly like a semaphore. Her face was alight with glee and she was mouthing words at me. I looked puzzled. She pointed beneath her and tried to drag something out from beneath her to show me. Why, she was sitting! Then I lip-read 'Box! Get a box!' Wonderful! I flashed her a smile of acknowledgement and darted away to a pile of fruit cases I'd seen earlier in the day. I dragged one back to my sink and stood it on end. It was just the right height. My body at ease, I bent to my task with a joyful heart.

My thoughts were far away when the box went flying from under me, kicked by a neatly-laced shoe, and Miss Lewis hissed in my ear: 'Stand on your own two feet and *work*!'

-oOo-

The day dragged on, uninterrupted but for an unnoticeable break for lunch. Five o'clock saw us streaming to the hostel for the bath rush.

Lola detached herself from the crowd and called languidly to us: 'How about coming to a dance at Tatura Camp tonight, you two?'

'Are you serious?' said Shirl astounded.

'I'm going to bed,' said I weakly.

'Got you down has it? First day's always the worst. You'll be right tomorrow. There's a beaut dance next week. Try and come then. Bye.'

After a bath, change of clothes and tea, we could feel more objective about the Cannery. It already was remote. Only the memory of the dawn tocsin and the numbing cold remained as a foreboding.

'The trouble is,' said Shirl, 'that I run out of things to think about. I can't talk to my neighbour without cupping my hands and shrieking so all I can do is think.'

During the days that followed, we eagerly compared notes and passed on to each other any new subject for thought.

'I had a good morning,' Shirl said at lunch. 'I started planning the lay-out of my photo album. Thinking about each photograph and where to put it took nearly an hour.'

'Well, I sang this morning. Every song I've ever known. This afternoon I'll do poems. That should see me through until five.'

No one who has never worked in a factory can comprehend the soul-deadening monotony of it. To be bored and fatigued is bad enough, but to have a mind, devoid of thought, completely blank, is to become a true automaton. I understand now why most factories have recorded music relayed over loudspeakers in the workrooms. Not so much to encourage workers to work faster as to preserve their sanity.

After an Easter break when we rode to Echuca, we clocked in for work next day and found that peaches were off and we were to work pears for the last week of the season. This was wonderful news. Besides varying the monotony, pears are much nicer. They are cleaner, less oily and haven't the sickening smell of peaches.

This time Shirl was to operate a pear machine. She stood at this Gargantuan contraption and fed pears at regular intervals into a hole. ('Like giving peanuts to an elephant,' she said disgustedly). In due course they emerged, skinned, halved and cored and came bobbing along a belt where I was on guard. Although the machine had cut around the cores, sometimes they hadn't been dislodged so as to leave the smooth little hollow which tinned pears must have. It was my job, therefore, to prod the stubborn cores with a finger and make them pop out. I just stood with my two index fingers extended and as the pears came swiftly out of the chute, went stab, stab, stab at the cores. But the game had its hazards. From where the pears emerged from the machine to the place where they dived over a sort of waterfall and thence out of sight down a hooded tunnel, was a mere five feet. If a slow, steady stream of fruit came along, I could easily cope. But when a rush came, I panicked and desperately tried to attend to them all before they plunged over the fall and out of my life. I'd start near the chute, fingers stabbing wildly, and as some of the pears eluded me, I'd follow them along the belt and make a last stand by the fall, with new fruit banking up behind me. The only thing to do then was to sweep them all back to the beginning of the belt with my arm, and start afresh.

I have since seen a revival of Charlie Chaplin's *Modern Times* where he had the task of tightening nuts on a long belt with a spanner. He, too, used to pile up at the end of the belt, just before the nuts disappeared into the bowels of another machine. I don't suppose any international incident would have been created if I'd let one core go to Britain in a tin of pears but at that time it seemed a heinous crime.

-oOo-

Our social life had burgeoned, and every three or four nights we went with a bus load of hostel girls to dances in the neighbouring towns. Muffled in our warmest clothes, and packed tightly on the long seats, we sped through the frosty night singing, laughing and swapping stories. Lola with tales of her conquests, Blue with an uproarious account of her Easter weekend in Bendigo. She was such a happy person, she could hardly tell her stories without going into gales of laughter herself. When we were all aching with mirth, she'd call for a song. I can still see her round pale face shining out of the gloom of the bus, eyes vanishing into slits as she flung back her head and roared:

> *Let 'im go, let 'im tarry, let 'im sink or let 'im swim.*
> *'e doesn't care for me and I don't care for 'im.*

We joined in and swayed to the rhythm, stamping our cold feet:

> *He can go and get another that I hope he will enjoy,*
> *For I'm gonna marry a far nicer boy!*

One of these expeditions took us to the Tatura No.1 Internment

Camp. There were many POW camps scattered through northern Victoria at this time but this one housed civilian internees, nearly all of whom had been apprehended in Persia. There was a lively dance in one of the camp buildings and then we all trooped into the Sergeants' Mess for supper. There was an abundance of food on the table and as usual, Shirl and I were the last to finish eating. We were at that stage of late adolescence when we could eat unlimited amounts of food. We were not yet sensitive to the warnings of beauty columnists and diet was a thing to deride.

The mess orderly was a quiet, good-looking internee. When he started removing dishes near us, rather pointedly, I asked if he were German. He said he came from Düsseldorf in the Rhineland but hadn't been there for nineteen years, having lived in Persia all that time. We spoke together in German although my German was as hesitant as his English. He was so pleased to speak to someone new and I suppose he hadn't spoken to a girl for years. I told him what Shirl and I were doing and hoped to do and his eyes flicked with that spark of interest and envy which we were to come to see so often – in the eyes of all schoolchildren, most adolescents and some adults under thirty.

'I should like to write to you,' he said hesitantly. 'If you'd reply, that is.'

'I'd like to. You'll have a job keeping up with us but I'll try and tell you our route in advance so that you can write to the Post Offices along the way.'

His name was Karl Frisch.

-oOo-

We had been working at the Cannery for only a fortnight when the season came to an end. We had been very late arrivals.

I wasn't sorry. After a week on the pear belt I felt there was nothing more for me to learn about pears. I knew every one of them, they all knew me and had been prodded by my vicious finger. I felt I could live a full and happy life if I never saw a pear again.

I watched the last one traverse the belt and slide out of sight. I let it go without lifting a finger.

NEW SOUTH
WALES

• Broken Hill

Tweed
Heads

Grafton • • Maclean

Newcastle

Orange •
Katoomba • ← □ SYDNEY

Mildura •

CANBERRA
Tumut •
ACT

Albury
Echuca • Bateman's Bay
Kyabram Tallangatta Cooma
Mt
Kosciusko

Chapter 3

UP INTO THE HIGH COUNTRY

From Kyabram we could have reached Sydney within a week by following the straight, uninteresting Hume Highway. But time was of no importance to us and we were tempted by what lay in the unfamiliar pocket of country between the inland Hume and the coastal Prince's Highway.

It is romantic country. The Great Dividing Range, the huge backbone which runs down the east coast of Australia for over 1,500 miles, cuts through this territory before swinging west into Victoria. The Snowy River, known to every school child from bush ballads, has its source there. So has the mighty Murray River which forms the border between New South Wales and Victoria. Lord of all the mountain peaks and indeed of Australia, is Mt. Kosciusko. A not insignificant 7,305 feet, Kossy is crowned and mantled in snow throughout winter and its great variety of slopes attracts advanced skiers.

I had been brought up on tales of mountaineering and skiing. My two elder brothers, Geoff and Phil, had pioneered the wild Grampians in Victoria while still boys and later, with my third brother Peter, had called the Australian Alps their second home. My head spun with wonderful spell-binding names like Bogong, Feathertop, Hotham, Geehi, Dargo High Plains, Kosciusko, Razorback, Staircase Spur, St.Bernard Hospice and so on. I used to eat my heart out with envy when I saw my brothers setting off on one of their trips. Dressed in ski trousers, wind jackets, heavy boots reeking with dubbin, they'd pile their bulging rucksacks into an old car and strap their precious skis on the roof. The skis were what fascinated me most. Made by the boys themselves, they represented hours of patient work – steaming, bending, planing, rubbing and waxing. Then the bindings had to be fixed and lastly, the alpenstocks with their pretty leather lacings were made. I watched these proceedings silently and with a worshipping admiration. My brothers were surely the most wonderful in the world!

Australia is primarily a temperate country and its snowfields are remote from the big cities. Skiing had only become available to the average citizen since the 2nd World War. In the thirties and forties it was reserved for the very rich or the very intrepid. (The former made their headquarters in the comfortable chalets or hotels which existed at some mountains; the latter roughed it in huts which were scattered through the wilderness.) One just didn't see skis in an average Melbourne home and to me they became a symbol of remote journeyings and high adventure.

I was excited when the boys set off in their battered car. I was bursting with pride when they returned weeks later with stubbly beards, blistered faces tanned to that peculiar shade of yellow-brown by sun and snow. Over their first civilized meal they would tell wonderful stories of excitement and accomplishment, of privation, exhaustion and disaster, of good 'grub' in camps and ordeals in blizzards or illness. The seed of my wanderlust was already pushing up sturdy sprouts.

So, of course, we had to go to Kossy. Our route was a strange one. Traced on a map it resembled a drunkard's meandering. From Kyabram we rode north to the Murray at Yarrawonga, crossed into New South Wales to ride east along the river to Corowa, back into Victoria and along the river to Howlong then back into N.S.W. for a quick trip to Albury.

Albury is a lovely town. It is like coming into an oasis after travelling through the summer-parched paddocks of Northern Victoria. Beautiful gardens and trees abound and in autumn the colours are breathtaking. We found our way to the home of a girl we had met at the cannery. Kay and her sister Leila had a small farm. When we arrived she was busy milking the cows. Cows! Our eyes lit up. That meant cream! Our progress along the Murray had been highlighted by the dairy farms we'd passed and we were already putting on weight. There was a definite procedure to be followed. We used to call at a farm at milking time ... the hum of the milking machines was the sweetest music ... and ask if we could buy a bottle of cream. (An empty bottle was always conveniently packed on top of my haversack!) The farmer's wife would hesitate and say ... 'Well, we're not allowed to sell it ... here, give me your bottle and I'll give you a drop.' We would take the spoil away, camp under a tree and have a wonderful feed of bread and jam and lashings of cream.

After helping Kay with the separating we had hot baths, dressed warmly and sat down to a colossal tea of pickled pork, salad (dressing made from cream) and mashed potatoes. Then preserved nectarines and cream; bread and cream and sugar; bananas and cream; and lastly some little cakes. That night we slept soundly in a real bed.

In the morning Kay brought in a copy of the *Border Morning Mail* and I looked for our article. We always reported to the newspaper office on arrival in a town. There was a great spread and a ghastly photo of us.

'Look at this Wen. **Strange Traffic on Hume Highway.** We're not the only cranks. 'Two Tivoli acrobats creating a Sydney-Melbourne 1 h.p. record on motorscooters, and a young Melbourne hairdresser, walking from Melbourne to Sydney with a Shetland pony and pony cart, on a wager, passed through Albury today.' Crikey, he's doing it the hard way.'

'I bet he'll be in Sydney before us! Come on, we'd better get going.'

We said goodbye to Kay and Leila and rode on to Wodonga and Tallangatta. That was a homecoming for me. My mother came from Wodonga, my father was a Tallangatta boy and the three eldest of our family were born there when Dad was a young teacher at Mitta Mitta. My grandfather and then my father had run the weekly *Upper Murray and Mitta Herald* for nearly 70 years but we arrived the day after the paper had gone to press so the office was quiet.

I never think of Tallangatta without nostalgia. Maybe because it retains the essence of my childhood in its gentle valley. It was never my home, but most of my school holidays were spent there.

> *Where Tallangatta lies sleeping*
> *And the Mitta rolls along.*

Winter days of sparkling sunshine and nights of biting frost. Summer, with a rocketing temperature but low humidity. The wide, wide main street, bare of traffic and people, quivering in the heat; the cool verandah of the *Herald* Office house, laced with luxuriant vineleaves with heavy pendulous bunches of grapes like stalactites; the high brown hill rising straight out of my aunt's fowl-yard, bare but for occasional gaunt ring-barked trees and clumpy grass, a dead sheep left to the flies and the crows. Yes, always the crows with their harsh, stricken cry. Lazy days spent swimming in the brown Mitta Mitta river or the creek winding through the weeping willows which fringed its banks; hot still summer nights when everyone trooped to the pictures if it were a Saturday night or sat out of doors in cane chairs, fanning and slapping at mosquitoes.

How many people know about Tallangatta? And how many grieved when it was destroyed? For Tallangatta was doomed. Ever since the 1st World War there had been talk of flooding the valley in order to enlarge the nearby Hume Reservoir. The old residents fought desperately to save the little township but its fate was inevitable. After the 2nd World War the decision was finally made to flood it. A site five miles away on the shore of the Hume Weir was selected for a new town and the great move started. Those buildings which could be moved were taken on the back of large trailers and deposited at the new site but many brick buildings stayed to sink silently beneath the flood. Poor little lazy, busy, sunny, contented Tallangatta.

We rode out of Tallangatta at 4 o'clock – our usual 'early start'. This early start business was to become a stock joke with us. People always expected us to rise with the lark and be on the road by 7. But we loved sleep next to food and, if left to ourselves, did not even wake until we had had enough sleep – usually at about 10am. Then we had a sort of brunch – maybe a bar of chocolate and an apple, explored the town where we happened to be, dutifully inspected whatever the town wished us to inspect, then packed up and set off again mid-afternoon. This invariably meant a reshuffle of our plans. We regretfully relinquished the hope of reaching a town fifty miles away and aimed instead for one ten or twenty miles on. Then just as we had adjusted to this change, along would roar a truck to take us to the fifty-mile town after all. Such an exhilarating experience! One felt one was cheating the clock.

So it was that when we left Tallangatta, we resigned ourselves to overnighting at Granya, fourteen miles on, instead of Burrowye which was forty-one miles away. A mile out of Tallangatta we hailed a truck and learned that it was going to a farm twelve miles short of Burrowye. Overjoyed, we helped the driver bundle our laden bikes into the back and clambered up after them.

'Pigs!' said Shirl distastefully.

We picked our way through the messy straw, sliding on the slippery floorboards as the truck got under way, and stood leaning on the cabin. With a grinding of gears we forged up Granya Pass in a very short time and exulted at the thought of how we had been spared a long walk. The countryside was beautiful. Soft green valleys unfolded at each turn of the road and huge purple and green mountains hemmed us in.

'*Gnarled and bent with age they stand, leaning on the troubled land,*' I declaimed, inspired.

'What?' bellowed Shirl, above the wind.

'Oh nothing.'

'WHAT?'

The wind leant against us and pushed. My eyes streamed with tears, and the ends of my head kerchief slapped and cracked like a stockwhip. No one can understand the supreme exhilaration of speeding effortlessly on a powerful truck who hasn't known the frustrating slowness of pushing a heavily-laden bicycle.

By the time we had reached the driver's farm and gone in to meet his wife, had some tea and started riding again, it was pitch dark and bitingly cold. We pulled long trousers over our shorts and rode on five miles, then turned along a sidetrack for two miles. We were looking for the home of Mr. and Mrs. Cheshire – he being the brother of a lady who'd worked opposite me on the pear belt. We kept a sharp watch for their house and were beginning to think we'd missed it when a utility truck approached. We hailed it and asked where the Cheshires lived.

'Right here,' said a cheery voice. It was they. They were off to a party but turned around and drove us back to the farm.

'Why don't you come too? It's a farewell to the local school teacher.'

'They won't want strangers there, will they?'

'Don't worry, the more the merrier. You won't be strangers for long.'

So these hospitable people, who had known us for only five minutes, took us into their house for a bath and change and then drove us off into the night to meet their friends. Australians are like that, from Hobart to Darwin. Open-hearted, open-handed, they make one a part of their life, no strings attached, no questions asked.

Well, not many. The people we met at the party knew about us already. Burrowye is within range of the Melbourne *Herald*. I was absorbed into a little group of residents and being asked about our plans as soon as I had crossed the threshold. After chatting for a while, I looked about for Shirl. I found her sitting listlessly in a chair in a quiet corner and hurried over.

'The Great Weariness has struck, Wen. I just can't keep awake.'

'I know, it's been a long day. But try and buck up. Supper will be on soon. You know country suppers Dunc. Cream!' I hissed softly.

Supper was certainly worth missing a little sleep. How I love country dances or parties, where the women vie with each other in bringing the most delectable cakes, sponges, sandwiches and trifles. This party was no exception, and we came alive sufficiently to do justice to the wonderful spread. A feeling of cat-like content pervaded us as we jolted home in the utility and, as I crawled between the cool sheets and let my weary limbs relax on the soft, so soft mattress of Mrs.Cheshire's spare bed, my first and last thought was simply, 'Heaven!'

-oOo-

We spent two days with the Cheshires, two glorious days of sunny laziness. North-eastern Victoria has wonderful weather. The air is still and hot, bees drone happily among the flowers, the horses in the home paddock switch their tails at persistent flies, a contented clucking comes from the fowls in the shade of the peppercorns and an occasional idle zephyr brings to one's nostrils the fragrance of sun-hot hay, the cool scent of green vines on the verandah, a whiff of roast dinner from the kitchen window and just the faintest suspicion of cows.

We sat about, wrote letters, washed all our clothes, boiled handkerchiefs and towels and washed our hair. Hair-washing was, next to teeth-cleaning, our most sacred duty. We would go to great lengths to find hot water once a week. If we were not enjoying private hospitality when the day arrived, we'd go to the nearest hotel and ask for the use of a bathroom. Because of the different kinds of water along our route, some hard, some soft, we always asked for a little vinegar or lemon juice to add to the rinsing water. This eliminated a dulling white film on the hair and made it squeak. I set my hair by pushing it into waves but Shirl had some equipment consisting of a roll of cotton wool which she put under her hair and pinned at her temples. Then she placed a ribbon above the roll, tying it on her forehead. Over all this she placed a hairnet. This resulted in her hair turning under in a beautiful pageboy style, with a ridge where the ribbon had been.

On our last afternoon at Burrowye, Bruce Cheshire, a lad of about ten, rounded up three horses and Shirl and I went out with him on a round of the rabbit traps. The trapping was Bruce's own thriving business. He set the traps, collected the rabbits and sold the skins. We had been out only an hour when darkness fell. The traps were scattered in likely places all over the surrounding countryside and our way led up steep hills, down rocky slopes, along creek beds, through patches of fern and bracken and over fallen logs. As it became darker, I was nervous lest my horse stumble, but sure-footed and steady, he picked his way carefully past the obstacles in his path. In a little while, the moon came up. It was glorious riding through the night. The sky was a-foam with stars and the mountains ringing the valley were black and silent. The only sounds were the gentle creaking of saddle leather, the ting of metal as the horses champed on their bits, a kicked stone rolling down the slope and a dog barking from a distance at our progress.

We left the next afternoon for Jingellic and ambled pleasantly along the Murray River which flowed gently so as not to disturb the reflections of weeping willow and poplar. On arrival, we went straight to the Cream Factory, as we had heard that the cream trucks plied regularly between Jingellic and Tumbarumba – a particularly hilly road. We arranged with a truck driver to be ready at the unheard-of hour of 6.30am and then sought the manager to enquire about accommodation for the night. He showed us some places on the river bank nearby which would be suitable for camping but Shirl and I weren't over-enthusiastic. Our love for the Great Outdoors had rapidly waned since the approach of winter. Romantic dreams of sleeping on hay under the stars are all right on a balmy summer night but not when you awake to find your sleeping bag wet with dew or stiff with frost. Just then, another chap came up and offered us one of the factory sheds. It was the case-maker's domain, stacked to the roof with 3-ply but we cleared enough room on the floor and unpacked.

It never ceased to surprise me how much gear we managed to compress into our haversacks. We each carried a total swag of about sixty pounds. Of this, sleeping bag and a combination groundsheet/rain cape/tent were strapped to the handlebars. The haversack went on a back carrier. In it were changes of underwear, handkerchiefs, a couple of blouses or cotton jumpers, two pairs of shorts (one pair of utility navy ones for riding, and one pair of white or coloured ones for 'best'), a pair of long trousers, a heavy woollen skirt, fleece-lined windcheater and knitted jacket for warmth and a gay cotton dirndl (not the Cannery one) for dances or parties. Then there was a pair of Joyce casuals to go with the glamour clothes (we rode in strap sandals), socks, gloves and kerchief, rain hood and eyeshade for extremes of weather, toilet gear and a towel; bike accessories such as a lamp, torch, repair kit, length of rope, pieces of string; writing materials, a bottle of ink to fill my fountain pen, diary, maps and an assortment of books. I carried half a dozen music books (Chopin waltzes, Schubert Impromptus, Grieg Lyric

Pieces, some Bach, Mendelssohn and a book of sonatinas) and three well-worn books of poetry – Methuen's *Anthology of Modern Verse*, a book of Australian poetry *New Song in an Old Land* and a slim volume of my sister Marj's verse entitled *Rainsongs*. I also carried a Bible, not because I was religious but because I had started reading a chapter each night when I was at school in order to lessen my ignorance of it; I was now reading it for the second time. Shirley was the photographer and had a good little Voigtländer camera.

We never carried food or cooking implements for the simple reason that neither of us could cook. Tradition demanded that we should at least carry a billy for making billy tea on a campfire but neither of us liked tea. We lived off the land, were invited to private homes for odd meals and filled in space with chocolate, fruit, raisins and malted milks. One two-glass serving of malted milk was as good as a meal and cost only sixpence. We usually had a malted for brunch and in the evening, when we were cold and tired, we'd buy three pennyworth of potato chips or a piece of fried fish. (We had a communal purse for when we were buying the same things…..a sensible idea given to us by that inveterate traveller, my brother Geoff. When it was depleted we'd each subscribe more cash.)   I don't remember ever buying a meal in those days. We couldn't afford to. We had to live on something like ten shillings a week.

'Shirl, how much cash have you left?'

'I've still got the fiver I left home with – and the travellers' cheques but I'm not touching them – and I've got £1.12.0 left from the Cannery wages.'

After two weeks board had been deducted, we'd collected a miserable cheque for £2 from the Cannery for two weeks work.

'Yes, I've about the same. It's pretty serious Dunc. We're taking so long to reach Sydney. We've been almost a month so far. I think we're going to take more than six months to do this trip – especially if we go to Darwin.'

Although originally we had merely planned to go to Queensland for the winter, now we were beginning to talk about Darwin, the capital of the Northern Territory and the most northerly point we could reach.

'Well, six months or a year, what's it matter? Our time's our own.'

'My mother will have a fit!   She thinks we're just going to Queensland.'

'We'd be mad to turn back from there Wen. With that lovely road going across from Townsville to the Territory.' (We weren't to be disillusioned about that road until much later!)

'Oh, I want to go all right. But we'll have to think of a way to earn some more money. And earn it as we go. We can't sit down in a place for a month or two to replenish our funds.'

'If only Malvern Star would sponsor us! After all, they're going to get an awful lot of incidental publicity. They should pay for it!'

We were both riding Malvern Star bicycles, ordinary girls' bikes with no gears and no trimmings. A dress net covered the top of the rear wheel. The little clips which attached it to the hub and the mudguard kept falling out and then the net would flap in the spokes. My bike was eight years old. Malvern Star knew about our trip, and had contacted all their agents along the route, in case we needed repairs in a hurry but there was no question of payment.

'Let's get on to them again when we reach Sydney. Perhaps, when they see that we mean to keep going, they'll come around.'

There was a knock at the door and Mr. Coughlan came in. He was the man who had found the room for us.

'How about coming over to my place for a while?' he said. 'The wife's got a good fire going and you can have a hot wash if you like.'

'Wonderful! We'll just change and be over in a minute.'

We put on our dirndls and went to his house. Mrs. Coughlan let us in.

'I'm just putting the children to bed. You sit here by the fire and make yourselves at home.'

We had nearly thawed out when she returned with some jugs of steaming hot water for our wash. As we were splashing happily in it, she called out: 'There's a dance on tonight. Why don't you go?'

'Any good! We haven't had any social life for ages. Where is it?'

'Only about a mile from here. You could ride there in a jiffy.'

We perked up at the sound of this. Country dances are great fun. So when we had dressed again, we went back for our bikes.

'It's terribly cold,' said Shirl, her teeth chattering. 'I'm going to dress up.'

That meant putting everything on that she could muster. Under her dirndl she had her woollen skirt; on top she wore a windcheater and a woollen cardigan. On her head and hands were kerchief and gloves and on her legs were her so-called 'leggings'. While I had been earning some money picking apples before setting out from Melbourne, she had done some piecework for a knitting factory. She used to take home piles of men's socks for finishing. A by-product of all this labour was a quantity of tubes of grey stocking waste. Ever prudent, she had brought these with her and now wore them around thighs and calves.

I hooted. 'You look like a racehorse!'

'I don't care. I'm warm. Come on, hey for the Ball!'

We rolled out to our bikes, laughing hysterically, and pedalled weakly to the dance hall. Diving behind a bush, we divested ourselves of our surplus clothing and, shivering in cotton dresses, peeped into the hall. It was very dull. About six couples were dancing half-heartedly to the plonking of an inharmonious piano. There was not a preponderance of men.

We gloomed darkly.

'There might be a beaut supper,' said Shirl hopefully.

'Not worth it. Let's go home.'

So we turned tail dejectedly, dressed again behind the bush and rode back. We took off our frocks, put on jodhpurs, windcheaters, jackets, long football socks, gloves and kerchiefs and went to bag. The floor was very hard and the air icy.

-oOo-

The cream truck was punctual. We crawled out into the grey dawn, packed our gear on the back of the truck and set off to Tumbarumba. Lovely name! It is aboriginal for 'thunder' and I can just imagine the reverberations rolling off those hills. It would have been a very scenic trip, except for the dense fog through which we drove. As we ascended a few thousand feet, we emerged into sunlight and the fog looked like glistening snowfields or sun-sparkling sea beneath us. We should have had a dreadful time on our bikes as the road was terrifically hilly with a wretched surface. As it was, we sat snugly in the cabin, lulled by the drone of the engine, and tried to sleep. Our driver was very friendly and talkative. He didn't often have passengers to beguile the tedious journey. He was a typical lean, wiry, hatchet-faced Digger. (Australian soldiers in the Great War were called Diggers.)

'How'd yer come to take up bike riding?' he enquired chattily.

I feigned sleep and waited for Dunc to answer. She didn't. I peeped between my lids and saw her, eyes closed, head slumped on her chest. I knew she was awake. Her lashes were quivering. The dog!

'Well…' I took a deep breath. May as well pay for our passage with good humour. 'We used to do a lot of hiking … Y.W.C.A. and Bushwalkers Clubs and so on. Then we did a two-day hike, staying overnight at a Youth Hostel. But, we thought, how much further we could go on bikes! So we tried it, and the trips became longer until we ran out of places to go. So then we just had to leave our jobs.'

'Gee, you've taken something on now though. How long d'yer reckon it'll take yer?'

'Oh, getting on for a year probably, though we may be home for Christmas. We want to go to Darwin and down through the Centre to Alice Springs and Adelaide, then home.'

'You want to be careful there. There's some mighty long stretches up by the Alice. I know.'

'Ah yes, but there are also droves of mighty big trucks thundering down the North-South Road.

'Garn, that's cheating! You're supposed to be riding bikes.'

'No, we're not,' I answered a little primly. 'We don't set ourselves up as cyclists or record-breakers. We're merely tourists. If we had one, we'd go by car. But we haven't. So it's bikes. But if we can hitchhike, so much the better. The bikes merely serve as luggage-carriers.'

'Well, rather you than me. Better wake Blue there. We're coming into Tumbarumba.'

I dug Shirl in the ribs and whispered 'The danger is past.' She sat up brightly and said 'Where are we?'

We pulled into Tumbarumba and parked outside Roth's Store. Mr.

Roth came out, saw us unloading our gear and hurried up.

'Welcome to Tumbarumba girls! We've been expecting you. I'll bet you were glad to get a lift this morning.'

'Gosh yes. It would've taken us hours to walk. Don't suppose you know of anyone going on to Tumut, do you?'

'No, I don't. But I'll make enquiries. How're your bikes? Want anything checked? Malvern Star asked us to help you in any way we can.'

'Mine needs some oil,' said Shirl.

'Well, bring it in and while the boy's going over it, you can tell me a bit about your trip.'

'Go on Dunc,' I said with malice. 'I'll wait here and keep an eye out for trucks.'

When she returned she was carrying a long scroll under her arm.

'Look what Mr. Roth's given me!' She waved it and it unrolled.

'What is it? A calendar! What do you think you're going to do with that?'

'Take it with me. I'm always wanting to know the date. And it has a lovely picture on it.'

Mr. Roth came out, beaming. 'Here girls. Better put these in your packs.' He gave each of us a quarter pound block of chocolate and half a dozen packets of P.K. chewing gum. Chocolate was still fairly scarce and was the most expensive item of our diet so we were grateful.

Just then the local reporter arrived and got our story. As we talked to him, we started unloading our gear from the bikes.

The sound of a heavy vehicle approaching made our ears prick. Round the corner swept a lordly truck.

'Hey!' We ran out on the road. 'How far are you going?'

'Only about five miles. Wanta lift?'

We raced back to the bikes and grabbed our gear.

'Goodbye Mr. Roth. Thanks very much for everything. Goodbye' – to the reporter – 'You will send copies of the paper on to us? Thanks.

Goodbye. Goodbye.'

Another minute and we were moving off, leaving a rather stunned little group, looking after us open-mouthed.

Such a friendly little place, Tumbarumba!

-oOo-

When we got off the truck we changed into shorts and set off for Tumut, 40 miles away. It was a dreadful road – merely a rocky track – and the hills were so steep it took all our strength to walk our bikes up them. Suddenly Shirl stopped and dived into a pocket of her haversack. She pulled out a small booklet and waved it gleefully.

'I'll read to you as we walk. It'll take our minds off the road.'

'What is it?'

'*The House Not Made with Hands*. I found it at the Cannery and thought it might be rather funny.'

'You ass! Get started then. I'm bored stiff with this road.'

The House Not Made with Hands was a gentle little story designed to tell children in the most reverent manner about the facts of life. Shirl balanced the book on top of her sleeping bag and began to read in a flat, factual voice. The narrative tells of a sunny garden. The little birds are nesting, the flowers are budding, the bees plying between the flowers and their hives. New life is bursting forth on all sides.

Shirl's voice changed to a gush of elocution.

'And lo! We bow before the miracle of birth!' She broke off into shrieks of laughter then assumed a pious air.

She went on to describe the little chicks breaking out of their eggs, the growth of the tadpoles in the pond, the baby animals with their mothers. She stopped walking and, flinging her arm wide in a gesture which encompassed the whole fertile earth, declaimed grandly:

'And lo! Once again we bow before the miracle of birth!'

We were just graduating to humans when I glimpsed a little settlement ahead. It was Laurel Hill. We had pushed our bikes on foot for five miles.

'Time off,' panted Shirl.

We stopped outside the timber mill and strolled inside to see what was going on. The foreman showed us around. We saw them making oars, handles for tools and other cunningly shaped wooden implements. I love timber mills, the whine and screech of the great cross-cut saws and the heady resinous smell of fresh sawdust, huge logs waiting to be sliced and orderly piles of sawn planks stacked for seasoning.

I also love timber trucks. There was one standing in the yard, ready to leave for Batlow.

Batlow is the centre of a large orcharding district, an extremely pretty sight. As the truck driver unloaded our bikes from the back, he said: 'Sorry I can't take you all the way to Tumut. I sometimes do that run, but not today. My wife's just had a baby, and I'm off to see her.'

'And lo, once again …,' Shirl piped ecstatically.

'Come on,' I interrupted quickly. 'To horse, to horse.'

After some more hill-walking, we struck about six miles of glorious down-hill, where the surface of the road fortunately improved too. We swooped down the road, curving around corners by the slightest lean of body to either side. I can think of nothing in the world so thrilling as exhilarating speed through no effort of one's own. Cycling downhill, surfing, horseriding, skiing, gliding, … all offer the same intoxicating thrill of effortless motion.

Shirl was a bend ahead of me and when I glimpsed her again, I saw a haze of blue smoke emanating from her back hub. Her brakes were smoking hot. Just as I made this discovery, I smelt burning oil from my own. Steep slopes and continual cornering play havoc with back-pedal brakes. I managed to spare them a little by clamping on and off, on and off, at the most essential places, but when we reached Wondalga on the flat, we hopped off to let them cool. The hubs were sizzling.

Once again we were lucky. A utility truck picked us up and took us the remaining twelve miles to Tumut. The driver, a pleasant young man, ex-RAAF, gave us an idea which we adopted for the rest of the trip. He asked what record we were keeping of our journey.

'We both keep diaries. Have done for years.'

'Yes, but you ought to have a record of the towns you visit. I read about some touring cyclist on the Continent, who collected a badge from each country he visited and had it fixed to the frame of his bike. It was a mass of souvenirs when he'd finished.'

'That's all right for Europe. But our towns don't have badges.'

'What about postmarks? You could have a notebook and get the stamp of every town you visit. Date as well. It'd be a good record.'

'That's a wonderful idea. We'll start with Tumut.'

We each bought a little book at a stationer's and then marched into the Post Office. The postmark stamp was standing on its ink pad on the counter and we said politely to the clerk:

'Excuse me, would you mind stamping our books? We're the girl cyclists and we want to keep a record of our trip.'

'Oh no, can't do that. It's against the regulations,' he said grumpily.

'But surely ...'

'No.' he turned away to discourage further argument.

'Well, of all the miserable bureaucrats! As if a couple of mouldy imprints would hurt anybody!'

'Never mind Dunc. Let's see if there's any mail for us. I haven't had a letter for ages.'

There wasn't a single letter for me. Not even from Mum. I felt forsaken and depression numbed me. I had been corresponding with a young man from my broadcasting station. Tall, dark and cerebral, he worked in the Programme Department and I found him mentally stimulating. He introduced me to lots of new music and his favourite author was The Beachcomber, of whom I'd never heard. He used to phone me regularly too, phone calls having to be booked through Trunk Calls. Then the calls and letters stopped. I was very upset. I wrote to Estelle, the 3KZ telephonist, and asked if she knew what was the matter. Estelle replied, gently suggesting I forget about him as a girl from Trunks used to ring him every day and have long conversations!

Shirl had a couple of letters clutched in her hand and was reading another avidly. At last she breathed a deep, happy sigh and folded the letter.

'Does he still love you?' I asked dully.

'Mmmm. Gee, Wen. That's the only snag about this trip ... not seeing our beloveds for so long.' (Shirl had a boyfriend in the Air Force and my long-time friend Keith was on a ship in the Navy.)

'You're not weakening are you Shirl?'

'No fear,' she said resolutely. 'If we don't travel now, we never shall. Once we get married, we're sunk.'

We both felt strongly on the subject as, before us like a grim warning, was the example of our erstwhile companion, Sharpey. She had been as travel-mad as both of us but she had just become engaged and now wild horses wouldn't drag her from Melbourne. So, firmly putting all thoughts of such entanglements behind us, we went outside and stood in the mellow sun.

'Next thing is to get our sandals mended.'

They bore battered testimony to the dreadful condition of the New South Wales back roads. We had walked further than we had ridden.

We found an odd-jobs man who promised to have our sandals ready in a few hours. This was wonderful. But it meant we shouldn't be able to go any further that afternoon so we relaxed, did a bit of shopping, saw a reporter from the *Tumut Times* and then went down to the Tumut River and sat on the bank. Glorious hot sunshine poured down on us and soothed our senses. We lazed contentedly, at peace with the world. The river was a beautiful blue, sun-sequinned. Drooping along the banks were graceful weeping willows and rows of golden poplars reached up to the sky like sticks of barley-sugar. Some pompous ducks pottered busily about the grassy banks.

'I like Tumut,' I decided.

As we walked back to the shops, people stopped to talk to us. They had all seen a photo and an article about us in Sydney's *Sunday Sun*. We felt like celebrities and I began to lose my forsaken feeling. Now we had to find a home for the night.

Just before six o'clock, we went to the town's camping ground. The caretaker, a dear old man, showed us a good place, right next to the river, with a little bark shelter nearby containing table and benches. In no time we had unpacked and strewn our gear over the latter. The old man raked together a huge mattress of dead leaves on the ground, one foot deep, and gave us a supply of firewood.

'Yer should be cosy enough with that,' he chuckled. 'Full moon tonight. It'll be pretty nippy later on.'

With our camp made, we took a change of clothing and went to the Commercial Hotel for a bath. We washed our bodies, our hair and then our blouses and undies and finally left an hour later, radiantly clean.

On our way out through the back – we couldn't face the hotel guests with our lank wet hair – the woman cook invited us into her cosy kitchen. She told us she knew a man who could probably give us a lift up the dreaded Talbingo Hill and maybe on to Yarrangobilly in the morning.

'How marvellous!' I exulted. 'Can we fix it definitely? It'd be dreadful if he went without us.'

'I'll ring him now if you like,' said one of the maids. She was back in a minute.

'You're in luck. He's going to be round here at nine in the morning. Don't keep him waiting.'

'We'll be here at seven if necessary. Anything to save us walking up Talbingo. Gosh, seven miles of it! Just imagine!'

We rode back to camp feeling very elated. The caretaker met us.

'I've made you a nice fire girls. Thought you'd be pretty cold when you got back.'

'Bless you! We'll be able to make some toast for our tea. Oh, before you go, could you wake us at seven? We just don't wake unless we're called and we must get up early.'

'Right-oh. Hope you have a good sleep.'

This was the loveliest camp we ever had. It was also the last. We had planned to be in Queensland for the winter, yet here we were, still dawdling around the backblocks of New South Wales. It was very cold. The night was clear and frosty. The stars were so numerous and so bright that the sky was white rather than black and the matronly moon had a hard job pushing her way through them.

We sat by the fire and munched sardines on toast. The river gurgled a few feet away. The luxuriously soft mattress awaited us. Our sleeping bags were warming by the fire. We looked at our little home affectionately.

'I couldn't wish for anything more,' I said. 'All home comforts.'

'No, not quite.' Shirl leapt to her feet with a shout of glee. 'I nearly forgot.'

She burrowed amongst her scattered belongings and produced the calendar. Unrolling it with a flourish, she hung it on a projecting twig on the tree above our bed. The gay little picture conjured up visions of cosy farm kitchens.

'Home is where the heart is,' I murmured.

'Home is where the calendar is,' said Shirl, satisfied.

-oOo-

The caretaker woke us at seven and we dressed and packed. We were at the Commercial Hotel by a quarter to nine. The truck was a large Army one with a canvas cover. Already it was heavily laden and there was a lot more gear to go in it, including a sulky and a dog. (A sulky is a light two-wheeled one-horse vehicle for a single person.) The driver took off the wheels of the sulky and threaded it into the truck, with its long shafts poking out over the tailboard. Then our bikes were lifted up, our packs wedged in and we clambered up after them. The dog was tied to the sulky. Very slowly we started to move. I flashed a delighted glance at Shirl. 'Heigh ho for Talbingo!' and then we stopped. I peered out and found we were parked outside the Tumut Café.

'What's the matter?' I yelled to the driver.

'I haven't had my breakfast yet. Do us a favour and order some sausages and eggs for me, will you? I've got to get some petrol.'

We finally left Tumut at half past twelve. Talbingo Hill was as bad as everyone had told us, steep and winding, with a dusty surface. After we had driven 46 miles the truck stopped. The driver came round to the back.

'This is the Yarrangobilly turn-off. Are you sure you want to get off here? I could take you right through to Cooma.'

These were always very tempting proposals, but we were firm. 'No thanks. We want to see the Caves and then we'll go on to Kossy.'

'Right-oh. Hand me down your stuff.'

We set off on the four mile descent into the Caves valley but had gone only a hundred yards when the extremely steep grade and sharp bends made us stop.

'Cripes, this is dangerous,' panted Shirl. 'I'm scared I'm not going to take one of these bends tightly enough and go rocketing over the edge.'

We broke off some large branches from the thick scrub and tied them by long ropes to the back luggage carriers. The drag of the branches was a very satisfactory brake and we coasted gently down to the valley. Looking down, we could see a cluster of picturesque houses nestling on the floor of the valley.

Yarrangobilly Reserve covers nearly six square miles and, apart from the attractions of the Caves which honeycomb the limestone belt, it is a sanctuary for bird, animal and plant life. I knew nothing about it until Shirl found it on the map and said she wanted to go there. She had met the son of the guide at a party in Melbourne and had made a note of his name in her address book.

We dumped the bikes and went for a short walk along one of the many delightful tracks to explore a bit before nightfall. We followed a lovely creek until it flowed into a large pool about thirty feet square.

Shirl was excited. 'This must be the Thermal Pool. It's supposed to have an all-year-round temperature of eighty degrees.'

I tested it with my finger.

'It's beautifully warm! Let's have a swim tomorrow.'

'Rapture!' Her face clouded. 'What'll we wear?' We had no bathing costumes. 'We could wear shorts but what on our tops?'

'When I was about twelve, my sister rigged up an outfit for me. Mind you, it didn't much matter at that age. She took a triangular kerchief, tucked the apex through a necklace and pinned it, then tied the base ends around my back.'

'I don't know if my kerchief's big enough.'

She whipped it off her head and draped it around her.

'It might do,' she said dubiously, 'but then, we haven't any necklaces.'

'We could use string.'

We rambled on until dusk, then came back and prowled around the hotel, Caves House, looking for outbuildings suitable for us to sleep in. There was nothing so we saw the manageress and asked if she could suggest something.

'You see, we only want a floor to lay our bags on and it's much too cold to camp out.'

'I know,' she said brightly. 'Just the thing! The Caves Parlour Coach should be here any minute. When the passengers have taken their luggage out, you can sleep in it. The seats will be quite comfy and you'll be warm enough.'

'That'll be wonderful! Thanks so much.'

It was dark by now so we sought out the guide, Mr. Hoad, and asked if we could light a fire to cook some food.

The old chap was very friendly.

'Colin told me you might be coming this way but I thought you'd be past here by now.'

'I'm afraid we take our time. We like to detour to see interesting places.'

'You should find Yarrangobilly interesting enough. I'll be taking the guests on a tour of the Jersey Cave at half past seven. Wonderful formations. You ought to come.'

'We'd like to, but we'll have something to eat first.'

'Oh yes, the fire.'

He dashed away and came back with an empty kerosene tin. He put some kindling and wood in it and soon had a blaze.

'There you are. Let's know if there's anything else you want. See you at 7.30 in the vestibule.'

We made lots of piping hot toast soaked with butter and ate it with sardines or peanut butter.

Five young boys from the Caves House gathered by our fire and talked to us. Of all the people we ever spoke to of our travels I much preferred talking to children. They were the most appreciative listeners as we were having the sort of adventure they dreamed about. I wonder if any of them were inspired to see beyond their home town or State.

The bell rang for Cave Inspection. We went to the ticket office, paid four shillings each with a groan and joined a large party shepherded by Mr. Hoad. The Jersey Cave was lovely but caves always invoke comparison. It all depends if you've seen others before. Shirley always declared that nothing could touch the Jenolan Caves for magnificence. I swore by King Solomon's Caves in Tasmania. See one, you've seen the lot. Is there a cave which does not have the likenesses of carrots, a rasher of bacon or a striped bath towel? Only once did we find one which surpassed all others but that comes later.

We came away at 10 o'clock and shifted our gear into the parlour coach. The driver had put some of the seats together making a wide bed and good Mr. Hoad brought a beautiful wallaby rug in case we were cold. He also asked us to hot Sunday dinner the next day.

We didn't wake until nine next morning and just as we were clearing away our beds, Mr. Hoad came and asked if we were ready to go to see the Jillibenan Cave. We said we weren't going.

'Not going!' he said incredulously.

We looked at each other in perplexity. We just couldn't afford another four shillings each.

'Er, we've got a lot to do this morning.'

'But you can't leave Yarrangobilly without seeing the Jillibenan. I discovered it, you know, in 1910 and I've been looking forward to showing it to you. It's better than the Jersey. I'll be terribly disappointed if you miss it.'

We felt dreadful but remained adamant.

A truck pulled up alongside us and we eagerly asked the driver if he were going to Cooma.

'No, I'm staying here. Where're you headin'?'

'Kosciusko, if we can. But we'll have to do it in stages – ninety-five miles of pretty dreadful road and not much habitation.'

'Ha! Just the thing for you! George Day's here seeing his sister – he's Manager of Kossy Chalet you know and he's going right through to the Chalet this afternoon. Maybe he'll take you.'

Right through to the Chalet! I was speechless with the wonder of it. Cheating the clock again. Ninety-five miles of appalling backroads in one afternoon. Kosciusko, my Ultima Thule, tonight! I couldn't believe it.

We rushed to Caves House and found Mr. Day who agreed to take us.

'I'm leaving at half past one sharp though. It's a long rough road and I'll be going fairly slowly. I'm taking a horse along.'

'Okay, we'll be ready. Thanks ever so much.'

It was now noon, so whooping wildly we rushed to the thermal pool, put on shorts and triangular scarves and had a swim. The water was wonderfully warm. The sun was shining. Kossy tonight! The world was a good place.

Back at the bus, we changed our clothes, packed our haversacks in readiness for a quick departure and then presented ourselves at Mr. Hoad's house. His wife heaped huge helpings on our plates, delicious roast pork and vegetables, then plum pudding and thick cream.

We couldn't savour it to the full. Mr. Day's car pulled up outside and we had to take our leave.

We stared at the car in dismay.

'Are you sure you can take us?' said Shirl. 'Where'll you put the bikes?'

'On top.'

George Day was a man of few words but considerable initiative. A skiing champion and mountaineer of many years standing, he had had worse problems to solve in his life.

So the bikes were rigged on the roof of the car, lashed down with yards of rope, the packs went in the back seat and we crowded in the front. In a trailer behind the car was a wild, unbroken horse he was taking to Kossy.

'What will you do with the brumby?' I asked as we started moving.

'Break him in and then train him for riding. After skiing, our interest is horses up the mountain. In the spring we have a big Rodeo and then during the summer there are riding parties for the guests. It's very nice in the summer. Some people prefer it to the winter season. The mountains are covered with wildflowers, there's trout fishing, good hikes, the lakes – oh, plenty to do in the summer, but I prefer the winter for the sports.'

I had heard of George Day from my brothers. He and his wife and his two young children were a champion ski team and usually scooped prizes for cross-country, slalom and other events.

We settled down for the long trip. It was uneventful. The country thereabouts, at the foot of the Alps, is not pretty. It is dry, sparsely grassed, bare of trees and incredibly stony. Innumerable mountain streams flowed across the road, and the car and its heavy load bumped and splashed through them.

After fourteen miles we passed through Kiandra, a collection of rickety weatherboard huts in the midst of some old goldfield works and at dusk we reached Jindabyne, a beautiful little township perched on the banks of a river with plenty of green grass to soothe our eyes and a clump of poplars by the water.*

'There's the Snowy for you,' said Mr. Day, as we stopped at the hotel.

'The Snowy River,' I said reverently (memories of Banjo Patterson's poem returning) and raised my eyes expecting to see a majestic peak somewhere above me. There were hills all around us but no majestic peak. I wasn't to be disillusioned about that until later.

Mr. Day went in to the hotel for dinner. We bought bread and butter

*Jindabyne was also flooded during the early stages of the construction of the Snowy Mountains Hydro-Electric Scheme.

to take with us and at half past seven we set off on the last lap … 27 miles to the Chalet.

Kiandra is 4,600 feet above sea level, Kosciusko is 7,305, so we had to gain a lot of height. Mr. Day had told us of a hut where we could camp, a few hundred feet above the Chalet at Charlotte Pass.

'But listen!' he admonished severely. 'The winter season will be starting soon. If it starts raining or snowing, you pack immediately and go down the mountain as quickly as you can. The road can become blocked or at any rate very treacherous and we don't want to have to send out rescue parties for you. Kossy's no place for novices.'

'We're not novices,' said Shirl indignantly. 'We've each had a week's skiing at Buffalo.'

'Buffalo!' he snorted. Mt.Buffalo is Victoria's social ski resort, the operative word being social and not ski. 'You're novices and you get down to the Hotel before the road's closed.'

We nodded obediently, feeling like chastened schoolchildren. We passed the Hotel and looked at it scornfully out of the window. It was situated twelve miles below the Chalet and was much more civilized. It was the safe place to which we had to withdraw when the season started. It had an all-weather road to Jindabyne. Its windows ablaze with lights shone through the trees. It looked warm and gay. But our more spartan aspirations were fixed on the Chalet where the experienced skiers went and the summit. We just had to go to the summit.

At half past nine we reached the turn-off to the Chalet and piled out of the car.

'There's your road,' said Mr. Day. 'It goes on four miles to the summit. About 300 yards along you'll find the hut I was telling you about. It's not locked. You'll find firewood and an axe but be sure to replenish what you use. First rule of the mountains. If there's anything you want, come down to the Chalet. I shan't untie your bikes now. You can pick them up tomorrow. Goodnight.'

The car and trailer dipped down the side road, leaving us alone in the black, bitter cold. I felt I could reach out and touch the stars and I thought of Banjo Paterson's lines about Kosciusko…

Where the air is clear as crystal, and the white stars fairly blaze
At midnight in the cold and frosty air.

'Gosh, we're actually here Shirl. To think that, at this moment, we're the highest people in Australia. The Chalet's below us.'

'Yes, but let's find that hut. I'm frozen.'

We lugged our packs along the track and soon saw the dim outline of the hut ahead on our left. A good hut. A solid-looking hut. A warm and comfortable hut. Our hut. We quickened our steps.

'What's that?' I stopped dead.

'What's what?'

'I heard a noise ahead. A sort of tinny noise as though someone had clinked a billy can or a saucepan.'

We peered suspiciously at the black hut looming ahead. There was no glimmer of light from its windows, no trail of smoke from its chimney.

'There's no one there. You must have imagined it. And if you didn't, we're still going to investigate. We can't stay out here all night. It's a perisher!'

We plodded on, the earth road hard as iron beneath our feet. Our breath plumed about us. The hut was still and deserted. My spirits rose again as they always did when we were embarking on a new adventure. As we reached the hut, Shirl flashed me a smile and called out brightly, as a joke, 'Anybody ho-o-me?'

A deep male voice said 'Hullo! Come in!' and the door swung open.

Chapter 4

ON THE ROOF OF AUSTRALIA

We shrieked in unison. The room inside was dark but by the light of the moon outside, we could just discern the shape of a man at the door. We stood rooted to the spot, aghast at this unexpected development.

'Well, aren't you coming in?' said the shape.

We stepped inside with trepidation and, walking through the hut, found another shadowy form sitting by a fire.

He stood up. 'Come in and have some fire.'

I breathed a sigh of relief. If their voices were anything to go by, we had nothing to worry about. They lit a candle and I looked at them. They were obviously the hiker type, young and keen on the outdoor life. I relaxed. They were like my brothers.

The taller, Rick Francis, was very good-looking, dark, with a small moustache. The other, Walter Scott, was also handsome, though not in the Hollywood manner.

As we were summing them up, they were looking at us, astonished.

'Where've you come from?'

We told them.

'You mean, you're not from the Chalet!'

'Hardly,' I said, pointing at our haversacks. 'I'm afraid we've come to stay. We didn't know the hut was occupied.'

'Obviously!' laughed Rick. 'I wouldn't have missed that scream! Well, as it happens, we can put you up. There are four beds next door. But if anyone else comes, they've had it.'

I liked the matter-of-fact way they accepted us. Many people might have been doubtful about sleeping under the same roof but with hikers and skiers there is no problem. If there is only one shelter in the wilderness, then obviously it must be shared. I remembered staying a night in the Cleve Cole

Hut on Mt. Bogong when Sharpey and I were allotted palliases in a bunkroom with twenty men.

The outside door of our new home opened straight into the bunkroom, which contained two double-decker wire beds. A connecting door led to the kitchen/living room, where Rick and Scotty had been preparing their supper in front of an open fire when we arrived. Scotty was still holding a blackened pot which he was vaguely stirring with a spoon. He remembered himself with a start and put the pot on the fire.

'Have you had your tea?'

'No, but we're not hungry. We had a terrific lunch today.'

Rick shook his head. 'You've got to eat up here. Plenty of good grub, lots of exercise during the day and then a good night's sleep.'

Scotty stood up and reached for a billy. 'You'd better come with me and I'll show you where we get our water.'

'You go Wen,' said Shirl, toasting her bottom at the fire.

I walked along the road with him to where a spring gurgled amongst some smooth stones. He filled the billy while I stamped my feet.

'What are you two doing up here?' I asked.

'We're just having two weeks holiday from school. We came out of the RAAF last year and now we're doing Matric. under rehab. Then I'm going to do Architecture and Rick's doing Engineering.'

'Where are you from, Melbourne?'

'Sydney.'

I had forgotten we were in New South Wales and Sydney was now the focal point.

I walked to the edge of the road and looking down, saw a blaze of lights below us in the valley. The Chalet! Excitement gripped me by the throat.

We clomped back to the hut. Shirl had unpacked and Rick was frowning disapprovingly at the spreading confusion.

'Look,' he said, 'you two put your stuff in this corner. We have to keep the table clear for meals.'

'Right-oh,' I said, 'but I'm not going to spread until I can see what I'm doing. All I want to do now is sleep. Which beds do we use?'

'Those two,' Rick pointed. 'They're not a bit comfortable ... put some spare clothing under you to pad them a bit. And take my tip ... put stacks of newspaper on the wire under you. The temperature goes down around zero at night, but paper keeps you pretty warm.'

(I'd learned that lesson in my cradle. 'Swagmen,' said Mum, 'always wrap themselves in newspaper for warmth.')

So we made our beds. I used one top bunk, Shirl was underneath. Rick was next to me on the other upper and Scotty below him. The beds were only shelves of trellis wire, which creaked and zinged when any weight was placed on them.

The boys offered to go for a walk outside while we got ready for bed. That didn't take long as we only removed our blouses and put on all our jumpers, an extra pair of football socks and leggings.

Then we got into our bags. The boys came back, got ready in the kitchen by the fire and went to bed too. The din caused by four creaking beds was terrific.

It was the most ghastly night I'd ever spent. I had just found a comfortable position where the wire didn't stick into me, when a flea started to bite me on the right thigh. Very stealthily, because each movement dragged a groan from the bed, I undid my jodhpurs and scratched the bite. Five minutes later, it bit me again. I could feel the large weals swelling under my finger. The irritation was intense. I tried to think how I could alleviate the itch and more important, how to catch the flea. During the next hour it migrated from my right to my left thigh and travelled inexorably down to my knee. I was panic-stricken lest it get down to the close-fitting calf of my jodhpurs. My mind appreciated the subtle torture which this would be. Not to be able to get to the irritated spot, not to be able to scratch! Oh Lord, no! I writhed and twisted in torment. The treacherous wires underneath me zinged happily as though they had been plucked.

I lay awake for hours for a second torture had begun. Cold! It was literally freezing. My feet were completely numb and yet aching. I wanted to draw my knees up and huddle but the bed protested loudly and besides, when I moved it threw Rick about as the same piece of trellis wire continued along his bunk. The flea had withdrawn by now, either because it was sated and just wanted to sleep or because my icy legs offered it little comfort.

And then, as the final problem, I wanted to go to the lavatory. I tried to concentrate on sleep but it was no use. At last I could bear it no longer. I must restore the circulation to my feet. I must go outside! To hell with the bed! I swung down to the ground, put on shoes, opened the door noisily and crept outside.

I came back, climbed stealthily back to bed and snuggled down into my sleeping bag. A warm stupor began to creep over me and I was just sinking into a blessed doze when there was a loud thump as Rick leapt out of his top bunk.

He stamped into the kitchen and soon there were cracklings and snappings of twigs and a wisp of smoke assailed my nostrils. Then he came back.

'Rise and shine Scotty m'boy. Seven o'clock.'

'Muh!' grunted Scotty.

'Ah, there's nothing like a good night's sleep.'

I groaned and turned to the wall.

We stayed in bed until the boys had breakfasted and left on a hike and then, still in our sleeping bag cocoons, hopped across into the next room and huddled by the fire. I reached an unwilling hand from the bag and ferreted in my haversack for chocolate. My fingers touched something of incredible coldness. It was my bottle of ink. The ink in it was frozen solid. (We learned later that the temperature had been 13°F below freezing.)

We made some toast for breakfast then went to the spring for water. My first glimpse of the strange new landscape was not inspiring. How different my impressions were, arriving in darkness. Last night everything had seemed exciting, magical, a new world awaiting me. The hard light of morning revealed a stark, bare and inhospitable landscape. The mountains surrounding us were not jagged and Alpine looking. They were still the rounded Australian hills which we'd seen all our lives but instead of being thickly covered with gum forests, they were merely dotted, here and there, with patches of dwarf snow gum. Above the tree line there were only outcrops of rock to break the monotony. There was no colour but the dull sage-green of the stunted gums and the sparse grass, the brown rocks and a leaden sky.

I felt disappointed. Where was the exhilaration we had felt last night? We were actually at Kosciusko but it looked no different from a Victorian mountain. Bleaker, lonelier and more dispiriting. We were supposed to be within four miles of the summit, but where was the awe-inspiring peak? Australia is ancient, so old that once-giant mountains have been worn down to undulating hills by the weather.

The spring was frozen over. With wooden hands I chipped the ice away and filled the billy. I was still engrossed in my moody thoughts when Shirl called to me in a peculiar voice.

'Wen, come and look at this.'

She was standing at the edge of the road, looking down into the valley. I joined her and my throat tightened with last night's excitement.

There was the Chalet.

I suppose I had expected something like the Hotel, a conventional chalet, with steep-pitched roofs, wooden beams and balconies but this was so strange, so bizarre and so utterly unexpected that I just couldn't believe it. To find anything so un-Australian appearing magically on the bare Australian hills wasn't possible. An air of fantasy surrounded it from the beginning.

Imagine a castle of Moorish design. Low stone-arched doorways, a round stone tower surmounted by a dome, and walls incredibly harlequined with pink and white diamonds, the whole glistening in the early sun like a frosted birthday cake.

My exhilaration returned. I looked at the scene transfixed.

'Gosh, let's go down Dunc!'

We hurried back to the hut, tidied up, then scrambled down the hillside to the Chalet.

-oOo-

General Tadeus Kosciusko, a Polish military engineer, was a contemporary of Lafayette and Jefferson in the War of American Independence. He returned to his native land and in 1794 undertook the military leadership of Poland against threatened occupation by the Russians. At first his campaign was successful but eventually he was defeated, wounded and imprisoned for two years in St. Petersburg.

Admiring his indomitable spirit, Czar Paul I liberated him and offered him a commission in the Russian Army which he declined. He went to Switzerland where he remained in voluntary exile until his death in 1817. He was interred with royal honours in the Polish capital, Krakow, and in his memory the population raised a tumulus overlooking the city.

In 1840, Sir Paul Edmond de Strzelecki, a distinguished Polish traveller and explorer, while preparing the first geological survey map of New South Wales, explored the Muniong or Snowy Range and named its highest peak Kosciusko. In his report he said; 'A pinnacle, rocky and naked, predominant over several others, was chosen for a point of trigonometrical survey. This eminence struck me so forcibly by the similarity it bears to a tumulus elevated in Krakow over the tomb of the patriot Kosciusko, that, although in a foreign country, on foreign ground but amongst a free people who appreciate freedom and its votaries, I could not refrain from giving it the name of Mount Kosciusko.'

-oOo-

We went under the frowning arches, swung the heavy door open and climbed a circular stair inside the tower until we emerged in the lounge. It was luxurious. Planned on hunting lodge lines, it offered the comfort longed for by the weary skier, returning after a day on the mountains. Wood panelling and smoked beams inspired the feeling of a friendly inn. Touches of rough stone-work reminded one that it was primarily a mountain lodge. There was a large buffalo skin on the wall, a huge open fireplace in another. There were long sofas piled with soft cushions, gleaming dark furniture ornamented with carved lions' heads. Very comfortable.....and so warm.

Shirl ran and bounced on one of the sofas.

'Heaven,' she breathed. 'Oh to sleep here instead of on those wire bunks.'

'Look! Even a piano!' My eyes lit up.

We had already planned to ask for the loan of some blankets but the sight of all this luxury gave me another idea. We went to the office and met Mrs. Day, a handsome woman in her thirties, with vivacious dark eyes.

'Hullo girls, come for your bikes?'

'Yes please. And also – we were wondering if you could possibly lend us some blankets. We nearly died of cold last night.'

'I suppose you did. Coldest night we've had so far. Norman!'

She called to a tall fair young man who was polishing some glasses in the bar.

'Ask Mrs. Clapton to let me have four grey blankets, will you? Now girls ... Shirley and Wendy isn't it? Is there anything else you need? Food? You can get provisions at our store you know.'

'Yes, we'd like to buy some tinned stuff. And Mrs. Day ...' I faltered, but the thought of that warm lounge drove me on. 'Look Mrs. Day, we want to stay up here for a couple of days and do some hiking and I was wondering if, in the evenings, you'd like me to come down and give you some music. Dinner music, you know, while the guests are in the dining room. I used to play in a Melbourne restaurant.'

'That's a wonderful idea ... the piano's going to waste. But you'd better come down and have dinner with us first – both of you – and then you can play afterwards.'

We looked at each other in rapture!

'Ah, here are the blankets. Thank you Norman. Will you show the girls the way to the store now? See you tonight.'

Norman grinned as he led us down the passage.

'Finding it a bit cold? This is nothing! Wait till it starts snowing!'

'Do you think there's any chance? Soon, I mean. Gee, if the snow came, we'd stay on for some skiing. Wouldn't it be wonderful!'

'Well, it's cold enough. You never know your luck. Here you are ... the storeman will fix you up. Be seeing you!'

He gave us a friendly nod and went back to the bar.

We bought some tinned sausages, peanut butter and some honey. We still had plenty of bread and butter in the hut. Then we located our bikes, loaded our acquisitions on the back carrier and pushed them up the winding track to the summit road where we had left Mr. Day the night before. From there we managed to ride along to the hut.

After a snack, we set off at last on the trip to the summit. It was a gradual climb and we had to wheel our bikes all the way. The country was not very interesting. No timber softened the bare, rocky hills. Little springs flowing by the road were encrusted with ice and in places where the water dropped over a ledge or pile of stones, the cascade was a sparkling curtain of icicles.

We passed the Seaman Hut, a solidly-built granite shelter, erected on the spot where the body of Laurie Seaman was found in 1928 after he had perished in a blizzard. His father built the Memorial Hut as a refuge for future skiers who might experience adverse weather conditions which frequently set in without warning.

By the time we reached the summit, the view was completely obscured by rolling cloud. A freezing wind whistled over the top and we huddled under the cairn of stones, eating chocolate and waiting for the sun to come out. We had to have a photo taken on the summit of the highest mountain in Australia.

'Not,' said Shirl bitterly, 'that it's much of a summit. It just happens to be a few feet higher than the other peaks.'

'Still, it *is* the highest point and we must have a record of it. I wish some other people would come and take a photo of us both.'

We cowered in misery, debating the chances of another party arriving before we died of exposure.

'Imagine the headlines,' said Shirl, ever publicity-conscious. 'Plucky cyclists frozen on Mt.Kosciusko. Bodies found at summit. Nation mourns loss!'

I dwelt on this melancholy prospect. I imagined the effect on my family and friends. 'So young to die,' they'd say. 'So tragic! Such a promising career!' My mind nimbly skipped the obstacle that I had no career in mind, let alone a promising one.

A car rattled around the last bend and steamed to a halt. I relinquished thoughts of a dramatic death and asked the driver if he'd take a photo of us. We climbed to the top of the cairn, posed stiffly with what we hoped was an intrepid expression but which merely registered as a ghastly leer then hopped on our bikes and started the glide home.

It was unbelievably cold. My nose just wasn't there and my hands were so frozen, in spite of gloves, I couldn't feel them at all and had to look to see if they were still grasping the handlebars. I couldn't help crying out with the great pain of it. And that started further dramatic thoughts about frostbite of the fingers, emergency amputations with rusty knives and having to take up singing instead of the piano.

Three miles from home I heard a 'Hoy!' and saw Rick and Scotty coming towards us across the hills. We waited for them and gave them a dink home. The ruts on the road near our hut were hard and icy and we skidded dangerously. We fell off in a heap outside the hut and stiffly limped inside. It was cold and cheerless.

'Ah, home sweet home!' boomed Rick. 'Tell you what girls – we'll chop the wood and light the fire and you can cook us some grub. How's that, eh? Fair's fair.'

'Except for one small error,' said Shirl smoothly. 'We can't cook you some grub; (a) we don't know how to, and (b) we have a previous engagement.'

'Really Madam.' He raised his eyebrows. 'Do you wish me to bring the car round at eight?'

'No thanks, we'll walk. We're having dinner at the Chalet.'

'Dinner at the … How's their form!' Two jaws dropped. 'Pretty quick work, Scotty my boy.'

'In fact, dinner at the Chalet every night,' said Shirl, rummaging for her washing gear.

'How's their rotten form!' breathed Scotty admiringly.

'What's the catch?' said Rick.

'No catch,' I said. 'I'm to work my fingers to the bone on the piano and we get our grub thrown in.'

'There!' said Rick enviously. 'Why couldn't we think of something like that?'

'Maybe Mrs. Day would be co-operative if you went and did some of your axe-swinging down at the Chalet.'

'Ready, Wen?' called Shirl. 'Let's go. I must have a hot bath before I get stiff.'

'A hot bath! Oh no!' groaned Scotty. 'I can't even remember what one is. Is that part of the contract too?'

'Don't see why not,' said Shirl. She was struggling into her voluminous groundsheet/tent/cape (a large green rectangle with a hole in the middle for putting one's head through, the hole being closed by a drawstring when it was used as a tent). She picked up a string bag bulging with her best clothes and shoes, towel and toilet bag. 'Heigh for the merry throng, bright lights, sumptuous repast and sparkling conversation.'

'All right, all right,' snarled Rick. 'Don't rub it in!'

They came to the door to watch our departure.

'How's their dirty rotten form!' said Scotty, shaking his head in wonder. They turned back into the dark, cold hut.

We plodded down the track, looking like two Wild Women of Willygoree. Waterproof capes hanging in dismal flapping folds to our ankles, kerchiefs on our heads, a stuffed stringbag in one hand and a bicycle lamp in the other.

We let ourselves unobtrusively into the Chalet through a basement door and found ourselves in the ski room, a vast, chilly area, the walls of which were lined with racks of skis and stocks and shelves of boots. It smelled of dubbin and grease and sweat. A drying room opened off it on one side and another door led into the house. We found a ladies' room and began to strip.

After wonderful hot baths (the benison of hot water indeed!) we put on our thin cotton frocks, knitted jackets and casual shoes. Shirl sported a bandeau on elastic (very fashionable) and I wore a bangle.

'Ah glamour!' I sighed. 'Who would've guessed, if they'd seen us arrive, that out of those drab utility rags we should emerge beautiful and radiant as the butterfly from the chrysalis?'

'Who indeed,' said Shirl absently, applying a dusting of powder to her freckles.

We bundled our outdoor clothes neatly into a corner and, with a last uncertain look in the mirror, went upstairs to the lounge.

-oOo-

Dinner was over. We had dined magnificently on Purée Cream of Celery, Fillet of Whiting, Devilled Steak, Prime Rib of Beef and three vegs., Apple Pie and Norwegian Trifle. We pushed back our chairs and beamed contentedly at the sprinkling of guests in the dining room. There were no more than a dozen.

'A cup of coffee now and I'll be right,' said Shirl.

'What miserable selfish types we are,' I said guiltily. 'Filled to overflowing with all – all this...,' I gestured to the pile of empty dishes surrounding us and involuntarily the word 'locusts' came to my mind, 'and never a thought for those poor boys up there in that miserable hut, cold and hungry. Is this the way to repay their kindness in letting us share their roof?'

'You're right Wen,' said Shirl righteously. 'Let's take them something.'

We looked anxiously at the table. There were a couple of bread rolls which we had ignored during the soup course. Nobody was watching us. We quickly slit the sides of the rolls, piled butter inside and slipped them in the little leather wallets that served us as handbags.

'It's not much,' said Shirl as we hurried out, 'but it's the thought and not the action that matters.'

'Be nice toasted,' I comforted myself.

As we finished our coffee, sunk in the deep chairs in front of the blazing fire, Shirl looked brightly about her at the other guests and said ... 'Right Wen, off you go and pay for our dinner. I'll – er – do my bit by mixing with the guests and being sociable.'

I hadn't touched a piano since we left the cannery and eagerly sat down to try the Chalet one. I started with quiet, unobtrusive classics and semi-classics, but one or two chaps wandered over with requests for popular songs. Soon we were having a lively session.

I glanced around. Shirl had been cornered by a Dear Old Duck (anyone over 40) who was no doubt asking her all about the trip. Shirl was talking mechanically, her eyes flicking restlessly to the group around the piano.

'What about *In the Mood*?' asked a hep cat.

'Never heard of it!' I said blandly and struck up something else. It was my stock answer. I loathed playing *In the Mood*.

'Let's have a drink,' suggested someone, and waved to Norman who was hovering, resplendent in white jacket, black tie and silver tray. 'What'll it be?'

'Lemon squash for me thanks.'

'Same for me thanks,' said Shirl who had magically materialized at one end of the keyboard.

'What's the matter Dunc? Finished your social round already?'

'No, just thought I'd help swell the community singing,' she said urbanely.

It was a successful evening. Mrs. Day smiled approvingly whenever she passed through the room. The fire was deserted, the piano merely a mass of swaying bodies. By now we were on to *Old MacGregor* and *Little Brown Jug*. Yes, a successful evening.

But at ten I caught Shirl's eye and shut the piano lid firmly, amidst a chorus of protests.

'More tomorrow. See you then.'

We hurried downstairs to the basement changing room and reversed our earlier procedure.

'Off with the glamour, on with the utility,' sighed Shirl regretfully. 'Cinderella had nothing on us.'

Laden with our bundles again, we made an inconspicuous exit through the ski-room and gasped as the night air struck us. Up the winding track to the summit road we went and along to the hut. Rick and Scotty were sitting morosely by the fire.

'Hullo you gadabouts. Had a nice time?'

'Wonderful thanks. Do you want us to tell you, or shall we spare you the most agonizing details?'

'Tell us about the grub,' said Scotty dully.

We told them.

'And two sweets, with lashings of cream! In the coffee too!'

The boys were silent. I signalled to Shirl.

'But we brought something back for you.'

'Well, that's very decent of you. What is it?'

'Some beef?' asked Scotty hopefully.

'A slice of apple pie?' suggested Rick.

'With cream - ', prompted Scotty.

I looked at Shirl whose mouth was twitching dangerously.

'You tell them Wen.'

I opened my bag. 'It's a beautiful bread roll,' I stammered.

They stared bewildered.

'It's the thought that matters,' said Shirl in a small voice.

'Nice toasted,' I added miserably.

Rick broke the silence. 'Oh well, it's something. Very good of you to bother.'

Scotty reached for his. 'Fresh too. And butter. Well, well.'

They both sat, munching their rolls avidly.

We watched them for a minute, then went into the freezing chamber which was the bunkroom. We wrapped ourselves in blankets like mummies then threaded our way into our sleeping bags.

Blissful warmth. I slept.

-oOo-

The next day we went for a hike around the lakes and came back to the hut in the afternoon. It was another bitter day and we found the boys had already returned from their explorations. We all sat by the fire drinking mugs of steaming black cocoa and inevitably a spirited argument sprang up between Shirl and Rick This time it was the perennial argument about hunting. Rick had started it by lamenting that shooting wasn't allowed on the mountain.

Shirl's eyes steeled. 'Shooting what?' she asked casually, but with ice.

'Birds – maybe some animals ...' said Rick, not recognizing the danger signals.

'I think shooting and hunting are disgusting!'

'Rubbish!'

It was on. Scotty and I sat on the sidelines, merely throwing in a word or two when the conflagration showed signs of lessening.

'Dear little trusting birds,' Shirl was saying. 'Ducks on a pond – or pigeons – or ...' her voice sank to hoarse depths of incredulity – 'kangaroos!'

'Kangaroos are a pest.' Rick was on firm ground. 'Cost the country millions a year in crops and fencing.'

'I don't care,' said Shirl illogically. 'How men can do it, I don't know. Have you ever seen a kangaroo close up, with its soft brown trusting eyes?'

Rick hooted.

'There it sits, probably with a young roo in its pouch. It looks at the men calmly. And then out come the guns and bang! She's done for!'

'Don't be so soft. The things are pests, I tell you.'

'Ducks and wild game aren't pests. Yet you go out and call it sport to bring them down.'

'Certainly. A bit of wild duck or green pigeon's very tasty for tea.'

Too much for me. 'But you don't do it because you're hungry! You don't stop when you've shot one or two for your tea.'

'Now look ...' Rick controlled himself. 'You make it seem as though we just bag sitting shots. Do you know just how hard it is to pot a bird on the wing or a kangaroo travelling at speed?'

We didn't. But Shirl had a trump card.

'Do you know that in Tasmania there's a place called Swan Lagoon where thousands of swans nest, and They ...' she covered the word with venom ... 'They used to have an open season for shooting them. Swans! Anyone who'd shoot a swan must be a low beast.'

'And what about the slaughter of koalas before they were protected?'

'Well, of course, that was bad ... but they don't do it now, so don't be irrelevant.'

'I'm not. What's the difference, in principle, between shooting a koala and a duck? You just love shooting defenceless creatures. And only because you have superior weapons. I'd like to see you get down on all fours and fight the creatures on equal terms. Oh no, but that wouldn't be sport. You might get hurt!'

Rick sprang to his feet and paced the length of the room. He opened his mouth to say something, then shut it and shook his head instead. His shoulders etched a shrug and the palms of his hands were eloquent.

'Well, I reckon that's a draw,' said Scotty cheerfully.

'Nonsense,' snorted Shirl. 'Point, game and set. Come on Wen, time we were away.'

I grinned over my shoulder at Scotty. 'Like us to bring you back something for supper?'

He threw a spoon at me.

We went to the Chalet, changed into our 'glamour' and sat by the fire in the lounge until dinner. Some of the ladies were eyeing us in a speculative way and conversation was polite and inconsequential. It seemed to me that they would've preferred to talk about something else.

Then one middle-aged lady leant across to me and said solicitously: 'How are you getting along in that hut?'

So that was it! They had heard about the boys.

'Very well thanks,' I said airily. 'It's a lovely hut, very solid and quite dry. Pretty cold but that's to be expected.'

She caught the eye of her companion and said gently: 'Are the two men still up there?'

I felt the eyes of the company on me. Conversation had ceased and they were all listening like a jury.

'Oh yes. They're up here for a fortnight. We don't see much of them, they're out hiking every day.'

A ripple of chatter ran around the circle. I was laughing inwardly, knowing quite well what they were all longing to know. Shirl's face betrayed her amusement too and a glance between us decided our course of action.

Another woman lifted her eyes from her knitting and asked Shirl, just a shade too casually: 'How many rooms are there?'

'Two – quite large ones.'

The company breathed with relief. 'Then you two have one room and the men have the other?'

Shirl was enjoying herself. 'Oh no. One room's a kitchen and the other's a bunkroom. There's a nice big fire in the kitchen, table and benches, cupboards ...' she prattled on, teasing them with unwanted details.

'And the bedroom ...,' the woman prompted softly. 'How are the beds arranged?'

Really! I wanted to throw back my head and howl with delight. These so nice people with their gentle inquisition, bursting to know what went on in the hut at night. I almost wished we could have shocked them with something spicy but nothing more blameless could be imagined than our association with the boys. I thought of the way we went to bed, fully dressed and swathed in blankets. (No wonder Eskimos have the lowest birth rate in the world, I thought *en passant*.) But then, they weren't to know that. I suppose they thought Shirl and I had haversacks crammed with seductive satin nightgowns and that, attired in these, we drifted around the hut, snapping an occasional icicle off the window, reclining languorously on the wooden benches, a blackened tin mug held delicately in one hand, a long cigarette holder in the other.

I was about to say something very rude to squash all this pettiness when a young girl burst into the room.

'It's snowing!'

Shirl and I looked at each other in wild delight then hurled ourselves at the windows. Noses flattened against the glass, we saw gentle eddying flakes drifting down, so softly, so lightly, gone almost before they'd touched the ground.

I thumped Shirl excitedly on the back.

'It's snowing, it's snowing! Just think! We'll be able to ski tomorrow. We'll be able to stay on here for weeks and ski every day! What incredible luck!'

Everyone was talking at once, with fresh shouts of jubilation as someone discovered from another window that the snow was starting to settle.

It needed the dinner gong to drag us from the windows.

-oOo-

Discussing the new turn of events over dinner, we realized a complete change of plan was necessary. We couldn't afford to stay on for weeks with no income, nor did we relish further nights in the hut with the temperature below zero and snow banked at the door and windows, an efficiently sealed icebox. The Chalet was obviously the desirable place to be but we couldn't stay there as guests.

'No Dunc, there's nothing for it, we'll have to work. It's about time we took another job.'

'But then there'll be no time to ski.'

'Yes there will. The waitresses have all the afternoon off and one free day a week. And they have their boots and skis provided. I think it's the answer. Let's go and see Mrs. Day now.'

Mrs. Day was in the office, her shining head bent over the books. I had a momentary qualm. We were always asking her for something. She looked up brightly and said: 'Well girls, I suppose you'll be away tomorrow. Looks as though the season's starting.'

'No, that's just the point. We want to stay. We're mad on skiing and the snow's come just in time. What we'd like to do is come and work at the Chalet. We'll be waitresses or housemaids or anything. Have you any vacancies?'

'Have you any experience?' Her eyes were sparkling.

'Well – no, but we'd learn quickly. I'm sure we'd be all right.'

'As a matter of fact, I could use you. The house will start filling up once the news gets through to Sydney that the season's started and our skeleton staff won't be enough. But I don't suppose you'll want to stay the whole season? No, I thought not. Well, I'll tell you what we'll do. I'll take you on until we get our regular winter staff. It may only be for a few weeks, but that'll suit you, won't it?'

'Wonderfully. What do you want us to do?'

'Housework I think. You'd have to have some experience for the dining room and you'd have to have black frocks. No … Mrs. Clapton needs you more. The whole house will have to be prepared for an influx of guests. When will you move down?'

'Tomorrow morning … that's if we can get back to the hut tonight.'

'Yes. Well, if it's too wild tonight, you'd better stay here. Your two friends from the hut have just been down to hire skis. You can't go far without them in this weather. Better move down as soon as you can in the morning. Oh – one more thing – once you're on the staff, I'm afraid you won't be able to use the living rooms any more.'

'No, of course not. Goodnight Mrs. Day.'

We hurried away to mull this over. The cosy lounge was doubly attractive to us now, knowing that tonight was our last night of privilege. Tomorrow we'd be banished to the second-floor back or the basement or wherever the staff lived.

'Housemaids! What fun!' said Shirl gleefully. 'I haven't a clue have you?'

'None whatever. My mother's one of those brisk efficient types who always thinks it quicker to do everything herself. She never taught me any housework.'

'Mine too. Mind you, it'll be wonderful training for us Wen. We'll need to know all about it when we get married.'

'I suppose so. Only thing is ... it's not very - well - glamorous is it, trotting around with buckets and brooms ... I mean, if we meet any attractive males.'

Shirl meditated a moment on this dilemma. Of course we would meet attractive males, the place would be swarming with them soon but they'd hardly have eyes for two housemaids when the female guests were sauntering past, dressed to kill in their David Jones ski suits.

'Only thing to do is treat it all as a joke ... it's just a temporary job. We don't need the money ... just doing it for the novelty.' Her countenance fell. 'But I know what you mean. You don't look your best down on your knees, scrubbing a floor.'

The snow continued to fall, gently but steadily, and Mrs. Day wouldn't hear of us going back to the hut. There were some spare beds in a room occupied by some girls whom we'd already met so we moved in with them.

The bedrooms, like the rest of the Chalet, were comfortable yet practical. Each had its own shower cubicle with hot water and lavatory. The beds were in the form of tiered bunks, but a much improved version of those in our hut. The limited hanging space was quite adequate for guests whose wardrobe consisted mainly of trousers and jackets. Central heating ensured a delicious warmth throughout the house. We just had time to crawl between the sheets before the slow dimming of the lights indicated 10.30 lights out.

The next morning we slept in until the girls came back from their breakfast. They had brought us some fruit which we ate as we dressed. It was nearly ten o'clock and we had a busy morning ahead of us.

The view from the window was enchanting. The landscape had been completely transformed overnight. The snow had stopped falling but a soft blanket, so ludicrously like cotton wool, had covered everything in sight. Familiar landmarks were unrecognizable, the road had vanished, the fencing around the rodeo corral was merely a circle of twigs. Everything was strange and exciting.

We set off on the trek to the hut, but before reaching the Chalet gates we were stumbling ankle-deep in soft fresh powder snow. We wore only lightweight walking shoes and the snow was over the top and melting inside them in no time. Going up the sloping road to where we guessed it joined the summit road was even worse, as we sank up to our knees. It was easier when we trod in the holes already made by Rick and Scotty the night before. But when we reached the main summit road we encountered what skiers call breakable crust. It bears one's weight for a fraction of a second then breaks. We sank to our thighs and sometimes pitched forward up to our waists. It was the most amazing sensation to be standing on supposedly firm ground and then to fall rapidly some four feet or so, as through a trapdoor, leaving one floundering in a little foxhole. For a little way we stepped in the holes made by the boys but then they must have put on their skis for the flat stretch to the hut.

At first we laughed uproariously as the snow gave way beneath our feet leaving us with each leg sunk to the groin in a different foothole. But we soon grew exhausted from climbing out of one deep hole into another, which was all it amounted to, and we were becoming colder and wetter. We left the road and clambered along the bank, hoping the going would be easier amongst the scrub and light timber. The snow wasn't quite so deep there but we still made very poor headway as we had to circumnavigate each tree or climb through it. We seemed no closer to the hut and I visualized us, days later, still grimly tunnelling our way, with no one suspecting our plight.

'Dunc,' I panted, nearly weeping with exhaustion, 'we'll have to get the boys to come and help us. We'll never get there otherwise.'

'Yes, we can stand on the back of their skis and then we shan't sink. Let's get out on the road again and start hollering.'

'Rotten messy snow,' I muttered. 'To think we were longing for it before!'

'Wait till we get some boots and skis and then we'll enjoy it. You must have proper equipment for this game.'

We reached the road and promptly made two great bear pits. We leaned out of them wearily, only heads and arms visible, and yelled to the boys.

No sign of life. We yelled again desperately.

We knew they were there as their skis were propped against the hut. Our third cry of anguish brought them out. They stood looking along the road at us then turned and went inside again, shutting the door.

We were astounded! Did they think we were fooling about up to our necks in snow for the fun of it? We screamed again, calling for help in anguished voices. After a full five minutes, they emerged again, fastened on their skis and plodded down the road to us.

'What the devil do you think you're doing!' growled Rick as soon as they were close enough.

'Never heard such a row,' grunted Scotty.

They seemed to be rather nettled. We gasped a pathetic explanation.

'No need to kick up such a fuss about it.'

'But we've been trying to make you hear. Why didn't you come the first time?'

'Had to put on our blasted boots, didn't we?'

'We thought you just weren't taking any notice of us and we had to have some help.'

'Well what do you expect us to do about it?'

They couldn't have been more uncooperative. We ate umble pie madly.

'We thought you might take us to the hut on the back of your skis.'

'What! And break the damn things? Not likely.'

'But you must! Please! We can't go on like this. We've been two hours already. We wouldn't break the skis; crikey, they carry much heavier people than us.'

Scotty gave in. 'We'd better get them home Rick. They'll keep on screaming otherwise.'

Rick shrugged and did a nifty kick turn to face the hut. We climbed on behind them, lifting our feet when they lifted theirs and we covered the last two hundred yards in ten minutes.

We were wet through and frozen. The boys were still in a vile mood and the atmosphere in the hut was very tense. Shortly afterwards they stomped off to Charlotte Pass and that was the last we saw of them. They left next day.

An hour later we were ready for the grim trip back to the Chalet. We had changed into dry clothes, had something hot to eat and drink, packed our haversacks and tidied the hut. Our bikes would have to stay there until the snow was hard enough to wheel them to the Chalet.

We stood outside the hut and closed the door finally. We looked at the snow without enthusiasm. We would make bigger holes this time as we were burdened with heavy haversacks on our backs.

Suddenly Shirl let out an excited cry and, dropping to her knees, started digging furiously in the snow with her gloved hands. I thought she'd gone berserk.

'What on *earth* are you doing?'

She didn't reply, but worked feverishly for a few seconds and then triumphantly dragged out a wire griller.

I gaped. 'How did you know it was there?'

'I remember seeing it outside the door before the snow.'

'But what ...'

She was bending over it, gloves off, fingers working diligently. It was a bi-valve griller such as is used on campfires, composed of two layers of interlaced wire between which one puts a slab of steak and latches the two halves together.

She undid the fastenings so that she had two identical rectangles of wire with handles, and placing one under each foot, struck an attitude.

'*Et voilà*! Snowshoes! Now for a little string to tie them on my feet. Here, get some out of my haversack pocket, will you?'

I was consumed with envy. What a wonderful idea! To think that she would now plod merrily down the road while I floundered alone. No, it was unthinkable. I must find something myself. I looked around.

Opposite our hut were the remains of another hut – derelict and unused. Its walls had been planked, but there were many gaping holes now, perhaps due to a too efficient search for firewood by frozen skiers. And then I had my idea, a beautiful, simple idea. I got the axe and strode purposefully to the other hut. One of the planks came off in my hand, a blow of the axe bisected it and I had a pair of crude skis. Wonderful! I lashed them to my feet with rope.

And we set off.

It's funny how seemingly insuperable difficulties can be surmounted in such a simple and absurd fashion and yet prove to be so stimulating. We were exhilarated by pride of achievement as we manoeuvred along the track. What did it matter that we looked like two humped horrors from another world with our groundsheets flapping over our haversacks. It was a matter of no concern that snow seeped through and gradually collected on the mesh of Shirl's griller until she was carrying a couple of pounds with each foot. She just stopped every twenty yards and shook it off. (I was minded of Mischa Auer trying to rid his feet of the sticky flypaper in *Hellzapoppin*). Nor did it bother us that the wire mesh cut through the slender string which bound it to her ankles and we had to continually knot and re-tie. Now that the main ordeal was past, these pinpricks were funny. Uproariously funny. We howled our erratic way down to the Chalet, covering the whole distance in three-quarters of an hour.

'Well! I bet I could teach Hannibal a thing or two after this. Anyone could do it on an elephant!'

I undid my planks and cast them from me. Shirl's overburdened string gave a last despairing tug and broke again. I think that griller should find its last resting place in the National Museum at Canberra.

Chapter 5

THE WAITER AND ......THE UPSTAIRS MAID

The next day we started work. Mrs. Clapton, the housekeeper, called us at seven and when we reported for duty in the lounge, found her and some other women already at work.

Mrs. Clapton was a small, compact woman with Eton-cropped greying hair (at a time when page-boys were the fashion) and horn-rimmed glasses which accentuated a cast in one eye. She was only five feet tall but her bearing was formidable and she was all powerful on the domestic side of the house. Her eyes missed nothing, she moved silently and pounced swiftly. Her tongue was a flay.

I was detailed to brush the staircarpet with a small whisk, taking care to get well into the corners. From the top of the stairs I looked down and giggled at the strange sight of Shirl shifting furniture and sweeping vigorously. When she'd finished that, she proceeded to polish the floor and the already-burnished furniture. I took so long doing the stairs and banisters that there was no time for anything else before breakfast. We trailed disconsolately to the cheerless staff dining room, feeling we'd already done a day's work but after a breakfast of porridge then eggs and bacon, we had to return to the house for the main labour of the day.

The guests were now at breakfast and we had to hurry to make the beds before they returned. Most rooms had three double-decker bunks to make, which made quite an obstacle course. One had to perch on the lower bunk and grip with one's toes (oh for a tail!), using both arms for turning the mattress and airing the linen before making all tidy again. After that, at a more leisurely pace, we would sweep the floor, dust, do the handbasin unit, scrub the floor of the shower and lavatory cubicles and clean the lavatory.

We dreaded being found at some degrading task and always contrived to be doing something genteel when the guests started trickling back, such as flicking gently with a duster or smoothing a bedspread. But if they lingered in the room or started to talk to me, I couldn't afford to waste any more time and was forced to pick up a wet cloth and start on the handbasin.

I enjoyed doing this. It was finicky work and I liked taking time over it. There was the basin itself to wash free of soap and grease-rings. The chrome taps, plughole, mirror and wall brackets had to be cleaned with an ingenious little preparation called 'Duzit' and rubbed till they shone, the tooth glass to be washed and dried, the toothbrush holder to be wiped clean of white droppings and finally, the basin to be wiped dry. (Oh, the tragedy of a late guest returning with an apologetic 'Just want to clean my teeth' and a gushing of taps!) Yes, a satisfactory task, a rewarding task. I was proud of my gleaming chrome and spotless porcelain.

But always Mrs. Clapton was hot on my heels. 'You've been too long on that basin. What about the lavatory? And the shower cubicle? Try to work quickly. I want this floor swept and oiled and then you can do the bathroom next door.' A whisk of slim, tailored skirt and she was away to hound Shirl and the others.

Floor-oiling was a most arduous and tedious task. First of all the floor had to be carefully swept, using a stiff broom to flick up puffs of dirt hiding between the cracks of the floorboards. Then I had to shake a few drops of oil on a mop and rub it on the inhospitable timber until a faint brown stain began to appear. And then finish a room twelve feet by twenty!

My arms and back were aching unbearably and I leaned on my mop to rest. Shirl's head popped furtively around the door.

'She's mad!' she hissed, looking over her shoulder. 'She's got me washing a floor next door and won't let me use a mop. Says I've got to get down on my knees and do it. Mad!' She darted away.

That, we discovered, was Mrs. Clapton's strong point. No slovenly long-handled broom or mop methods. Oh no! Down on the old knees and work your arm vigorously over a small area of floor, crawling under beds and splashing water and sandsoap everywhere. Then go all over it again and wipe it with a cloth.

A variation on this theme was the concerto for bucket and brush. The floors of bathrooms, shower cubicles and lavatories were supposed to be scrubbed each day, using a scrubbing brush and a bucket of water. Shirl and I couldn't bear to get down on our knees in the confined wet space of these cubicles, so we swished a mop over it. It looked just as clean. But one day as I was leaving one of the luxurious suites usually booked by honeymooners, Mrs. Clapton materialized at my elbow and the thin steely voice slid past my ears like a rapier.

'You haven't done the bathroom floors yet, have you?'

I said blandly: 'Yes, I've finished everything.'

'But you haven't done the floors yet. You haven't your bucket with you.'

I realized my error and admitted I'd forgotten to do the floors.

Thereafter we became crafty. We walked ostentatiously down the hall, clanking a bucket with a scrubbing brush, passed Mrs. Clapton with a submissive and obedient expression on our faces and entered a bedroom. Shutting the door, one of us mounted guard while the other hastily mopped around the cubicles. Then we exited, our haloes rampant, our buckets just as full and the scrubbing brushes quite, quite dry. So long as we had our buckets with us, we could have drawn noughts and crosses on the floor.

-oOo-

Half an hour before lunch one day, I ran out of work. The bedrooms were all spotless. The handbasins shone from applications of 'Clever Mary' and I had run along the hall carpet with a carpet-sweeper. I lowered myself into a chair but the thin voice deftly interposed.

'Just time to fold some sheets in the laundry. Come with me please.'

The laundry was a dank, steamy place in the basement. It was the undisputed realm of a wonderful character called Bella. As we entered, she turned to glare truculently at us, one massive arm, as thick as a leg of lamb, flung across the mangle at which she was working. She was, I think, the ugliest woman I'd ever seen. She gave me the impression of a bulldog ready to spring with her jutting lower jaw (which bore two stunted central incisors), pug nose and small eyes. Her face was red and moist from the steaming coppers and short, lank hair was pulled back behind her ears with large hairclips. Her figure was fat and dumpy. I learnt later that she could swear like a trooper – an Australian trooper – and her narratives were vivid and lusty. She was always outspoken about her opinions but, although as rough as bags, she was sincere and I liked her bluntness from the start.

She eyed Mrs. Clapton malevolently and, though the latter didn't quail, she conceded her ground with discretion and withdrew.

'Come on in love. What's she want yer to do?' She lit a cigarette and eased her ample bulk on to a laundry hamper.

'She said I could fold some sheets for you till lunch.'

'Ha!' She loosed a great shout of derision. 'Bloody nice of her, I must say. Nothin' else to do in the house so someone thinks of Bella! Doesn't matter if I sweat me guts out the rest of the time. Oh it's all right ... nothin' to do with you. 'ere – sit down while yer can.'

She waved me to another clothes basket.

'What about the sheets?'

'B——- the sheets. I'm not all that busy today. Only a few guests in the house. But you just wait till Sydney hears about the snow. We'll be burstin' at the bloody seams – like some of the piller slips when I've finished with 'em.' She grinned maliciously, her two teeth splendid in their isolation.

'Yeah – full up soon. Then we'll see if Bella gets any help. Oh what's it matter anyway. I keeps to meself as much as possible. I hate women! Can't stand 'em! Rotten sneakin' lot of b——-s. Bella's no good in a crowd. You'll always find Bella on her own.'

'Anyway, what about you and your girl-friend? Where're youse goin' next? Will youse be goin' to Newcastle? Y'oughter go t' Newcastle! I've got friends there. I'll give youse the address. Just say Bella sent youse and y'll be right.'

It was time for lunch and I raced off but on several occasions after that I went down to help Bella and learned how to operate the ironing machine, a gigantic monster into which one fed the sheets. Woe betide if I inadvertently fed a fold into the slot and it emerged knife-creased. The whole lot had to be done again with Bella's language smoking around my ears.

But one day she grudgingly admitted 'This'll stand yer in good stead if y'ever want a job. Now yer've learned the laundry business, y'll be right for a job at a laundry any time.'

She was kind, was Bella, in her rough way. I believe she had a daughter in Sydney or somewhere. That surprised me, and yet ... I think she might have been beautiful with a baby in her arms.

-oOo-

We now slept in one of the rooms for female staff. It contained three double-decker bunks, which meant that six women were falling over each other in a room fourteen by ten. We had to get up and dress in relays. Most of the floor space was taken up with lockers (one each), wash-basin, travelling cases and clothes. There was no hanging space so all clothes were draped over the bunks, making the room look like a second-hand junk shop. As in all the bedrooms in the house, we had a shower-room and a lavatory cubicle, the lavatory being of the push-button flushing type. It never worked so finally the push-button was removed and a chisel inserted. With considerable practice, it was sometimes possible to manipulate the chisel so as it opened a valve and let in the water. As no one could ever work this except the plumber ('What's the matter with you girls? Look, 'ts easy' .... WHOOSH!), we had a bucket of water handy. The chaotic state of affairs in our room was bad enough, without having someone dashing out of the lavatory, standing the bucket under the shower, tearing back and pouring the water down the bowl, back to the shower, back to the lavatory and so on. I preferred to go down to the ladies' room in the basement. It was quicker in the long run.

Sharing the room were Rosie and Gwen (waitress and pantrymaid); they had been in the Army and had taken this job for the fun of it. They were very pleasant girls and seemed to spend most of their spare time reading poetry. (Rosie would read out loud at bed time and I loved Christina Rossetti's *The Blessed Damozel*.) Mrs. O'Donnell, a sweet-faced, grey-haired old dear who did housework, and Flo, the staff's waitress, were the other two. Flo was simply terrific and brightened our whole day. She was nearly forty with badly-permed frizzy hair and rouged cheeks. She laughed at everything she said, whether funny or not. We laughed politely and thus encouraged she went into fresh gales of mirth, holding her hand over her mouth to conceal her slipping dentures. This only made us laugh more and soon everyone was rolling and hooting with merriment. She used to come in late at night after lights-out, find the room quiet and everyone apparently asleep, yet start loudly haranguing us. She'd splash her noisy way through a face-wash, stumble over everything on the floor and leap gaily into bed, shrieking with laughter and carrying on a conversation with whomever cared to listen. By this time, we'd all be awake anyhow and we'd go through the laugh routine all over again.

That was our nightly diversion. Our morning one was worse. Each day I was awakened by a hoarse, guttural voice at my head, coming from Frank, a mournful-looking middle-aged Italian. He was the dairyman and during the winter was in charge of the Samoyed dog team. According to

Rosie, Frank was 'like a father' to her and Gwen. He was certainly devoted but I wouldn't have said his interest was paternal. Rosie slept on the bunk above me, and at the same time every morning, the door would open and Frank would loudly exhort her to 'coom on; giddup; loogadtheclog, id's vive minutes to zeven; coom on now Rosie, lift your 'ead an' loogadthe sonrise.'

This monotonous voice when I was foggy with sleep seemed to me like the trump of doom. I snuggled into my blankets but the voice went on relentlessly.

'Rosie! Gan you 'ear me Rosie? Id's vive minutes to zevun; you'll be lade Rosie.'

'Mmmm ... all right Frank. I'm awake.'

'You awake Rosie? Loogadthe beaudivul sonrise; lift your 'ead Rosie, gan you see the sonrise?'

'Rosie, for the love of Mike, lift your head and look at the blasted sunrise,' I'd moan, trying to tunnel myself into sleep again.

Shirl and I protested vehemently against this daily invasion of our room. We even stealthily locked the door one night but Rosie was so indignant next morning when Frank had to stand at the door and bellow his summons that we had to resign ourselves to the violation of our privacy.

Frank wasn't the only member of the male staff who entertained us. Norman, the friendly drinks waiter, had been a prisoner of war in Germany and now filled the air, night and day, with passionate renditions of German love songs. The electrician and the carpenter never met each other without snapping to attention, extending their right arms and bellowing 'Heil Hitler!'. Then there was the plumber who snored so loudly that no one would share a room with him, so he had to sleep in a partitioned part of the corridor, and the dear old kitchen man who used to sneak food for us when the chef wasn't looking!

We were always hungry. There was great dissatisfaction in the staff room about the quality of our meals. The chef maintained we had the same food as the guests. We did, the left-overs from the day before. Furthermore, the guests always had three or four choices; we had to eat what was placed before us. We had no fruit, no cake, only occasional scones and stale bread and jam to ease our hunger.

After we'd had our tea at 5.30, Shirl and I dried dishes in the kitchen until eight o'clock. We liked doing this as it gave us a chance to fill the aching void. We sucked in our cheeks and looked pathetic until the chef, grudgingly, flung us oddments of food which we carried away to a corner and devoured eagerly. The culmination of our predatory activities was a cup of black coffee with a tablespoon of whipped cream floating on top. Exquisite!

Sometimes I was let off the kitchen chores and summoned by Mrs. Day to give the guests some dinner music. I can never play *The Waiter and the Porter and the Upstairs Maid* now without having a mental picture of Shirl and Norman dancing recklessly in the deserted lounge, Norman in his impeccable white mess jacket, Shirl with her apron tucked up and her eyes watching for the first guests to emerge from the dining room.

After eight o'clock we were usually so tired that we went straight to bed, greedily grasping at a little sleep before first Flo and then Frank woke us.

Our afternoons were just about our own. Until two o'clock we had to help in the kitchen, laundry or sweep the upstairs carpets ... ('Look girls ... make your broom *work* for you ... bend it so that it springs up and whisks the dirt along. Use force, don't just stroke the floor!'). Then we rushed to change into ski pants, jumpers and boots and shot down to the ski room for our skis. Away then to the slopes – hundreds of them, where one could pick a fresh run each time. If there were even one set of tracks down a run, it was spoiled in our eyes. Hardly anyone came out to these slopes.

Now that snow had fallen, the older guests had all gone down the mountain and the young sporting types who were beginning to arrive were usually marshalled in a line on the nursery slopes under the watchful eye of an instructor. Learners are advised to join instruction classes before taking steep slopes and, by gaining ski-control, avoid accidents. All very laudable but our time was too precious. Let those with leisure learn their snowploughs and stem turns by the hour. We could not satisfy our hunger for the broad, glistening expanses of virgin snow in the meagre time at our disposal. We herring-boned wearily to the top of a hill (the ski-lift wasn't working) and then, pushing off, whistled straight to the bottom. Our only safeguard was the fact that we did a sort of snowplough all the way down. A guest we knew told us that one day as we shot past the class on the lower slopes, the instructor said to them: 'Now, that's how not to do it. Your skis should leave a single track, not tramlines!' We were very amused at this story but though not technically correct, our 'tramlines' saved our necks as not once did we come to grief, even when we became more ambitious and started including jumps in our runs.

We had a full day off each week and, taking a cut lunch and anything else to eat we could lay our hands on, we usually went to the wonderful unfrequented Sugarloaf runs, a couple of miles along the valley from the Chalet.

Unfortunately, other members of the staff had days off too and on Gwen's holiday, we had to stand in for her in the pantry. What a dreadful job! She stood at a sink washing dishes for hours, finishing one lot only when another meal was due to start. Breakfast was the worst. Each guest had a separate tea or coffee service, consisting of silver-plated pot, sugar basin and milk jug. There were thus about sixty of these articles to be treated. Not just washed in soap and water but put to soak in a sink of water containing soda, methylated spirits, plate powder and squares of aluminium. And then each piece had to be polished! Glasses too! I learned the first morning the secret of sparkling glass ware. I had rinsed a whole batch of glasses in very hot water, thinking that was the logical way to achieve a greaseless crystal clarity. I was so crestfallen when I saw the cloudy film over them that Gwen burst out laughing.

'Cold water dear! Never hot.'

I had been brought up in the tradition of piping hot washing-up water and couldn't concede this point but I only had to try one glass to see the difference. It sparkled like a diamond.

All this and dirty dishes too. Horrible eggy dishes. There was no such thing as detergent then. At 11.15 we finished and at 1 o'clock started the luncheon dishes. They came in their thousands until 4 o'clock, when we staggered away and collapsed on our bunks. Then the dinner round from six until nine. What a business! I almost began to believe that food wasn't worth it.

-oOo-

Shirl was busy in Room 12 one morning. Its occupant was Stewart Pennington-Smith, a Royal Navy rating with whom we had been skiing a few times and whom Shirl had bagged as the only personable unattached male at the Chalet. She usually contrived to be about when he returned from breakfast, in order to have a few words 'accidentally' with him. But on this particular morning breakfast had been over for some time and Stewart hadn't come back. Poor Shirl had finished the room except for the unmentionables. She was desperate.

'Look Wen. I'll have to get on with the cubicles. Mount guard for me will you?'

I was sweeping the hall carpet. 'All right. We'd better have a danger signal. I know ... I'll sing *I'm Fair Titania* if I see him coming.'

She scuttled into the bedroom with a sigh of relief. To be caught cleaning a lavatory, *his* lavatory, by the beloved was just too embarrassing to contemplate.

The male prospect hadn't been as bright as we'd imagined. True, the house was only now beginning to fill up, but so far there hadn't been any *bon hommes* worth mentioning.. (Shirl and I spoke a hideous hybrid dialect of schoolgirl French and German which attained such a state of inaccuracy as to be quite unintelligible to others. We spoke of 'doing our horses' when we meant doing our hair ... a simple play on *cheveux* and *chevaux*; and lipstick was always *lèvrestück*). No one really as nice as our beloveds at home. But then, if we could leave the latter for an unspecified period of time with only a slight pang, could it be the real thing?

I was debating this serious question when, up the stairs, two at a time, bounded Stewart.

'Hullo there!' he nodded, 'keeping you busy?'

I came to. Horror! Already he was striding past me. 'Yes, you bet. *I'm fair Titania, la la la, lardy dardy da ...*' I warbled wildly.

'I beg your pardon?' He turned, startled.

'Just singing. What are you doing this afternoon?' I ran along beside him. *'La de dardy dah de de de tralala la la ...'* (Confound the thing. Why didn't it have any words!)

'Thought I might climb Mt. Stilwell ...' he broke off, confused by my running obbligato. He'd reached his door and now stood with his hand on the knob.

'I'm fair Titania,' I bellowed with my last breath as he disappeared inside.

I leant on my broom, exhausted. After a few minutes Shirl emerged, her face flaming.

'You might've warned me!' she said, fuming.

-oOo-

The Chalet was just about full now and it was obvious that we shouldn't have much leisure time for skiing. The prospect of one day off a week just didn't compensate for six days drudgery. We decided to move on.

But first ... one more day to ourselves on the mountain. Once we had ceased being staff we couldn't remain in our bedroom so there was nothing for it but to spend the night in the mountain hut. So we packed our haversacks and trudged up the road.

The hut was half full of snow which had seeped through the windows and under the door. I tried to sweep some of it away but there was too much of it. The temperature must have been well below zero. We thought of making a fire but the woodheap outside was snowed under. Anyway, neither of us was much good with an axe. So we left it and went out on the slopes.

The snow was icy and after a couple of falls I lost my nerve. It would be too dreadful to have an accident on our last day. So I trailed back to the hut by myself, feeling cold and hungry and miserable. Shirl roved about the mountain all day, exulting how perfect it was and hinting that we should stay another day. Completely without fear, she didn't share my feeling of possible disaster. I lay in my bunk all day, wrapped in blankets and at teatime we slunk down to the Chalet and crept up to our old room. The girls were very sympathetic and Flo smuggled us a hot meal. Greatly cheered and warmed, we set off for the hut.

Instead of going the long way round by road, we herringboned laboriously up the steep side of the mountain. The night was dark, with a moon breaking through now and then. I was shrouded in the trailing drapery of my tent/cape and Shirl leant weakly on her alpenstocks, laughing helplessly because I looked like a great bat spreadeagled against the white snow. The climb warmed us and we went straight to bed on our old squeaking bunks, swathed in blankets inside our bags. We were a little chilly at first but soon fell asleep, praying we'd survive the refrigeration.

The next thing I remember was a terrific pounding on the door and angry cries of 'Come on! Out of our hut! What're you doing in *our* hut? Unlock the door!'

I woke up clawing wildly and groping for my torch. I wasn't sure where I was. Shirl roused herself and bellowed 'It isn't your hut. It's ours!'

'Get up! Come on … unlock the door!' continued the yells.

'It isn't locked!' yelled Shirl in a fury.

With that, the door burst open and hordes of people fell into the room. I couldn't believe my eyes. The beam of my torch picked out face after unexpected face. Three of the girls on the staff, six of the men and three male guests whom we knew. Still foggy with sleep, I couldn't understand what on earth they were doing up in our hut on the snow-covered mountain in the dead of night. Actually, it was only nine o'clock, but it seemed that we'd been asleep for hours.

They dragged us out of bed and demanded to know where the wood was. I waved weakly in the direction of the shed and tried to explain that it was buried in snow but nothing loth, they staggered back with a long iced log and proceeded to chop it with wild, erring strokes inside the hut. Then they built a roaring fire and from a haversack produced beer, soft drink, glasses, apples, bananas, oranges, salted peanuts and chocolate. We stood and gaped. It was so unexpected. One of the men was a sixty-year-old kitchen hand and one of the girls had a weak heart but they'd come straight up the side of the mountain in thick snow to give us a send-off.

We crowded around the fire and ate and drank, sang and joked. It was unbelievably cold even near the fire – and I began to dread going back to my bunk. Someone suggested we go down to the Chalet and smuggle ourselves into one of the girls' bedrooms. We packed up again, shouldered skis and plunged down the slope through deep drifts to the Chalet. Assembled in the ski-room like a lot of naughty schoolchildren, the girls decided it was too risky to conceal us in their rooms. So we spread blankets on the concrete floor of the drying-room and dossed there. The kitchen man brought us a pot of scalding coffee and slabs of apple pie. Making sure that we were comfortable, he tiptoed away, shutting doors and turning out lights. It was the most comfortable night we had had for weeks. Gloriously warm and quiet! We fell asleep, snug and secure, with rows of dangling socks and mittens hanging over us.

In the morning we rose at seven, dressed and officially arrived at the Chalet. Flo brought us some hot breakfast to our old room. Then we went the rounds of Staff and guests saying goodbye. At half past ten we were ready to go. We were planning to ski the twelve miles down to the Hotel, disdaining offers of transport on the tractor as we thought the long downward glide would be heaven. (Our bikes had already been taken down to the Hotel.) Outside, we were amazed to find it snowing steadily. There was a strong wind whipping the snow into our faces and in a few minutes our woollen cardigans were completely iced over. We plodded through the Chalet gates feeling very intrepid and waved an heroic farewell before turning into the blizzard.

Chapter 6

SUNNY SOUTH COAST

The long glide turned out to be wishful thinking. The road was level and consequently we had to hike most of the way. Walking on skis is a laborious and wearying business. We covered the 2½ miles to Betts Camp by one o'clock. There we found our friend the Chalet plumber working and he cooked up a wonderful hot dinner for us. Off again at two o'clock. The gale was increasing and the snow blinded us. We rested at Perisher Hut, had a look at the nearly-finished stone hut at Rock Creek and staggered into Smiggins Holes Camp (four miles) at four o'clock. The Chalet tractor was there, waiting for the Hotel truck to arrive and transfer its passengers but it was long overdue and at half past four several people arrived on foot to report that the truck was bogged half a mile away. It didn't sound promising so we said we'd ski on and ask the driver to pick us up.

We set off at five o'clock; darkness fell and everything was grey and misty. We could discern only one snow pole at a time, indicating the position of the road. After a while we met the truck bogged down in the snow. We continued along the track. We were covering only two miles an hour as the road was still level and there were even slopes to climb. Our heels were blistered and sore from the ski bindings. We kept looking back for the lights of the truck but as time went on and the miles passed, we half hoped we could reach the Hotel under our own steam. At last we reached the top of Daimers Gap and suddenly, rapturously, felt our skis tip over and pointing downwards, start moving under their own power. We realized we were at last losing height and just 'sat in' on our skis, hurtling down. The road, or what we hoped was the road, was just a gleaming expanse, with no ruts or mounds to give it third dimension. On our left was a cliff face and on our right a drop. Everything was white and vague, with gaunt, dead trees rising like spears out of the gulch. We zipped along through the darkness for two miles, sliding effortlessly around the corners and then, to our unbounded joy, saw the friendly twinkle of lights through pine trees. It was the Hotel.

We felt so proud as we passed through the gates. We didn't know which part of the building to enter and eventually found our way to Reception. Our jumpers were thoroughly iced and our feet soaked. The

Manager, on hearing we had been working at the Chalet, directed us to a Staff bedroom. We were having a very welcome hot roast dinner in the Staff dining room when the Manager's wife swept in wearing evening dress and apologized for her husband. He didn't realise who we were and would we care for a guest bedroom. Of course we would! After a hot shower we dressed in respectable clothes and mingled with the guests at a dance, trying to smother our weariness and evoke some enthusiasm for a Mad Hatter's Dance. After trying vainly to make a silly hat from some spare bicycle tubes, we gave up the idea and went to bed.

At about this time, we heard later, the truck driver returned, cold and weary. After the truck had been dug out of the drift, it had broken down just out of Smiggins and the driver had walked all the way back to the Hotel.

The next morning we went out for a last fling on the snow. We were keen to pass a Preliminary Test in skiing and the Hotel instructor, Bill Harris, an ex-A.I.F. Commando, examined us – or rather, passed us. It appeared that he knew my brother Phil and most of the time he reminisced or talked to us about our trip. Then he'd say hastily: 'Oh well, you'd better try a Stem turn.' We'd do it and he'd say 'Yes, that's all right. Now where are you going after Brisbane?'

Finally he said; 'Right, shall we go?' and sped down the Kerry run. We followed and catching him up asked when we should do the test.

'Oh, you've got it. You're OK.'

Jubilant, we promptly sewed the badges on our jackets and wore them proudly thereafter.

-oOo-

We arrived in Cooma after dark that night. While we were leaving some films to be developed at the chemist's, he said he knew a man who'd like to meet us, and took us over the road to Norris's Garage. There we met Frank Norris and Stan Dykes, who conducted a very popular yodelling session on Radio Station 2XL. Mr. Norris was the Mayor and also the agent for a brand of cycle which he advertised on his yodelling session. He was delighted to see us and invited us to feature on his session that night. He was, in fact, about to leave for the studio. If we would just step outside to board the mayoral carriage. We went into the street and saw a battered two-seater called the 'Airflow' for obvious reasons. Wrecked during the V-J Day celebrations, it lacked a hood, none of the doors worked and had to be snibbed shut. It was an old-fashioned, high-backed vehicle and the rush of air was terrific. We climbed over the doors and huddled on the floor of the back seat, trying to escape the icy wind and sleet. We tore rowdily through the streets with skidding tyres and screaming brakes. An uproarious, hilarious journey, especially when, in order to clear the windscreen of rain, Mr. Norris rapidly worked the screen wiper with his hand.

The session consisted of several yodelling records requested by listeners, interspersed with phone quiz questions and commercials. We gave an account of our trip to date and Mr. Norris implied that we were on his brand of cycle. We let it pass – we were under no obligation to Malvern Star.

Mrs. Norris had offered us shelter for the night and when we went to the house after the session, found she had made up comfortable beds on the lounge floor and sofa. It was a beautiful room – exotically furnished with dark, carved Chinese furniture, tapestries and silken hangings.

-oOo-

Three days later we rode into Canberra, the Federal Capital, and promptly lost our way. Apparently everyone does. We had been warned and were, in fact, en route to the Tourist Bureau to buy a map but we couldn't even find the shopping centre. Most of the Canberra residents didn't know where anything was.

In 1912, eleven years after Federation, Chicago architect, Walter Burley Griffin, won first prize in the international competition to design the proposed Federal capital. The site, diplomatically chosen to placate the two main contenders, Sydney and Melbourne, was situated almost half way between them. New South Wales ceded the chosen area to the Commonwealth to become Australian Capital Territory. Despite one suggestion of Sydmeladlperbriho as its name, it was decided to retain the original name of the area.

Canberra is built on a system of concentric circles with connecting rods radiating out to join other circles. Riding around the outer circumference of a circle, you must follow a spoke to reach an inner circle, ride around that till you find the correct spoke to take you out again to the circumference and away to another group of circles. The only solution is to have a Tourist Bureau with piles of maps situated on the road from Queanbeyan, so that visitors are firmly orientated before they start gyrating.

Canberra was a queer place, but I loved it. It was so beautiful even in winter, when the trees were bare (being mainly imported trees) and piercing winds arrowed across the Monaro plains. The spring blossom of the ornamental cherries and their autumnal foliage would be glorious.

But what a strange place! It was really a model city; not model in the sense of being perfect but like a model of a city which one sees in an architect's office, a blueprint of the future. Everything was planned, though perhaps unrealized. We passed notices on vacant blocks reading 'Site for C.S.I.R.' or 'Site for R.C. Cathedral' and we tried to visualize the finished product when all those noble buildings filled the streets. But would they fill the streets? I hoped there would be a planner with a sense of humour who would retain a few paddocks for the flocks of sheep which browsed so contentedly a stone's throw from the dignified Parliament, which skipped nimbly out of the way of the ponderous diplomats driving sedately to Yarralumla and stared with amused tolerance at portfolioed Cabinet Ministers frowning over their speeches as they hurried to the House. I liked Canberra's sheep. They gave an air of rustic simplicity and unsophistication to this would-be city and an urban politician, watching them from his window, might well be reminded that Australia's economy was founded on the sheep's back.

So much for the city of the future. The present nucleus was promising enough. Every building was modern and beautifully designed. Here there were no conflicting architectural styles to rear their Corinthian heads as in Melbourne and Sydney, no Victorian towers and turrets, no pseudo-Tudor, no Regency. Eveything was clean and bright with paint. There were no slums or shabby houses. Gardens abounded and all thoroughfares were tree-lined. Everywhere there were beautiful buildings, the National War Memorial and Museum, the wonderful Institute of Anatomy, the National Library, the University, Ainslie Model School and dozens more.

Mark you, Canberra wouldn't please everyone. Some might say that in its extreme youth it lacked character. It has plenty of character though it may not have the charm of old age but those circles would drive me crazy if I had to live there!

-oOo-

We dutifully did the rounds in Canberra. We had coffee with Senators' wives at the Kurrajong Hotel, we were taken for a scenic drive in a Legation car positively plastered with gilt crowns, we looked over the House, where dozens of workmen were cleaning in preparation for the Opening of Parliament the following week. Sound systems were being installed for the controversial innovation of broadcast debates. We paused outside Government House at Yarralumla and a couple of policemen came racing across the lawn to drive us away as the Duchess objected to our staring.*

I envied her the large residence. We were in a desperate position as regards accommodation. The bitter wintry weather precluded camping. The first night we asked if we might stay at the YWCA Leave House.

'Certainly,' gushed a typical Y.W. organizer. 'We charge two shillings a night, one-and-six for breakfast and lunch, two shillings for dinner. Ten shillings for a full day and night.'

So that was out. We finally managed to secure luxurious quarters in the staff room of a school. I had a letter of introduction from my father, Principal of Melbourne Teachers' College, and when we were at our wits' end this managed to secure us friendly help from schoolteachers along our route.

We were in Canberra on the 10th June for the Victory March. Huddling in Civic Square, we watched Prime Minister Chifley, muffled in a camel-hair coat, taking the salute from a thin column of servicemen. How we longed to be in Melbourne or Sydney or London where there would really be a Victory celebration. That was the funny thing about Canberra. It had such an important role to play and yet it was little more than a country town.

-oOo-

The next stage of our journey was to be east to the coast. At Queanbeyan, we found we had just missed a fish truck going right through to Bateman's Bay. It would be making another trip the next day, so we decided to stay the night. The boss of the iceworks, whose trucks did the fish run from the coast, said we could sleep in one of the sheds. He took us to the biggest one which consisted of two rooms, one full of machinery and one full of stored furniture. He pulled away a stack of chairs and revealed a double bed with a magnificent nine-inch, super-sprung mattress, just waiting for us!

We dumped our gear and spent the afternoon at the Horse Sales, where thirty beautiful cavalry horses from Duntroon Military College were being sold to cut down Army expenses. Perched on top of the high log fence,

*The Duke of Gloucester was then Governor-General of Australia.

I had difficulty in restraining Shirl from bidding with the rest of the people. I tried to make her see that we had too much gear already and couldn't possibly put a horse on the carrier.

'But they're so cheap!' she wailed. 'Only £4 for that glorious chestnut! Why, we could give our bikes away and continue on horseback. Think of all the extra gear we could carry!'

'Think of all the trucks we'd miss!'

In the evening we went to a dance. Clad in our eternal dirndls we still had to go through the ritual of dressing up for the cold ride to the dance hall. Whenever we went thus attired to a dance, we gleefully envisaged the possibility of being escorted home and of our saying demurely: 'Just a minute while we get our wraps.' We pictured the expression on our partners' faces as we emerged sartorially magnificent in grisly leggings (which kept falling down in a grey woolly mass about our ankles), woollen skirts showing beneath our floral ones, and muffled to the eyes with other warmth. And then, the amusing moment when we'd say: 'Well, this is where we live. Goodnight!' and dive furtively into a clump of bushes to our concealed camp. We longed for this to happen. It never did.

The next day we sped eastwards on our fish truck. A wonderful thing had happened. There was warmth in the air for the first time in two months. There had been a severe frost during the night but the day was cloudless and hot. We peeled off windcheaters, scarves and gloves and gloried in the strange sensation. Stopping at Braidwood while the driver went to pick up a load of potatoes, we sat in a park and wrote letters. It was a never-ending struggle to keep up correspondence, not only with our families but with the dozens of people we met along the track. There were thank you letters to people who had given us hospitality, there was a growing list of people who wanted us to drop them a line from Darwin and always our diaries. There was no escape from this duty. If sheer exhaustion drove us to bed without writing, it meant two days to write on the morrow. And if we went to a dance or stayed with a family on the second night, then it was almost impossible to catch up on three days' doings. Each day covered two or three closewritten pages of a large exercise book.

I had received a letter from Karl Frisch. It was written in rather faulty English and so that he should not be embarrassed by his mistakes, I suggested that I should write to him in German and each of us should correct the other's mistakes. This proved to be my only mental exercise for the duration of the trip. To write an account of my travels without the aid of a dictionary or grammar pricked my brain into action. Karl's written English improved immensely and an Australian sergeant at the same camp with whom Shirl corresponded, told her that Karl's morale had sky-rocketed.

At three o'clock the truck returned and we drove through magnificent country to the coast. Beautiful mountain ranges, thickly wooded, fell away into dark, silent fern gullies and up from the depths rose spindly cabbage palms, soaring to burst their fronds above the roof of the forest. We wound down the superb Clyde mountain and at dusk came to the Clyde River at Nelligen. The river was a wide expanse of gleaming opalescent water, with dark brooding forests fringing its banks and purple mountains softly ranged behind. Above the crest of the hills a full moon was rising. I gazed, rapt, and thought of Paul Verlaine's white moon .... *"C'est l'heure exquise!'*

There was no bridge across the water – it is more like a lake than a river at this point – and we crossed in a ferry, truck and all, moving slowly without ripples, like a swan. A great melancholy and nostalgia fell on me, and glancing at Shirl, I saw she was feeling the same.

'If only the beloved were here Wen!' she sighed and looked across the water. I knew she was picturing a rowing boat drifting beneath the overhanging trees. I was.

The jolt of the ferry against the bank and the noisy coughing of the truck engine snapped us out of it and we said nothing more as we sped through gloomy forests and reached the coastal Princes Highway at last. Our six weeks' detour through the Alpine backblocks was over. From here, it was a straight run through to Sydney.

The truck dropped us near the recreation ground at Bateman's Bay where there was reputed to be a good shed. We headed for it, across the moonlit field with its four ghostly goalposts straggling at each end. Shirl reached the hut and pushing open the door, stepped inside. Fumes of alcohol and a hoarse voice from the floor greeted her.

'Come on in! I'm 'ere, but wot's the difference!'

Shirl jumped backwards. 'Who are you?'

'Well,' answered the voice, 'beggin' yer pardon fer the language, you bein' a lady, I'm just a bum-off-the-road. But wot's the difference ... come on in!'

The swagman has not yet disappeared from Australian roads though this one was not a good example of that fine breed of itinerant travellers.

We again sought shelter at a school and the schoolmaster and his wife couldn't do enough for us. He made a fire in the schoolroom, lent us a lamp, spread two kapok mattresses on the floor, left us matches and firewood and told us to come to the house in the morning for a bath and breakfast. We fell asleep with the sound of the sea lapping the shore. I was very glad to reach the coast as I love the sea.

The next morning I saw it. Incredibly blue water, sparkling in the sun. Fishing boats and yachts were dotted over the harbour and islands off-shore looked as though they were painted on a stage backdrop. It was the most glorious, perfect day. The sky was cloudless and blue and the sun drenched everything in gold. We felt exhilarated and longing to get on the road. I put on shorts and sandals for the first time since Tumut and they always made me feel free and unhampered. We said goodbye to our kind hosts and set off, pedalling light-heartedly. The beautiful bitumen road stretching northwards was a signpost to perpetual summer. What a day! This was what we'd left home for.

And then a utility truck came along. From force of habit we hailed it. It was going to Nowra, seventy miles away, and our brave mood paled. We simply had to reach Nowra that night, in order to reach Wollongong the next day, so as to reach Sutherland the day after (Monday), ready to meet Sydney reporters there first thing Tuesday morning. This was the first and last time we ever attempted to keep to a schedule. It took all the joy out of exploring new country.

So we piled on board the truck and tore off at fifty miles an hour. The windstream was terrifically strong and I could hardly keep my eyes open. Peering through veiled slits, I was aware of the breathtaking scenery The road wound through forests and ranges and though we didn't see the ocean at all until nearing Ulladulla, there were forested mountains with rivers and lakes shining in the sun. We reached Ulladulla at 1 o'clock and the truckdriver and his friend went into a café for lunch. We were neither hungry nor financial so we went for a stroll along the pretty beach. The road through the town was planted with coral trees which were now in full bloom. The flaming scarlet of their spiky blossoms against the bare grey branches with a background of impossibly blue sky was wonderful.

We unloaded our bikes from the truck at Nowra and were just standing on the side of the road debating whether to go to the railway station or school for the night when a woman crossing the street called out: 'Going far?' I told her who we were and asked if she knew where we could spend the night.

'You're welcome to use my verandah if you like. Or I could shake you up a bed on the sitting-room floor.'

Something always turned up. Our only problem each day was where to stay the night and as soon as that was settled, Shirl and I would look at each other exultantly and mentally shake hands. Our luck was extraordinary. We were besieged with lifts and offers of hospitality.

This time it was Mrs. Hanley, wife of the editor of the *Shoalhaven and Nowra News*. She told us that Malvern Star had sent them notification of our trip weeks ago but as there had been no sign of us, they had concluded that we had passed through unnoticed.

'Malvern Star sponsoring your trip I suppose?'

'No they're not!' I replied vehemently. 'Everyone assumes they are. We don't get a penny from them.'

'But they're getting a lot of incidental advertising from you.'

'I know. Everyone asks what kind of bikes we're riding. And if they don't ask, they can see the star insignia from yards away.'

'I'd stick up for my rights if I were you. When you go to Sydney, go and see the manager and if they don't come to terms, change your bikes.'

That sounded all very well but we couldn't afford to change our bikes and there wasn't another cycle firm so well-established in every State. We knew Malvern Star was our only hope and they knew too. We thrashed the matter out with the Hanleys and resolved to do battle when we reached Sydney.

The next day we wanted to get away as a heavy day's riding to Wollongong or Bulli was ahead of us but the Hanleys were set on taking us for a car drive to see the wonderful view from Cambewarra Lookout. We realized how foolish it was to cut short our stay in beautiful places such as Nowra just to be in Sydney by a certain date. Blow the schedule! So we went in the car for a drive through superb mountain scenery, reminiscent of the Acheron Way near Melbourne – ferny gullies and dense forests of cedar and myrtle and gum. As we climbed higher we caught glimpses of the country beneath us, culminating in the magnificent panorama from the summit. As far as one could see from left to right was an unbroken vista of patchwork fields bordered by the wide ribbon of the Shoalhaven River (a wonderful sight for anyone from Victoria, where the rivers are mainly narrow and rocky), serpentine creeks, proud mountains, nestling farms, then the glorious ocean with Jervis Bay, Pig Island, Point Perpendicular and Goodnight Island away in the distance.

It was three o'clock before we pedalled out of Nowra. We thought it impossible to reach Bulli now, unless we were given a lift and, as it was a Sunday, that was improbable. There were plenty of cars on the road but no trucks. We were not in the best of shape. Shirl had eaten something that disagreed with her, I had a headache and my thighs were being chafed by the rough woollen skirt I was wearing, it was very warm, the packs were heavy and the road long and hilly. We were praying for a lift.

Then I heard It! The heavenly sound of a heavy vehicle labouring up a hill. I stood panting, Shirl sat on the ground looking ill and we waited expectantly. Over the brow of the hill groaned a truck laden high with timber. We thumbed madly and it stopped. The driver could take us to Wollongong at the foot of Bulli Pass. Rapture! We climbed up and relaxed on the timber.

From our rearguard position we idly watched a utility truck approaching and just for fun made signs to the driver to enquire where he was going. He passed us and slowing down, forced our truck to stop. He was going all the way to Sydney. We explained that we only wanted to go to Bulli and transferred to his truck, leaving the lumbering timber truck behind.

What a contrast! Our new benefactor was a speed fiend, racing along at fifty miles an hour on the wrong side of the road, zipping around corners oblivious of the possibility of other traffic approaching. We sat on the edge of the seat, petrified with fear.

At dusk we passed through Kiama, an entrancingly lovely town aflame with coral trees. I should have liked to stay there for a while but the truck sped through and reached Wollongong at six o'clock. I was astounded at its size. What we had known merely as a name on the map was a city with crowded streets, neons and traffic lights. As we climbed the highway to Bulli

Pass, we looked back on a fantastic fairyland of coloured lights extending beyond Wollongong to Port Kembla.

We were dropped at the Panorama Hotel at the top of Bulli Pass. Mrs. Hanley had told us to look up Mrs. Gordon, the proprietress, and ask if we could sleep in the garage. We did so but Mrs. Gordon wouldn't hear of us sleeping anywhere but in a spare bedroom. We were able to have baths, wash our hair and our clothes in readiness for the triumphant entry into Sydney. The view from our window was breathtaking. Wollongong, with its parallel lines of lights, was stretched out beneath us. Behind it was the placid ocean, bathed in moonlight, with scalloped bays etched in lights receding into the distance.

Shirl, still unwell, went to bed and I sat by the fire in the hotel lounge to write up my diary. The only other occupants were two young couples who, by their awkwardness and studied gaiety, I adjudged to be newly-arrived honeymooners. They made polite but dull conversation, went to the window innumerable times to exclaim anew about the lights below and finally lapsed into an embarrassing silence. Then one of the wives noticed a large and splendid sports trophy on the mantelpiece and invited guesses as to the sport it represented.

'Swimming,' said one.

'More likely tennis up here,' said another.

'Or golf.'

'I say rifle-shooting.'

'Get it down Bert and let's see.'

Bert took it down from the shelf, grasped it by its magnificent carved handles and peering at the engraving, read bleakly 'Under 14 Broad-Jump Championship'.

They went to bed!

Next morning a maid woke us and asked if we'd like breakfast. We were very hungry, but not wishing to impose, refused. Ten minutes later, she reappeared with a tray of food and said: 'Mrs. Gordon says to sit up and get this into you.' We marvelled.

It was another beautiful day, and below us, through a slight morning haze, we could see the long curving beaches and bays, and the ocean, blue and devoid of ripples.

We rode all that day through enchanting country. As far as Bald Hill we had glimpses of the sea, but then turned inland and rode for eight miles through Stanwell Park along Lady Carrington Drive. The road was a soft dirt track, winding through dense moist forests with fern gullies at every bend and little creeks crossing the road every fifty yards. It, too, was similar to Melbourne's lovely Acheron Way, with the striking difference that here were palms. They gave a tropical aspect to the forest and it was hard to realise that we were only twenty miles from Sydney.

At five o'clock we reached Audley in National Park, a pretty little holiday resort. The creek broadens considerably here and it was covered with gaily-coloured rowing boats crowded with picnickers. Five miles further on we came to Sutherland, which is on the outskirts of the Sydney metropolitan area. Once again we were looked after by a Headmaster and his wife. We slept under a roof, had baths and ironed our clothes ready to meet the Press in the morning.

Chapter 7

CITY LIGHTS

After an interview with reporters and photographers at Sutherland, we rode into Sydney. In our shirts, shorts and sandals, we felt most conspicuous in the city streets and when we hopped off outside the G.P.O. and leaned the bikes with their towering loads against lamp-posts, we were immediately besieged by curious passers-by. Shirl was surrounded in a little clump five yards from my circle.

'Excuse me, where are you going?'

'Where have you come from?'

'You're not the girls we read about! Fancy!'

We tore away to collect piles of accumulated mail and after a great deal of trouble and an interview with the Supervisor of Mails himself, were given the Sydney postmark in our books.

Then we launched into business. We rang the Sydney manager of Malvern Star who had been pestered by reporters wanting to see us. He took us to the Harbour Bridge to have photos taken and then to an advertising agent to discuss terms. They wanted us to sign a contract giving them permission to use the photo in a Malvern Star advertisement in the next day's paper.

'We're willing to pay you four guineas each,' said Mr. Nabbs the manager expansively.

I read the contract. In it, I the undersigned, agreed to Malvern Star using the said testimonial and photo in any form of advertising. It seemed straightforward to me. I signed. I pocketed my four guineas. Two months later I realized how we had been tricked.

Hubert Opperman, ('Oppy'), Australia's road cycling champion, now worked for Malvern Star. He contacted the Sydney office to say that in our publicity photo Shirl's leg was too straight at the downward limit of her pedalling. He said her saddle should be lowered.

Then we bustled off to the Australian Broadcasting Commission for an interview on *Women in Sport*. We left our bikes at Malvern Star for an overhaul and took a tram to Bellevue Hill where dear Mrs. O'Donnell from the Chalet was waiting to look after us. A widow, she kept house for her three sons, Pat, Brian (who had almost finished medicine at Sydney University and was regarded as a brilliant student with a future in neurology) and schoolboy Bob. She had a pleasant flat and we had a room to ourselves.

The day after our broadcast I had a phonecall from Keith, my long-time Melbourne boyfriend. He was in the Navy but had left HMAS *Swan* and was now based at Watson Bay Naval Depot. Before I left Melbourne we had agreed to be 'just friends' during my absence. So I was rather perplexed when we met to find him most attentive and not at all platonic.

At nine o'clock one morning, Mrs. O'Donnell bustled excitedly into our bedroom to tell us that Peter Barry of 2GB had arrived to interview us for *Macquarie Newsreel*. We dressed rapidly.

'Don't forget Wen,' muttered Shirl, 'no mention of finances or my family'll hit the roof. And just say we had jobs at various places but don't specify what they were. Mum's scared of what people'll think.'

'Oh all right, but it seems to me all the fun's gone if we don't tell people about the odd things we've done.'

Peter Barry was of a very friendly and enquiring nature. Before the recording was made we chatted to him and confided in him the necessity for concealing the nature of our work.

His eyes twinkled. 'Right, let's make a start then.'

The spools of the wire recorder started turning and we began the interview. All went well until he said … 'And what did you do at Kyabram Wendy?'

Wendy:	Oh, we – er, we helped with the fruit picking. Yes, the fruit picking.
Barry:	And how did you find the life?
Wendy:	Oh, we just loved the open-air life!
Barry:	I bet you did. And Shirley, how did you pick the fruit? Did you use ladders?
Shirl:	(dithering and thinking of Tasmania) Well – no, we – er – had bags that we put the apples in. (*Apples*, mind you, at Kyabram, the centre of the stone-fruit industry!)

Barry: And what did you do at Kosciusko, Wendy?

Wendy: Well, when the snow fell, we wanted to make the most of it
            and – er – we went to the Chalet and worked there for a
            fortnight.

Barry: What work did you do there?

Wendy: (looking at him reproachfully) Oh, er, we just – er helped out
            around the house – ha ha.

Barry: What *exactly* though Wendy? I'm going to pin you down on
            this!

Wendy: (almost incoherent with laughter) I did some piano work and
            anything else that was needed.

Barry: And what did you do Shirley?

Shirl: (unable to conceal it any longer) I made hundreds of beds!

-oOo-

Frank Small of Malvern Star sat behind his large executive desk and looked
at us. We were dressed in our civilized clothes which had been sent on by
train from Melbourne. We were trying desperately to be women of the world
and show our business acumen. We wanted a contract for the duration of the
trip. He treated us with great charm and our defiance crumpled.

'You see girls, it's not that we don't want to help you. We like to
encourage these sort of ventures but you're not worth much to us at present.
You've had a certain amount of publicity here and we've taken advantage of
that. You've been paid separately and I think generously for that.'

'Well, we think that with a trip of this magnitude – we definitely
intend to go to Darwin now – which hasn't been done by girls on cycles
before, we *should* be worth more to you. Think of all the publicity you'll
get! Everyone along our route will know we're on Malvern Star bicycles.'

He shook his head. 'I'm sorry. Advertising must show results. If
your publicity snowballs by the time you reach Brisbane or further north,
we'll be only too glad to make further arrangements with you. But till then
.....' He rose and held out his hand.

-oOo-

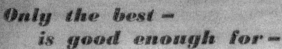

June 25th:

Not too good a day. Up at 8.30, breakfasted and dressed. Went up the street to local dentist. Have one cavity. Then into town at 10.45 to see Mary Evans Jones of Dept. of Information, who carried us off to the Botanic Gardens to have photos taken. At 1.00pm met Mary Campbell from Kossy and had wonderful lunch at Cahills. (She paid!) Then started a great round of advertising agencies. Nothing doing at Nestlés; they wouldn't even discuss the matter, curse their black hearts! But they agreed to sell us a dozen quarter pound blocks of chocolate. Yippee![1] Went to Horlicks and saw the Manager. No money, therefore no go, he said, but pushed us on to Mr. Carruthers at Thompson Advertising who handles many big accounts. He wasn't in. Went to Paton and Baldwin for modelling jobs but no luck. Enquired at shipping office for ships between Brisbane and Cairns but there aren't any. Tried to see snaps of us taken by street photographer but they'd been mislaid. Tried to pick up photos of the trip but they weren't ready. I was surprised to see in the photo shop's window displays of coloured photographs. Apparently you can buy coloured film now. No mail for us at GPO. Very footsore and weary. Asked Qantas Airways re a flight over the harbour. May be a chance. Went to Johnson and Johnson re advertising and told Manager we really do use Johnson's Baby Cream as a protection and cure for sunburn. He was very friendly and interested but couldn't help us. However, he gave us half a dozen tubes of Baby Cream. Any good! Then went to George Patterson to enquire about Cadbury's and Palmolive. All Cadbury's advertising is handled from Melbourne and the Palmolive representative said she'd make enquiries. Goldberg Advertising said Dunlop might give us £25 for three months' placard carrying. That is, £1 a week each. How funny![2] On our way home at 7.30, saw huge crowds milling about outside the State Theatre for the world premiere of *'Smithy'* (the life-story of Australia's famous Sir Charles Kingsford Smith, the great aviator). Flags festooned the theatre, bands were playing and a long line of limousines disgorged glamorous women, dripping with orchids and furs. Vice-Regal cars slid smoothly to a halt at the red carpet, and we had fun causing false alarms about the arrival of the Duke and Duchess of Gloucester. We'd spy a becrowned car containing an unimposing couple and we'd point and cheer until a crowd had gathered to see the Governor-General. Home. Cheese on toast for tea. Bed 9.00pm.

-oOo-

[1] Chocolate was still hard to find in the shops.
[2] They didn't.

1st July 1946

Dear Mum,

Once and for all, about Darwin. We aren't going to ride there. We'll work in Mt. Isa until a truck goes through. There's bound to be something some time. If not, we'll save up enough money to take a plane. And we'll do the same down to Alice and Adelaide. Heck! We wouldn't be fools enough to attempt it by ourselves. But I'm not going to miss it. There's no other place I want to see more than the Centre. Even if there's nothing at Darwin and the Alice, if it's the worst place on earth (which I don't believe), at least I can form my own opinions about it and not take another's word for it.

Besides, we don't want to come back the same way as we go. Hope this clears the air a bit.

Much love to you all. I miss you dreadfully.

Wen

-oOo-

Our financial salvation came when we tracked down a young man we had met in Melbourne. His father ran a publishing company which specialized in trade journals and farming books. Stan offered us the agency for some of these, with generous commissions on each sale. The idea appealed to us enormously as it would obviate the necessity for staying in towns for weeks at a time while we earned enough money to go on. This way we could earn as we went, spending perhaps half a day on business in each town. We would collect cash for sales and subscriptions, keep our commission and send surplus money and orders back to Stan.

Our range consisted of *Dairy Farming*, a concise modern manual for the Australian dairy farmer ('Make the cow pay or sell her!'), a book called *Pig Breeding*, a cheap little monthly magazine called *Hotel and Café News* and a *Radio Record*, in which we were to sell advertising space.

We were jubilant, and longing to get on the road again to try our salesmanship.

In the meantime we looked at Sydney. Of course, Melbourners and Sydney-siders are rivals, so naturally I am biased when I say that I don't think Sydney is a patch on Melbourne. It is wonderful for a holiday, with its harbour, sailing, surfing or mountains but to live there would drive me mad. Its scattered shopping centre, its one-way streets, its narrow, twisting roads which are merely macadamized bullock tracks, all irritate anyone from Melbourne where the shops are the best in Australia, the city is planned and orderly and where living is far more gracious and unhurried. Sydney is Americanized and cosmopolitan. She is a brassy coquette flaunting her charms. Melbourne disdains such advertisement and relies on her quality to attract.

But Sydney's charms are considerable. It is blessed by nature. How can it fail with mountains and sea, the perfect recipe? I remember the beautiful drive through Kuringai Chase to Bobbin Head where the lake sparkled and danced under sleek, skimming yachts and luxurious launches while visitors picnicked in the multi-coloured tents dotting the lawns; Church Point on Pittwater with its wattles blazing; the flying boats landing on the harbour at Rose Bay; Whale Beach and lunch at Jonah's on the crest of a cliff overlooking the ocean; Palm Beach and Narrabeen Lakes; the upper reaches of the Hawkesbury and the sand dunes at Cronulla (which made a very realistic North African desert for the film *Forty Thousand Horsemen*). To us, a sojourn in a capital city did not mean relaxing at resorts. Cities meant work, a bolstering of finances, an annoying but necessary interruption of our discovery of the country.

Brian O'Donnell had just finished showing us around the Medical School at the University. With morbid interest we had been through dissecting rooms and museums. Having left Brian, we were walking to the tram when we spied the offices of Fox Movietone News. We crossed the street and went in. The Contact Manager, Mr. Murdoch, was quite interested after hearing our story and managed to sell his boss on the idea. As we told him some of the sidelights of our trip, he became more enthusiastic and arranged for the filming unit to collect us and our bikes the day of our departure from Sydney.

They drove us out through Parramatta to Prospect, and found a quiet country road where they could film without interruption. We were dressed in shorts, shirts and sandals, bikes groaning beneath the heavy loads fore and aft. (We now had front carriers for our sleeping bags.) They took shots of us riding along the flat road, pushing our bikes wearily up a steep hill, thumbing a lift and unrolling our sleeping bags for the night. For a spot of colour, we cooked sausages (thoughtfully brought by the cameraman) over a few smoking twigs and rode along with our washing drying on a line stretched between the two bikes. Neither thing did we ever do in reality but it looked good and caught the public's eye. For a long time afterwards we met people who remembered us as the girls with the washing on the bikes.

Instead of a newsreel announcer describing the film, we recorded a commentary. It concluded: 'If you see a couple of highwaymen, don't worry. It's only us – trying to escape sunburn.'

With that we tied on head kerchiefs, fastened other triangular scarves highwayman-fashion across the lower part of our faces, put on sunglasses, mounted our unwieldy bikes, waved goodbye to the camera and sped, freewheeling, down a terrific hill into the distance. Slow fade-out.

We dismounted at the bottom, turned around and bent nearly double, trudged back to the top. We arrived panting and scarlet with exertion.

Murdoch met us, his face full of apology.

'Girls,' he stammered. 'I'm terribly sorry, you'll have to do that again. Bill forgot to take the cover off his lens!'

At last we shook Sydney dust off our tyres and headed west to the Blue Mountains for a short detour. The first stop was Penrith.

'And now to work Wen,' said Shirl excitedly. 'This is a good place to start … not too big.' She unhooked the canvas dilly bag from her handlebars and we headed for the first hotel. We found the proprietor in the Bar and introduced ourselves.

'G'day girls. Like a drink? What can we do for you?'

Encouraged, Shirl launched into an uncertain spiel about the excellent little journal we had for Hotel Proprietors; see – (flicking the pages of the sample copy) – recipes, bar suggestions, interior decorating, economy in the kitchen, and all for six shillings a year. Our eyes wide with hope and emphasizing the extreme cheapness of this obviously valuable asset to a publican, we waited. Without any argument he produced six shillings and we signed him up. Two interested listeners in the bar presented us with ten shilling notes to help us on the way. I looked delightedly at Shirl. Clearly a commercial traveller's life had incidental advantages.

With springy steps we tried a café. The woman proprietor browsed through our sample copy then handed it back.

'I don't think I'll bother girls.' Our faces fell. 'But take these along with you.' She handed us a loaf of crisp oven-fresh bread and three rolls.

'Poor Stan,' murmured Shirl without sympathy.

Progressing down the street we sold eight *Hotel and Café News*, one *Pig Industry*, one *Radio Record* and, late in the afternoon, sold a *Dairy Farming* to an old gentleman at the local Dairy Factory and Freezing Works. We felt on top of the planet. I was down to my last pound note so things had been pretty bad.

-oOo-

We managed to get a lift on a large truck right up the hilly approach to the mountains and, instead of stopping at Katoomba, it roared right through to Bathurst. Another truck took us to Orange, our most westerly point. We were delighted although I had expected to collect some mail at Katoomba.

The weather was colder than anything I had ever experienced. At Kosciusko there was snowy cold, still cold, but at Katoomba, Blackheath and Bathurst, icy winds spiralled out of the deep gulches and knifed their way through the towns. We were hopelessly inadequately clothed and suffered greatly. It is hard to remember what life was like before nylon and other synthetics. There were no padded anoraks, no thermal underwear, no light-weight waterproofs other than oiled silk. All we had for warmth were fleece-lined cotton windcheaters to keep out the wind and woollen cardigans. These were hand-knitted from 8-ply Totem wool.

At Orange we stayed with friends and enjoyed the luxury of a warm bed again. Since leaving Sydney we'd slept in a Sunday School Hall (very comfortable too, with matting on the floor, electric light, a sink and tap for our ablutions, a lavatory and even the ladies committee's tea-urn for boiling water) and a very dusty, greasy and refrigerated truck with only a laced tarpaulin along the sides to screen those bitter winds.

Riding down the main street of Orange after the weekend, I passed the Malvern Star shop and remembered that my cyclometer needed adjusting. I went in and told the manager that I was one of the girl cyclists. I have never seen such a reaction. He was not so much astonished as stricken. His eyes bulged, his jaw dropped.

'But ... you can't ... when did you arrive?' he gasped weakly.

'Saturday.'

His lips tried to form words, but instead of speaking, he rummaged through the papers on his desk and handed me a long letter from Mr. Nabbs, which said:

'The two girl cyclists are due to arrive in Orange on the 16th July. They will send you a collect telegram advising you as to the date of their arrival. This will be the signal for you to start operations immediately.

1. Arrange for members of local cycling club to meet them several miles out and escort them in.

2. Arrange for Mayor, Councillors and leading citizens to be present at reception in front of your shop.

3. Arrange with local women's organisations for the girls to address them. You will find them capable and interesting speakers.

4. Arrange for a microphone to be installed in front of shop for broadcast of reception.

5. Arrange for reporters to be present.

6. Book space in same paper for ad. featuring the girls on Malvern Star bikes.

7. Send me two copies of paper.

8. If you have a friend with a camera, get him to take some good snaps of the reception in front of the shop and send me two black, glossy prints.'

I was aghast! I raced out to tell Shirl who was similarly thunderstruck. Everything had fallen through because we hadn't sent a telegram. But we hadn't known we were supposed to. I realized there must have been a letter for us at Katoomba from Nabbs. It was really extremely funny, especially the fact that we had also sailed into Orange on a truck, thus beating our schedule by two days.

'Just imagine if the local cyclists had trooped out to meet us and we'd dashed past them on our truck!'

Then the manager found his voice. 'It's all very well for you to laugh but what about all the time I've wasted on this? What'll I say to the Mayor? What will the reporters say? I'm going to sit down right away and write to Mr. Nabbs in no uncertain terms!'

I pacified him and told him that we'd write and protest. 'We're not going to stand for this mass organization either. We can't possibly stick to a schedule. Anyway, what do they want for their four guineas?'

Slightly mollified, the manager gloomed a little longer. 'But what about the publicity?'

'It's all fixed. We've been to the newspaper and we're having an interview on 2GZ this afternoon – heck, in ten minutes. Come on, Dunc!'

We raced out of the shop, leaving a bewildered manager sitting dejectedly at his desk, his head in his hands.

-oOo-

"Attractive 21 year old redhead Shirley Duncan and brunette Wendy Law, 19, the two girl cyclists who are touring Australia, visited Orange at the weekend. Owing to unforeseen circumstances, a reception that had been arranged for them for today had to be cancelled. They arrived in Orange well ahead of schedule...... Arrangements had been made for

various social bodies in Orange to welcome them. An escort
by the Orange and District Cycling Club from Shadforth to
Orange was planned. Their early arrival prevented it......"
"Western Times" 15.7.46

-oOo-

On our third day in Orange, another guest arrived to share the hospitality of
our hostesses. She was Miss Monica Farrell, the Irish Evangelist, who was
to address a meeting of the United Protestants Union the next evening. She
was a small, dumpy woman, jovial and voluble, full of amusing anecdotes of
her life which she retailed with a strong Irish accent at teatime. After we'd
washed the dishes, Shirl and I settled by the fire and buried ourselves
unsociably in our diaries but we became so engrossed in what Miss Farrell
was saying that we sat and listened for nearly three hours and didn't write a
line. What a wonderful speaker she was! So frank, unpretentious and funny!

She was very interested in our travels and warned us not to sleep out
in the moonlight.

'Why on earth not!' I asked.

'Oh it's very bad, you know. The soldiers in Egypt during the first
war knew all about that. They used to sleep out with a handkerchief over
their faces. One man who didn't take that precaution woke up next morning
and his face had been dragged to one side as the moon passed across the sky.'

I stared disbelievingly and Shirl, who had a completely scientific
mind, let out a shriek of incredulity.

'Well, you know the moon's effect on the tides of the sea. And in
Psalm 121 you know it says 'The sun shall not smite thee by day nor the
moon by night.'

We laughed but she wasn't offended. Although we took it all with a
grain of salt at the time, I often thought of her words in the months that
followed.

We left Orange and turned back to Sydney. It was still miserably
cold and after riding six miles we decided to have a rest and eat some
chocolate. Invariably a truck came when we did this. Two minutes later,
round the corner roared a large truck with two Italians in the cabin. It was
so cold that we couldn't contemplate sitting on the back so we all squeezed
into the cabin, I sitting between the men and Shirl perched on the co-driver's

knee. They dropped us just out of Bathurst and we made a detour for business. Two farms for *Dairy Farming* and the Governor of Bathurst Gaol for *Dairy Farming* and *Pig Breeding*. The latter said no. I suggested they would be very good reference books to have in the prisoners' library but he said the prisoners didn't have a library. Very difficult.

We rode into Bathurst as darkness fell. We bought some fish and chips and ate them out of the piping hot newspaper parcel while sitting on the steps of the impressive War Memorial Carillon Tower. We were thinking of calling on one of the churches for shelter but decided to go to the Police instead. They were most co-operative and directed us to the Court House, where the caretaker allowed us to camp in the Lady Witnesses' Room. This was snug and warm and had a sink and tap, gas-ring and gas-stove. We made beds on the hard floor and used all our surplus clothing, hanky bag and towel as padding underneath. This proved most effective and we followed the same procedure for the rest of the trip. It was a clear and starry night when we went to bed but during the night there was a terrific rain storm and a fierce howling gale lashed the trees and whistled over the roof.

I was awakened next morning by the sound of bells from the Carillon Tower. On Saturdays and holidays they peal out a selection of songs commemorating the first World War – French folk songs such as *Il était une bergère, Sur le pont d'Avignon, Au près de ma blonde, Trempe ton pain, Marie* and lots of others we knew, as well as the *Marseillaise* and many classics by French composers.

We dressed and set off on our business round and it was 5 pm before we headed for Lithgow, forty miles away. It was almost dark and we expected to go only a few miles and stay at a farmhouse. However, three miles out, as we were trudging up a hill, Shirl panted: 'Eat some choc. Wen!' I dutifully nibbled three squares and round the bend swept a magnificent truck with a towering load of cauliflowers. I couldn't see how we could possibly ride on it but it stopped. The driver said he could easily put the bikes up so we unstrapped our packs and he disappeared among the cauliflowers and somehow roped the bikes to the already teetering edifice. We piled into the cabin with him and had a warm drive all the way to the Lithgow turn-off. He was actually going right through to Sydney and tried to persuade us to go with him.

'Why do you want to stay out in this neck of the woods? You come down to the big smoke with me and I'll get a friend of mine to make up a foursome and take you out one night.'

He was a handsome young man, but I explained that we were turning north at Parramatta and not going into Sydney again.

'Besides, we want to see Lithgow, Blackheath and Katoomba. We missed them on our way up because we were on a truck.'

So he reluctantly dropped us at Lithgow and we pedalled off in the ghastly cold. My nose was as numb and aching as it was on Kosciusko summit. Reaching the centre of the city, we looked for churches. The Salvation Army Citadel loomed into view but there was no one in residence. Then we tried the Baptist Church and spoke to the Minister but he was about to commence a service and couldn't talk for long. So we rode on to the Methodist Church, where the Rev. Whitbread and his wife made us welcome. They opened the church hall, lit a coke stove to warm the room, moved tables together to serve as beds and then invited us into their home for supper by a blazing fire.

They were a very interesting couple who had done several years of missionary work on an island off Suva. They even had a couple of whale's teeth hanging on their wall, like the one which was presented to my father when he went to Fiji.

Mr. Whitbread banged on the door at nine o'clock next morning.

'Are you awake girls? I've got a reporter from the *Mercury* with me. He wants your story in a hurry.'

I sat up, bleary-eyed and dopey and felt as much like an intrepid adventurer as a novice taking her final vows.

'Let him in,' I said resignedly, clutching my sleeping bag about me. With its hood up and its quilted green body tapering from broad shoulders to narrow feet, I looked like the *Alice in Wonderland* caterpillar and felt I should be toying idly with a hookah.

The reporter, a spry energetic chap, practically leapt on top of the tables in his enthusiastic desire to get a story. We swayed in our bags, arms imprisoned, and looked at him dispiritedly.

'Hullo girls! Top of the morning! Welcome to Lithgow!'

He gaily swept off his dripping raincoat and a spray of water flew through the air. As each drop hit the floor, I swear it had turned to hail.

'Now then, let's start from the beginning. Where have you come from?'

'We've come from sunny Melbourne and we're going to sunny Queensland. Right now, we seem to be stuck in the doldrums.'

'And what made you come to Lithgow?'

'I can't imagine,' croaked Shirl dully.

'Oh come now, Lithgow's a lovely city. You don't want to let a bit of cold weather worry you. This is a very rich district. Yes, plenty of money around here. Our coalfields are the largest ..... the richest ... the blackest ....,' his voice ran on as my eyelids drooped. '....... why, most of our male population is employed by the collieries.'

'It's probably warm in a coalmine.'

'Ha ha, very good. Well, you're heading north. Queensland's the place if you want heat. Ah, beautiful, beautiful Queensland!' He threw his head back and stared at the ceiling as though already he were leaping up papaw trees and gambolling on the Reef.

'I was up there in the Army and loved every minute of it. Mind you, it's not all tropical paradise you know. Where we were camped, the scorpions were as big as crayfish and the black widows ....'

'The what?'

'Black widows – spiders, you know. Deadly. Absolutely deadly! And of course, the trapdoor spider too, though you stand a bit of a chance with her. And you mustn't go walking around without something covering your legs. The snakes up there - brrrr! – well, the death adder's so small you really don't see it till it's bitten you, and the tiger snakes.....'

'Where – was – all – this?' Shirl looked as pale as a snake's belly.

'Well, we were up the York Peninsula, but you get these things all over the State. Ticks too,' he added brightly.

I mentally inked out Cape York on my map and forced my mind to dwell on visions of long curving beaches, quivering sun and palm-fringed islands.

'Another thing,' his eyes lit up, 'always shake your sleeping bags before getting into them. During the wet season you'll get all sorts of caterpillars and leeches creeping in to keep dry. You can't be too careful.'

We promised to be careful and begged him to get on with the interview as we had a busy morning ahead of us.

'That's all right. I think I've got all I want. I can check any details from the Sydney papers. I'll whip something up and send you a copy. Keep cheerful!'

I ducked as the shower sprayed again and the door opened and banged. It took six squares of chocolate to cure the jaundice of my eye.

In the afternoon we were taken over the Cobar Colliery by the manager, Mr. Genders, who assented readily to our request to go down a mine. He produced a boilersuit for me and a dustcoat for Shirl. Then we each put on a miner's helmet with lamp attached, powered by a battery strapped around one's waist. We giggled self-consciously and hurried behind our guide into the black, forbidding tunnel. There was no shaft or hurtling cage in this colliery but I think the entrance was even more impressive. I thought of the Pied Piper of Hamelin and waited for the mountain to close behind me. The roof was so low we couldn't walk erect but crept along through the peculiar-smelling earth, down a gradual slope until we reached a level track. Looking back, I could see the entrance as a faint glimmer way back and up. The ground underfoot was moist and muddy and we walked along the sleepers of a small railway. Coming soon to a long line of horse-drawn coal trucks or skips, we climbed into one and squatted on the bottom. With a sudden jerk we were off. The horse went quite fast and we clattered through the dark tunnels, rocketing round corners with neck-breaking jerks.

'This is better than Luna Park,' screamed Shirl above the racket.

When the train stopped, we hopped out and walked on a little further until we came upon a group of men. Clad only in athletic singlets and trousers, they were sitting talking, waiting for the empty skips to arrive. It was very warm. We explored lots of tunnels, saw the men shovelling loose coal into the skips and tried our hand at it. How difficult it was! I was exhausted after three shovels full. Shirl tried her luck with a pick and after some hit-and-miss blows at the coalface dislodged a small nugget. She seized it joyfully and capered around the tunnel.

'I mined it all by myself,' she crowed. 'I'm going to keep this.'

I groaned, thinking of the way our packs were already half full of souvenirs, pamphlets, pressed flowers and other sentimental acquisitions.

'We're just going to fire a charge now,' said Mr. Genders. 'Who'd like to light the fuse?'

We tossed for it, and I won – about the only time I can remember winning. He lifted me on to a high petrol-drum and I lit the fuse. The men assured us we had plenty of time but we panicked and fled around the nearest corner. The men roared with laughter and we felt very sheepish as time crawled by and nothing happened. Then there was a long, muffled explosion and we groped through the dust to see the result. A good fall of coal lay piled on the ground.

We walked back along the tunnels which were mainly propped up with thick timber supports. The strain was so great, however, that several of them were splitting and buckling under the terrific tonnage of earth above.

When we reached the skips, we had to adopt a different method of riding back, as the trucks were now full of coal. Our guide showed us how to crouch low on the buffers between the skips. Off we tore again on our rocketing journey and I sympathized with the miscreant whom W.S.Gilbert's Mikado condemned 'to ride on a buffer in Parliamentary trains.' The skips took us out of the mine and up a ramp to the tipping platform, where we had to leap off before the coal was tipped down a chute onto the sorting grilles. These were perforated metal platforms, which slid backwards and forwards with jerky movements which propelled the coal along them.

That being the last stage of the mining process, we went and had a lemonade with Mr. Genders. As we were about to leave, he asked us when did we have our last cooked meal. I hurled my mind back and decided it was four days previously at Orange.

'Would you like to come to my cottage and help me cook the dinner?' he asked timidly. 'I'll provide all the food and you can have a hot meal and sit by the fire and listen to the wireless.'

The prospect was so tempting by comparison with our cold church hall and cold tea and he was so courteous that we assented. He said he lived by himself and would like to have someone to talk to.

For the rest of the afternoon we flew down the main street doing the hotels and cafés with our books and then at half past five presented ourselves at Mr. Genders' cottage. He had just returned from a shopping expedition and showed us a case containing cauliflower, brussel sprouts, potatoes, eggs, licorice allsorts, steak, home-made butter and three honey jars of cream!

'Do you think that will do us?' he asked anxiously.

Shirl and I tied teatowels around our waists for aprons and set to work. We stewed apples, grilled steak, boiled cauliflower, brussel sprouts and potatoes and sat down to the most wonderful dinner. Then came two huge helpings of apple covered with cream. Then I had two mashed bananas and cream followed by two cups of coffee with cream. Then I was done. We staggered from the table, washed up and cleaned the kitchen and, sitting by the fire, ate licorice allsorts while Mr. Genders played his piano-accordion. He was a very pleasant man, quiet and well-mannered, who had had a lot of unhappiness in his life. He seemed genuinely pleased to have some company in the house for a change.

Supper of biscuits and cheese and coffee came up at 10 o'clock and we could hardly ride home afterwards, we were so full of good food. The night was freezing again and a gale was still blowing. No wonder Marjorie Jackson, the 'Lithgow Flash' and champion woman athlete, smashed world records for running six years later. Anyone living in Lithgow would have to be able to run; anything moving slower than six miles an hour would undoubtedly freeze.

-oOo-

Lithgow, Blackheath and Katoomba remain in my memory as one unbroken stretch of misery and cold. In Blackheath we cowered in a schoolroom while the windows rattled and the wind howled outside. At Katoomba we had shelter in the Methodist Church kindergarten where we actually slept on a mattress. There was also a piano.

In Sydney we had seen the film *The Seventh Veil* and for the first time I heard Beethoven's *Sonata Pathétique* which ran through the film as a theme. I managed to buy the music in a Katoomba shop and spent the long cold evening practising. That was the beginning of my reconversion to classical music. As a child I had learned the piano from a first-class teacher but I loathed the drudgery involved and was delighted when, at fifteen, I was allowed to stop lessons and go my own way. My heart was in modern music for my three brothers played nothing else and my greatest pleasure was playing for dances with my brother Pete on clarinet and two friends playing trumpet and drums. In 1943 we inevitably became involved in the revival of Dixieland Jazz as preached every Thursday night at the Palais Royale by Graeme and Roger Bell. By now Pete was teaching himself the slide trombone and was befriended by Adrian ('Father Ade') Monsbourgh, an outstanding musician in the Bell band, who played valve trombone, trumpet, piano, tuba and sang his own songs. When Ade formed his own band, he recommended Pete to take his place with the Bells. Pete played with them for many months in and around Melbourne but in 1945 he graduated in Engineering and went off to Borneo to work on the Shell oilfields, just missing the fantastically successful European tour the Bell band made. In Borneo he formed a swing band and organized all the dance music on the oilfields for the next eight years. In Melbourne I consoled myself in Pete's absence by playing with another small jazz group.

However, once away on the trip with Shirl, jazz didn't satisfy me. It is essentially a form of music played by a group and although it can be played by one person, it is most enjoyable for the performer when played with others. A solo pianist can sit for only so long playing blues by himself. I tired of my jazz, or rather, I couldn't give it full expression and when we camped in a church at night, Shirl would invariably say 'Play me some nice soothing classics Wen.'

The dozen or so works which I remembered from my student days became monotonous and I began to buy more music. We had access to a piano or organ nearly every night of our journey so I was able to keep in practice.

The Methodist Minister at Katoomba, Rev. Harper, also started something. Before we left the town he produced a sheet of paper.

'I've given you a list of the men of our church in every main town as far as Brisbane. I know them all. Just say I sent you. It'll be some contact in a strange town.'

When we reached Brisbane, another minister gave us the names of the men north to Cairns and so on. Though neither of us was a Methodist, we completed our travels under the wing of, in the main, the Methodist Church and were always received kindly and given every help. In these church halls there were frequently issues of a little temperance magazine called *Waterwags Own*. We found it hilarious and memorized many of the mottoes and verses. '*A devil lurks in every berry of the grape!*' and

Leave the liquor alone, boys,
Leave the liquor alone!
A man full of malt isn't worth his salt
So leave the liquor alone.

and

Purple clusters on the vine,
Pluck and eat them, they are fine,
Press the juice, if you incline,
Into glasses, yours and mine.

If we drink it when we should,
When it's fresh and sweet and good,
Health and strength and joy combine,
In the grapes but not in wine!

Of course we saw Blackheath's and Katoomba's magnificent sights. Perched as they are on the cliffs of the Blue Mountains' incredible gorges, any path will lead you to breathtaking views like that at Govett's Leap. Numerous picturesque stories account for this misleading name but Govett was a Government surveyor who discovered a remarkable waterfall in 1831. It was named after him in accordance with the English practice of calling a waterfall a 'leap'. Riding along the Cliff Drive at Katoomba with the wind behind us was very pleasant with wonderful limitless views of the Jamieson Valley opening up at each turn. Then we left the Drive and followed Prince Henry Walk. This was only a rough walking track which wound around the edge of the cliff with no protective fence. As the cliffs fall sheer to the timbered floor of the valley a thousand feet below it was rather exciting. We rode wherever possible but had to walk over the steeply graded parts and also where there were steps. I swear we lifted our bikes up two hundred steps that afternoon. At Leura we each bought a sheath knife for 5/6d. We wore them threaded on our belts.

And so to Echo Point and the famous Three Sisters, photographs of which must be in nearly every Australian home in some form or other, whether on souvenir pottery, spoons, artificially-coloured postcards or in photo-albums. However hackneyed the photographs, the reality is stupendous, a trio of huge crags rising hoarily out of the great chasm and looking with ageless eyes across the wide, wide canyons and forest canopy. I peered over the rails of the look-out to the carpet of trees far below. It looked like moss from this height and the sense of space made my head spin.

'Gosh Dunc, I don't think I could ever take a glider off the ground or any aircraft for that matter.'

I had been learning gliding in Melbourne before I left but had advanced only to the stage of lifting the glider to grass-top height.

'I'd be scared stiff if I looked down and saw all that space under me.'

'I don't suppose you would. By the time you were flying around at this height you'd have done a heck of a lot at lower altitudes and it just wouldn't bother you any more. Wouldn't it be *magnificent* to swoop right down there like a bird!'

We were both dead keen on flying (Shirl even swore that she would make a parachute jump before she died) and to me a glider seemed the nearest approximation to the flying of birds, noiseless, effortless, part of the wind.

We turned away dejectedly, climbed on our heavy clumsy bikes and rode slowly back to the church. I spent the evening working on two poems. The 'tussocks' theme I had been toying with on the West Coast train in Tasmania developed into a triolet. The other was quiet and tranquil and I called it *Song of the Night*. I copied them out and posted them to the Australian magazines *Jindyworobak* and *Meanjin Papers*.

We left Katoomba the next day and with the wind behind us rode downhill through Wentworth Falls, Lawson and Blaxland. These three townships are named after the explorers who found a way across the barrier Blue Mountains in 1873 and thus opened up the vast land to the west of Sydney. It seemed strange to me as I pedalled easily down the winding highway that the early settlers had ever been imprisoned by the great mountain range which today is a tourist paradise. A little further on we came to luxurious Lapstone Hotel. This was the venue of a big UNRRA Conference in 1945 and I wanted to see it. Shirl thought we should sell them a *Hotel and Café News*, so we went in and wandered through the elegant lounges, dining room and ballroom, and saw the swimming pool set in beautiful gardens. While we waited for the Manager, the barman offered us lemon squashes and talked about the trip. Then in swept the Manager, his wife and four guests, all twittering with excitement and bore down on us with hands of welcome outstretched. More drinks all round and a detailed account from us of our adventures. After that, we didn't think we should bring up the *News* question. They invited us to stay to tea and even for the night but we had to reach Parramatta that evening so declined.

Darkness was falling as we sailed down the mountain to Penrith, gliding swiftly through the night. A truck took us the remaining twenty miles to Parramatta. The driver astounded us by asking weren't we the girls he'd seen on the newsreel.

'When?' we shrieked.

'A couple of days ago.'

We looked at each other aghast. It couldn't have been screened so soon. When we reached Parramatta, we rushed into a cinema to make enquiries and were told that the newsreel had been showing all the week and was due to change that very evening. We persuaded the manager to give an extra screening for us and, sitting tensely in the theatre, we waited. There were three other short features before ours but finally there we were. There was my voice, strange and unrecognizable, describing our activities. There was the rear view of us vanishing down the great hill and a slow fade-out as the male announcer (Jack Davey) said cheerily: 'Yes, these Sheilas are venturesome freewheelers!'

We sat on the edge of our seats, silent and amazed. Behind us, a lady said to her companion regretfully: 'And they look such nice girls too.'

There were still a few things to be done in Sydney. We tried to change our bicycles, but the Advertising Managers of other brands of cycle all shook their heads and said we could be of no use to them as they sold their product only in New South Wales. Malvern Star was the one brand which flourished in all States. It looked as though we were stuck with them.

Then we had an eleventh hour bonus. We signed a contract with Bonox (a beef extract) and within a week our photo appeared in the papers with the following diverting conversation underneath.

Shirley: We're travelling light, but there's always room for a bottle of Bonox in *my* pack.

Wendy: Mine too! There's nothing like a cup of hot Bonox to keep us warm when we're camping out this weather. It gives us a lift when we're tired too.

Chapter 8

NORTHERN RIVERS

At last the way was clear to Queensland. With Sydney behind us, we became more and more impatient to reach the sun and dispense with the drab woollen garments we'd been living in for three months. Riding and hitch-hiking we sped north along the coast, passing through the green slopes of orchards around Gosford and Wyong where rows of dark green trees covered with oranges basked in the sun. Nearing Newcastle, Lake Macquarie placidly reflected the mountains behind it with all the delicacy of a Chinese watercolour.

Our only contact in Newcastle was the name given us by Bella at Kosciusko, a Mrs. Pilchard. Bella's words rang in my ears. 'Just say I sent yer. She'll give yer a bed for the night.' We found the house, one of a row of terraces, dark and depressed-looking, the front door of which opened straight onto the street. Mrs. Pilchard was a small plump woman of about forty. She was very surprised to see us. Yes, she'd heard of us from Bella but thought we must have passed on by now. We followed her into the house.

'Ah yes, poor Bella,' she replied, when we relayed a message. 'We feel so sorry for her. And she's proud to call us her friends. You see love, she's not like us. Isn't it funny the way she goes around saying we're her friends?'

This was disconcerting. If they weren't really good friends we could hardly impose. However, Mrs. Pilchard called her nineteen-year-old daughter Mary to talk to us and busied herself in the kitchen. Very soon we were sitting down to fried eggs on toast with a pot of coffee sizzling on the stove.

Mrs. Pilchard brushed away our thanks. 'That's all right dears. I'm a good Holy Catholic and always try to help people. But you must take me as you find me and not mind the house. That's right Mary dear, just put the tray over there. Isn't Mary a sweet girl? Everyone loves her, she's a dear little thing.'

Tea over, we made a move to bed. Shirl put in a good word with Mrs. Pilchard about letting us sleep in next morning; how we needed our sleep, riding was *so* exhausting. Our hostess agreed, to our relief.

'There's nothing like a good lie-in,' she said.

She took us to a front room. Mary was to sleep on a couch there. I could see no other bed and asked Mrs. Pilchard where we should sleep. She crept across the room like a Tragedy Queen, drew the curtains, and in a hoarse whisper adjuring us not to tell a soul about it, she let down a three-quarter bed from the wall in a curtained recess. We solemnly swore on all we held sacred not to divulge the presence of the spare bed and crawled into our sleeping bags.

I was woken at half-past six by the wretched milkman. Because the house was built flush with the street, delivery was simple. He pushed up the window loudly, clanking his milk cans with joyous abandon and plonked a billy-can and several bottles on the table inside our room. Crash! Down with the window again and cans rattling on to the next house.

I stared disbelievingly at Shirl who had raised herself blearily on one elbow. She shrugged and buried herself inside her bag. Then, Mr. Pilchard started moving about the house and, apparently wanting milk for his breakfast and not wishing to come into our room, he went out into the street, pushed up our window with a jarring crash which vibrated across the room, groped across the table and removed the milk can and bottles, one by one. The window slammed down again, the street door banged and Mr. Pilchard started to make his breakfast. From then on it was impossible to sleep. Mrs. Pilchard rose and prowled around getting her husband off to work. Mary, in our room, arose and went off to early church. Her young brother, aged two, came in and wandered around the room, pawing my face and making baby talk. With determination I maintained a mask of slumber and he toddled away. Then just as sleep was dragging my eyelids shut again, Mrs. Pilchard bustled in and told us it was nine o'clock and what a *lovely* lie-in we'd had, and had we slept well, and my, but we must be refreshed!

Only nine o'clock! I moaned softly into my pillow and Shirl replied, without conviction, that we'd slept like logs. Ho hum! Fancy letting us sleep so late!

After breakfast, we packed up and thanking Mrs. Pilchard for her hospitality, set out to look for more permanent quarters. We were taken in by a motherly woman, Mrs. Maggs, and her husband. They had lost their only son in the war and to fill the gap had taken into their home as boarders five young employees of Broken Hill Proprietary. The Maggses looked on these young men as their sons and the warmth of their hospitality to us was only tempered by their anxiety that the boys' studies at the Technical School might suffer from our presence in the house. Certainly we had a wonderful time. We played tennis and went to dances with them and roared around Newcastle on the pillions of their motorbikes.

I had my 20th birthday while in Newcastle. Shirl gave me the music for Debussy's *Clair de Lune* and I had telegrams and parcels from home. Mum had sent me a new style of summer frock called a Jigtimer. There were buttons down each side seam so it could be opened out flat for ironing, I recklessly splashed some of my meagre funds on a trunk call to my family in Melbourne. My mother made her usual attempt to persuade me to come home without tackling the road to Darwin but I firmly assured her that our plans for the north-western section of the trip were already made and that our route home was through Alice Springs.

'How much longer do you think it will take?' Her voice came sadly over the eight hundred miles of distance.

'Oh I don't know … another six months or maybe a year.'

It was a constant surprise and delight to Shirl and me to be able to plan ahead with no deadline to limit our wandering. We were completely free and time meant nothing to us. Years later I read William Hazlitt's words: *'The soul of a journey is liberty, perfect liberty, to think, feel, do, just as one pleases."*

How we loved Newcastle! Not the city itself, nor the great steel works where we trudged around for one whole day looking at spectacular leaping flames and glowing ingots of steel, listening to guides with the light of intelligent interest in our eyes and the slump of utter weariness in our bodies, but the warmth and friendliness of the people.

One day, while we were standing in the street, some girls in white smocks ran over from a beauty salon opposite and wanted to know were we the girls they had seen on the newsreel. They dragged us back to the salon to meet the rest of the girls and the manageress and the latter asked briskly: 'Well, what would you like girls? Shampoo? Cut? Set?' Shirley had red-gold hair, I was a brunette. We wore our hair sweeping our shoulders in the fashionable page-boy style. I plumped for a haircut and shampoo and Shirl emerged from her cubicle, totally unrecognizable, with her usually smooth and flowing hair set in a high pile of waves above her forehead and clusters of curls framing her face.

On another day we received a fearful badgering at breakfast from the Maggs brood when one of them read aloud from the morning paper that 'the famous cyclists will be pleased to autograph any purchases made in the Stationery Department of Scotts Emporium this morning.' We reported for duty on the tick of nine o'clock and found a great placard on display, featuring a map of Australia and our names in bold lettering. There was another in the window.

We sat down at a table impressively weighted with ink, pen and blotting paper, all set for a busy morning. We assumed our most intrepid expressions and waited. At half past nine we signed a writing pad for one of the salesgirls. By ten we'd signed another for a shopwalker. Then I read all of the *Ancient Mariner*, browsed through Ion Idriess's *Crocodile Land*, two English women's magazines and a book on palmistry. By then it was twelve o'clock and we'd signed about sixteen purchases, all for worshipping children or fond parents. However, it was a nice idea. With a pound each in our pockets we trotted home contentedly.

A fruit juice factory presented us with bottles of fruit cordial and a bottle each of heavenly chocolate sauce. An icecream factory gave us a large parcel of icecream and told us to be sure and get more on the day we were leaving Newcastle. We had free steaks at Keith's Kitchen, afternoon teas at the Bowery and a magnificent dinner at the palatial Great Northern Hotel. Then the local Aero Club offered us a flight over the city. Shirl and I stalked around the house like Cassandras contemplating the insecurity of life and wondering if we'd survive the flight. Everyone was vastly amused and Mrs. Maggs damped our morbidity with her forthrightness.

'Go on – off with you, and don't be late home for lunch!'

Shirl stared into space and intoned dully: 'Tragic air crash! Plucky girl cyclists killed. Trip suspended. Nation mourns loss!'

The boys chased us out.

I had caught my shirt on something sharp and there was a small three-cornered tear on the sleeve. I asked Mrs. Maggs for her iron and produced my packet of Iron-On, a thin rubbery tissue which I used to stick a patch underneath the tear, the heat of the iron melting the tissue. Mrs. Maggs was intrigued and regaled everyone with the story of how I glued my clothes together.

By now Shirl was madly, obviously, keen about one of the Maggs brood and hinted darkly at further postponing our departure but Mrs. Maggs said with some asperity that the boys had set aside the weekend to swot for their exams and mustn't waste any more time. I explained hastily that we really had no intention of staying any longer and the next day we strapped up our bikes. Wearing blouses and shorts which a sun with a hint of warmth in it made possible, we waved goodbye to the Maggs brood and set off. Before we had ridden one block, the boys swept by us on their motorbikes, one by one, on their way to work. Shirl was nearly in tears. I thought desperately for something to cheer her.

'I know Dunc ….. let's go and collect that icecream!'

-oOo-

The next day was very hot and blustery and about half a mile out of Raymond Terrace we boarded a truck. Some weeks later we felt guilty on reading in the local paper '…. *They left yesterday, pedalling determinedly with their heads down and battling a nasty wind, confident of themselves and secure in the knowledge that, although all things come to those who wait, they come a lot quicker to those who go out after them.*'

Our road now led through Gloucester's green paddocks and heavily-forested mountains (where one can still see the cave of Thunderbolt, the notorious New South Wales bushranger) and, lying on top of a load of beer barrels on the back of a truck, we drove through the warm balmy air of a lovely evening. The wind had dropped and the sky was already covered with stars. There was very mountainous country on all sides now with little farms nestling on the lower slopes. At last we crossed the broad silver ribbon of the beautiful Manning River and pulled in at Taree. We climbed down from the truck and, leaning our bikes against the fence of a house, combed the tangles out of our hair. The lady of the house was sitting on the verandah and called out to see if we'd like a bath. Hospitality indeed! An offer of a mattress on the front verandah followed and as I was unpacking, there was a dreadful cry of anguish from Shirl. Her bottle of glorious, thick, syrupy chocolate sauce had broken inside her pack and everything was a sticky mess – clothes, bike pump, books. It took her two hours to wash everything.

Port Macquarie is another historic town, thick with convict ghosts.

In the old Church of St. Thomas, we saw the tell-tale arrows on the bricks and shuddered at the dividing doors which closed on each prisoner as he took his seat in the pew, separating him from the man who sat next to him. The crumbling cemetery of the early Colony is still to be seen with tombstones dating back to 1826 and huge trees growing out of some of the graves.

Northern New South Wales was then in the grip of a serious drought. No rain had fallen for four months. As there was no water supply at Port Macquarie, each house having the usual rainwater tank to supply its needs, the residents were desperate. Every tank was empty except that at the Seventh Day Adventist church where we were staying. There was a dreadful stagnant well on the roadside which some of the women used for washing clothes but apart from this, there was no water at all. As it always seemed to rain wherever we went, I assured some of the townsfolk that their worries were probably at an end.

In Kempsey next day we saw our first aborigines. Both men and women were completely civilized, the women rouged and lipsticked, with elaborately rolled hair, smart frocks, fur coats and spike heels. The children were enchanting with fine, intelligent faces.

That night we thought it was time to have some recreation and donning the glamour we presented ourselves at the local dance. We could never have afforded weekly entertainment in the form of films or dances so we had a sure-fire formula for gaining admission for nothing. At the ticket box we'd ask for the Master of Ceremonies, introducing ourselves and saying that we had been told to make ourselves known to him. The convenience of passive speech! Not one M.C. ever pinned us down as to who exactly had sent us along. This stratagem usually took us past the door. We didn't always find the M.C., or if we did, he might just say hullo and tell us to make ourselves at home. But usually he would rush up to the stage, smash the drummer's cymbal a stinging blow and hold up his hand for silence. While we stood in front of the assembled dancers feeling foolish, he would make a speech and get the company to applaud and sing *Jolly good fellows*. We suffered this embarrassment as the price of our evening's enjoyment.

After we had run the gauntlet of curious stares at Kempsey, we were rushed for dances. This was a dubious honour as nice chaps usually hung back and either old men or wolves (called 'loups' – French for wolves - and pronounced 'loops' by us) or spotted youths dared by their friends, advanced on us. In Australia one must never refuse an invitation to dance. This time, an old drunk shadowed me most of the time. He said he was from Tex Morton's touring show.

'Yesh – and I'll tell you something. I can do everything that Tex doesh. The lasso-ing and the Circle of Death and all that. I c'd do it blin' fol'.'

I expressed dutiful surprise.

Then he switched to a new line and tried to persuade me to join the troupe as a dancer and singer. 'You'd do good-oh, you would! You can certainly swing the Cossack.' He flung me across the room, twirling me round and round and, catching me on the rebound from a pained-looking couple, hugged me to him like a python.

'Eh?'

'Swing the Cossack .... fling the flipper ..... plant yer plates .... use your feet! Cripes, don't yer understand English?'

'Oh,' I said faintly, reeling under the blast of alcohol-laden breath.

The music stopped and I thankfully made for my seat. He followed, still talking.

'And don't forget what I told yer. You and me'd get on fine. Yesh, you can certainly swing the Cossack ....'

I think the most wonderful view on the whole of the New South Wales coast is to be seen from Smoky Cape lighthouse, near South-west Rocks. We rode along a rough track, leading through very pretty bush culminating, nearer the beach, in almost tropical vegetation. We climbed a high hill and had a sublime view of a sweeping beach, fourteen miles long with rows of rolling breakers crashing on the golden sand. About us were hundreds of tall palms lifting their fronds above the gums. Lantana flowered amongst the sombre undergrowth and luxuriant creepers swarmed over the trees. I was amazed at the profusion of lantana, which in Melbourne is a cultivated shrub much used for hedges. I now know that lantana is an ineradicable weed in the tropics.

On our way to Macksville we stopped at a farm and tried to sell *Dairy Farming* to the owner. We launched into our sales talk.

'See Mr. Meehan, a farmer's guide to bigger and brighter cows ...'

'Just step this way my girl,' he said with twinkling eyes and led us into a room, the walls of which were festooned with huge bunches of prize ribbons won by his cows at every Show in the State every year.

'I think I know my business by now! But never mind, come and have a look at the farm.'

He showed us the chaffcutter in operation and we climbed a vertical rung-ladder to the top of the silo where a drowsy owl started up in panic and flapped past us. He dragged out a large box of Queensland nuts and told us to eat our fill. The Queensland or Bush nut *(Macadamia)* is the most wonderful thing, about the size of a large marble and extremely hard. We sat on the ground smashing them between two stones and ate dozens. Then we filled our string-bags with oranges from his trees. His wife appeared then and asked us in for a snack of bread and jam and cake. We were very hungry, having had no lunch. Mr. Meehan took us to the dairy and filled our jar with cream. We inspected his prize calves, cows, bulls and boar and watched the cows being milked. I tried my hand at the process but failed dismally. Back at the house we filled bags with nuts and laden with these, our oranges and our cream, staggered away at four o'clock.

Once out of sight of the house we stopped by the side of the road and cracked some more nuts. What astounding luck we had! Our books secured us introductions to farmers and hotel proprietors even though we did not always sell them copies and all the time our publishing firm back in Sydney was patiently waiting for the orders and money to roll in.

At Macksville we paid a visit to a tattooer who had pitched his caravan on a spare block. He was a small grey-haired lively man of seventy-five and a great talker. He told us he had been touring Australia in his caravan for the last twenty-six years. His wife, a tall, angular, toothless woman was a Californian. They offered us a cup of tea and we sat down in the caravan and listened to dozens of stories about his life and profession. Yes, he had all sorts coming to him to be tattooed – women as well as men (with a sharp glance at us); lots of young chaps did it for a dare or when they were drunk but the majority did it for sentimental reasons. He pulled out his chart of designs to show us. There was an up-ended ship, wreathed in roses, Union Jack floating overhead and an extravagant scroll bearing the legend 'A Hero's Grave'; there was every variation involving anchors and wreaths, with 'Mother' inscribed; there were lilies, Red Indians, naked women, hearts pierced by arrows and dozens of other pictures.

'What about it girls? Run you up a nice map of Australia with a bike inside it?'

We declined hastily and he and his wife stood at the door of their caravan laughing loudly as we departed.

From Macksville to Grafton the country was enchantingly lovely and the road heartbreaking. Nambucca Heads for lunch ... a quietly beautiful place, with a combination of mountains, pounding ocean and quiet inlet and river, all a deep blue. The road was hilly, gravelly and treacherous, made of fine stone, piled up in ruts three to four inches deep. We'd hurtle down a hill and then skid into this deep gravel, wobble and fall off. We made very poor progress and finally managed to get a lift into Coffs Harbour.

The road to Grafton led through bush and at one turn, out from the thick gum forest came two aboriginal girls. One was about twelve years old and the other seven, both clad in faded cotton frocks. It looked so natural for them to be walking out from amongst the dappled trees. They were beautiful girls. I said hullo and waved. They replied in low, melodious voices and continued waving until we were out of sight.

Half way up the next hill we saw our first banana plantation. I cannot describe the intoxication of spirit which this gave me. For five months we had been striving to reach the tropics, making but slow progress through New South Wales's interminable winter and dreaming of the sun. Now at last, here were signs of approaching Queensland. It was a beautiful sight. The sloping hillside was covered with the green, frayed, silken fronds of the banana trees. But how disappointing they were as fruit trees! I'd been visualizing huge hands of fat golden bananas hanging under the leaves but not one did I see. Bananas are usually picked green and ripened artificially.

As we rode into Grafton, across the long bridge spanning the Clarence River, we were caught up in a swirl of excitement and festivity. The Jacaranda Festival was in full swing. Grafton's streets are planted with jacaranda, that heavenly Brazilian tree which in springtime covers its bare branches with masses of pale bluish-purple bells. Down Jacaranda Avenue the huge trees met overhead making a blue awning and the blossoms which fell carpeted the road underneath. Each year, when the jacarandas are at their best, Grafton celebrates for one week. There is a Race Meeting, a decorated floats competition, a Regatta, children's displays and folk dancing in the Market Square day and night. The festival has been held every year since 1935. We could hardly wait to join the fun in the morning. We found a home at the Methodist Hall and made up comfortable beds on the stage with some long padded kneeling cushions.

The next day was a public holiday. We went to call on a friend of my father and his wife let us loose in her garden to deck ourselves with flowers. I was wearing a green floral skirt and white blouse, so I picked some vivid crimson and orange gerberas. I made a lei for my neck and pinned a few in my hair. Shirl tucked cornflowers over each ear to match her blue seersucker dirndl. At ten o'clock we rode to the Market Square. A large crowd of merrymakers was already assembled on the lawn around the central, flower-bedecked maypole. Heavily-laden jacarandas fringed the green on three sides and shed their blue bells on the ground in a thick carpet. All the girls were dressed in bright floral skirts or frocks, with hibiscus in their hair and leis of brilliant flowers around their necks. The men wore short-sleeved open-necked shirts and slacks, with coloured streamers twined around them. The Dance of the Seven Steps was announced and we dived into the nearest circle. This is an amusing Scandinavian dance in which, chorus by chorus, one does an extra action until at the end one is in a crouching knees-elbows position, head down, bottom up. We did it with great abandon. Then they announced the Jacaranda Dance. This was danced in concentric circles around the Maypole. It is the only authentic Australian folk dance and is based on the steps of the brolga, a graceful long-legged grey bird which, like the lyre-bird, is an accomplished dancer. The Jacaranda Dance was easy to learn but very tiring, especially as some Department of Information cameramen were busy filming the festivities in colour and we did the dance ten times. The song to which we danced was pleasant, the first line being: *As I dance beneath your spreading boughs of lovely misty hue, I see each bell a fairy sweet in jacaranda blue.* However, the woman organizer, instead of singing these words, sang instructions for the dance over the amplifier. So now, whenever I think of the song, instead of hearing the poetic words, I find myself singing:

> *Now four to the centre and four back again,*
> *Now eight skips to the left, six seven eight;*
> *Then set to the right and set to the left.*
> *And turn your partner round;*
> *Then set to the right and set to the left –*
> *It's Jacaranda time*!

Another delightful dance, possibly of Australian origin, is the Papaw

Patch. We each grabbed a partner and did it merrily. Then came the Helston Floral Dance. My partner and I and Shirl and her youth formed a four and tore off behind the column of dancers. They led us out of the Square, around the Clock Tower in the centre of the main street and back again, everyone one-two-three-hopping with gusto.

> *Each one making the most of his chance.*
> *All together in the Floral Dance.*

The only difference between the Grafton version and the Cornish being that we did not kiss as we danced along.

We were exhausted by this time so we left the Square and strolled down the main street towards Jacaranda Avenue. Parked on one side was a vivid yellow and red truck with lions' heads on each door and the magical legend 'Silvers Circus' painted on the side. We ran across to ask the driver if the Circus were in town but he said he was merely the Advance Unit and Publicity Manager. A young man, he was busy bill-posting in preparation for the opening night. He invited us to come to his caravan for supper after the dancing at the Showgrounds that evening and, over toast and lumpy coffee, he talked about the circus. He had been in the business all his life and was a tumbler and aerial acrobat.

'Listen,' he said. 'Why don't you join the show? I could teach you tricks in a few weeks and you'd be paid while you're learning ... probably get from £6 to £12 a week when you're finished.'

I looked at Shirl. What fun!

'I'd like to be a trapeze artiste,' she said excitedly.

'Yolita – the equestrienne exquisite,' I said, my eyes on one of the posters.

Our host leapt to his feet.

'Here,' he said with sudden energy, 'let's see what you can do. Are you supple? Can you touch your toes?'

'Of course!' I said loftily, 'I can do the bend-back.'

In the confined space of the caravan we did bend-backs and hand-stands and he coached us in acrobatics and graceful movements.

'Now this is the way we bow in the Circus. No leg movement, just hands. You see? Make your hands expressive and acknowledge the applause. Now try it.'

We tried, giggling self-consciously. Shirl had the awkward grace of a young colt. Her arms were stiff and her elbows angular.

'No, that's too stilted. Be graceful! That's better! Bend like a tree!'

We tried to be trees but the effect was so ludicrous that I gave up.

'It's no use Dunc, we'll never be any good at it.'

'It's only a matter of practice,' said our host handsomely. 'What about it?'

I wondered what my mother would say if I told her I had taken to the road with the Circus and though I fancied the idea of riding around the ring on a coal-black horse, pirouetting daintily on one toe on its broad glossy back, it was altogether too nebulous. Another vision kept intruding … a 'look, no hands!' act in which I took one step too many and walked off the horse's back into thin air while using my hands like trees to acknowledge the tumultuous applause.

By the look on Shirl's face, she was visualizing herself missing the trapeze and plummeting to the sawdust because there was no safety-net.

'Thanks very much but perhaps we'd better not,' she said regretfully.

I forestalled another 'Nation mourns loss' pronouncement and said goodnight.

Each day in Grafton passed in a whirl of activity. There was the Regatta when Shirl and I entered the ladies' motorboat race. We managed to pass one boat and crawl home second last. There was dancing every night, either at the Showground or in Jacaranda Avenue. This famous avenue was a little disappointing, probably because the trees are so old the blossom grows high up over one's head. At eye-level there are only brown trunks. One morning we rode over the river to South Grafton. Its avenue, in my opinion, was far superior. It was longer and the trees being younger, the blooms were closer to the ground.

At the end of the Avenue we came to the airfield where a plane was standing on the tarmac. Remembering Newcastle, we ran to ask the pilot if he would take us up for a joyride. He named a price and after a hurried look in our communal purse, we agreed. I went first and pulled on helmet and goggles. I asked the pilot if there were dual controls in the plane as I'd like to feel the movements of stick and rudder.

'Well, we don't do it usually but as a special favour ...'

I climbed in the rear cockpit and took hold of the stick, with my feet on the pedals. He took off at a good speed with very little run, and through the speaking tube told me what he was doing and why. I was conversant with the theory of it after my glider training but was completely taken aback when he said: 'Now I want you to try and keep her on a straight course. She's all yours now!' and lifted his hands in the air to show I was in sole control.

It was the most thrilling experience I have ever had. Not that it was dangerous or difficult. That was the strange thing. It was all so terribly easy. There was not a breath of wind to complicate matters and it was just like driving a car. I banked and levelled, glided and climbed while he gave me directions: 'Turn her to the left now – left rudder and left stick – now level up – keep the nose on the horizon,' and round she'd go, plunging a little until I could level her. I felt I could have flown solo anywhere. I remembered the doubts I'd had in the past as to whether I'd be scared of the height. This was so reassuring; I hadn't a qualm. At last he cut off the engine and I took her down in a long spiralling glide. He put her down and it was all over. I climbed out, flushed with success. Shirl, waiting impatiently for her turn, rushed over to where I was chatting with the pilot and behind his back made frantic signs at me. I looked down at myself and saw with horror that the slipstream from the propeller had wrenched open my blouse (the same one which had similarly embarrassed me in Tasmania) leaving me standing in a most unglamorous cotton singlet. The perfidious garment did not play the same trick again. I sat up that night sewing up its buttonholes.

It was at Grafton that we discovered how Malvern Star had taken advantage of our inexperience in drawing up the Sydney contract. The day after our arrival, the newspaper sported the same photograph and testimonial which we had agreed to let them use in Sydney. We confronted the Grafton manager and asked for an explanation.

'Why, those were my instructions,' he said. 'I thought you were under contract to the firm.'

'We signed a contract for Sydney but not for all the towns on our route!'

'What did the contract say?'

'It just said that we gave the firm permission to use this photo in any advertising. That is, any form of advertising they might think suitable.'

'Oh no ... you've got it wrong,' he said triumphantly. 'The key word is 'any'. They can use it anywhere, any time and anyhow.'

Realization dawned and we foresaw an endless chain of advertisements in hundreds of towns around Australia. All for the paltry four guineas we'd been given. The light of battle gleamed in Shirl's eyes.

'Well, that's too bad because we're negotiating with another firm,' she said grandly and we made our exit.

After that the fight was on. We were determined not to give the company a whit of publicity until they met our demands for a full-time contract. We wrote a rather wild and incoherent letter along these lines to the Head Office and sat back to await results.

Grafton is the gate to the Northern Rivers district of New South Wales and if there is a lovelier stretch of country in the world I should like to see it. The lordly Clarence River sweeps down to the sea but before losing itself at Yamba on the coast, it adorns itself with a jewelled chain of islands. This district is a little patch of Queensland dropped by mistake into New South Wales. The sugar country, which does not start in earnest until Bundaberg, 300 miles further north, puts out a tentative feeler along the Clarence and to keep the cane company there is a liberal sprinkling of tropical vegetation. The weather is made to match and with the sun soaking down from a deep blue sky, we rode into Maclean agog with the surprise of it. We crossed over a bridge to Woodford Island (the largest island in the Clarence and reputedly the largest inland island in the world) where we had an invitation to stay at the farm of Mr. Ken McDonald. His daughter-in-law, Marj, was my second cousin and before her marriage was Marj Hopman, sister of Harry Hopman, the pillar of Australian Davis Cup tennis. She heard us broadcasting over Grafton radio and quickly sent us a note to stop by at Woodford. Old Mr. McDonald was a kindly man, genial and hospitable, and after Marj had settled us in the spare room of the lovely home built on the banks of the river, he took us on an inspection of the garden.

We walked in the shade of great flame trees and lofty mango trees, while on the ground marched orderly rows of pineapples, seemingly growing upside-down. Then we saw *monstera deliciosa,* the Mexican fruit-salad plant, reckoned by some to be the most heavenly fruit ever created. This long, cucumber-shaped fruit with a skin like a crocodile's is not designed to whet the appetite, but hang it up for a week or so, until the small hexagonal sections of skin loosen and drop off, then bite into the soft white pulp inside. The only thing I know to better it is the *durian belanda* or soursop of Malaya. At the back of the house there were growing custard apples, a dozen ragged banana trees actually bearing ripe bananas and, of course, the inevitable cane....... field upon field of the palest, freshest, yellow green sugar-cane, springing from red soil and reaching up above our heads to the blue sky.

Sugar country has an atmosphere of its own. The golden sun drenches everything with heat and colour and makes the still air quiver and leap. The cane fires crackling under their smoky pall strip the standing cane of its dead foliage and leave the blackened stems glowing fitfully at night during the burning-off season. The cane-barges, heavily laden with towering piles of megass (the fibrous residue after sugar has been expressed from the cane), float slowly down the wide, placid river and the air is heavy with the sweet, sickly smell of molasses from the crushing mills. One feels at the same time stimulated and enervated.

We were having lunch when someone came to the door and excitedly told us that there was a cow in the river. We went to look. The poor beast was lying helpless on her back, only prevented from slipping into the river by the thick bramble bush beneath her. The bank was steep and she must have rolled down. Marj's husband Alex tied a rope below her horns and pulled her round into a sitting position but she made no move to get up, probably because of exhaustion. So they let her rest a while then started pulling on the rope. We couldn't budge her and discovered that her hindquarters were bogged in the sticky mud at the edge of the river. As she was no longer resting on the bramble, she was gradually slipping into the river and getting more securely bogged. Then a man came along in a car and, tying the rope to his car, tried to pull her out but she stayed in the mud bellowing in terror. Old Mr. MacDonald came in his car. A second rope was tied to the cow and his car and both cars pulled. The cow didn't move but the first man broke his axle. So Alex went for his tractor. This time the cow's neck stretched out to twice its usual length, the sinews taut, and she suddenly emerged from the mud and was dragged up the rough slope. I couldn't bear to look. I felt sure her neck would break but she reached the side of the road safely and collapsed making little noises of distress. She was absolutely exhausted and couldn't even hold up her head. Great tears dropped down her silky cheeks and Shirl and I felt wretched. We brought her water and some cane to eat but she didn't touch them. We sat petting her while Alex and old Mr. MacDonald talked gravely together. Apparently the cow was due to calve in a few weeks and they were afraid she might have some internal injury.

'Better try and get her on her feet Alex, and we'll see if her legs are all right.'

They put a rope around her body horizontally and we all pulled her up until she could stand. Though rather unsteady at first, she stood and after much urging took a step forward. It was very thrilling, like teaching a child to walk. Gradually she came nearer to the gate of the paddock and entering, stood by herself for the rest of the day, grazing. I named her Mosette, seeing as we had pulled her out of the rushes.

We felt quite drained by the stress of the rescue and Marj put the kettle on for tea. I told her Shirl and I didn't like tea.

'Coffee then?'

She produced a jar of brown powder and put a spoonful in each cup.

'What's that?' I asked.

'Instant coffee. Nescafé it's called.'

We couldn't wait to taste it when hot water was added. It tasted just like coffee but saved all the tedious brewing process. What a wonderful invention! The only alternative to brewed coffee previously was appalling coffee essence. We resolved to buy a jar of Nescafé.

In the afternoon Shirl and I made a great decision. We had arranged to go to a dance at Ulmarra in the evening and, unpacking our haversacks, we looked critically at our cotton frocks. Fashion was on the move again and our skirts were just that little bit too short. We suddenly felt ashamed of our knees. The hems had already been let down to their limit. Shirl, the home dressmaker, thought of a solution.

'Ribbon,' she said. 'Stiff ribbon, like petersham.'

We rushed out and bought some at the general store and spent an hour stitching it on by hand. The result was magnificent. We pressed the frocks and then asked Marj for a bath. She initiated us into the mysteries of the bucket bath. In spite of the proximity of the great river, the household had very little water for domestic purposes.

'It's quite easy,' said Marj cheerfully, setting a bucket full of water in the bath. 'You kneel on this pad, wash yourself out of the bucket and when you've finished pick up the bucket and pour the water over you to rinse off the soap.'

It was easy and surprisingly efficient. We continued having bucket baths all the way to Brisbane.

The Ulmarra dance was an ordeal. There was absolutely no talent, all the men being callow and uncouth. Besides, seventy-five per cent of them were drunk. To make it worse we were both terribly tired, our eyes sore from sewing and we didn't know how we could keep awake until two o'clock when the Maclean bus was to leave. At last came supper. Shirl went in with a small insignificant, ingratiating chap and when no partner had come for me, I trailed in with them. There was the usual good country supper and we brightened. I started talking with the girl next to me, a bright, rouged girl from Grafton who gave her views on Ulmarra in a loud voice.

'Yeh, one of them yelled out 'look at 'er showin' off.' Hell! That ain't showin' off. I like dancin' see! I was learnt dancin' an' I can dance good, see! They're just ignorant, that's all. I paid me money to come and enjoy meself an' that's what I'm doin'. Huh! Ulmarra!'

We ate steadily in silence for a few minutes then she turned to me and let out a shriek of laughter.

'Hell! Didjer hear that? Someone at the other table said – 'look's like we'll be runnin' out of food by the looks of the people at that table.' Well, we'll show 'em. Eat up girls! Eat till you damn well bust. The idea! Fancy tellin' us what we can eat and what we blasted well can't.'

A little later she caught sight of Shirl's escort and whispered loudly in my ear: 'You keep well away from that bloke! He's not a nice chap at all. You mark my words, he's known in Ulmarra. No one will have nothin' to do with him!'

I raised my eyebrows and stole a glance at him. He didn't look very dangerous but then you never could tell. Some of these mild-looking, inoffensive men turned out to be criminal types, razor-slashers and so on. We'd never known a razor-slasher…I panted for more information.

'Hell, he's mad! Quite mad. When he's dancin' with you he's quite likely to hug you or kiss you or anythin' else. I tell you, don't have nothin' to do with him!'

I passed this information on to Shirl and we were grimly amused at the way we always seemed to collect the local freak. She managed to evade him after supper and nothing untoward happened.

Riding back to the farm in the early morning, we passed a tall mango tree at the side of the road and a cloud of black shapes, disturbed, rose from the branches and winged silently away. We hopped off our bikes to watch.

'What were they?' asked Shirl.

'Flying foxes. It only needed that.'

Every night before we went to sleep I used to read to Shirl from the books of poetry I carried with me (a habit acquired from Rosie and Gwen at the Chalet), and our favourite was Lucille Quinlan's *North Queensland Lullaby* which always increased our feverish longing for Queensland. Yet, now, line by line, we found it applied to Maclean. Only one thing was missing.

'*And see across the pale sky, dark shapes swoop – the flying foxes, leather-winged, the silent troop …*,' I quoted dreamily, watching the quiet, effortless beating of their wings. We rode home fulfilled.

Five days on the Clarence at Maclean were all too short and when we at last moved on, the district continued to charm me. Just past Maclean we boarded a punt for Harwood Island where there is a large sugar mill. From there we hopped across to Chatsworth Island which is the loveliest place imaginable. The town itself is in one street on the banks of the Clarence and is shaded by a row of huge shade trees and flaming coral trees. All around it are fields and fields of cane, yellow and green, tall and waving. And that, with a deep blue sky above, is enchanting.

Another ferry from Chatsworth brought us back to the mainland north of the Clarence and the way was clear to the Queensland border. With eager haste we spurred on, now that our main goal was in sight. Through the fertile hills and valleys of Lismore, on to the coast at Byron Bay and then along the heavenly sweep of beaches to Brunswick Heads.

I decided that Brunswick Heads would be my choice for a future holiday. The blue Brunswick River broadens at its mouth into a placid inlet and high blue ranges encircle the township, two volcanic-looking peaks frowning above the lesser hills. Both the river and the ocean offered wonderful opportunities for fishing, we were told, so we hurled ourselves on our haversacks with gladsome cries and withdrew tangled masses of knotted linc, hooks embedded in clothing, sinkers rattling around amongst spanners and oilcan. A fishing enthusiast in Grafton had given them to us.

'What! Going along the North Coast without fishing lines! You don't know what you're missing! Here, take these!'

For a fortnight now we'd been carrying the wretched things, stowing them neatly each morning, cursing each night when we found them inextricably confused with our gear. Periods of rest on the road were now devoted to untying knots instead of dozing in the sun. Now they should earn their keep.

We bought sixpenn'orth of whitebait and sixpenn'orth of worms then found a likely-looking place on the southern bank of the channel. We loaded our lines and proudly threw them in. After a while, Shirl reckoned she had a bite but no fish appeared. My line didn't even twitch and I was maddened by the supremely indifferent way it disappeared into the water, keeping its submarine life a dark secret. A passing boatman rowed us to the other side where it was sheltered and sunny and the water was deeper. He showed us how to float the bait for flathead and caught one fairly soon. It looked much easier that way as the float bobbed under when the bait was taken.

We started throwing in at different spots. I tried several throws but couldn't get my line out far enough. So I unwound a longer length of line from the piece of wood which served as a reel and swinging the weighted end round my head several times, let it fly right out into the middle of the river. It was a magnificent throw! I watched it with pardonable pride as it drifted downstream with the current and then discovered I had thrown the piece of wood away too. I stumbled frantically into the water but it was out of reach. I watched it sail calmly away on a life of its own down to the ocean while Shirl staggered about on the bank, shouting with laughter at my discomfiture.

That night we spent in a church. There was no hall and the vestry was nothing but a tiny porch so we had to lay our bags in the aisle. Long experience of hard floors had made us connoisseurs of church furnishings. Shirl always made a beeline for the opulent red plush tasselled cushion from the lectern while I claimed as my right the comfortable long cushion from the organ bench. Cupboards often yielded piles of flags and bunting and there were always hassocks or long kneeling cushions from the altar rails.

We had received an answer from Malvern Star to our hysterical letter demanding a contract. They were, it appeared, prepared to grant us a contract, paying us one guinea a week each but laying down such a list of conditions and provisos that we would have been hamstrung, slaves of the trip, instead of being free to plan, amend or change itineraries. With reckless confidence we wrote to the Brisbane office requesting three guineas per week each for the Queensland publicity, otherwise we would cancel all arrangements. At Brunswick Heads a reply awaited us. 'Regret our offer unacceptable are unable agree your proposal can only suggest you regard yourselves entirely free negotiate elsewhere.'

We were grimly amused at our failure, but at least the fencing was over. Now we knew where we stood. We wouldn't give them any more publicity. So at Murwillumbah, our last New South Wales town, we clamped down and gave no mention of Malvern Star during our radio and press interviews.

Murwillumbah is a pleasant town, nestling on the foothills of the mighty MacPherson Range which forms the NSW/Queensland Border, with magnificent Mt. Warning, Captain Cook's landmark, frowning imperiously in the background. When we rode out and headed for Tweed Heads, the hills were indistinct and shrouded in smoke from the bushfires which had been raging all the week. We nearly wilted in the fierce heat which came up in waves from the scorching bitumen beneath our tyres. We were therefore a trifle shaken to receive copies of the Lithgow article which declared in a bold black heading **Girl Cyclists pedalled through the Snow**. Not a flake of snow had we seen but I suppose that's journalistic licence. It had been cold enough for it and that only two short months ago.

Soon we came into the cane district again, field on field of golden green with the broad Tweed flowing beside them. The Northern Rivers of New South Wales surely embrace some of the loveliest country in Australia.

We rode into Tweed Heads at noon but, wasting no time there, crossed the border straightaway into the twin town of Coolangatta on the Queensland side. Our first goal had been reached but only after five months travelling. Instead of spending winter in the tropics as we'd planned, summer was advancing with sticky hands and a hot breath to welcome us. But still, warmth was far better than cold and we could remember only too vividly those bitter weeks in New South Wales.

'All I want,' said Shirl excitedly, 'is to find those 'glorious sandy beaches drenched and soaked and quivering in pagan sunshine' that the guide book talks about.'

On our way to Kirra Beach we stopped to collect mail at the post office. Shirl opened one from her mother and grinned.

'Listen to this Wen. 'From now on, you must both be especially careful. Remember, you are now in Crocodile Queensland! Every river spells danger ....'

'What, crocodiles! At Coolangatta!'

Chapter 9

BEAUTIFUL, BEAUTIFUL QUEENSLAND

Kirra Beach lay curved and golden before us, majestic rollers crashing on the sand, the sun shining, pretty girls and wonderful-looking men, bronzed and virile, strolling up and down or lying on their backs in sun worship. A feeling of carnival was in the air.

We had been in Coolangatta for nearly a week and couldn't bear the thought of moving on. We were comfortably camped in a church hall, we had been invited by the proprietress to have all our meals at her Guest House and through contacts made there, we were having some social life. A boat picnic to the Terranora Lakes ended hilariously when we had to push our boat home, our escorts straining like Volga boatmen at ropes attached to the prow because there wasn't enough water to float it and we kept running on to sandbanks. There was open air roller skating by day and night, dances, films and of course, swimming every day. There was one young man whom Shirl had been worshipping from afar and at lunch she had plucked up courage and asked him how the swimming had been that morning.

'Wonderful!' he'd replied. 'We're going down again after lunch.'

So we hastened to change our clothes and rode to the beach immediately. A little later he and his friend arrived and dumped their towels a little distance from us. We pinned up our hair and ran into the surf. (By now we had sent for our swimsuits from Melbourne.) The water was very cold at first but once in, we felt invigorated. Shirl vowed she was going to stay in until Leslie came in, even if she died of cold and exposure. (His name was really Arthur but Shirl thought he looked like the film star Leslie Howard). However, they weren't hurrying. In fact, they were embroiled in a conversation with two glamour girls from the Guest House for whom we immediately conceived a desperate hatred. We stood in the water up to our necks and glowered.

'Well, act disinterested and let's get on with our surfing.'

The sea was extremely rough with huge waves crashing in quick succession. The undertow was very strong and it was impossible to get out into the deep water. Each wave would knock me off my feet, thus losing any

ground gained between waves. The idea of surfing is to get out where the great breakers are curling and then to launch yourself in front of the wave so it carries you, straight and sure, into the beach. But, if you stay in the shallows, you are pummelled and dumped by the turmoil of thrashing water and foam, the surge of the undertow dragging at your legs.

We had been carried several hundred yards down the beach when, to our dismay, we saw the men disengage themselves from the sirens and, cantering into the water, take a header beneath the first wave.

'Quick!' gulped Shirl. 'Out!'

We struggled out with the sand sucking at our ankles and, as nonchalantly as possible, made full speed up the beach to the place where we had entered before. At last we distinguished the men a hundred yards away from us and, allowing ourselves to go with the undertow, we shortly found ourselves near them.

'Oh hullo!' called Shirl in surprise and embarked on the long-awaited conversation.

I contented myself with being thrown vigorously on to the beach, panting and spitting salt water, my bathers full of sand, time and time again and getting nowhere. At last by great strategy, I reached the place where the waves were curling. Then followed intensive and exhausting efforts to surf. Some experts near me explained patiently what to do but each time they sped into the shore on a wave, I was left splashing and bewildered in the depths. So I gave up and retired to the beach to rest, soaking in the sun.

Ten minutes later Shirl flung herself down beside me. I opened one eye and looked about for her companions.

'What's the matter? Have you drowned them?'

'He's engaged,' she said listlessly.

-oOo-

We were forced on by rain. The quivering pagan sunshine hid itself behind thick black clouds and the heavens poured down torrents for days. At first we sheltered in the hall, writing up back diary, catching up with correspondence, washing and mending clothes. Shirl had read in a women's magazine that the latest fashion foible was gaily-studded shoes. We bought a packet of gold studs and spent one afternoon hammering them around the edge of the soles of our shoes. They looked most effective. The trouble was they weren't fixed very firmly and kept falling out when we walked. Another item of fashion which we simply couldn't ignore any longer was the cap sleeve. Extended sleeves had been ousted by the tailored sleeve towards the end of the war but now both were completely outmoded. Besides, cap sleeves were so much cooler in hot weather. So out came our scissors and we cut our sleeves in half, binding the edge with bias binding. With the petersham ribbon around our hems, we were now dressed *comme il faut*. Or as we thought *il faut*.

One morning there was a hammering at our door and, clutching my sleeping bag around me, I hopped across the floor and opened it. A woman and a small girl stepped in, shaking the rain from their coats.

'I'm a music teacher,' the woman explained. 'I use the piano here two mornings a week.'

Our hearts sank. It was only eight o'clock. Further sleep was out of the question so we sat up and did some writing. I was seized with an idea and rummaged in my pack for the music of *Clair de Lune* which Shirl had given me. I simply could not understand how one could play music written in nine-four time. When the lesson had finished I diffidently asked the lady if she would explain it to me. She looked at me as though I were some interesting biological specimen and said it was really quite easy, you just had to count one and two and three four and ..... She made stabs at the manuscript with her pencil, handed it to me without another word and bustled away with her pupil.

At the first break in the weather, we packed up and set off for Southport but the spell of Coolangatta was so strong that, even after reaching Southport, we hitchhiked back to have another weekend on the border. Coolangatta had that wonderful gift of being gay with a perpetual holiday atmosphere without incurring the opprobrium of a tourist resort. These days, the Gold Coast of Queensland is the place. Surfer's Paradise, sixteen miles further north, has become the darling of holiday-makers and the joy of real estate investors. When we saw it, it was a sleepy little hamlet, bearing on its golden fingers one sparkling solitaire. The Surfers Paradise Hotel, forerunner of all the swanky establishments to come, the bistros, the espressos and continental cafés, the exclusive clubs, the towering apartment blocks and millionaires' weekend houses, gleamed with chrome and luxury fittings. We timorously proffered a copy of *Hotel and Café News* but the proprietor laughed and said he already received it.

Adjoining the Hotel was a tropical garden and zoo. We wandered through the gardens enjoying the cool leafy shade and petted the zoo babies – two beautiful week-old kids, three baby kangaroos and some bantam chicks. Nearby in the monkey cage was a very human Capusian monkey which gripped our fingers through the wire, diligently searching them for food. Shrieks of disbelieving delight from us when he started picking at Shirl's leg and, peeling off a flake of dried skin, ate it avidly. We stood there for a quarter of an hour while he closely examined all her arm and leg for tidbits then started picking off the fluff from her jumper. We progressed along the row of monkey cages and saw a dear little baby. It was like an awkward, mischievous child, playing tricks, swinging, pulling other monkeys' tails. Its mother had the most terrifically inflated and red *derrière* I had ever seen. I was horrified a moment later to see Shirl extend a tentative finger through the bars and prod it. I have never seen anything so funny as the mingled looks of indignation, anger, confusion and outraged modesty which showed on that monkey's face! Unless it was the look which appeared a second later on Shirl when she discovered that a couple several yards away had witnessed the scientific experiment.

While canvassing Southport with our books, we tried to sell the proprietress of a fish café a subscription to *Hotel and Café News*.

'Sorry girls, I'm not interested. I'm selling out this month and going back to farming. I've got two hundred pigs out on my property.'

'Pigs? Really? Well I'm sure you'd be interested in this ...' Shirl quickly swapped books and produced *Pig Breeding*. 'Every thing you need to know about pig breeding .... sties, feeding problems, mating, castration ...' (we had been reading this book on the road, albeit with some revulsion, so knew quite a lot about the subject.)

'What! For breeding!' laughed our client but she bought one.

At the smart Pacific Hotel we sold the proprietor a *News* and I sold him a pianist. For a week I played music in the dining room and Shirl and I both had dinner afterwards.

The first post-war Federal election took place while we were in Southport. Shirl, from the superior status of her twenty-one years, professed disinterest in anything but sheaves of election literature which she perused carefully. I, though very interested in the contest, could only stand on the sidelines, chafing with frustration. Came the great day and Shirl, acting as though she were carrying the whole future of responsible government on her shoulders, went to the Polling Booth.

'Registered here madam?'

'No, I'm travelling through.'

'Have you your electoral form?'

'Er – no – it hasn't come back from Brisbane.'

'I'm sorry, you can't vote without it.'

'But I'm entitled to a vote!'

'No form, no vote.'

Labour swept to victory by a large majority. I tried to console Shirl by pointing out that her vote would have made no difference either way, but she felt betrayed.

To our great surprise we discovered Silvers Circus was in town. In Grafton we had met the advance agent, the young man who had tried to get us to join the circus and had taught us to bow in the circus manner. Now we should be able to see the show. We were welcomed and given seats. I was greatly impressed by the standard of the performance and by the youth and attractiveness of the artistes. I think I had expected them to be hard-bitten show-biz performers from long-established circus families. We had supper afterwards with some of the girls who were charming and natural.

From Southport we planned a detour off the main road west to Lamington National Park. We packed up all our surplus belongings and sent them on by rail to Brisbane, leaving our packs light for hiking. Then we bought up sufficient food for a fortnight. We had become madly health and diet conscious since reading some magazines at a Nature Food Clinic. Besides, my sister Noel, shocked by my diet, had censured me.

'If you won't consider your own well-being, think of your unborn children!' she stormed in a letter. Lunch now consisted of lettuce, carrot, turnip, apple, oranges, bananas and passionfruit. They cost us a fortune.

'One thing about unhealthy foods,' I wailed, 'they're cheap.'

'But health food is so delicious!' said Shirl as she tucked into mashed bananas, passionfruit and cream.

She acquired a stray cat and bought a pennyworth of milk in a saucer which the fool cat refused to drink. An obliging dog got rid of it for her.

'See! Dogs are far more intelligent than cats. I'd rather a dog any day.'

'Yes,' she agreed. 'I think I would too. They're more company than cats. I wonder if we could take one with us.'

'It'd have to be small enough to be carried when it was tired.'

'...yet big enough to be able to run a lot.'

'It must be a savage watch-dog, ...'

'.....yet friendly to people whose homes we visit.'

'It'd have to kill snakes....'

'.....be intelligent and devoted...'

'.....be able to retrieve things we drop ...'

'.....and be omnivorous ... and able to swim...'

We burst out laughing. Where, oh where could we find such a paragon? We decided to look around in Brisbane and left it at that.

We arranged with a cream truck driver to get a lift nearly to Binna Burra, the guest house at the northern end of the National Park, and at two o'clock in the afternoon we set off. It was a slow trip, as we stopped frequently to pick up and set down cans. At one stage, while discussing the transport problem, our driver horrified us by saying:

'Buses run up here. They charge twelve shillings return. We only charge six bob.'

Shirl shot me a panicky glance. For a journey of about thirty miles, it wasn't really expensive, but we hadn't realized it was a commercial proposition. We could have had a lift on other trucks. We whispered to each other in Dog Latin, the secret language which we used in public when we didn't want others to understand us. The atmosphere was rather tense until we reached Beechmont. The driver pointed out the School of Arts to us and suggested we camp there so we unloaded our gear from the truck while he squatted on his haunches and waited. Uncomfortable silence. When we couldn't delay our departure any longer, Shirl said: 'Well, what happens? Do we have to pay you or what?'

'Yes, that'll be two bob each – if you've got it.'

We were aghast. Nothing like that had ever happened before but I suppose we had had things too easy too long.

The School of Arts is a splendid Queensland euphemism used to identify the village hall. In Victoria it is called a Shire Hall or Mechanics Institute but in Queensland it is always the School of Arts. These institutions are to be found in many country towns and were founded to provide information, education and culture for the country working man who had missed out on education through leaving school early. They were very much a part of the social life in the country and were the venue for Friday night pictures, Saturday night dances, Mothers' Clubs afternoon teas, wedding receptions, Smoke Nights and evening lectures on all sorts of topics. The Beechmont School of Arts was a small hall, showing traces of Saturday night's dance. The well-powdered floor was covered with raffle tickets, broken streamers, matches and cigarette stubs. Two kerosene lamps hung from the ceiling, there were a few benches and tables and that was all. We settled in, dressed up for bed as the mountain air struck chill and, after I had played the piano for half an hour by torchlight, we went to bed.

Next day we made our way by timber truck and under our own steam along the Binna Burra road. There were exquisite views on our left where the range dropped away sheer. White roads laced the green valleys below and the mountains all around us were a deep blue. We came at last to the end of the road known as the Dump. Seven hundred feet above us towered a craggy mountain surmounted by Binna Burra Lodge. From the Dump to the Lodge, a wire stretched across the gulch and some Forest Rangers told us it was part of the flying-fox mechanism for taking visitors' luggage and stores to the house. We left our bikes and packs and walked up to the Lodge by a fairly easy graded track. On each side there were glimpses of smoky blue valleys and mountains. On a flattened space at the top was a pleasant collection of small cabins and one large communal block. Sitting on the lawn in comfortable chairs we could see far out to Southport on the coast. A door opened and a woman bustled out of the house to see us. She was very friendly and asked how long we were going to stay and where. We weren't too sure ourselves but thought we'd probably camp in the Ranger's hut at the Dump.

'Well,' she said, 'there's an unused hut out the back, it's half full of tools and junk but there are a couple of beds in it … if you don't mind roughing it.'

We went to see. It was a dear little hut with a notice over the door reading 'Honeymoon Cottage'. Inside were two beds and mattresses. We were enchanted. By dint of pushing a lot of the junk down one end, we managed to get some more space around the beds. What could be better!

We decided to bring our bikes and gear up by the longer, more manoeuvrable track.

'Nonsense!' said our benefactress. 'We'll send the flying fox down for your luggage, then you can come up empty handed.'

We ran down the mountain to the Dump, locked our bikes away in the Ranger's hut and laboriously tied our packs and sleeping bags on to the flying fox wire. We felt very anxious lest the straps should break and precipitate our precious belongings into the ravine. We tied dozens of knots then prayed fervently as the bundle moved slowly out of reach. The suspense was awful but when the swinging packs had safely topped the cliff we set off up the path again. It was six o'clock and a beautiful pink sky was merging with the blue mountains and a new moon and Venus shone brightly through the trees.

I went to the hut to unpack and a moment later Shirl rushed in with the news that we'd been invited to tea. We changed our clothes and went to the dining block. There was a large crowd of young people seated at long tables. Informality was the keynote. We filed past a hatch in the kitchen wall and collected each course in turn. After some lovely rich soup we had a huge serving of tender lamb and vegetables. Then we went to the hatch for our sweets.

'What'll you have,' asked the girl, 'apricot sponge, steamed chocolate pudding, jelly, raisin custard and prunes or a 'yes please'.'

'What's a 'yes please'?' I asked innocently.

'The lot!' she answered with a wide grin.

'Yes please,' I said delightedly.

After tea we settled down virtuously to write, but were dragged away to play progressive table tennis and other games.

Day followed day in a succession of hikes and food. Lord, how they ate at Binna Burra! We were invited to have morning and afternoon tea as well as dinner each night for the rest of our stay. For morning tea we'd have fresh, hot scones and honey and for afternoon tea delicious cakes. Then the huge meal two hours later, ending up with a 'yes please' consisting perhaps of lemon blancmange, vanilla custard, jelly, stewed apricots, fruit salad, jam roll and steamed pudding!

After returning from hikes, tired and stiff of limb, there were deep baths of piping hot water in which to soak for half an hour. The bathrooms were on one side of a long block. On the other side, overlooking a deep ravine and fine prospect, were the lavatories. I have known no others so aesthetically satisfying as those at Binna Burra. To sit there peacefully with the door open, contemplating the vast blue distance and the deep gulch at one's feet, with eagles lazily wheeling in the still air and the forest loud with birdsong, was something which I remember even now with delight.

Then came the expedition to O'Reilly's. Situated towards the south-western end of the Park, the O'Reilly homestead, Green Mountains, was probably better known than Binna Burra. Bernard O'Reilly's books* about his pioneer family and the tremendous hardships involved in settling their land in the then unexplored Lamington Range would have made the family known to most Australian homes even if it hadn't been for the Stinson

*Green Mountains and Cullenbenbong

airliner disaster of 1937. Bernard was the man who, by reasoning and intelligence, started looking for the missing aeroplane in a completely different area from that in which eyewitness reports indicated it should be and then, when he had seen one brown and dying gum tree on the slope of a mountain several valleys away, by faith and superlative bushcraft, made his way alone through untracked jungle to the place where the remains of the plane lay. Then followed his epic journey to obtain stretcher parties for the wounded survivors, his third trip to bring the rescuers to the plane and his fourth journey back to Green Mountains.

We got up at eight o'clock to prepare for the 14 mile walk and repacked our haversacks. Apparently I wasn't ruthless enough as my pack was still terribly heavy. There was my sleeping bag and groundsheet and a stack of tinned food, torch and other indispensable things. Nothing else could be jettisoned but how my back hurt! The Binna Burra guests were perturbed because we hadn't set out earlier and warned us that darkness would overtake us if we weren't careful.. Nevertheless, it was half past ten before we left.

We had been walking for only five minutes before our packs were giving us trouble. At the first milepost we lay on our backs and rested for five minutes. We decided to have a five minute rest after each mile, even though it would mean over an hour wasted by the end of the day. The path was well-graded fortunately and very beautiful, leading through luxuriant rain forest. It was surprisingly gloomy, sunshine only penetrating in tiny patches on the leafy paths. The sky was almost completely blotted out. In the struggle for light and air, trees and clinging water vines (which when cut yield quite palatable water to the thirsty traveller) had pushed upward to the sun and formed a dense canopy overhead. Here were the ancient Antarctic beeches, thousands of years old, with their huge roots forming buttresses extending eight feet up the trunk. These great trees grow straight up for fifty to sixty feet before branching out. Usually the living tree is a sucker sprung from an old root system. It is found in only a few parts of the world, the west coast of Tasmania, the south island of New Zealand, Tierra del Fuego in South America and in southern Queensland in the Macpherson Ranges. Incredibly knotted 'Tarzan' vines from the strangler figs looped from tree to tree in great contortions until, reaching the light, a luxuriant umbrella of foliage spread out in a great fan. Huge clumps of orchids bloomed profusely and around our feet grew lichens and mosses and the pale luminous fungi which shine in the darkness with an unearthly glow.

There was an abundance of bird life; we could hear the metallic cling-cling of the bellbirds, whip birds cracking, brush turkeys scratching under the bushes, parrots screeching overhead, kurrawongs with their strangely human wolf-whistle and dozens whose songs I did not recognise. At one stage, suspecting the presence of a lyre-bird by the variety of different bird-calls emanating from one spot and by scufflings in the undergrowth, we hid in the bush and waited silently for a quarter of an hour. The lyre-bird is a wonderful mimic of all sorts of sounds ranging from the calls of other birds to the sound of wood chopping, sawing and other noises it hears. However, apart from a few small birds, we saw nothing.

At three o'clock we stopped for lunch by the Wollongara Lookout, having gone a little more than half-way and it was four o'clock before we turned off down the Tooloona Creek. We shouldn't have done this as it entailed an extra mile and we had only two more hours of daylight and five miles to go. However it had been recommended to us as an extremely beautiful walk. The track led downhill for the first three miles and we travelled very quickly trying to beat the darkness but we didn't seem to be getting anywhere. It was a pretty track though, leading through glades with hundreds of lacy, fragile ferntrees. Every so often we passed a waterfall as we were following the creek downstream. At six o'clock we picked our way on boulders across the creek and thereafter knew we were on the right track. From there it was a straight path through to O'Reilly's. We passed Elabana at sunset and started the gradual ascent of the mountain. It became quite dark but fortunately there was a half moon. My pack had bruised my back unmercifully and I strove to support the weight with my hands, thus lessening the drag on my shoulders. In our feverish race up the mountain, sweat poured from me and my hair was wet and clinging to my temples. It was in this state that we burst into O'Reilly's at seven o'clock and only just in time. No sooner were we under shelter than a terrific storm broke with lightning, tremendous crashes of thunder and torrential rain. Molly O'Reilly hurried out to welcome us and showed us to an empty room. Shirl and I rubbed our stiff limbs with methylated spirits and fell into bed.

It rained and stormed all the next day, except for a short period in the afternoon when we poked our noses out and went for a walk, so that we were unable to see much of the Green Mountains end of the plateau. The whole of Lamington Park is glorious and we had covered large areas of it while based at Binna Burra, so next day we retraced our steps to the Lodge and made much better progress, the track being mainly downhill and our packs lightened by some steady eating.

On our return to Binna Burra I found a telegram awaiting me. The week before Shirl had told me that her mother was sailing up to Brisbane to meet us. I promptly wrote off to my mother suggesting she do the same. The telegram told me that she'd been unable to get a berth but would be flying up. I was very excited at the prospect of seeing her after an absence of nearly six months and that night I wrote her a letter giving a long list of summer clothes I wished her to bring up to me. It was time to send home my much-worn winter garments.

Before reaching Brisbane however, there was one more place I wanted to see, Mount Tamborine, eighteen miles away.

Tehambreen the natives called it,
Mountain of the wild lime tree,
Mountain of the white cloud nestling,
White cloud and the wild lime tree.

Where the sky is always red-stained at the slaying of the day
And the mountains are a dream-blue with the cold that evening brings,
Bluer than the distant sea, blue with breakers curling,
Curling like the first notes of the bell-bird when it sings.

Where the kurrawong cries sadly as it flies among the shadows,
And the people have the light of laughter always in their eyes.
There the days are long and sunny and there's music in the air,
Flowing softly down the mountain to Canungra, where it dies.

Where the scent of orange blossom fills the air the whole day long,
Floating gently on the west wind as it wanders on its way.
As it wanders on the red road through the languid waving grasses,
Lush green waving grasses in the golden haze of day.

Tehambreen the first men called it,
Tehambreen, the wild lime tree,
Tamborine the magic mountain,
Mountain of the wild lime tree.

The road up the mountain from Canungra was extremely steep and we had to literally push our bikes up. The sun was hot and we didn't know how we would ever cover four miles. Then, just as we were having a rest and an apple in the shade, a huge truck lumbered up the road. It was piled with iron, wood and other building materials bought at an auction sale but we managed to get our bikes up and perch on top. The road from there was ten times as bad as the preceding stretch. It sloped at an angle of forty-five degrees and was very stony. At the south end of the mountain, one of the men showed us an empty house which we could use for camping. It was a very large bungalow, surrounded by wide verandahs on all sides, with spacious rooms inside. We were just unpacking our belongings when the man came back and offered us a double bed in his home next door. Only he and his mother were home and we were welcome. Though we liked our big house, it had no light or water so we packed up again and went next door. And there was Gran.

Granny Young, at 81, was a remarkable woman. A pioneer of the district, she had now assumed the position of matriarch in the community. People still came to see her and ask her advice. Diminutive but sprightly, she was dressed in black, her silver hair worn in a bun. She had had a stroke two years previously and her left hand was paralysed. Despite this, she kept house for her son and a young farm hand, cooking, washing and cleaning with all the energy of a woman fifty years younger. She insisted we stay for tea and, in fact, stay with them for as long as we liked.

We refused her offer of linen on the bed and spread our sleeping bags on the mattress. Gran didn't think they looked warm enough so she insisted on bringing in some blankets in case we needed them in the night. No sooner had we gone to bed than we were set upon by hordes of fleas. The elusive flea at Kosciusko had been torture but here we were oppressed by the feeling that no matter how many of them we killed, there would still be dozens more to fill the ranks. I kept a lamp burning throughout the night and by morning the tumbler of water on the dressing table was dotted with floating corpses I had drowned. We felt very diffident about telling Gran and tried to shake our bags and blankets unobtrusively out the window. But what to do about the mattress? The next night was just as bad. Emerging from our room in the morning, haggard from lack of sleep, we decided politeness must go by the board.

'Gran, we had a flea in bed last night,' said Shirl with admirable understatement. 'Have you any DDT? We'll have a spray around.'

'A flea, eh? We get quite a lot up here. They seem to come in from under the house. Drag everything out on the verandah and leave it in the sun.'

We gladly obeyed, sprayed the whole room and that night slept soundly.

We spent the days riding over the plateau along the red earth roads which wound through orange groves and flower farms. The scent in the air made us drowsy and we would lie down by the side of the road in the grass and doze or stop at a patch of berries and pick fruit until our hands were stained. Then home to one of Gran's huge afternoon teas, a meal in itself, and while we were washing the dishes she would talk. We heard wonderful tales of the old days when, as the only midwife for miles around, she used to be called out at any time of day or night. With her instrument bag in one hand and a hurricane lamp in the other she would climb the mountain to some isolated cottage, deliver a baby and be back cooking breakfast for her husband by daylight. She had been married three times and outlived each husband, even the last one, younger than she, who used to jokingly call her 'old 'un'.

When it was time for us to leave, she wouldn't hear of our saying goodbye.

'We'll just say ta-ta… perhaps you'll be back some day.'

The enchantment of Tamborine Mountain has stayed with me for years and I would dearly love to go back but it wouldn't be the same without Gran.

It was five o'clock in the evening before we left North Tamborine and started the wonderful 7½ mile descent of bitumen road to Tamborine township on the flat. We covered the distance in twenty minutes in a thrilling ride. The road wound through magnificent tropical forest, thick with palms and lush vegetation. (The giant Macrozamia palms are believed to be the oldest living things in the world today.) We attained a considerable speed and had to be extremely wary of upcoming traffic at the sharp corners. I sang with exhilaration until I had to devote all my attention to the road. Three-quarters of the way down I caught up with Shirl and beheld a merry little cloud of smoke billowing from her rear hub. I yelled to her to stop and shot two hundred yards past her before I had slowed down sufficiently to jump off and run my bike to a standstill. The brake was red hot and belching forth smoke. A smell of burning oil sickened me. We waited ten minutes but, as the sun was nearly down, realized we'd have to go on. Fortunately there was only another half mile of hill and then the road flattened out. We rode into Tamborine township as the sun was sinking in a sea of flame and, finding the local school, we spread our bags on the grass under a spreading camphor tree. It was a lovely clear night and a blinding moon shone on us as we slept.

I had a moment's panic wondering if Miss Farrell's dire predictions of facial disfigurement would come true but the only disaster was the discovery in the morning that a possum had stolen a new half pound of butter, a packet of cheese and a bag of biscuits, leaving torn-up paper scattered over the schoolground.

The next day we rode to the outskirts of Brisbane and stayed the night with some friends. The only preparations we made for the grand entry into the capital were – apart from the usual hair wash and ironing of clothes – effecting a complete disguise of our bikes. With a roll of sticky brown paper tape, we covered every part of the frames. The forks, which bore Malvern Star's emblem, the bars which bore their name, all hid their identity behind the anonymity of brown paper. With intense satisfaction we rode into Brisbane.

Chapter 10

THREE'S COMPANY

When I collected my pile of mail from the GPO I found several frantic notes and telegrams from my mother who, it appeared, had been in Brisbane for three days. She had no idea of my whereabouts and, with only ten days holiday at her disposal, had been trying to find me. A telegram to Binna Burra had been returned, she had left little notes at every place she could think of, including the Railway cloakroom where our dust-covered suitcases were waiting. The police were on the lookout for us, so was the Tourist Bureau. We were eventually reunited in the office of the *Courier Mail* and with glad cries and tears fell on each other's necks. It was Mum's first long trip away from home by herself and she was as excited as I. She was staying at the Canberra Private Hotel so we accompanied her there and dumped our luggage in her room until we could find a home of our own. In fact, throughout the duration of her stay, we practically lived there. (Mrs. Duncan had been paying £1 a day tariff at Lennons Hotel. Mum was paying only 6/6d at the Canberra so Mrs. Duncan moved in too.) We would dash in, shower and change our clothes and rush out to some appointment. We used the writing room and dining room, I played the piano in the lounge every evening and, until the day we left Brisbane, the porters and liftdrivers thought we were guests.

After a few desperate days of home-hunting, during which we solicited the help of the Lord Mayor, the YWCA and various churches, we miraculously met a young minister and his wife, Newton and Margaret Bagnall, who invited us to stay as their guests at the Missionary Training Hostel for Young Men which he conducted. It was situated only five minutes by tram from the city, we were free to come and go as we wished but always welcome to have our evening meal with our hosts and the fifteen personable young men who boarded at the Hostel. An ideal arrangement!

But even that could not last. Our days in Brisbane stretched into weeks and the weeks into a month and still we could not get away. As in Sydney, our time was spent desperately trying to earn our expenses. Though our mothers bought us a meal whenever they could, we did not ask them for further help. The blocks and blocks of city shops were a potential source of income to us and we had to strike while the publicity iron was hot. Hotels and cafés and booksellers were canvassed for subscriptions to the books we carried; radio stations, newspapers, theatres and the Speedway were approached for interviews and personal appearances; department stores, photographers, watchsellers and shoe shops were tapped for advertising purposes. There was hardly a commodity which could not have its sales boosted by our sponsorship – provided we could sell the idea to its producer. Sportswear shops had a logical tie-up, so did beauty preparations ('we keep our complexions creamy by using …'). Kodak films for the camera and chocolate for energy could also be relevant, but we had a hard and frustrating apprenticeship in the chancy science of advertising and it wasn't until a year or so later that we graduated with honours.

In the meantime we spent day after foot-slogging day around the city while our hosts must have wondered what could be keeping us so long. Kindly as they were, there came a time when we felt we simply couldn't impose any longer and set out to look for another home. We spent a few isolated nights with families we had met, a couple more on the floor of Mrs. Duncan's room at the hotel and then, in desperation, tried to get hotel accommodation (although this perpetuated a vicious circle, as it meant we should have to work longer to get more money to pay the tariff.)

It was Test cricket week in Brisbane and the Canberra like every other hotel was full. The only place with vacancies was the depressing People's Palace opposite, run by the Salvation Army. We booked a small double room at seven shillings a night. Naturally, we'd still spend all our spare time at the Canberra, where we were regarded as semi-permanent fittings. Clanking a huge room-key, we hurried upstairs to look at our new home. The first thing I saw as the door swung open was a caged window overlooking a dingy, slateless roof and fanlights. Next to it was a huge patch of wall, denuded of paint, the grey plaster underneath covered with pencil scribblings and lewd drawings. Two steel beds, a washstand with garlanded ewer and basin, a combination wardrobe and dressing table with a small mirror, more distorting than any in Luna Park, completed the view. We subsided weakly on the rock-like beds and waved our legs in the air, convulsed with laughter.

And just across the road was the Canberra with its quiet, elegant comfort. We drifted back there like homing pigeons each day and skulked into our tenement bedroom at night.

Brisbane has many attractions. The tempo of life is much slower than that of the southern cities. The glorious sun makes one feel lazy and holiday-minded, palm trees remind one that this is the threshold of the tropics and poincianas and jacarandas blotch the landscape with vivid colour. Cold drinks, fruit and icecream fritter away half one's spending money. Clothing is very informal and the Australian male has a degree of freedom in his attire unheard-of in other capitals. Informality, in fact, is the keynote of Brisbane. One strikes up conversations with people in the tram or milk bar and then, a week later, wonders at all the familiar faces in town. I remember waiting for a tram one evening; it didn't slow down as it approached me and I realized the tram stop was 200 yards further on. With desperate energy, good dress, high heels and all, I did a creditable sprint alongside the tram, cheered on encouragingly by the passengers and conductor, the driver clanging his bell to set the pace.

One of the Brisbane shops had an eye-catching window display of colourful raincoats made of something new called plastic. They were in vivid scarlet, emerald, daffodil yellow, royal blue and candy pink. Unheard of! Raincoats had always been beige oiled silk or black mackintoshes. What a marvellous waterproof material this plastic was!

A luncheon at Parliament House with the Under-Secretary of State and the Minister for Transport, Mr. Walsh, was interesting, the latter putting the fear of God in us with his snake stories. Despite the cordiality of this occasion, they let it cut no ice with them when we subsequently tendered through official channels a request for a free pass on Queensland Railways! The answer was no.

If you want to be a tourist, there are plenty of delightful places to visit in Brisbane. At Lone Pine Sanctuary we cuddled koalas and received the cold, but definitely not clammy, embrace of a large carpet snake. We saw Brisbane by night from Mt. Coot-tha and the incredible Glasshouse Mountains. (The guide book defines these as 'gargantuan plugs of trachyte pockmarked by the attrition of a million eras'! They reminded Captain Cook of the huge glass houses or furnaces of his native Whitby, not, as many suppose, because of any resemblance to a garden greenhouse.) You can go up the river to Mandalay or down it to the sea and the offshore islands Stradbroke, Moreton and Bribie.

Then there was the millionaire atmosphere of the Oasis Gardens and Swimming Pool. This was a public resort but very select. The owners could refuse admittance to anyone they thought undesirable. We passed scrutiny and went in. Walking through luxuriant, cool ferneries, we came to velvety lawns set with blazing flowerbeds, exotic poinsettia, banks of flowering mesembryanthemum and blossoming shrubs and trees. Three pools were set amongst the gardens and surrounded by ferns and palm trees. Gaily-striped umbrellas shaded tables and chairs at the water's edge. There were enclosures containing koalas, emus and other birds and four obliging peacocks with their tails spread all the time strutted proudly before a barrage of cameras. After swimming, we lay in the sun on the grass by the pool. I was just sinking into that delightful state of sun-drunkenness when, through half-closed eyes, I saw the notice. I sat up and looked more carefully. On the top line, in large type, were the words 'COUPLES MUST LIE APART' and in smaller type 'in these grounds'.

I nudged Shirl and asked her what she thought it meant.

'I don't know. It's most ambiguous. In the first place, why does it say that couples must lie?'

'And does it refer to *one* couple – or that two or more sets of couples must lie apart?'

'And why does it priggishly suggest that one can do it anywhere else but not *in these grounds?"*

We were delighted with this and other moralizing placards scattered through the gardens but felt they spoiled the sophisticated atmosphere. I wondered what Dior's visiting French mannequins thought when, several weeks later, they came to the Oasis to disport themselves in their sensational abbreviated swimsuits. (Within a few months these were being called bikinis as the world's fifth atomic bomb had been detonated at Bikini Atoll in the Pacific in July. What connection the daring swimsuits had with the test bomb I don't know.)

If you feel like climbing the intimidating Jacob's Ladder from the heart of the city up to Wickham Terrace and then turn along past the old windmill and treadmill, you will come, as we did, to a delightful square of land where old men were playing draughts on a large open-air board. Basking in the delicious sun we sat and watched them walking across the outsize squares, shifting their giant 'men' with iron-hooked sticks. They invited us to play and for half an hour we did so, enjoying the gentle pastime.

But we couldn't relax for long. There was always work to do. A photographer in Coolangatta had given us the name of his young daughter who ran a photography business in Brisbane. About nineteen years of age, Josie was a very glamorous teenager, bearing in her clothes and her accent the indelible impression of the recent American military presence. Her hair was worn in a long page-boy bob, and round it, instead of the commonplace bandeau, she sported a thick silken cord, knotted under one ear with two large pendent tassels swinging on her shoulder. At this time we were favouring the Queensland hair-do, cool and practical, in which the front and side hair was rolled off the face and the back hair plaited into one braid and taken up to the crown of the head. We were greatly impressed with Josie's glamorous style and yearned to copy it but for the moment business was our object. We wanted to work for her as street photographers. She quickly explained the workings of the Leica camera and sent us out with a film to practise. It was marvellous fun. We went first to the GPO, situated in the main street, and asked the Mail Counter girls to come outside. We took their photos on the steps, then some of ourselves and some passers-by, then sauntered through to Anzac Square. Few passers-by stopped though so we moved up the steps to the Station. It was amazing the number of refusals we had. We couldn't take walking shots with this camera, the subject had to stop and pose. The women who said 'Certainly not! The idea!' to my saccharine invitation, sent us into peals of mirth. Mrs. Duncan came out of her hotel to have her photo taken but unfortunately Shirl forgot to wind the film and she subsequently appeared splashed on a genial fat man in a steamroller. We snapped the roadworkers and a man leaning against the parapet eating sandwiches and, duly finishing our film (thirty-six exposures), we proudly returned to base. Josie fell on our shoulders and gave us a greater welcome than that accorded the Prodigal Son.

'You haven't been taking photos commercially! Oh my Lord! I only meant you to take photos of yourselves! I didn't think you'd have the nerve to go on the streets. Someone just came in and asked who were my two new photographers and I nearly died! And a woman has been in already asking when she can see the proofs. Every minute I've expected a policeman to drag you in and I'd have to pay the fine.' (Actually, it wasn't the taking of photographs which was discouraged but the handing out of cards to the subject which constituted illegal distribution of literature.) I quietened her and explained that as we'd frequented the main street, the steps of the General Post Office and other obvious places, the police hadn't seen us. Fools rush in ...

Meantime, we were busy book-selling. Our publisher employer from Sydney, Stan, visited Brisbane and congratulated us on our successful salesmanship. Urging us to greater efforts, he introduced us to a book wholesaler who gave us a huge pile of new lines. We were aghast at the number of samples we were expected to carry, but a quick inspection made us realize that we could soon jettison half of them. Our new employer noticed the dubious look on our faces and hastened to explain.

'Some of them are a little – er spicy you know, but spicy humour's what sells. You'll get orders for dozens of those. And of course the children's books are a good line.'

He showed us an excellent range of children's books, Australian animal books and nursery rhymes; a line of book comics bearing the exciting titles *Desert Dragon*, *White Eagle* and *The Hidden People* and sporting Westerns like *River of Blood*, *Golden Gulch* and *Mesa Gold*. Then there was an hilarious book on astrology which we loved reading, various souvenirs, leather tobacco pouches, key-rings etc. Lastly, hanging their heads, were the lurid yellowbacks – heart-touching romances variously titled *You and I*, *My gambler husband*, *Kelly my Irish lover*, A *Bendigo Lad*, *Reunion in Albury* (nothing like a spot of local colour), *Sweethearts of the Fighting Forces* and so on. Right at the bottom we had a dreadful volume called *One good time* which we rarely and apologetically produced, a *Sunbathing Review* which we never showed, and *Alma WAS Nice* – spicy humour to put it mildly but with some very funny drawings. A dull stretch of road could not fail to be enlivened by readings from this.

The main string on our fiddle was, of course, Malvern Star. On the day after our arrival in Brisbane, the usual advertisement was splashed in the newspaper. Sharpening our claws for battle and talking darkly of lawsuits, we went to their office.

'We've got them now,' I exulted, 'We've their telegram saying that we're to regard ourselves as entirely free and to negotiate elsewhere. If we did have something on the carpet with another firm, this could be most embarrassing.'

On being shown into the manager's office we had a surprise. Mr. Nabbs, the erstwhile Sydney manager, rose from his desk with extended hand and a cordial welcome. Our thunderous countenances cleared only to be succeeded by expressions of suspicion. Mr. Nabbs beamed at us, his whole attitude conciliatory.

'Now girls, let's talk this thing out. I'm sure we can come to an arrangement satisfactory to both sides. This feuding is rather senseless, don't you think?'

With similar disarming sentiments, he bade us sit down, ordered some ice-cold malted milk and soon we were bitterly unloading our grievances. He nodded understandingly then put his firm's case.

'You make us seem a very black-hearted lot but we've got some grouches too. If you were doing a quick-fire record-breaking trip around Australia, where there was tremendous public interest – and sustained interest, you'd be of great value to us. But you amble along, disappear for a month or so at a time, turn up again in an unlikely place and don't let us know when or where to expect you. How can we derive any benefit from that?'

'We don't want to be tied down to a schedule,' said Shirl sullenly.

'Fair enough,' said Nabbs, 'but you can't expect three guineas a week each for that sort of casual travelling. Now, I suggest ....'

At the end of a long discussion, we emerged wreathed in smiles, clutching a contract which stipulated a weekly fee of one guinea each (A$2.58) in return for which we should give publicity to Malvern Star whenever possible in interviews, public appearances and private conversations and cooperate with managers in main towns. Our time would be our own, our rate of progress as slow as we wished but we must keep them informed of our itinerary. An amicable settlement. We felt as though we'd inherited a fortune, the guinea a week being that blessed thing we had been striving for – a regular income. We had security! We could just about live on a guinea a week. Anything we earned over and above that would be clear profit. Why, perhaps we could even buy a meal now and then!

Mr. Nabbs had an even more wonderful idea. He said he was hoping to sell us to Peters Icecream, the biggest manufacturer of icecream in Australia. They might even be persuaded to come to the same arrangement. Our senses reeled at the idea of two guineas a week. But it would be up to us to impress our personalities favourably on the manager of Peters at a personal interview. We could hardly wait.

-oOo-

We had been invited to lunch at Lennons with a doctor whom we had met at Surfers Paradise. He was middle-aged and almost bald and instinctively

Shirl's eyes had telegraphed to me the category '*Loup*'! Still, he seemed civil enough and a luncheon at Lennons was a pleasant thought. As we were waiting for him in the lounge Shirl said: 'I wonder what sort of specialist he is. I bet he's a gynaecologist. Hope not!'

'Why on earth?

'I don't know. They always embarrass me.'

Just then our host arrived, bringing a friend to complete the foursome. He was introduced as Clarence and was no more prepossessing than our host. He also was older than we, stuttered a bit and had a receding chin. Clarence. We drifted into the dining room after declining the offer of drinks.

As the soup dishes were being removed, there was a hiatus in the conversation and Shirl, turning to Dr. Sullivan, who sat there benevolently evil in the Alistair Sim manner, asked brightly:

'And which branch of medicine do you specialize in Doctor?'

We both waited tensely for the answer and the moment seemed very long.

'Gynaecology,' he said, with an ingratiating leer.   Shirl's face flooded with crimson and I dropped my napkin under the table.

After lobster, icecream and coffee, Dr. Sullivan looked at Clarence and then at us and suggested we might like to go up to his apartment to clean up. I saw Shirl stiffen at the word 'apartment' and she looked askance at me. We followed him, muttering cautious words to each other. Oh, the anguished uncertainty of girls who know themselves to be wildly out of their depths! We were twenty and twenty-one but knew very little of the world and less of sophisticated men. But perhaps we were exaggerating the melodramatic atmosphere of the luncheon?

'After all,' I said to Shirl, when the men had left us alone in the bedroom, 'they're behaving quite respectably. Dr. Sullivan only suggested we come up here to give us the chance to go to the bathroom if we want to.'

Shirl shook her head dubiously. 'I don't like it Wen. I'm very sensitive to atmosphere and this one is charged. But charged. He's a *loup*, I bet you.'

'Well, wait and see. I expect we'll just go home now. There's nothing to worry about.'

We had just convinced ourselves that we'd imagined the atmosphere when the men returned.

Dr. Sullivan smiled slowly at us and said, very softly:

'Well now, what would you like to do – rest a while, or go for a car ride, or rest then ride?'

('Horreur!')

'Let's go for a ride to some place we haven't seen,' said Shirl with forced gaiety.

'How about a run up to the mountains then?'

We agreed. A car ride seemed safe enough.

'Do we need a rug?' he asked with solicitude.

Wham! There was that darned atmosphere again!

I laughed hollowly. 'A rug? Oh no, it isn't cold.' (We were almost in the tropics after all.)

After the merest pause, he said: 'Oh we might want to lie on the grass and sleep.'

Still *horreur* and still forced vigour from Shirl and me.

'Oh no, we'll be climbing cliffs ....'

'Jumping from crag to crag ....'

'Leaping the streams ....'

We spent a strained but uneventful afternoon driving through beautiful country, Clarence crowding me in the back seat, Shirl talking brightly in the front. Whenever we stopped, Shirl and I jumped out of the car and ran hither and yon, admiring nature and marvelling at the sights. No, we weren't a bit tired thanks, it was all so *refreshing*! (My shoes were killing me but I'd have died rather than admit I wanted to rest.)

Dr. Sullivan and Clarence looked a trifle crushed but perhaps it was our over-sensitive imagination. After all, who did we think we were! Why, dear Dr. Sullivan was old enough to be our father. He probably had daughters of his own and just wanted to give us an enjoyable outing. Of course. He was very kind really – that luncheon, that drive …

'That rug?' asked Shirl.

We told a Brisbane friend about it afterwards. Her brow puckered for a moment.

'What did you say his name was?'

I told her. 'He's a gynaecologist.'

Our friend screamed. 'Oh NO!'

'Why, what's the matter? Do you know him?'

'Oh girls, he's the most *dreadful* man! Everyone knows about him! Even his professional conduct has been criticized. And to think that you've been out with him all afternoon!'

'You see,' said Shirl, smug though shaken. 'I told you he was a *loup!*'

-oOo-

Whenever we had a chance we looked for a dog. A visit to the Lost Dogs Home provoked sympathy but no great enthusiasm. Then one day, en route to our important interview with the Peters Manager, we passed the Happidog shop and there was our dog in the window. Just like that. We went straight inside and bought him for thirty shillings. He was a Queensland Cattle Dog, or Blue Heeler, a pretty pup about six weeks old with a short mottled grey coat which looked blue in the sunlight, black spots and markings and a white blaze on his forehead. The breed was established in 1890 when a dingo/dalmatian/collie/kelpie cross resulted in a dog which could run long distances and was highly intelligent. It was an excellent watchdog, had plenty of stamina, was lightly built and had a short coat suitable for hot climates. The salesman assured us he came of small parents and so wouldn't grow very large. He seemed perfect in every way and we loved him already. After arranging for the shop to board him until we were ready to leave Brisbane, we departed feeling very excited.

Mr. Christophersen, the Queensland General Manager of Peters Icecream, was a Great Dane. A huge man, tall as well as broad, with a fine leonine head and blue Nordic eyes, he included in his activities the function of Danish Vice-Consul. We felt very small sitting on the other side of his enormous desk with Mr. Nabbs but proceeded to be as charming as we could in an effort to win him over to our cause. He wasn't quite sold on the idea, thinking that public interest would flag as our tour was so leisurely but Mr. Nabbs carried all before him. Now that he was on our side, he spared no effort to help us, pointing out to Chris the advantages of Malvern Star and Peters both sponsoring us. He outlined wide and simple plans and volunteered to do all the organization himself. Chris looked impressed and said he'd think it over and let us know.

He asked if we'd like some icecream and a girl brought in some of Peters famous Arctic Delicacies. I had heard of these wonderful things but during the war icecream had been strictly utilitarian. My eyes goggled at what I saw. On Shirl's plate lay a perfect peach, its skin faintly orange flushed with red, the condensation on the surface giving it a peach-like bloom. I had a delicate pear, yellow with brown shading.

'You mean we have to eat these? I've never seen anything so beautiful!'

Chris looked pleased. 'They are good aren't they? And flavoured according to the fruit.'

He then showed us a chart of designs which had been regular lines before the war, icecream cakes, ships, shoes, 21st birthday keys, baskets of flowers, birds in nests, all made of icecream.

As we ate, we talked to Chris about our trip and I could see him becoming interested in spite of himself. He was surprised to hear how much luggage we carried.

'I thought swaggies got by with a blanket roll and a billy,' he laughed.

'We're not very good swaggies I'm afraid,' I said. 'We don't even carry a billy because we don't like tea. But we have got a dog.' (The traditional swagman carries a pup in his billy.)

'What's this?' Mr. Nabbs pricked up his ears.

Explanations came tumbling out. 'We've just bought him. Today. And he's the most beautiful, adorable pup you've ever seen.'

'What are you going to call him?' asked Chris with a twinkle.

Shirl and I looked at each other. We hadn't thought of that. After a whispered consultation, we turned to Chris and said:

'Peter.'

One evening as we were out on the Canberra's roof garden, cracking some Queensland nuts with a stone, we heard gay dance music emanating from the 9th floor and went to investigate. The lift driver had told me earlier that I couldn't go up as there was something special on. So we asked for the 7th floor to trick him and ran up the stairs to the 9th. We peered around the corner and saw that a lively dance was in progress. I asked a Dear Old Duck what it was all about.

'It's a dance run by the Lancashire Club dear,' she said genially in the unmistakable accent of that county. 'Go and enjoy yourselves!'

We were delighted and rushed off to change our clothes first. Our cases were still in Mrs. Duncan's room so we hurriedly put on our best dresses and after I had chased around to find a porter to hammer a nail from my shoe, we entered the lift and asked for the 8th floor. The driver turned on us.

'Where are you going? You can't go running around floors where you don't live.'

'Ah,' I said in admiration. 'You're sharp! Can't put anything over you! Well, as a matter of fact, we're going to 9.'

'You can't go to 9.'

'Oh yes, we can. We've an invitation.'

'Who from?'

'The Lancashire Club.'

Very dubious, he took us to 9, disgorged us from the lift, then stood watching to see if anyone would accept us. No one did. The D.O.D. had gone. Revelling in our discomfiture, he sent an official to ask if we had an invitation. I did some fast explaining and caught the ear of another D.O.D. who, on learning who we were, caught us – figuratively – to her bosom and made such a fuss of us that our disgruntled liftdriver rattled his doors shut and plummeted out of view.

Our sponsor hustled us along to have our photos taken by a photographer. Then she grabbed my arm.

'Listen dear, four of the English cricketers are here. I'll get them to have their photos taken with you.'

She looked around the crowded dance-floor and bustled up to a red-faced, sandy-haired man who was the centre of interest in one group.

'Oh, Mr. Pollard ....'

She spoke to him for a minute and he referred her to their manager, white-haired Major Howard. He was very interested; so was the extremely handsome dark man next to him, John Ikin. They were about to leave, so we preceded them to the foyer where the photographer waited. But a swarm of women hovered around them for the same purpose, and the D.O.D. organized everyone in a loud Lancashire voice. She arranged the four cricketers (Washbrook had now joined them) as a background then whipped a grinning female in front. The camera clicked, the woman was removed and another substituted. This went on for three or four minutes till the men were looking very bored and uncomfortable and their smiles were becoming wooden. We despaired of ever working to the head of the queue so darted around to the other side and hopped in front of the men. The resultant photograph is one which I treasure, not so much as a snap of visiting celebrities but as a triumphant memorial to adversity overcome.

Chapter 11

THE TROPICS BECKON

At last we were ready to leave Brisbane. All our business affairs were in order. Peters had agreed to give us a contract which, besides stipulating a payment of one guinea a week each for the duration of our stay in Queensland, produced the far more valuable gift of a pass to obtain icecream free all over the State. We were in raptures! To be able to eat as much icecream as we wished! Why, we'd eat nothing else in the tropics! I could see our cost of living dwindling to a negligible amount and our future based on a rock of security. We were eager to get on the road.

A complete reorganisation of our belongings had been necessary. It was now the end of November and all warm clothes had been sent home. Our cases of good clothes had been sent on to Mackay. We had bought a huge jungle-green mosquito net shaped like a bell tent from an Army Disposals sale and a couple of Army pint pannikins. We had also acquired two water bottles left behind at the Canberra by American soldiers. To complete the metamorphosis from a tourist outing to a serious expedition, we had changed our riding clothes. Blouses and shorts would be no good to us in the fierce tropical sun. We now wore men's shirts, Navy disposal bell-bottomed trousers made of khaki drill, and wide-brimmed khaki felt bush hats. They were actually Women's Air Force summer hats of the type which earned for the W.A.A.A.F. the sobriquet of 'Curtin's Cowgirls'. We fancied we looked like Daphne Campbell, star of the successful Australian film *The Overlanders* which we had just seen. She had worn a hat like that, as did all the stockmen, and already we were visualizing ourselves riding down the fabulous North-South road to Alice Springs, mounted on iron steeds instead of hairy ones.

The day before our departure, we hurried excitedly to the dog shop to collect Peter. To our joy he had hardly grown and it seemed likely that he would always be a small dog. The shopman lifted him out of the window where he'd been lying forlornly in one corner. He had a large head with 'ears like errant wings', quite out of proportion to his tiny body. His ribs were prominent and his belly pendulous. His eyes were watering.

'He's all right, isn't he?' I asked the man. 'Why are his eyes sore?'

'Oh, it's a bit bright in the window. The glare .....I've wormed him already but you'd better take a bottle of syrup with you and do him again in a day or two. He'll be right.'

So we bought some worm syrup, flea powder, a collar and leash and dog biscuits.

'I don't suppose he'll eat many of these, we're going to feed him on icecream.'

'Icecream! You're mad! You'll give him colic!'

Our faces fell. Our main publicity point was that Peter ate icecream too, Peters icecream. Well, we should see. I looked down at him fondly. He crouched on the floor, snarling savagely at a broom which a boy was wielding energetically at the back of the shop.

'The darling! He's going to be a good watchdog.'

'Oh, he just likes a game,' the man said hurriedly.

Pete wasn't playing. This hatred of brooms persisted all his life and I think he had been pushed around by one when he was a pup.

When we had packed up next morning, Shirl tied him on her front pack with strips of fabric torn off the bottom of the mosquito net. He wasn't too secure but she managed to ride slowly to the GPO for our send-off. Mr. Nabbs was there making sure the reporters and photographers were doing their stuff. We had had an awful job removing the brown tape from our bikes but now, cleaned and overhauled, they were a credit to Malvern Star. Crowds of people milled around us, eager for a look at Peter, marvelling at the towering luggage on both carriers and wishing us luck. The girls from the Mail Counter took our redirection forms and said business would be slack after we'd gone.

We pushed off and groaned at the effort needed to get the bikes under way. It was very hot and beneath our felt hats our faces streamed with perspiration. On the outskirts of the city we stopped at a café to try our Peters pass for the first time. After a plate of four scoops of icecream drenched in chocolate sauce and then a malted milk with a sixpenny icecream in it, we felt better. Shirl asked the woman for a cardboard carton for Pete and strapping it on top of her front pack, made a steady perch for him. She cut a hole in the front of it so he could put his head out in the breeze. His ears flapped like Dumbo's.

Our route now lay west across the Darling Downs before swinging away north to rejoin the coast road. At Ipswich we camped in a church hall and used our mosquito net for the first time. Tying one end of a rope to the peak, we threw the other end over a rafter and hauled until the net looked like a wigwam, its ends trailing on the floor. Then we pulled out the sides and weighted the bottom with haversacks. That night, for the first time, it was too hot to sleep in our bags. Clad only in underwear we lay on top of them and were devoured by clouds of mosquitoes which streamed in through gaps so in the morning we cut the net in half longitudinally, each of us having the responsibility of protecting herself. The solutions we devised were ingenious. After spreading out our padding and sleeping bags, we tied strings transversely to any convenient object at shoulder, waist and knee level. Attaching the portion of mosquito net to these by large safety pins ensured a long green tunnel of safety. The strings were tied at a height of about eighteen inches so that the net was kept off our bodies. Otherwise, if there were any point of contact, mosquitoes would bite through the net. It was extremely stuffy but we were to become used to sweat.

We never became accustomed to flies. The scourge of Australia, the bush fly is persistent and maddening. (Most houses have their doors and windows fly-screened.) The archetypal Australian bushman has a hat with corks bobbing around the brim although I never actually saw one. We were driven to buy fly veils which we draped over our hats. Failing that, we were obliged to use the Cloncurry Wave, the regular brushing away of flies from the face. (Years later I saw a newsreel of the Queen visiting the Outback. She was speaking to children on the School of the Air radio network. Every few seconds she passed her hand across her face. The British must have wondered what she was doing. It was the Cloncurry Wave!)

We were worried about Peter. He was apathetic and couldn't keep any food down. It has been said that a baby is a biological system of uncontrolled apertures. Pete was still a baby and we were kept busy cleaning up his various messes, binding kerchiefs around our noses to exclude the stench and desperately carrying out diversionary measures if our clergyman host should call – I hastily intercepting him at the door, directing his footsteps here or there as we talked; Shirl, on her knees, frantically scraping with a knife and mopping with clumps of newspaper, her face a mask of suffering, her nostrils almost closed in protest! Peter, probably choosing this very moment to wander in from outside and perform anew.

Every evening he would get a great hunger, which had to be utilized before it abated. We would rush out and buy some minced meat or other scraps, hurriedly cook it in one of our pannikins over the gas ring in the hall and put it in front of him. At first he wolfed the lot and brought it all up again.   So then we fed him small amounts at quarter-hour intervals. Sometimes he would snuffle around in it for a little, and then, his appetite waning as quickly as it had come, he would lose interest.   One Sunday evening we were desperate. The great hunger had come, the shops were shut and we had nothing for him.

'Come on Wen, we must sink our pride and beg some scraps from a hotel or café. It's for the little boy, remember.'

We tried a hotel first and the proprietress clucked her tongue sympathetically and brought back a large parcel. 'There's the end of our

Sunday joint in there,' she said. 'You should be able to get quite a bit off it for the little chap.'

We thanked her profusely and carried it away. On the next corner we stopped under a street light and opened it. There, nestling in the paper, was a goodly quantity of glorious white pork, little bits of golden crackling curling temptingly on the outside. I looked at Shirl. Shirl looked at me.

'Let's ask at another place,' I said, reading her thoughts.

Trying to justify our action by assuring each other of the unsuitability of rich pork for little pups, we managed to secure some scraps of cooked meat for Pete from a café and carried the pork home for our tea. It was delicious.

The café proprietor had taken one look at Pete and said that he had distemper.

'Look at those runny eyes!' he said. 'You'd better watch out or you'll lose him. Pups haven't much resistance.'

'Then he must have had it when we bought him,' I said indignantly. 'That dastardly dog man said it was the glare in the window.'

At a small town further on, a man came up to us and, pointing to Peter, said 'That dog's got distemper!'

'Bright boy,' Shirl murmured.

'Well, I'm the Distemper King around these parts and if you give me that dog, I'll have him back in five minutes and he'll be better in a day.'

'Why, what're you going to do to him?'

'Well y'see, distemper's nothing more'n a ulcer in the back passage. All I do is break that ulcer and your dog's as right as rain.'

Shirl snatched up Pete and put him in his box.

'No one's jabbing knives in this dog! What absolute rubbish! Distemper's a form of flu.'

On reaching Toowoomba, we took him straight to a veterinary surgeon and had him injected with serum. Shirl, despite her hospital experience, made a hasty exit. I found her sitting outside, her face pallid.

'I can't stand seeing needles going in,' she said apologetically. 'I thought I was going to faint.'

We repeated the treatment two days later and I had to hold the little pup myself while the vet drove a coarse blunt needle into his flesh. Little Pete bucked and yipped and the needle came out bent like a button hook. The serum fixed him. He started to pick up and we rejoiced. He began to eat regularly and fortunately showed a great liking for icecream!

Our meals now consisted of a dish of four threepenny icecreams which we garnished with sliced bananas, passionfruit or papaw, the whole swimming in orange or mandarin sauce supplied by the obliging café proprietor. For a change we sometimes had vanilla icecream topped with chocolate or coffee sauce. To finish the meal we bought malted milks with threepenny icecreams in them. Little Pete had a scoop in one of the pannikins.

In Toowoomba, city of beautiful gardens, we were overwhelmed by hospitality. As we rode into the town along the wide, tree-lined streets, people waved from their front doors and shouted 'Welcome!' We made our home in a church hall and were glad of the shelter when the weather changed and pouring rain turned the red clay roads into bogs. It was the worst storm in years and washed out the Test Match in Brisbane.

We did a radio interview for a progressive fruit merchant who promised to give us a send-off from his shop laden with a pound's worth of fruit and a Turkish Bath establishment offered to give us the works in return for using our names in their advertising.

'Well, that's something new, let's go!' said Shirl. Assuming her testimonial voice she burbled: 'Contrary to popular belief, cycling doesn't keep us slim. We depend on regular Turkish Baths to retain a trim figure. At Steaminhot Salon the service is ......'

'Come on, let's see what it's like.'

We were welcomed by a woman attendant who ushered us into a small room and told Shirl to strip for the steam bath. She undressed and hopped into a hot-box, only her head visible above a necklet of towels, whilst I looked on with glee. The steam was turned on and when Shirl was starting to produce a moist glow with little trickles of perspiration running down from her hair, the woman beamed.

'Right!' she said, rubbing her hands. 'Now we'll get the photo-rapher to take the photos.'

'Photos!' shrieked Shirl. 'You didn't tell us! I thought you'd just use our names.'

I could imagine her legs dancing a frantic fandango inside the box.

'You'll look very nice dear, I'm sure.'

I roared with laughter at poor Shirl looking her photogenic worst, neck-deep in the box with steam billowing in clouds around her, her face scarlet and shiny with heat, her hair lank and dripping.

The photographer bustled in and took a photo. I stood swathed in a towel next to the steam box and assumed a nonchalant 'we do this often, it doesn't hurt a bit' attitude while Shirl glared balefully through her steam.

'There, that's lovely!' said the attendant. 'Now you get undressed so we can take your photo being massaged.'

'*Massaged!*' I looked suspicious. 'Where?'

'Don't worry, you'll have a sheet on.' She hurried away to find one.

I lay on a couch with one leg bared and crooked for massage. Shirl emerged from her box sweating profusely and, desperately clutching her sheet around her, sat at my side. As a bit of cheesecake the resultant photo wasn't too bad but I doubt if it would have enticed any new customers to the establishment.

When the weather cleared we left Toowoomba, laden with grapes, cherries, apples, oranges, bananas, pineapple, cantaloupes, papaw and passionfruit from our greengrocer benefactor and two family bricks of icecream from a Peters café. Our load was so heavy that, when a truck had taken us ten miles out and dumped us in the middle of nowhere, we settled down to do some solid eating. I demolished my cantaloupe and family brick but even so the rest of the pack weighed like lead. Our way through Dalby then north through Bell to Kingaroy was punctuated by frequent stops at the side of the road, trying to reduce the pile of fruit. All this and Queensland hospitality too! At Dalby we got off a truck on the outskirts of the town and leaned our bikes against a fence. A woman came out of the house and promptly asked us to stay the night. In Kingaroy the offers of food were so numerous and the chance of refusing them so slight that Shirl and I met our Waterloo. We staggered limply from huge morning tea to sumptuous lunch to delectable afternoon tea to three-course dinner, eagerly snatching at a night's sleep to recuperate before the busy round recommenced next day.

Kingaroy, besides, is the home of the peanut industry. Coming in from Bell, the red soil road wound through green fields of waving maize and young crops of peanut seedlings, the deep blue sky glowing behind and warm, flowing sunshine enveloping everything. We spent a day on a peanut farm and a morning inspecting the peanut factory. A dusty, tiring morning when we traipsed around after our guide, climbing up to the top of the huge concrete silos. Naturally there were mountains of peanuts around but all uncooked! Nevertheless we ate stacks of a variety called Spanish Reds which are edible raw and carried pounds of other types away with us. In Gympie, we found that the Malvern Star shop sold electrical appliances so we borrowed an electric griller and roasted all our peanuts.

That was the only saving grace of Gympie. How we hated it! I had read that Gympie was picturesquely set upon verdant hills. What I didn't know was that there isn't a flat stretch of road anywhere. I have never seen anything like Gympie's hills and the school where we were to camp was situated on top of the Palatine Hill, the worst of the lot. It was so steep that my sandals were slipping on the road and even when I was having a rest from pushing my bike, it was an effort to stop it rolling back. It took us fifteen minutes to reach the top, Shirl having let Pete out of his box to lessen the weight. Then we discovered that the nearest hotel where we hoped to have baths, was down in the main street. After mountaineering in this fashion for a couple of days, we rode out of Gympie with nary a backward glance.

Then Fortune tossed us Maryborough to compensate. Beautiful Maryborough where the life of the city revolves around the cyclist. The broad flat streets are made for cycling, the kerbs are lined with either wooden parking racks for bikes or notched to take the front wheel. Everyone rides a bike. It was a frightening and exhilarating experience to be in the main street during the lunch hour or five o'clock exodus when wave upon wave of wheel-borne humanity swept down the thoroughfare. Trying to find a vacant telegraph pole or verandah post to lean my bike against was just as much a worry as a city motorist's parking problems. We were in our element and if it hadn't been for little Pete, sitting up proudly in his box and the towering packs on our back carriers, we shouldn't have been noticed.

It was Christmas week and the drift to the Bay had begun. Every weekend all the young folk in Maryborough went to the beach resorts on Hervey Bay, an hour's trip by rail, to dance and swim. The proximity of Christmas had doubled the number of visitors. We thought it as good a place as any to spend the festive season so we joined the throng. It was eight o'clock at night when we got out at Torquay station. The train roared on leaving us standing on the deserted platform. Most of the passengers had got off at Pialba and Scarness. We found our way to a school and settled in on the verandah. Now that the summer holidays had started, schools were a better bet than churches. After a wash and change of clothes, we rode along to the dance at Scarness, about a mile and a half along the beach road. Even in the darkness the chain of townships looked very pretty, the road being separated from the beach by a belt of trees dotted with the lights of tents.

Inside the hall I was struck dumb by the sight which met my eyes. The men wore mainly khaki or white shorts and coloured shirts – very informal and sensible. But the girls! Some wore shorts and shirts which was surprising enough. Others sported shorts and bare midriff tops. But the majority wore brief flared skirts like skating skirts and sun tops or midriff tops, long legs emerging from the scanty covering, all dancing around as unconcernedly as though they were on the beach and not in a ballroom. Our eyes bulged at each fresh discovery.

'Can you imagine going to a Melbourne dance like that!' gasped Shirl. 'Even at a beach resort!'

I looked down at my conservative dirndl and felt positively old-fashioned.

Surprisingly, next day when we rode along the front, dressed in bathers and shorts – Shirl wore only her bathers in her desire to emulate the half-naked women of Scarness – not one underclad female did we see. Every girl wore a frock or a skirt. Mortified, we hurried to the beach.

We were beginning to train little Pete. In the first weeks after leaving Brisbane we used to lift him out of his box and call him to follow us but he just stood there idiotically staring after us. Now, as we rode along the hard sand on Pialba beach, he kept up very well. Then we tried to introduce him to the water. He followed us to the edge of the sea and stood there yelping. I tried dipping him in the shallows but he wriggled out of my grasp and trotted disconsolately back to our belongings.

'It's a bit hard starting him in salt water. Perhaps we'd better wait till we come to a river. Anyway, it's lunch time.'

We made our way to Bowd's Store which had become our headquarters. It was an excellent community store comprising a newsagency, grocery, small goods, toy shop and café, all in one. Mr. Bowd had placed a large order for books with us on our first day, he sold Peters icecream and had a piano. So, after finishing my icecream I was always invited to give them a tune and the music drew lots of holiday-makers in from the beach. It was good for business and Mr. Bowd was always pleased to see us.

Standing at the counter was the young trombonist from the Ambassadors Orchestra which played at all the Scarness dances. In the friendly Queensland fashion I engaged him in conversation.

'Are you by any chance a Dixieland enthusiast? The sign-off to one of your choruses the other night sounded very suspicious.'

'Am I!' He whirled round, his eyes wide. 'I've only got the best collection of jazz records in Queensland!'

I told him about the record of the Original Dixieland Jazz Band I had unearthed in a Toowoomba junk shop and then we discussed the relative merits of bands and performers.

'I'd like to hear your records some time.'

'Sure!' he answered. 'Any time ….all day long we've got them going on the stage in the dance hall. I'm going back there now as soon as I've got some drinks for the boys. How 'bout coming?'

I agreed with alacrity, Shirl having been invited to go for a swim. The trombonist, Bill, introduced me to the rest of the band who were sitting around the stage listening quietly to records. There were Ron the trumpeter, a youngster of about nineteen, and Leo the saxophonist who also did wonderful vocals, and Ted the second sax. The pianist and drummer weren't there so after a while I timorously suggested we have some live music if they had their instruments with them.

'Why, do you play?' asked Leo.

I sat down at the piano and started the introduction to a very Graeme Bell-ish *Making Believe*. At the end of three choruses there was a momentary silence and Leo said 'Well!'

They pulled their chairs into a closer circle and we settled down to a jam session. We played all the old jazz standards and I taught them *Spain*, *Blue turning grey over you* and *Sister Kate*. It was exhilarating. For the first time in eight months I had a mental spring-cleaning, a real brain test in which split-second improvisation had to be transmitted to hands without the loss of a beat or the slip of a finger. After two hours, I rode home feeling exalted.

That night at the dance I sat in with them for a few choruses and afterwards we all went to have supper at Bowd's. Young Ron the trumpeter was quiet and listless most of the time, absentmindedly stirring his coffee and gazing into space. It appeared he had girl trouble and the others ragged him unmercifully. I had seen him at the dance, hurrying down from the platform between numbers to talk to a slim, pretty young girl called Pat. Now he was miserably wondering why she'd left the hall before the end of the dance. After half an hour of listening to his maunderings, Leo leant across the table. He was a man of about 35 and so considerably older than the others.

'Listen now Ron. You've got to snap out of it. This isn't doing your music any good. How serious are you about Pat?'

'I want to marry her,' said Ron defiantly.

'Well now, you're pretty young to be thinking along those lines just yet. May be just a flash in the pan – (he waved away Ron's indignant protest) – but say it isn't. Say it's the real thing. All right. Now have you stopped to think how Pat would like being married to a bloke in a dance band?'

'Pat's all right. She loves music. Don't have to worry about Pat.'

Leo shook his head wearily as though from bitter experience. 'Maybe not now Ron. But take it from me, music and women don't mix. Not unless your wife plays too. Just think ….you get married. Right. You shelve engagements for a while just so's you can be together. Then you start hankering to get back with the band. Comes Saturday night you get a booking. Right. She comes along to listen to you but after a while she gets pretty bored with just sitting and listening so she'll start dancing with other men. That's all right, you think, I want her to enjoy herself. But, sitting up there on that stage, you get to thinking about the chaps she's dancing with. Isn't she having rather a lot with that smooth, flashy bloke who dances wonderfully? And when she goes out with him for a drink, you'll be watching the clock to make sure she's not away too long. Ah ah, bad for your music son. And then, maybe, one night you'll have a row about it and she'll get mad because you don't trust her and when you've made up, she'll say 'well, never mind darling, I won't go to the dance. I'll stay home.' But even that doesn't work because now you're wondering what she's doing at home. Perhaps it was better when you could keep an eye on her. You get to worrying about it and then you take to the grog and you feel lonely without her but you don't want to give up your music. So what happens? One night at the dance, one of the boys brings along another sheila to make up the numbers for supper and the next thing you know she's looking at you sympathetically with big gooey eyes and you're telling her that your wife doesn't understand you. Oh Ron boy, I've seen it happen. Women and music, son, just don't mix! I'm telling you.'

He took a deep swig at the mug of coffee and we all sat silent, pondering the hazards of women and music. Ron suddenly stood up and pushed back his chair.

'Maybe you're right Leo. But Pat's different. She's wonderful …you just don't know. I know it'd be different with her. Think I'll go round to her place now and see if she's in…just gotta see her.'

He nodded goodnight to us and walked swiftly out of the café.

'Yeah,' said Leo drily. 'She's different. They always are.'

The next day, it was Christmas Eve and we'd promised to put in an appearance at the Pialba Diggers Dance. Someone told us it wouldn't be very good so we planned to move on after an hour to the Scarness dance. Our informant was right. There were hardly any men but plenty of girls and old folk sitting around the walls. The President of the Returned Soldiers League came to greet us and dumped us with his wife.

'Don't forget now, have some dances.'

'Heavens! We will if someone asks us,' rejoined Shirl hotly.

He said he'd fix that and, to our discomfiture, began to make the rounds of the men, soliciting someone to dance with us. Nobody was forthcoming and we stewed in embarrassment. We decided we couldn't stick it for even an hour and told the President we must be going shortly. He panicked and dragged us up to the stage to be introduced to the crowd. He bellowed trite remarks about 'brave girls' whilst we tried to look modest. Any comments we made were inaudible in the babble of voices in the hall. He concluded the interview by bawling 'I hope you have some dances girls!', intended I suppose as a reminder to the men to ask us. We went back to our seats and the Secretary and the Treasurer promptly came forward, primed to do their duty.

It was a Jolly Miller waltz and we changed partners, dancing with all the other men. Several times I was trapped with a bucktoothed, beer-sozzled youth who leered bloatedly over his teeth and convulsed me with laughter. I waited till Shirl got him, caught her eye and attendant look of misery and was completely broken up. Oh, the grisliness of it all! We made our excuses and were just creeping out the door when we were accosted by a man who directed at us a stream of high-pressure talk.

'You them two girls? Well listen, listen now! I'm a drover I am – from the Northern Territory, I know all that country, been everywhere. Now listen, you going up there, you need a water bottle, for crisake take a water bottle, take two water bottles or else you'll die. Now I *know*, I been there, my God you've no idea what you're heading into, you know I've wanted to meet you and just then I heard your names from the platform, I couldn't believe it, I've been wanting to talk to you all about it. Now which way are you going? Through Isa, Camooweal …well now listen! Don't you get off that bitumen road, there's a good bitumen road from Isa to Tennant Creek, don't get off that bitumen! For crisake don't get off that bitumen! I got off it once, wandered around for days – lost meself, but don't you get off that bitumen road and don't forget – take two water bottles!'

All this was delivered non-stop with short gasping breaths in between each sentence. He spoke with a slight American accent and was called 'Kansas'. He'd been a Digger and now he couldn't settle down so had gone to the Territory. We said we would take his advice then made our escape. We had ridden two hundred yards down the street when we heard pounding footsteps and muffled shouts behind us. Kansas was trying to catch up with us. We stopped and waited for him.

'Hey,' he panted. 'Give us a double into Scarness, will yer?'

A 'double' is Queensland idiom for a 'dink' which is Victorian slang for a lift on the back of a bike.

'Sorry, our tyres are too soft.'

He was holding the carriers of our bikes and the situation was becoming rather difficult when a bus came round the corner.

'There's a bus for you!' I called and as he turned to look, we spurred away leaving him standing in the middle of the road, still yelling: 'Don't forget, take two water bottles and don't get off that bloody bitumen!'

The Scarness hall was packed with a gay throng dancing to the infectious rhythm of the Ambassadors' music. Shirl was snapped up by a lad she knew and, as I stood out, someone nudged me and there was Kansas. My heart sank. He started talking again, the same words going on and on like a buzzing fly and I looked away in misery. To make it worse, the band started to play one of the latest hits, a sentimental tune called *I'll buy that dream* which Leo sang wonderfully. I tried to listen but the torrent of talk was still pouring into my ears. Just when I thought I should strike him, a girl nearby turned around and greeted Kansas. He transferred his attention to her. I collapsed with relief on a chair and heard the end of the song. It made me feel very lonely and homesickness enveloped me like a Melbourne fog. I had the next dance with Shirl's partner and after that a drunk shambled up and asked me. That was the last straw. I couldn't even talk to him civilly. He kept on saying 'Merry Christmas' to which I replied 'I'm not a bit merry', all the time becoming more and more miserable. I thought of *Carols by Candlelight* which would be in full swing in Melbourne now, the tremendous outdoor festival which my boss Norman Banks had originated nearly ten years before and which I'd worked on for the last three Christmases. I thought of the girls at work and my family and my boy friend Keith until my eyes started to prick with tears and my face began to pucker. I decided I couldn't see Christmas Day in amidst the rowdy throng so I sneaked away quietly and rode home. I let little Pete off his rope and as he jumped up joyously to lick my face, I burst into tears. As I kissed and petted him, the bells started ringing and in the distance I could hear muffled cheers and shouts. Our first Christmas away from home and, please God, the last.

Chapter 12

SUGAR COUNTRY

New Year's Day, 1947. Nearly nine months out from home and here we were, only as far as Bundaberg. Not that I was worried. Our time was our own and though we'd cheerfully estimated to be home for Christmas, it was obviously Christmas 1947 we'd meant. What did a year or two matter?

My Christmas Eve depression had vanished by morning and we'd had a wonderful time at the Bay with a festive dinner at Bowd's with a lot of holiday-makers, followed by music around the piano. A few days later we were riding comfortably on a truck from Maryborough to Bundaberg through thickly-wooded country. The road was very corrugated but we were reclining on mattresses under a green canvas awning which softened the glare of the sun and made the gumtrees and the dusty road look red and mauve. Childers township was lovely with lots of trees along the streets and then the country opened out into long, undulating fields of soft green cane laced with a red dirt road.

Our obliging truck driver dumped us on the outskirts of Bundaberg and, as we were tying on our packs, a welcoming carillon rang out. Just like the one at Bathurst, it rambled merrily through many familiar songs.

Two little boys stopped near us and speculated curiously on our business. When we told them we were going to Darwin, they just laughed derisively and wouldn't believe us. It was funny to see how, although they openly doubted us, they were only half certain and felt that maybe we were telling the truth. When one of them asked a question about the trip, the other would wheel on him and say 'Hey, you don't believe these gypsies do you? You're mad if you do!' They were sure we were gypsies and kept their distance.

Bundaberg! The very name has magic in it. It conjures up pictures of hot sun and wide fields of surging sugar cane, green and gold sugar cane, golden sugar, tons of sugar, vats of molasses, black and viscous, barrels of syrup, limpid amber and prosaically stacks of soft-board, the by-product obtained from the crushed cane fibres. The glorious enchantment of sugar country which had flicked its sensuous veils temptingly at us in Maclean, was now to be with us for nearly eight hundred more miles to the north. It was a delicious prospect. Nowhere but in sugar country does one experience that sapping lassitude, the sun-drenched languor and the relaxing sloweddown tempo of everyday life. The air is sweet and heavy with the cloying smell of molasses, the heavily-laden barges float idly down the Burnett River. Even the funny little sugar-trains pulling their trucks of towering cane potter unconcernedly through the plantations, the red earth bright beneath their rails, the cane fresh and springing behind them.

Yet Bundabergians are not lotus eaters. They still manage to produce at least one celebrity each generation. Bert Hinkler, Gladys Moncrieff and Don Tallon, bright stars in the Australian firmament, came from Bundaberg.

We stayed there a week enjoying hospitality from many people and tasting our first mangoes. What an astonishing fruit! Its flavour has been described as a combination of pear, peach, strawberry, plum, apricot and cream mixed with musk and honey, coriander and aniseed, smothered with the scent of musk roses and blended with cider! It is very difficult to eat mangoes gracefully as juice pours down one's fingers. We were told we should eat them in the bath.

During our stay we camped in a large church hall. One morning I got up at eight o'clock, (sleeping in wasn't fun any more when a blazing sun came up at six and made my sleeping-bag feel like an incubator), slipped on a frock and started playing the *Pathétique Sonata* on the piano. Suddenly the outside door opened and a gaunt old man entered. I heard a surprised little squeal and beheld Shirl, who had just emerged from her bag, cowering in her singlet and panties. Disregarding her, the man said: 'Stop playing that piano!'

I looked at him as though he were mad. 'Why?'

'You just stop playing that piano. That piano's not to be played!'

'But – why?'

'You're only here for a few days, aren't you?'

'Yes.'

'Well don't play that piano. That's to be kept for the church only. I'm one of the Trustees and I've got to see the place is kept properly.' (This with a horrified glance around the littered room. I fancy he shuddered.)

'But the minister gave us permission.'

'He's got nothing to do with it. He should've referred it to the Trustees. He's got no right to give you permission.'

He stumped out breathing heavily. Shirl and I exchanged certain pithy remarks.

Five minutes later as Shirl was standing at the sink in her singlet washing, we heard footsteps coming through the big hall to the connecting door. Shirl snatched up a towel and said: 'Don't come in!' whilst I rushed to guard the second door. We heard heavy footsteps tramping around the stage and I thought it might be a cleaner but Shirl had a peep and saw it was the same man in his flannel shirt and braces. She pulled on a frock and a few minutes later, in he marched again.

Shirl's lips narrowed. 'Er – would you please knock before you come in. We were dressing before.'

Quite unabashed, he said: 'I'm in charge of this place. Got to keep it in order.'

'Well, you still should knock before you enter.'

He ranted on about trying to keep the place clean and we told him we'd clean up before we left. He stalked across the room then swung round belligerently.

'I suppose you're using the gas-ring too!'

'Oh no,' said Shirl. 'We never cook.'

'Well, what's the teapot doing there!' he pointed triumphantly. (Shirl had boiled her hankies in it the day before.)

'We just heated some water yesterday but we don't use it habitually.'

'Huh!' he turned to me again. 'Didn't you see a notice on the piano saying it wasn't to be played?'

'No, there's no notice on it.'

He immediately sought other cause for complaint and pointed accusingly at Pete. 'That dog stay in here?'

'No, he's chained up outside all day.'

I tried to bring him back to the piano question and asked where was the notice but he wouldn't answer and strode away.

Queensland was in the grip of a crippling drought. The countryside was parched, the livestock in poor condition and the landowners desperate. Some spent large sums on the services of water diviners in their efforts to locate underground springs and on other stations the stock were driven out to find grass where they could. As the weather had been breaking behind us all the way up the east coast, we comforted the unhappy squatters and assured them the rain would soon come.

Between Bundaberg and Gladstone we had 144 miles of dusty road with only half a dozen tiny hamlets. We set off with our quart water bottles filled to the brim. It was a searingly hot day and the road was very hilly. When we were forced to walk the perspiration ran down our faces from the leather bands inside our wide hats and our shirts stuck to our backs. As soon as the road levelled out however, we jumped into the saddle and the windstream was deliciously cool. At one stage Shirl dropped behind by about half a mile so I sat down under a tree and waited for her. I drank some of my water and had a precious orange. When Shirl arrived she was nearly out of water so I gave her a few gulps from my flask. I punched a dent in the crown of my hat and poured some water into it for Pete. He drank greedily. There was no traffic going our way at all though plenty going to Bundaberg. We decided to hail the next vehicle and ask for water. A large truck approached with a pony in a cage on the back. The driver gladly gave us what fresh water he had, about half a flask each. Then he offered us food and we accepted as we didn't know how much longer we'd be on the road. Sitting at the side of the road we devoured some thick slices of bread and butter and a goodly hunk of corned beef, followed by some gingerbread. All the worst thirst-provoking foods! The driver lifted a five-gallon kerosene tin from the back of his truck.

'Look, I've got this full of water but I don't know what it tastes like. I only rinsed out the tin this morning and it still smells of kerosene.'

I tried it and it did taste of kerosene but we each downed a cupful with an effort before waving goodbye to our benefactor. The next vehicle was a car driven by a station owner. He had no water but told us not to worry about drinking what water we had as there was a windmill about a mile on where we could fill our flasks, have a wash and give Pete a swim. We hastened on joyfully and saw the vanes of the windmill through the trees a little way off the road. We leant our bikes against trees and walked across the paddocks to it, clutching flasks and pannikins..

I turned the tap of the tank and waited. Nothing happened. I knocked on the side of the tank and the iron boomed hollowly. Climbing up on the stand, I peered in the top of the tank. It was quite empty except for slime in the bottom. We looked at each other, speechless. It was 55 miles to the nearest settlement at Miriamvale and the full heat of noon was blazing down. At that moment, I felt a *frisson* of fear. We had often joked about hunger and thirst but this was it! We hadn't a drop of water and could think of nothing but how thirsty we were. I was thinking of long tapering glasses of icy lemon squash and lemonade, the glass wet and frosted.

'Oh for a three-glass, thick chocolate malted!' crooned Shirl. Little Pete whined and ran around in circles, sniffing.

And then a miracle happened. I felt a cool breeze on my damp forehead and, looking up, saw the trees stirring gently. Then I heard a strange creaking noise. The vanes of the mill began to turn slowly at first then faster and faster and began to pump water from the well. Shouting with relief, we grabbed our flasks and pannikins, stumbling in our anxiety to get to the inlet pipe. The receptacles brimming, we buried our faces in the cool liquid. It tasted peculiar.

'Ugh!' Shirl spat. 'I can't drink that, it's vile. It tastes of something bad …I can't think what.'

When I got a whiff of it, I recoiled in horror. It smelt of dead and decaying animals. Probably there was a carcase or two in the well.

Plunged in gloom again, we sat under a tree to have our 'heat of the day' rest. The heat was brittle and a curious silence lay in the air. The little breeze which had sprung up at our behest had died again. Massed on the north-west horizon were heavy black clouds.

'Thunder!' I shouted. 'We're going to have a magnificent storm!'

'Might be a false alarm,' said Shirl dubiously. 'We've been tricked before. Still, better be prepared.'

We put our bikes under the tree and unpacked rain capes and hoods. The clouds gathered for about a quarter of an hour then large drops began to fall. We donned our voluminous capes and draped the folds over our packs. Like patient cattle we stood mutely while huge rain belted down. Then came hail, hopping and bouncing off our bodies on to the ground. We opened our mouths to the sky and let the sweet water pour down our throats. Our pannikins, left out in the open, had an inch of water in them within ten minutes. When the storm had passed, we stretched our stiff limbs and took stock of the position. The ground was steaming. Pools of water lay everywhere. Little Pete crept out from beneath the tree, shook himself vigorously from his head all the way down to the tip of his tail then raced around ecstatically, lapping at puddles, leaping with renewed energy, dashing back to lick our wet legs.

Refreshed, we set out on the road again but after a few yards an ominous grating noise from the back of my bike indicated a flat tyre. I pumped it for a while to test it but the pump wasn't gripping and in a few seconds it came apart. Shirl's pump was packed at the bottom of her front pack and to get it she would have to unstrap Pete's box. She didn't want to do it but I couldn't go on without it. While we stood there fuming, a truck came our way. It was a timber truck with a long plank-like rear portion and the driver doubted if he could take us. As he was going all the way to Miriamvale, I assured him we had had lifts on these trucks many times before and soon we were perched on top. Off we raced over the muddy road. With great excitement we saw our first wild kangaroos bounding over a fence and away across a paddock. Several more appeared along the road. We flew past a herd of white-faced cattle ambling along the road, their drover slouched in the saddle, slapping at flies, his dogs circling the herd and urging on the beasts if they stopped to graze.

Also on our truck were two men hitchhiking around Australia and that night, at a vicarage, we met a Melbourne couple, Mr. and Mrs. Fletcher, who were caravanning through Queensland. I began to think all Australia was on the move. Mrs. Fletcher embarrassed us considerably by asking what we did for ministers in return for the privilege of sleeping in church halls.

'I just want to know if you've ever thought of it. (I hadn't) Everyone just bots on a minister because he *is* a minister and supposed to be a friend to the needy. Yet he's the lowest-paid public servant.'

She gave me pause for thought. I suppose we had been imposing on our benefactors although frequently we addressed their youth groups or Mothers' Clubs.

From Gladstone's meat works and steaming heat, it was a comparatively short hop to Rockhampton, the next big city. Riding in a truck, we saw dire evidence of the severe storm we had experienced. Every tree was damaged, branches scattered all over the ground, many trees snapped off half-way up the trunk and others uprooted. As a contrast to this wild scene, there were lovely lagoons covered with purple waterlilies and alive with flocks of ducks and swans. I dozed frequently and Shirl was reading *We of the Never-Never*, the Australian classic about the Northern Territory by Mrs.Aeneas Gunn. Once, as I half-opened my eyes, I saw a post whizzing by bearing the magical inscription:

TROPIC OF CAPRICORN

Temperate Zone   Torrid Zone

'STOP!'

My shriek brought the truck to a halt as the driver jammed on his brakes. The others stared at me as though I were mad.

'The line! The line!' I stammered excitedly. 'Get your camera Shirl!'

We always took a photo to commemorate the crossing of a State border but this was far more exciting. We tumbled out of the cab, combed our hair and stood in front of the post holding Pete while the driver took our photo. Then I placed Pete on the other side of the line.

'Well, little fella - how do you like the Tropics?'

We drove on, feeling very elated and very torrid.

Three miles from Rockhampton, we stopped at the Balmoral Hotel and the driver took us in to meet a friend of his.

'He's a terrible larrikin,' he said as we sat in the parlour waiting for lemon squashes. 'You'll probably see him without a shirt or shoes.'

When this singular man came in, he was wearing a shirt but no shoes. He settled down in a chair and after we'd sold him a magazine, he started talking.

'Shoes!' He snorted. 'Never wear them! Bad for your health! I reckon my pub's the most widely known one in Queensland. From Townsville to Brisbane everyone knows about the barefooted publican. Why, I was in Brisbane a few weeks ago and went into a barbershop. The barber caught sight of my lower half in a mirror and straight away said: 'Hullo, I bet Cope's in the shop!' See, naked feet!'

I was horrified. 'You don't go barefoot in the city, do you?'

'Why not? Cities aren't any different from towns. Shoes are only convention.'

I looked at him admiringly. I hated wearing shoes myself and short of bare feet, was only happy wearing the broad, strap sandals in which I rode.

'I used to be a butcher before I came here,' he continued, 'and one day a Health Inspector came in and ordered me to wear shoes. I refused. So he wrote to Brisbane. So did I and I got a letter back saying 'butchers must be fully clothed and wear an apron but shoes not being classed as clothing, it is not compulsory to wear them.' Did I have the laugh! Anyway, if they start splitting hairs about cleanliness, feet are much cleaner than shoes. I wash my feet several times a day and other people don't wash their shoes. If I dropped blood on my feet, I washed them but blood stays and dries on a boot. Filthy habit!'

After our driver had had several 'for the road', we set off and soon drove into Rockhampton. It was dark and the brilliantly lit streets and shopping centre looked lively. We were just wondering whether to find a home first or have something to eat when I said: 'Where's Pete?'

'Didn't you put him in the back?'

'No, didn't you?'

'We must've left him behind!' Shirl wailed.

We tortured ourselves with dreadful visions of Pete seeing us drive off without him. We imagined him trotting gamely after us only to be knocked down by traffic. We begged the driver to turn back. He wisely suggested we ring from the Post Office and see if he were at the pub. We did so and he was. The publican said he would bring him to Rocky next day. We had a great reunion then. Pete was frenzied with joy to see us.

We stayed in Rockhampton for a week, each day spent trudging wearily from shop to shop, from hotel to café, trying to earn enough money to carry us on to Mackay. By now we had devised a new form of advertising which we were to repeat profitably for the duration of the trip. On arrival in a new town we always went straight to the newspaper office to give our story to a reporter. Then we visited the local radio station, if any, and arranged an interview on air. When the newspaper came out next day we were instantly recognized. After appraising the various clothes shops in the shopping centre, we picked the most modern one – we could tell by the quality of its window dressing – and then sought out the manager.

'Good morning girls! What can I do for you?'

'We wondered if you'd like to use our names in your advertising. You know, only the best quality garments are suitable for us. They must be durable, hardwearing....'

'Yes,' he said. 'Sounds interesting. How much would you want?'

We looked modest and said we didn't ask for money but maybe he'd like to help us on our way with a small garment...a shirt, a pair of shorts....'

'Right,' he said. 'Run along and see Miss Smith in the Sportswear section.'

We wrote a testimonial which appeared in the next issue of the newspaper and departed with our new acquisitions. This proved very lucrative although, as we already had hard-wearing, indestructible shorts and shirts, we usually migrated to the better frocks department. If the dress were too expensive, we would either pay the difference or find something cheaper. The 'free garment' enterprise really came to fruition later as our expertise increased and our presentation improved.

During our stay in Rockhampton we were the guests of the proprietor of the Royal Hotel and it was through him we met Captain 'Skip' Moody, the owner of the Barrier Reef resort, Day Dream Island. Capt. Moody was a very tanned, grey-haired, slow-speaking man who talked to us of the beauties of his island. He said he would reserve a cabin for us if we telegraphed him when we expected to arrive. Shirl and I were delirious with excitement.

'Day Dream! It's the most attractive of all the islands, I believe. And we can see the Reef through glass-bottomed boats and swim and sail...and they have aquaplaning!'

'I wonder if he means us to come as guests? It'd cost a packet to go as tourists.'

'Yes, it's rather awkward. Still, we can't do anything about it now. We'll ask him about it later when we tell him we're coming.'

At towns along our route we occasionally found a Peters icecream factory and we always made time to visit it. There was one at Rockhampton.

Although we professed an interest in inspecting the works and learning about the manufacturing process, our ulterior motive was to sample the icecream! Not the frozen finished product but the heavenly molten stream which came out of taps on the great vats. During the war icecream production had been limited to vanilla flavour but now we were tempted by chocolate, strawberry, pineapple, passion fruit. The manager would produce two tumblers and fill them. We ate the delicious chilled cream with a spoon and then moved on to the next flavour. I could never decide which I liked best.

While in Rockhampton, we climbed Mount Archer one day and on another took the train for a trip to Yeppoon on the sea. We arrived at the station just as the train was leaving. The porter said to ride ahead and catch it at the next station. I looked at him incredulously but he was quite serious. The railway line in Rocky goes sedately down the middle of a street with no fence or barriers to separate it from other traffic. We rode off furiously and beat the train by four minutes.

At Yeppoon wonderful long ocean rollers came sweeping in to the beach in a flurry of white frothy foam. We set off along the road to Emu Park. Little Pete was running alongside and after a short distance we stopped so Shirl could lift him up on her pack for a rest. Suddenly she screamed.

'Wen! A tick! Pete's got a tick!'

We looked at each other in consternation. Our way north had been punctuated with notices, prominently displayed, setting out the various dangers which beset the traveller's path. There was a particularly frightening poster which told one everything about death adders, trapdoor spiders, black widow spiders, leeches and ticks. In each section were listed the symptoms and necessary treatment. In nearly every case the patient would turn blue and collapse. And now to think that Pete had a tick. We raced into a house and begged a little kerosene. I poured it over the tick which one must not pull out for fear the head will break off and remain buried in the skin. The tick dropped off and, greatly relieved, we continued on our way.

We had ridden about two miles when we saw a police patrol car approaching. It stopped and the two men started chatting to us about our trip. I told them we were trying to reach Emu Park but would never cover fourteen miles in this headwind. I laughingly suggested they turn around and take us there... it is so nice at Emu Park, surely they'd like to see it again? To my surprise, after a few seconds' discussion about how they'd get the sack if caught, they agreed. We strapped our bikes on the back and drove off along the pleasant sea road. Every now and then we passed groups of gaping campers and the police would mutter uneasily.

'Look, if you're reprimanded, why not say you picked us up for some minor offence – vagrancy or something?'

'What? And not charge you?' our driver grinned.

Out in the open bush again, one of them thrust the microphone into my hand and asked for a song. I racked my brains then burst into the Policeman's song from *The Pirates of Penzance*. Over the quiet bushland came the loud mournful assertion that 'a policeman's lot is not a happy one.'

At the beach we found a heavy surf running. I pitted my puny strength against the waves but couldn't get a shoot at all. I was merely whirled about, arms and legs flailing wildly and deposited on the beach, limp and exhausted after five minutes of it. We gave Pete a short swim in the shallows and roared with laughter at the way the undertow would draw him backwards while he was still swimming furiously towards the shore. On his face was a look of pained surprise when he couldn't make any headway.

-oOo-

The most wonderful thing had happened. Shirl burst out of the telephone booth, her eyes wide with excitement, to tell me about it.

'Mrs. Barrett would be delighted to have us come and stay at the Station for a while. She says to come on Saturday as her maid is away till Friday. My dear! Class and distinction! Ride our horses! Muster our cattle! Eat our cream!'

'Did she say that?'

'Well, not exactly but heavens, it's the biggest Station this side of the black stump. Oh, what heaven... horses, cream...!

'Cattle aren't quite the same as dairy herds, I don't think,' I said doubtfully.

'Well they *must* have some cows. Don't tell me they don't have their own butter and milk.'

'Mm...maybe. What else?'

In reply, she struck an attitude, heaved a deep sigh and looked dreamily into space. 'There is a son. An eligible son! And he's right there on the station. Moonlight horse rides...boat picnics, strolling by the river...'

'What, all three of us?'

She withered me with scorn. 'No fear! I bags him.'

'Ha! What about me?'

'You can talk to Mrs. Barrett.'

Saturday found us waiting at the tiny shop which served as general store and Post Office to the surrounding district. We were just trying to wheedle the postmark from the postmaster when a man of about thirty-five came up to us, smiling.

'I don't think you'll be able to get the stamp but let me introduce myself. My name's Paddy Barrett.'

So this was the eligible son! He was pleasant and friendly but too old! I didn't dare look at Shirl. I could sense her crest falling.

'Would you like to ride on ahead? I have to wait a bit longer for another visitor...a doctor's son from town. Please yourself.'

I whispered to Shirl. 'You can have Paddy. I'll have the doctor's son!'

'No no Wen, I've always wanted to marry a doctor.' She turned to Paddy. 'All right, we'll go on but pick us up if you pass.'

We followed a dirt road which wound through wooded country, over a dry river-bed, between paddocks and up a steep climb with the homestead at the top. Mrs. Barrett came out to greet us.

She was a gracious lady of about sixty with short grey hair and an aquiline nose. After refreshing us with iced drinks, she took us on an inspection of the house.

It was the original homestead which had stood there for over a hundred years. The beautiful timber of which it was built was spiked as nails were not available then and the roof, now made of iron, had originally been shingled. In the lounge was a great fireplace with a huge tapestry screen standing in front of it, flanked by a massive brass wood-box, fender and fire-irons. Comfortable green and gold brocaded chairs and sofas with gold cushions stood about the room and the long windows were shaded with green

Venetian blinds and green and gold curtains. A fine piano stood against one wall and in the corner was a large glass cabinet full of lovely plates, Chinese porcelain and silver. On the walls were other tapestries, brass and wooden plaques and a great Chinese Buddha occupied the end of the room.

Along the verandah next to a small office was Mrs. Barrett's room. It was most luxurious and furnished in blue and gold. There was a blue wall-to-wall carpet and a blue bedspread. Over the head of the bed was a gold canopy in which the mosquito net was concealed when not in use. The dressing table was covered with chased silver brushes, combs, mirrors and trinket jars. From this room opened the bathroom, small but modern, and a spare bedroom.

Back on the verandah, next to Mrs. Barrett's room, was Paddy's which featured dark wood and pink and burgundy furnishings. Around the corner of the verandah was the dining room. Down the middle of the room ran a long, glass-topped table of dark wood. It was set with crisp linen place-mats, napkins and centrepiece, gleaming silver, long-stemmed crystal goblets, beautiful china plates and tea service. Around the table stood high-backed chairs heavily carved. In front of the yawning fireplace stood a great Chinese gong suspended on a black wooden frame. Mrs. Barrett told us it was looted from a Chinese temple by one of her ancestors in 1846 during the Boxer Rebellion. Standing in one corner was an 1820 grandfather clock.

We then came to our room. It was rather small but beautiful with a colour scheme of deep vieux rose. The bed was made up with pink sheets, blankets and quilt topped with a heavy brocade spread. A rose canopy with a rose mosquito net billowed above. There were rose curtains and carpet and dark red plum furniture to match the timbered walls and sloping ceiling. Everything was tastefully prepared for us. Some travel books and a few digests were on a bedside table, two thick soft towels for each of us (a pink face towel and a white bath towel) were on a rail; on the washstand were a ewer of water and basin, two cakes of soap and two stiff white linen hand towels, a pink jug of drinking water and tumblers. I looked around helplessly for somewhere to dump my battered, dust-laden haversack.

Mrs. Barrett tactfully offered us a bath and explained the procedure.

'We are having a dreadful drought, you know, so we have to use river water instead of tank water for all our washing. Come to the kitchen when you're ready and I'll give you a tin of boiling water from the stove, then fill a kerosene tin with cold water from the garden tap. It's a wretched nuisance but the best we can do in the circumstances. There are only a few water holes left in the river now and they won't last much longer.'

We joined her at the window and looked down to where a sinuous silver river coiled at the foot of a cliff. A few hundred yards lower down we could see where the water petered out, choked with weed.

I fetched water for a bath and revelled in the soft warm water then stepped out and disappeared into the snowy depths of my towel. I put on a clean dress and joined Mrs. Barrett where she sat on the cool verandah in a quaint Chinese basket chair with a back like a peacock's tail.

'Before we left town this morning, I met a young lad of about sixteen who said he was coming out to the station to work. Who would that be?'

'Oh, that's young Bob Wilson, Dr. Wilson's son,' Mrs. Barrett said. 'He's coming for a few weeks to help Paddy. Paddy's bringing him home this afternoon with Violet my maid and two stockmen.'

Shirl and I exchanged hilarious glances and when we had a moment alone I said to her: 'I'll be big! You can have Paddy *and* the doctor's son. I'll have the two stockmen.'

'You're taking a big chance.'

'Maybe, but chances are better than certainties.'

They weren't any better, it transpired, for when we helped wash the dishes afterwards, we met the newcomers. They were young too and fairly dull. I gave up the unequal struggle and Shirl resigned herself to the marked attentions of Paddy. He was definitely smitten and at night, when Shirl and I had retired to the luxurious depths of our soft bed with the mosquito net enveloping us like a pink cloud, we built extravagant castles in the air featuring Shirl as châtelaine of the station and I coming up to see her for holidays. The only trouble was his age but then Shirl liked older, more mature men and the thought of horses, an aeroplane and the gracious homestead was certainly tempting.

'They're either too young or too old,' I sang. *'They're either too grey or too grassy green...'*

A more crushing disappointment was the absence of cows and riding horses. The drought was so severe that all the livestock had been turned out to fend for themselves. Only three horses had been retained for the stockmen. One day we drove with Paddy to a paddock where a bore had been sunk. Each day he had to pump enough water to fill a long trough for the cattle who came here to drink. As we waited for the trough to fill, Paddy told us how a water-diviner had chosen seven locations in this paddock. They had unsuccessfully bored six of them and were nearly giving up hope when, on trying the seventh, they struck this wonderful stream only fifteen feet down. We were seized with enthusiasm to try divining for ourselves and tried to trace the flow of the stream across the paddock. The air grew thick with accusations of cheating as one or other of us managed to achieve a vertical forked stick. We found it could be faked merely by relaxing one's fingers slightly. Paddy then did some wonderful gumleaf whistling for us. We were speechless with admiration but although he told us how to do it and procured the right sort of leaves for us, we were unable to produce a sound.

After lunch we helped Paddy wash up and introduced him to the mystery of our dishmop which we'd been carrying since Kosciusko. So often did we enjoy private hospitality and naturally helped our hostess clean up after meals, that we had invested in our own washing-up mop. Neither of us could bear to use a cloth to clean the dishes and, if we perceived that our hostess had no mop, we would be struck by a sudden thought.

'Oh, you should have one of those mops on a handle! Just a minute and I'll show you.'

Ours would then be produced and used throughout the duration of our stay when it would be packed back into the haversack.

As we helped Paddy with the dishes, little Pete amused us by zooming through the kitchen, out into the yard, playing with Mick the big cattle dog then leaping the step and tearing back to us. Suddenly there was a terrific screech, (I thought at first it was the cry of one of the beautiful peacocks which strutted around the garden), and a thunderbolt flew through the kitchen and up the hall to the diningroom. It was Peter going for his life, yelping and crying piteously. We dropped our towels and raced after him, through the diningroom and around the verandah to the office. He continued to howl with pain and with a shock we saw blood running from his snout and lower jaw. Spots of blood were splattered over the floor. We were nearly in tears. I rushed to get a rag and asked Paddy to come and look. We thought he might have knocked out a tooth but Paddy examined him and said that Mick must have bitten him on the snout, both the upper and lower jaws being wounded. We wiped the blood away and tried to comfort the little dog. He crept into our room and lay in a quiet corner, very still and sick. In an hour he was quite unrecognizable. He had a large swelling under his jaws which made him look just like a pelican and another on his snout near his eye. Instead of his clean-cut, intelligent features, he was a puffy mess. I couldn't bear to look at him, he was so ugly. He was very docile all afternoon, sleeping fitfully, snuffling the blood in his nostrils as he breathed.

Mrs. Barrett had announced that we would have some music that evening so after tea we heard her playing the piano and went into the sitting room, discreetly armed with our diaries. I didn't dare open mine but during items Shirl, taking advantage of her position slightly behind Mrs. Barrett, wrote furiously. At the end of each piece, she shut her book and leant back, looking dreamily at the ceiling.

Next day we settled down to mending, washing, letters and other chores while we waited for Peter to recover. The swellings on his head had slightly abated but he slept quietly all day.

'Listen to this Wen!'

Shirl read me an extract from a newspaper. It was about a new method of delivering babies called Natural Childbirth, propounded by a man called Grantly Dick Read. He maintained that ignorance bred fear, fear caused tension of the muscles and tension caused pain. An understanding of the stages of labour together with relaxation and correct breathing could eliminate much of the trauma of childbirth.

'What would a man know about it!' said Shirl in disbelief.

I couldn't believe it either but six years later I embraced his principles with fervour.

In the afternoon Bob, one of the stockmen, burst in to tell us that all the horses were in the yard now if we wanted a ride. He had been agitating on our behalf all the week. We raced to the yard and Shirl mounted a beautiful chestnut. Digging her heels into its side, she trotted off and we saw her galloping rapidly away in the distance. Mrs. Barrett and Paddy were greatly concerned for her safety, Paddy standing a little apart, his face pale and drawn, his eyes straining to follow the disappearing rider but I reassured them and told them she'd practically been reared in the saddle. Actually, she hadn't had much riding experience and no tuition at all but her fearlessness enabled her to ride any horse. My mount was more docile and had the most comfortable canter of any horse I have ever ridden. Riding it was like sitting in an armchair. Instead of thumping about in the saddle, I just sat motionless and the horse moved under me. It was a wonderful feeling.

That was our last night at the Station. We felt rather melancholy at the thought of leaving the security and comfort of the homestead and heading for the unknown again. It was terribly hot in bed and I couldn't sleep so I got up to look at the night. Shirl came too and we sat on the step of our room in our underwear. There was a full moon and the night was radiant. The sky was thick with stars and the moonlight poured down on the sleeping Station, investing the palm trees with tropical magic. Near our door, suspended between the roof and a large bush were too huge cartwheel spiderwebs, each about three feet in diameter. These shone and glistened in the moonrays and everything was as light as day.

Chapter 13

PEDDLING NOT PEDALLING

On our road map of Queensland we were appalled to find warning signs printed along the coastal road. *Sandy, Submerged in wet season, Corrugated surface* finally gave way to a despairing *Advise truck car* over the 240 mile Rockhampton to Mackay stretch. We decided that heroics were all very well but where there was a train we'd use it. The only trouble was that it would cost us twenty-five shillings each for a ticket plus bike and dog tickets. Having worked hard in Rockhampton we were more financial than usual.

It was noon and the Stationmaster was in a great panic for fear we'd keep the train waiting. We had to unload the gear from our bikes, attach labels to everything, stow it in the luggage van and tie Pete up in the animal cage. During the journey I read several copies of *Tribune* which my sister Noel had sent me and when finished, I threw them out of the window to groups of rail workers shouting 'Pi-per! Piper!' They were asking for newspapers which passengers would throw to them when finished. In this way they would get the latest paper within a few hours of publication.

At St. Lawrence Shirl rushed off to feed Pete who was very lonely and bewildered in a small cage with a towering greyhound on each side of him. I dashed away to get the postmark but learned that the Post Office was a mile away. I got a stamp from the Stationmaster instead.

Up to St. Lawrence the land had been dry and brown with dead trees and empty creeks but after leaving it we passed through lovely wooded country surrounded by hills, crossed innumerable rivers and deeply-cleft gorges and some salt plains. We saw plenty of wallabies and at seven o'clock, as dusk was falling, saw our first troop of flying foxes in Queensland, rising in a cloud from the trees where they had been roosting all day, hanging upside down like old black umbrellas.

At eight o'clock we reached Mackay and, loading up, rode into the town. It looked lovely, clean and modern. We went straight to the Tourist Café where Mr. Malos, a genial Greek, gave us icecream and a superb malted milk. Then we went in search of the Church of England. It was most impressive, built in a Spanish Mission style of architecture with a huge hall just as big and a pretty residence nestling among palms and frangipani trees. The minister, Archdeacon Robinson, and his wife insisted we spend the night in their home.

The next day was beautifully warm with a fresh breeze. We were most impressed by the town which had lots of trees and nature strips planted down the streets. It was no use our hanging around enjoying ourselves, there was work to do! We went to see the Malvern Star manager, Mr. Mullen, who took us to the *Mercury* office to give our story. It took one and a half hours as a very keen reporter wanted every detail. After a lunch of three icecreams on a plate with pear and banana sliced over them, we went to the Museum to see Mr. Williams, Manager of 4MK radio station. He gave us a lengthy harangue on the life and habits of crocodiles, spiders and snakes that we might meet on the trip. Perhaps he saw we were looking rather apprehensive because he quashed all the wild stories people had been telling us and said we probably wouldn't see a crocodile or a snake.

Off we went to meet the Mayor, Ian Woods, a pleasant man very proud of Mackay. He had made it what it was despite a lot of small town opposition. He told us about beauty spots to visit and then turned serious.

'You'll have to be careful girls, you'll be running into the wet season soon.'

'What do you mean, rain?' I asked. 'There's been a drought everywhere we've been but rain always seems to follow us.'

'No, not rain. The WET! The monsoon season. That's not just rain, it's rain such as you've never seen. It'll rain for six weeks without stopping. The roads will be covered, the Burdekin river will be flooded, you won't be able to go anywhere!'

I raised my eyebrows at Shirl. We'd have to deal with the Wet when it happened.

We next met a local character, Alec McColl, who was organizing the imminent Australia Day celebrations. Mr.Woods had told us 'He is an old bush teacher, untidy, jovial, a well-known local identity.' He proved to be so and was tickled pink at our offer to ride in the procession through the town on the Monday holiday. He promptly invited us to a boxing display on Friday night, an A.N.A. banquet on Saturday night, a sports meeting at Eimeo beach on Sunday, a concert on Sunday night as well as the celebrations on Australia Day. He was very perturbed by our homeless state (we had only sought shelter with the Archdeacon as it was late when we arrived) and after driving us around the town in his rattletrap of a car, suddenly smote his thigh.

'I've got it! The Victoria Park School. The headmaster hasn't gone away.'

We found the headmaster, Mr. Fudge, watering his garden. He was very helpful, drove us to the school and showed us a room where we could sleep. We went to the station to get our suitcases of good clothes then back to the Vicarage to collect our gear and Peter and moved into the school. It was funny to see the Archdeacon, dressed in a long dust coat and driving gloves like an Edwardian chauffeur, lugging our haversacks on his back.

We left Pete playing with the cleaning woman and continued our round of the commercial establishments, selling our books and looking for a sponsor for our broadcast interview. We did excellent business with the books but the managers of the various shops were away on holiday or out. Then we met Mr. Comino, manager of a dress salon, who said he wasn't interested in advertising; he only had a small advertisement for a second shop featuring men's wear, sandals and so on. Sandals! We told him that we always wear them and people know we wear them so it would be very pertinent. We won him over and he gave us each a pair. I exulted as my old ones were past repair.

On Saturday night we dressed in the unaccustomed finery from our suitcases and went off to the A.N.A banquet. (A.N.A. stands for Australian Natives Association. It has nothing to do with the aborigines but was originally intended for white Australians born in the country. It was a very vocal and influential organization.) There were only a couple of other women there and we were introduced to all the men. In between courses of the meal speeches began. The first man made an excellent speech on 'The day we celebrate'. He seemed to be a Labor man and spoke about democracy, the Eureka Stockade and so on. After him a doctor spoke with veiled allusions to Russia and Communism. There were lots of toasts (for which I consumed large quantities of gassy, soft drinks) and the evening wore on. At one stage we toasted the Friendly Societies present – Masons, Caledonians, Buffaloes, Maltese – and one by one the representatives of these groups acknowledged the toast. When they had finished I stood up and thanked the A.N.A. for the privilege of attending and said that many people wanted to know why we were travelling. Was it a publicity stunt or what? No, we had always wanted to travel and particularly wanted to see our own country and benefit from contacts with our own people before we went abroad. At 10.30 Mr. McColl gave his speech. It was a rollicking, interesting picture of the 'hurly' days of the pioneers.

That was the end of the proceedings and we left to go to the dance at the Majestic. There was a large crowd and the air was made breathable by great swinging punkahs. I went up to speak to the trombonist in the band whom I had met before. He insisted I play a bracket so I did *Darktown Strutters Ball*, *Some of these Days* and *Alexander's Ragtime Band*. Shirl met a young man who accompanied us back to the school. I went into the classroom and left Shirl chatting to the man on the verandah. However I realized I couldn't go to the lavatory without going past the verandah so I just sat and waited for Shirl to come in. I played all sorts of songs on the piano to embarrass her... *Just a little love, a little kiss, L'amour toujours l'amour, Girls were made to love and kiss* (I knew she loathed this), *When Irish eyes are smiling* (he had an Irish name), *If I should fall in love again* and so on. Apparently it all went over her head as she could hardly hear the piano.

The next day we were driven to the beach at Eimeo by two young reporters from the *Mercury* and passed along a wonderful avenue of mango trees, old and shady, densely cool. We emerged from that and saw another avenue of lofty coconut palms, graceful and wind-blown, straight off a tourist brochure. All around the small settlement was dense vegetation. From the top of a nearby hill we saw a magnificent panorama of sea and islands and looking inland, the thick luxuriant mangoes and palms looked like a tropical island.

At two o'clock we went to the sports meeting where a large crowd had gathered. Shirl entered a lady's race and won it, winning three shillings. I suggested we enter the Siamese (three-legged) race and we won that. (Only two shillings prize). And so back to Mackay for the concert in the evening. I had not expected much in the way of talent but there were some very good items before we were ushered on stage for an interview.

Australia Day public holiday was on Monday. We didn't wake till half past eight and in a great panic dressed and decorated our bikes with streamers. We strapped on half our normal load and at ten o'clock raced into the town to the assembly point of the procession. We took up our position in front of a brass band, turned round and set off without a breather. It was extremely hot and my face was flaming and running with perspiration. Our bush hats, though shady, prevented evaporation from the scalp. Motor bikes preceded us and we followed at a respectable distance. Most of the crowd was in Victoria Street where we received a great ovation. Pete was riding on Shirl's bike, sitting up in his box and looking around, master of all he surveyed, like an emperor! I'd tied a blue bow around his neck and he created a sensation. The sun beat down mercilessly and at one stage when we'd got way ahead of the band, we raced into a shop and got an icecream then continued to the Showgrounds. Two circuits of the arena followed. We met our two reporter friends and went up in the press box with them to watch the events.

The Woorabindi Settlement aborigines then gave a display of corroboree, boomerang throwing and spear throwing. Afterwards, to our delight, we were each given a boomerang although we couldn't make them come back. (I remembered the old joke about the aborigine who wanted a new boomerang but couldn't throw the old one away!)

By now I was very attracted to one of the reporters, Allan. He reminded me so much of my Melbourne boyfriend Keith. He was musical, intelligent, even intellectual. He liked the same music as I and then I discovered he was into poetry. He even knew about *Meanjin Papers*, a periodical containing contemporary Australian poetry and he offered to lend me his Oxford Book of Verse. That made him perfect. Keith, I reckoned, had no 'soul'.

That evening, dressed in our best dresses, we went to the big dance. I had several dances with Allan. He, like Keith, had been in the Navy and like most sailors was a wonderful dancer. It was unbelievably hot and my good dress was soaked from neck to waist.

I saw Allan again the next night when he called to take us to see *The Man in Grey* with wonderful James Mason and divine Stewart Grainger. I was playing the *Pathétique Sonata* when he arrived and then switched to some Fats Waller pieces and *Sunrise Serenade*. Then he hummed a few bars of the Grieg *Piano Concerto* and said 'What's that?' This was Keith's and my song. I couldn't get over the similarities between them.

He produced the Oxford Book of Verse and then we started a discussion about Australian poetry and the Jindyworobak Club. My cup of happiness overflowed when he asked if I'd read any of James Devaney's poems.

'Devaney!' I replied in near ecstasy and began to quote from

Dedication, The Bunyip and *Dirrawan the Song Maker*. He said he knew Devaney who lived in Brisbane and was a wonderful chap. I told him about Shaw Neilson, the lyrical Australian poet and produced my books, *New Song in an Old Land* and the Methuen *Anthology of Verse*. We discussed our favourites, Rubert Brooke, Yeats and Edward Thomas. I felt as aesthetically satisfied as I did after a jazz session.

Then came the thunderbolt. He said: 'I got myself engaged just before I came up here.' Shirl expressed surprise and congratulations while I forced a sickly smile as my heart froze.

'Yes, it happened on New Year's Eve.'

He went on talking about her. He had frequently mentioned her but only as 'the girl I run around with in Brisbane.' I felt crushed and couldn't believe it. I guess I'd allowed myself to become pretty keen. He was everything I'd always wanted in a man. After that, although we still saw the boys, the atmosphere had changed. I felt constrained and tried not to show any interest in him.

The school term was about to start and we had to find another home. We had finished all our work in Mackay but before setting off north we thought we'd like to see the Eungella Range. The Methodist minister agreed to let us stay at his church on our return from the mountain. We therefore started sorting and packing our gear into three categories. Stuff that always went ahead by rail in our suitcases, things which normally went in our haversacks but wouldn't be going to Eungella and a small amount of gear to take to the mountain.

We'd heard of a milk truck that could take us at noon. We didn't wake until ten and then feverishly finalized our packing, cleaned the classroom and ladies cloakroom and rode into town. I collected mail from the Post Office while Shirl rode off to the dairy. She returned to report that the truck wouldn't be leaving till 1pm so we had a malted milk for lunch and bought egg and tomato sandwiches for the journey. Back at the dairy there was still no sign of the truck. We sat down and ate our sandwiches. At 1.30 the truck came but the driver said he wouldn't be leaving till four. We sat and wrote letters and diary. The truck returned at four but the driver said he wouldn't be going till six o'clock! We rode back into town, bought some fish and chips to eat on the way then loaded our gear onto the back of the truck and clambered up ourselves. There were about thirty empty cream cans piled in higgledy-piggledy and we perched precariously on them. Rain had been threatening all day so we took precautions. Dragging our haversacks near us we donned our capes.

It was a delightful trip through Playstowe and Marian. The sky was lowering and the pale green canefields were the only vivid splash of colour. I lay back and dozed until we came to the end of the bitumen and drove onto an unbelievable road...lurching down creek banks, splashing through water, bumping over areas of boulders, dodging fallen limbs, ducking under low-hanging branches.

Then came the rain. We put on our hoods, arranged our capes to cover the gear and huddled in the downpour. At Netherdale we started to climb. It was impossible to sit firmly on the wet, rolling cans and all I could do was hang on grimly while I was bumped about. Little Pete cowered dejectedly under my cape, hemmed in by heavy cans. The road was very steep and precipices yawned at our side. Through the valleys wormed long snakes of mist, giving credence to the legend of Eungella, Mountain of Mist. It was so eerie, climbing up in the darkness surrounded by clammy cloud, like Walpurgisnacht.

At 9.15 we reached Dalrymple Heights and stopped outside the Guest House. We had a letter to the owner and she showed us a room which we could use under the house. It was very bare and cellar-like with a cold stone floor and fibrolite walls but it was a home.

Next morning it was still raining steadily. Everyone said the Wet had started. I walked along to the shop and bought bread and cheese then came back and sat in our dark room. I started to write a poem about the Legend of Eungella, inspired by James Devaney, Mary Gilmore, Rex Ingamells and other Australian poets who acknowledged the aboriginal heritage in their poems.

Next day Shirl went out in the rain to get provisions at the store. She came back bubbling with news.

'It's raining from here to Brisbane, the Burdekin River's in flood already and the trains can't cross. The cream man doesn't think he'll be going down tomorrow if the rain continues.'

Trapped! We had seen nothing of the mountain but decided we'd leave that afternoon, hike down the road to Netherdale and get the train at six o'clock next morning. A little later however, we heard from the truck driver that he'd probably be able to get down the next day. So time dragged on.

The kind proprietress offered us lunch and we repaid her by helping with the washing up in the kitchen. I played the piano for the guests. It was still raining when we went to bed.

At 10.30 next morning we loaded our haversacks onto the truck. The rain fell in sheets. We clambered up and sat on the cream cans which were now full and didn't roll around as before. Gathering our gear about us, we spread our capes wide and huddled in this position for three and a half hours. I nursed Pete under my cape most of this time.

The trip to the foot of the mountain was accomplished safely and slowly though we saw a few boulders which had rolled down. Every now and then a leaping cataract splashed across the road. From Netherdale to Mackay practically all the land was submerged. I'd never seen so much water. The truck was forging through inches, sometimes a foot, of water and the bridges at Cattle Creek and Pioneer River were awash. It was very exciting. We thought we wouldn't be able to get through but we reached Mackay at 2.30pm.

Our position was desperate. We'd had plenty of time to think while bouncing around on the truck. We had finished our business in Mackay and should have been moving on but if the roads and rivers to the north were impassable, we'd have to stay in Mackay. To do that, we'd have to find other work.

After moving into the Methodist hall, we started looking right away. We tried the Child Welfare Centre but they didn't need anyone. We went to the Civic Theatre in the hope of becoming usherettes but there were no vacancies. We asked at two separate photographic shops to see if we could get a job tinting photos (a skill learned in Brisbane) but business was slow. We asked the Mayor, the Malvern Star manager and several policemen about jobs. They said they'd keep an eye out for us. We trailed home, wet and dejected. In the church hall we found a box of cakes, evidently the remnants of the Ladies' Guild afternoon tea. We waited until 7pm in case an owner arrived but as no one did we ate them, our consciences salved.

Next day we boiled up our filthy, damp and mouldy towels and handkerchiefs in the copper and washed blouses, skirts and jumpers. Our clothes were beginning to acquire the sickening stench of mildew and our cotton frocks were speckled with black. Our shoes were white with mould.

'Heavens knows when they'll dry,' said Shirl, 'but at least they're clean.'

Going into town at 2pm we bought papaw and bananas to have with icecream for lunch but the Tourist Café was shut until 3. Shirl decided to have a cheap 1/3d meal at a canteen in the street whilst I bought a piece of fish for sixpence. I rejoined her at the canteen where she was tucking into soup, pie and peas and potato with slices of roast beef and coffee. I ate my fish avidly.

At the opposite counter was a young, darkly handsome chap, obviously drunk, unshaven and in working clothes. He was truculently upbraiding a fat waitress for her incivility in not speaking to him. We were slightly amused and when he saw us watching, he left his seat and came around to our side, getting between Shirl and me and enlisting our sympathies against the serving staff.

'The old man – he's all right – good bloke. The missus (gesture of curling the mo'), the fat one…(holding his nose and spreading his hands downwards), the other one… not so bad.'

Then he gave us a lecture on the cheapness of civility and how, when the Yanks were here, it was a different story. The fat one then was all 'Ohhhhhhh'. Garn, the fat trollop!

We felt uneasy as the girls were looking at us but he kept on talking. Somehow or other he got onto the subject of a freak bull he'd exhibited once. I interrupted and proudly boasted of our Ferdinand in Tasmania whereupon, seeing as we'd been in the Show business, he began to enlarge on the peculiar qualities of this bull. He lowered his voice and said 'Y'see, it was both a bull and a heifer. Now you don't believe me! Well, it was a proper bull with two stones and a penis…(horrified blushes from us, noting which he said 'Well, you said you'd been in the Show business') and yet it had four teats.'

We evinced professional interest and sought to change the subject. He asked did we know anyone in the Show business and Shirl said brightly that we knew Sam the Boxer (fictitious!). No, he couldn't say he knew him but he'd made pots of money out of his bull.

-oOo-

We continued job hunting. Woolworths might have a vacancy next week. Penneys said trade was slack with no one coming to town. A woman might want me to play the piano for her dancing class. We tried a couple of chemist shops without luck. At Armati's the boss had just been brought a basket of freshly-picked mushrooms. What a great idea! We could go picking over the weekend and sell them around the shops.

'With the paddocks all under water?' said practical Shirl.

However the idea rang a bell somewhere in my mind.

The Employment Office had nothing to offer us. Dear Mr. Malos at the Tourist Café promised to take us on if his business picked up soon. Someone said Taylor's hotel had some vacancies so we rushed around there but they only wanted a barmaid. We were vastly amused at the prospect. What would Mrs. Duncan say! At another hotel the proprietress thought she could get Shirl a job mending sheets. She'd let us know. There were two advertisements in the paper, one for someone to do children's sewing and one for a girl to do light household duties. We trailed home in the rain and sat down to answer them.

Next day we tried the Harbour Board and Michelmore's with no success. Whilst cudgelling my brains for other lucrative ideas, I remembered a man in Bathurst a year before saying: 'In times of depression, you can always make money out of people's needs or their vanity. Food, haircuts, clothes or photographs. People have to eat and clothe themselves. Hair grows constantly and has to be cut. Parents always want pictures of their children before they grow up.'

My mind explored the possibilities. People have to eat. Office workers didn't want to go out into the pouring rain to get food. Why not take it to them? We could start a Cyclists' Sandwich Service. I suggested it to Shirl and she was enthusiastic. We began planning. We'd experiment tomorrow. Butter was rationed but we could use our own and continue if it were a success. We ordered bread for the next day and bought butter, cheese, ham, lettuce, onions, tomatoes, Vegemite and greaseproof paper then went around several offices preparing the ground.

Next morning we sliced the ingredients and rode to the baker's. The bread was steaming hot from the oven. We tried to get it sliced at Penney's but it crumbled so we took it to Zaglas's who had a wider gauge on their cutting machine. (There was no sliced bread then.) We sped home and started making the sandwiches. There was a great panic as we were supposed to deliver some to the Post Office and Michelmore's at 10.00am and it was already 9.30. We wrapped the sandwiches in greaseproof paper (there was no such thing as Cling Film or Glad Wrap) and packed them in a cardboard carton strapped on the front carriers of our bikes. With our capes spread over them, we rode out into the deluge. Beneath our capes we wore only shirts, shorts and sandals. It was easier to dry skin than clothes in 100% humidity.

The Supervisor of telephonists at the Post Office took only one sandwich instead of the six she'd ordered. We sold six at Michelmore's and got orders for more. After a few more offices we had sold our first batch of

thirty and rode home to cut more.

There we found a letter from the headmaster of the school where we'd camped the previous week. He said he was very disappointed that we had not left the school as we'd found it. The two mattresses from the reclining chairs had to be sent to the drycleaner (ten shillings) and Mrs. Mullens had to be hired to scrub the verandah and room again (ten shillings). Of course he expected us to meet these costs.

We looked at each other in dismay. The money part of it was bad enough. Where was it to come from when it was doubtful whether our sandwich trade would make a profit. But the shame and humiliation of it! We'd betrayed his confidence in us.

Shirl rallied. 'This is a test. The first day of a new enterprise is always harrowing.'

We determined to rise above all the setbacks. Desperately we made more sandwiches for the lunch rush, eyes streaming from slicing onions and, just as we were about to set out, discovered Peter wasn't around. A man had seen him pursuing a cyclist towards town. We dropped everything and raced off, imagining him under the wheels of the town traffic. We combed the streets and finally found him. By now it was half past one, we'd missed the lunch rush and had two boxes of sandwiches on our hands. Oh desolation!

We trailed around all afternoon trying to get rid of them. We went to the Dairy Company and the Steam Laundry and sundry offices. We got orders from the Government offices in the Court House for the next week and sold our last few to a couple of aborigines and a knot of men on a corner. Then there was a rush to buy provisions for the next day before riding home worn out.

I grabbed pen and paper and did the accounts. We had spent 11/4½d on ingredients and made approximately 25/- so we were in profit but out of that we had to pay £1 to the headmaster. All in all, it was a depressing day.

There was another problem. Butter was still rationed and we'd used up our own supply. I sent an urgent letter to the Rationing Commission asking for an extra quota of butter. If they didn't agree our service would peter out on Monday.

That night we were in the Tourist Café waiting for a sudden burst of rain to abate when a man joined us. He was about 44 and slightly drunk. He kept us convulsed with laughter especially when relating the story of a film he'd seen two nights ago.

'It was all about this lad who loved horses and he loved this girl, right?'

'Ah yes,' Shirl said profoundly. 'Young love. Isn't it beautiful.'

'Swunnerful,' he said. 'Young love. My wife and I remember.'

He digressed to tell us about his wife and kids then returned to the film.

'In the end, he loved the girl better than the horses.'

'Ah,' I sighed, 'true love triumphed.'

'Oh it was lovely. Young love and horses. That's what my wife said about it....young love and horses.'

'Ah yes, young love and horses, wonderful thing,' we reiterated several times and left him.

-oOo-

We had to move out of the church before Sunday and Mr. McColl came up trumps. He had a friend, a vet called Gennrick, who had a spare room we could use. We moved all our stuff round to his house where he and his 24-year-old daughter made us welcome. He reminded me of my brother Geoff, heavily built, balding, with an explosive way of speaking. It was wonderful to have a kitchen to work in and to have a day off on Sunday.

Monday was awkward as we had to wait till the bread was baked and then it was too hot to slice. Some of the sandwiches were like doorsteps, but at 10 o'clock we left with thirty wrapped bundles and headed to the Court House, the Bank, the Post Office and Harbour Board. A lad there gave us four butter coupons in return for four tea ones. This saved the enterprise as the Rationing Commission replied to my letter saying they couldn't give us extra butter unless we were ex-servicewomen who had been engaged in a similar line of trade prior to enlistment.

By 11 o'clock we had sold out and rushed home to make five more loaves for the lunch rush – which didn't eventuate. A break in the weather had sent people home for their food. Laden with surplus wares we trailed around the town, going into the hotel bars (men only of course) and even the town's den of iniquity, the billiard saloon, where there were about sixty gamblers. We sold our stock.

When heavy rain precluded our going out at all, we stayed at home writing diary, reading or, in my case, writing poetry. At Bundaberg two lines had come to me.

> *'There is no love within your heart,'*
> *He said, 'nor pity in your soul.'*

I lay on my bed all one afternoon writing the rest of it. It turned out something like Rupert Brooke's *The Great Lover* describing all the things I loved. I was pleased with it.

One morning I awoke feeling very tired. My ear ached. It had been tender the day before and now it felt blocked and throbbing. As a child I had been prone to abscesses in the ear but had had no trouble for years. By evening I felt very ill. My right jaw was stiff and sore and I couldn't open my mouth wide or turn my head easily. That night the pain was intolerable and I cried in misery. When I saw a doctor next day he said I had a boil in my ear. I had a temperature and he ordered me to bed, prescribed some sulfadiazene pills (a new drug) and some others to stop the pain at night. After a day on medication the ear was much better and by the time we were ready to leave Mackay, the rain having eased, I felt almost normal.

Chapter 14

REEF ISLANDS AND A SECRET JOURNEY

We headed for Proserpine from where we hoped to get the launch to Day Dream Island. Captain Moodie had said he'd reserve a cabin for us if we told him when we were to arrive.

It was 93 miles to Proserpine and on the second day we were struggling along an execrable road, rocky with potholes and ruts. I had Pete, which made my bike more unwieldy than ever. As we were walking up a hill, I heard a train whistle and a little later the unmistakable puffing of the train. We knew there was a siding at Wagoora a couple of miles further on so Shirl sped off to stop the train. At last, as I was slowly pedalling along a straight stretch, I saw the train crawling across the road.

'That's that then,' I thought and imagined us riding through the night to cover the remaining fifty miles to Proserpine.

Then I noticed the train was stationary and the station was at the side of the road. I pedalled on desperately, holding Pete's slipping box with two fingers. We loaded our bikes, put Pete in a cage and soon started moving. At the next station we got out to buy tickets. After cajoling the Stationmaster, he gave us tickets for five shillings and overlooked the bikes and Pete.

After some time we came to the hill described in Paul McGuire's *Australian Journey* where the train backs up half a mile and then takes a run to get over it! Leaving our bikes in Proserpine, we caught a bus to Cannon Valley and there was the *Hilma,* a trim launch riding at anchor. Its wireless was on and we were welcomed with sensuous Hawaiian music floating across the water. We headed towards the open sea which was specked with islands. Hayman, Hook and Whitsunday came into view then South Molle, Mid Molle and Day Dream (West Molle). I borrowed binoculars and eagerly examined Day Dream. It looked much prettier than any of the others, wooded with a white coral beach, a red-roofed house and cabins half concealed amongst the trees. At the north end were the 'precipitous pine-clad slopes' described in the brochure. The launch was able to go right in to the water's edge.

Skip Moodie and his sister greeted us and showed us to our cabin. (*Flirtation Flat – At her boy!* read a notice on the door). It was very comfortable. Skip took a party of guests off for a two-day fishing trip so we settled in and after a wonderful roast dinner set off to explore the island. We climbed the hill at the northern end then went for a swim. It was surprisingly cold in the water so I didn't stay long but picked my way gingerly across the coral beach. The words 'coral strand' conjure up romantic visions of gleaming white sand but I was so disappointed. Powdered coral is rough and abrasive.

When Skip and his party returned he asked if we were interested in aquaplaning. Of course we were! (Water skiing was unknown then.) We boarded the *Jane*, the Day Dream launch, and sailed to Shute Harbour, a lovely sheltered bay off the mainland. Alan Wilson, Skip's offsider, went first. He lay face downward on the board which was then lowered into the water and the rope paid out until he was about fifteen yards behind the boat. The *Jane* set off, increasing speed till Alan was skidding across the water. He was very good. After he'd stood up he did all sorts of tricks. He rode with one hand then turned and rode backwards. Facing forwards again, he proceeded to weave from side to side, riding over the waves caused by the wake and sending up walls of spray. When he was wound in, Skip looked at us and asked who was going first.

'Go on Wen,' said Shirl so I lay on the board, squealed when I was immersed and then found myself zooming along at nine knots with nothing between me and the sharks but a piece of wood and a rope. I cautiously stood up and then bent my knees to ride the waves as though I were skiing. I found it quite easy to keep my balance. Thus encouraged, I started transferring my weight onto one foot and was thrilled to see I could shuttle from side to side too, tracing a giant arc. After a quarter of an hour I was pulled in and everyone clapped.

Shirl then had a turn. She had said she didn't care if she fell in so she tried a few tricks. She managed no hands for a split second then turned around sitting down and went backwards. She finally fell in when trying no hands again. I was glad I hadn't taken a tumble as I didn't want to wet my ear. It had started to feel tender again.

Then Rupert, the skipper of *Jane*, dazzled us with his skill. He rode one foot and one hand; backwards no hands, then he stood on his head with legs upright, then with legs apart and finally with legs akimbo. We were very impressed.

That night after dinner Skip ceremoniously presented us with ornate Certificates advising all Twirps, Lounge Lizards, Wolves, Suicide Blondes and inhabitants of Sydney and Melbourne and other poor types that we were now entitled to place the letters M.A. after our names – Master of Aquaplaning.

We had been worrying about how much Skip would charge us for our accommodation and meals. When he told us he would let us off for half the normal amount, we were jubilant. We used to help out in the kitchen after meals and I played the piano every evening so I think we earned our keep.

Two days after aquaplaning, my ear was hurting horribly. I dosed myself with aspirin every four hours.

Alan said he'd take us out in the dinghy to see some coral. When we were only twenty yards off-shore he handed us the glass-bottomed viewing box and said 'There you go!' I looked at him in amazement. Surely there was no coral underneath us, this was where we swam every day. I lowered the box into the water and coral seemed to leap up at me. In fact, I thought the glass was magnifying it but it wasn't. The coral was thickly luxuriant like a forest on the sea bed. There was a lot of staghorn coral, branching antlers of it often tipped with pale blue or lilac. I was slightly disappointed as it wasn't as colourful as I'd expected. Alan said that we'd have to go to much deeper water or to the Reef itself to see brilliant colour. I saw lovely green soft coral, sea urchins with their black spines nine inches long, beautiful sea-anemones, their tentacles swaying languorously in the current, mushroom coral like an inverted fungus, skull coral (something like brain coral) and the incredible sapphire blue starfish, six inches across. As we drifted Alan pointed out strange things to us, beautiful fish coloured scarlet, turquoise and black and shoals of little black ones skimming through the coral.

Two days later, Sunday, the South Molle boat *Pearl* arrived bearing mail. I had written to Mr. Bauer, the proprietor of the tourist resort on South Molle Island, asking if we could go there for a few days. The skipper of the boat handed me his reply. It was very friendly. He said there'd be a big crowd there next week and he'd need some help. We went for a cruise on the boat, dropping passengers off at South Molle and continuing to Long Island. The sea was bright blue and calm and all the islands looked beautiful. My ear was extremely painful now and on the voyage back to Day Dream I lay down on a bunk and gave myself up to misery and tears. The nice young skipper was sympathetic and wished he could do something to help. I had a sudden thought. I ripped out a page of my diary and scribbled a note to the chemist in Proserpine explaining that I was in great pain, there was no doctor, no medicine, no sleep and beseeching him to send me some sulfadiazene tablets by Tuesday's launch. I gave the skipper the letter before disembarking at Day Dream and went straight to bed.

On Monday morning my left ear was feeling tender in the concha. Surely the trouble hadn't spread there too. I was now practically deaf in the right ear. I could hardly hear anyone and felt most isolated. At night I would wake up crying and groaning as the effects of the aspirin were wearing off. I'd always had a dreadful fear of going deaf. I'd think of Beethoven and worry. When I awoke at night, not hearing a thing, I'd think the worst had happened and would burst into wild tears. Shirl would wake then and have to reassure me.

In the brief periods when I was free of pain, I continued to enjoy the island. Alan took us to the southern tip to fossick around the rocks at low tide. He showed us giant clams with their colourful mantles and huge oysters, prizing them open with his knife. I found some pretty shells to add to my vast store of souvenirs and saw my first *bêche-de-mer* or sea cucumber, a revolting fat, black slug about two inches in diameter and a foot in length. When touched it squirts out portion of its entrails in a white stream. This is very sticky and presumably entangles the attacker.

By next morning my left ear was extremely painful but the right one had subsided somewhat. At noon on Tuesday the *Pearl* arrived from Proserpine bearing mail and, joy, my pills. The end of my five-day ordeal was in sight.

We left beautiful Day Dream and travelled on the *Pearl* to neighbouring South Molle Island. It was larger, more tourist-oriented and not as beautiful as Day Dream but it had a lively social life. The Bauer family ran the resort and every member was involved in making sure the visitors had an enjoyable time. One son was the skipper of the *Pearl*, another was in charge of entertainment each evening when we danced or played games. The Bauers had an inexhaustible supply of them – progressive ping pong (we were not yet calling it table tennis), blow ping pong, the broom waltz, Family Coach, Passing the Penny and many more. It was all very jolly but I couldn't jump around too much as my head was heavy and felt it would fall off. I was now deaf in my left ear and felt excluded from conversation. I felt unintelligent. It was also painful to speak as it hurt my ear. We earned our keep by helping with the washing-up after each meal and setting the tables.

A few days later I was almost cured. There was a full moon that night and I sat on the verandah to write my diary. I could see the sand sloping down to a rippling, sequinned sea, the land curving around like an arm to embrace the water, the two rocky crags like towers and the glorious moon floating above everything. A few graceful, leaning palm trees completed the picture. I wished Keith were with me!

On its next run the launch brought us mail. There were invitations to our friend Sharpey's wedding in Melbourne and a letter for Shirl from her boyfriend. Margaret Sharpe had been our companion on our first bike rides but had not come away with us to Queensland as she was in love. (Or 'sunk' as Shirl called it. Although we had boy friends we were both resolved not to marry until we had travelled.) We had thought about how wonderful it would be to go home for her wedding and surprise our families and friends but how could we afford it? We had even started buying Golden Casket lottery tickets.

Shirl squealed with delight. Her boy friend was going to be in Townsville in a few days so she decided to go on and see him, rejoining me in Bowen.

I caught the next launch over to Proserpine where I had to attend the hospital twice daily to have my ears cleaned and dressed with penicillin wicks. (Penicillin was a new wonder drug.) The doctor who examined them said the inside of each ear looked like a coral reef – full of green mullock. He said the infection was caused by coral 'bugs' in the tropical water.

It was a miserable time. I was in pain, I was lonely, I was hungry and very short of money. After two weeks on the islands my funds had dwindled almost to nothing. At one point I wanted to buy a nail file for threepence but couldn't afford it. Threepence would buy a piece of fried fish or some meat for Pete. Without Shirl, no one recognised me as one of the girl cyclists so there were no offers of hospitality. The nadir of my time in Proserpine was when I looked into the earth closet attached to the hall where I was camping and saw a vast, writhing mass of maggots. Utter revulsion swept over me and I succumbed to self-pity. Only little Pete's presence brightened my day.

As my ear healed so my spirits rose to their accustomed height and I was able to do some business in the town. Financial once more, I managed to pay 7/6d for a ticket and caught the rail motor to Bowen as there was virtually no road.

Bowen is known for its salt and its mangoes. I saw whole orchards of huge mango trees and the salt pans where the sea is allowed to flood. It was not the garnering season though I saw stacks of salt being bagged.

Pete greeted Shirl exuberantly and we travelled on by train. It was a very pleasant journey through lightly timbered country with lots of rocky outcrops, pools covered with purple waterlilies and lush, deep grass after all the rain. The so-called road made an occasional bashful appearance before plunging back into the scrub.

On reaching Homehill we left the train but it had no business potential so we set off for Ayr at four o'clock and had a delightful ride through green canefields. How I love sugar country! Little Pete was running behind us and became very hot and tired so we tried a new idea. He perched on Shirl's front swag and rode easily.

Very soon we came to the mighty Burdekin rivercourse and were amazed at its size. We rode for ten minutes over the dried-up, soft sandy bed, just following the ruts of traffic winding ahead. The floods from the monsoon rains had dwindled to a trickle. Then came a short causeway or 'bridge' which was nearly level with the insignificant flow of water. No wonder towns were isolated for weeks in the wet season as the smallest flood would engulf this bridge, let alone the roaring Burdekin. The train crossed on a much higher bridge but even that was impassable in the Wet. We rode on to Ayr through more canefields and waterlily-covered ponds and were greeted by the whirring of a thousand windmills. Ayr has a constant underground water supply and never suffers from drought. Every house has its own windmill.

Shirl celebrated her 22nd birthday in Ayr and we finally met our Waterloo with Queensland hospitality. We were doing business in a café when I saw a customer consuming a large pile of spaghetti. I love spaghetti so spent two shillings on some. Then we were due at the home of Mr. Paige, the Malvern Star manager, for lunch. The thought of more food daunted me but I ploughed through meat pie, potato, peas and beans followed by apple pie and custard.

After lunch Mrs. Paige and her sons told us astounding stories about Townsville during the war, of the constant coming and going of planes, the air raid signals and the bombing, the daily conveyance of corpses to the military cemetery. I was amazed. We never heard anything about this at the time. We knew Darwin had been bombed but not Townsville.

Leaving the Paiges we were taken by another host to Pioneer Mill settlement and soon we sat down to a large evening meal followed at ten o'clock by a huge supper of home-made cakes and tarts smothered in cream. Before we left they loaded us with two coconuts each, four custard apples and the remnants of two tarts. On returning to our church hall, a meeting had just finished and we were offered a plate piled with sandwiches and cakes which were left over. We refused!

On Sunday morning we went next door to church. There was a special Communion service with a procession of children. I took Communion and Shirl followed me although it was her first time. On regaining our pew I said '*Ce n'était pas vin!*' (She had been dubious about getting wine down.)

'No, it was beaut,' she said. 'I was wishing there were more!' (It was a sort of mulberry juice.) 'I had great trouble getting the bread down though. It'd be much better with butter!' Incorrigible!

We had heard of a man who could take us part of the way to Townsville in his utility truck. It had been raining during the night and was spitting as we left. Beyond Pioneer Mill the road became very greasy. Every now and then the truck slewed round sideways and skidded. In between holding my breath I was able to admire the scenery. The grass on each side was covered with a blue flower and creeper, perhaps morning glory, and there were bushes with yellow flowers. Lush green grass grew everywhere and occasionally there were Chloe-like swamps with trees growing out of the water and looking as though crocodiles were lurking in the murky depths, like a Louisiana bayou. Again there were lots of lagoons covered with purple waterlilies.

Our driver dropped us in a small town and we sat by the roadside waiting for another lift. A truck came which could take us about ten miles and would drop us near an empty house where we could shelter from the rain. We set off, enveloped in groundsheets, our bikes lying on the floor of the truck. There were three or four inches of muddy water lying up the front end which, as soon as we approached an incline, surged back wetting our packs and soaking our feet. As the truck lurched over the rutty road, we managed to stand our bikes up against the side structure. It was a hazardous journey. The driver was going quite fast and the truck slewed around in the mud as the utility did in the morning. He dropped us at the empty house and unloaded our gear. Immediately a thick cloud of vicious mosquitoes landed on us. I had *never* seen so many! Not even with both arms flailing could I keep them off me. I quickly pulled on my slacks and dashed into the derelict house where the driver was lighting a damp sack to smoke the insects away. He said he'd pick us up at seven o'clock if we hadn't got a lift by then.

As we were out of sight of the road, we decided to take turns keeping watch for traffic. Shirl went first and when I went out to relieve her, found her huddled in misery, wrapped in her groundsheet and swathed in scarves. Even so, the mosquitoes flocked to her face. I borrowed her kerchief, threw it over my head and cowered beneath it. When she came to relieve me she had her white fly veil swathed around her head and I left her sitting there like a Sikh. When I went out again, I threw my huge green mosquito net right over me and walked out looking like a wigwam or a woman in purdah. Shirl collapsed with laughter.

I sat down in complete isolation by the road. A truck passed me going in the wrong direction and I felt so foolish. Apart from my disguise, they wouldn't know why I was sitting on the road! Eventually a nice old Italian drove us to the outskirts of Townsville where we spent the night in the home of the Methodist minister and his wife.

The next day we made our official arrival at the Malvern Star shop where a little crowd soon gathered. The manager was a live wire and had arranged an interview on radio 4TO and another on a programme called *The Customer Speaks* broadcast from Lane's Café. It was rather on the lines of *The Voice of the People*, Norm Banks's 3KZ programme in Melbourne. At the end of the interview we were given a message that Jack Lane, the owner, would like us to be his guests at a house party on Magnetic Island over the weekend. It lies five miles off Townsville and is a popular and attractive resort.

The Malvern Star manager gave us an idea for a money-raising scheme which he had used on a tour years ago; a pamphlet with our photo and an account of our trip to be sold for a voluntary donation. We did not pursue this for another eighteen months.

We moved to the home of Mr. and Mrs. Hearn whom we'd met at Bundaberg and who had offered us hospitality.

It was now a week until Sharpey's wedding in Melbourne. Our lottery tickets had not produced prizes but we still thought constantly about training home. My sister Noel had managed to get the family to contribute £6 towards my journey. Mum had wired me earlier that she would pay half the fare if I would stay home permanently. Sadly I had to refuse.

We went to the railway station to price the journey. Usually £16.7.0, there was a special rate for Easter, the return trip being only £13.19.0. We decided to go. We would catch the train Tuesday night, reach Brisbane on Thursday, Sydney on Friday and Melbourne on Saturday at 11.30am. The wedding was to be at 5.30pm so it would be a big rush even if the train were on time. I wrote to Noel telling her to meet me and asking for the loan of one of her evening dresses for the wedding.

Mrs. Hearn gladly agreed to mind little Pete for us although we agonized about his sense of bewilderment when we disappeared. The whole trip would have to be shrouded in secrecy as Malvern Star and Peters must not know.

'We'll have to wear sunglasses and headscarves to disguise ourselves,' said Shirl.

We sorted our belongings into things to be left, along with our bikes and Peter, and planned to take on the train only a case of good clothes and a small bag of necessities for the four-day journey.

It had been raining heavily for our first few days in Townsville and once again the Burdekin was flooded.

'Gee, I hope we can get across,' I said to Shirl. On Monday night the water was five inches over the railway lines.

At the station next day we bought our tickets and a helpful traffic superintendent rang through to Brisbane and booked our onward seats to Sydney and Melbourne. (At each State border, one had to change trains as the States had never been able to agree on a uniform gauge.) We rushed home, finalized packing, said our goodbyes and made a slow and over-weighted trip to the station, catching the train as it was about to leave.

After leaving Ayr came the thrilling crossing of the Burdekin. To our immense relief the water had slightly subsided and was now lapping the undersurface of the bridge so we roared south. There were eight of us in the compartment and as darkness fell we disposed ourselves for the night. Shirl and I slept head and tail on one seat, two were on the other seat, two on the floor between the seats and two in the corridor. It was very cramped but at least we were horizontal. On arrival at Brisbane at 3.30am we learned that the train would only be in the station until 6am so we grabbed our sleeping bags and settled in the ladies' waiting room on the platform for the rest of the night.

The train for Sydney left from South Brisbane station at 11am and not long afterwards we were back in beautiful northern New South Wales – Grafton, Coff's Harbour, Lismore. We had been on the road almost a year and would retrace our route in four days. My mind boggled. With excitement we discovered at the end of each carriage a luggage rack three feet wide and as long as the width of the train. We tossed up our sleeping bags and then had to climb up ourselves. It was about seven feet high. I pushed Shirl from behind and then she hauled me up. The ceiling was only two feet above and we had to assume the most difficult positions to get into our bags and then to remove our frocks. At last we were settled and had a good night until people started moving around at 6am.

On the Sydney to Melbourne train, the famous *Spirit of Progress*, we waited until the conductor had made his last rounds then struggled up into a rack. It was narrower than on the previous train and we were very cramped. I got into my bag at last and Shirl was sitting bent up with her legs hanging over the side when a woman came along. She looked up and said with ice: 'Does the conductor know you're up there?' She was a Railways hostess!

'I don't think so,' said Shirl.

The woman stalked off in the direction of the conductor. Shirl quickly got into her bag, we lay as flat as possible and switched off the light. We decided I'd be sick and must lie down if there were any trouble.

In a few minutes the conductor strode down the corridor and said: 'Who took these globes out?'

Shirl said from her perch: 'We didn't take the globes out. We just turned off the switch.'

'You can't do that. People will be walking through here.' He looked up with interest. 'How did you get up there?'

We told him. He was very good about it and said not to tell anyone he'd allowed us up there. We swore to secrecy and he left. Five minutes later, he crept back and turned off the lights. What a kind man!

The *Spirit* pulled into Spencer Street and there was Noel. What a reunion! We trammed home talking non-stop and then we were at the College. Mum and Dad hugged their prodigal daughter while Noel ran a bath.

Four nights on the train, sleeping in corridors with minimal washing facilities, had coated me with grime. Noel was shocked and shuddered as she scrubbed me. There was a black ring around the bath. Then I washed my hair and black water poured out. Emerging pink and shining, I donned clean panties.

'Where's your bra?' Noel asked.

'I haven't got one.'

When I reached puberty Mum had never bought me one. Admittedly, I wasn't well endowed but Noel went and fetched one of hers. I dressed in her lovely cyclamen taffeta evening dress and at 4 o'clock trammed to South Yarra for the wedding. We had warned Sharpey of our arrival and she smiled radiantly at us as she walked down the aisle.

I was dying to see my boy friend Keith (now out of the Navy and living in Melbourne) and had asked Noel to invite him to be her partner at the wedding. He couldn't make the church but had said he'd come to the reception. I kept an eye on the entrance and finally saw him come in. He couldn't believe it when he saw me there. I was overcome. How lovely to be back home!

After two weeks we left Melbourne, refreshed emotionally and physically after our families had indulged us. Comfortable beds, hot baths and three meals a day ...how would we adjust to our Spartan existence up north? We wired Mrs. Hearn to let her know of our imminent return. We spent two days in Sydney, actually sleeping overnight on the verandah of Sharpey's honeymoon suite!

Three more days on the train took us to Townsville, baking in the shadow of its great red granite Castle Hill. We went to Mrs.Hearn's house. Walking around the side through the garden, I saw her dog Wiz and then a large dog raised its head from the grass.

'Peter!' I shrieked and flew to him.

He nearly went mad, leaping feet in the air, licking and whining and trying to demonstrate his joy. We nearly cried we were so glad to see him. Actually he wasn't so big but the first glimpse was so amazing. I had retained a mental picture of a puppy. Mrs. Hearn told us that when she let him off the chain every morning (he slept outside), he'd dash to the garage, leap up on the table and nose around our gear then dash to the lavatory and sniff around there, then shoot like lightning to the front fence where he'd sit all afternoon by the gate waiting for us to return. Every day for almost a month! The dear, faithful hound!

Chapter 15

JACKEROOS IN CAPRICORNIA

From Townsville we wanted to go by launch to Palm Island where we knew there was a large aboriginal settlement. At the wharf we were told we couldn't land on the island in shorts. I had a skirt in my string bag but Shirl had to borrow a bike and race back for one. It was a four-hour journey to the island, the sea was moderately rough and many people were sick. I think we must have been good sailors. Little Pete too, although we purposely didn't feed him in the morning so he had nothing in his stomach to vomit.

We rounded the point of the island at noon. It was very big and thickly wooded with no immediate sign of any palms, but then I learned that Captain Cook discovered it on Palm Sunday. We dropped anchor offshore and three small boats ferried passengers ashore. We had to wade through the shallows and then walk along the beach. The island was only occupied by aborigines. About four thousand lived in the settlement. The village was practically screened by an immense grove of coconut palms and seemed a very pleasant place to live.

We ate our sandwiches sitting in the grove and then went hunting coconuts. There were dozens lying around in the grass and we proceeded to open them on spikes driven into the palm trunks. We drank the juice and then ate the flesh.....delicious! What a wonderful plant is the coconut! Every part of it is useful, even the husk.

The aborigines put on a large corroboree, their faces and bodies painted in weird designs with coloured clay. They grind coloured rocks and mix the powder with water and oil. After painting their bodies they use feathers and animal skins to further embellish their appearance and look hideously fearsome. We had seen two corroborees before but we were fascinated by a tiny boy of about three, painted grotesquely and stamping, grunting and dancing like his elders. Other men provided an accompaniment of clacking rhythm sticks while the women droned in the background.

As we had only twenty more minutes till the boat left, we dashed away to see some of the settlement. A nursing sister took us to the hospital. In the maternity ward we saw several adorable pot-bellied babies, much more attractive than white babies. Surprisingly they are almost white when they are born, the pigmentation increasing as they grow older. We saw the single quarters, the houses for married couples, a school, a church and the store. Wading back to the dinghies, we collected several beautiful shells from the sand and returned to the launch.

On our way home it became very rough indeed. The launch was pitching and rolling as though she'd go under at any minute. All the other passengers vacated the bow and cowered in the stern but Shirl and I were revelling in the motion and stood at the prow. It was exhilarating. The boat would climb a big wave and we'd see a yawning cavern beneath us. Down we'd slide into it, often smashing into an oncoming wave on the way down, causing a huge cloud of spray to engulf us. Everyone thought we were quite mad, standing in the prow being drenched with chilly water and shrieking with laughter at each plunge. I was singing 'There is beauty in the bellow of the blast, there is grandeur in the growling of the gale' from *The Mikado* while Shirl was tunelessly entreating someone to carry her back to old Virginny. After each plunge, as the water streamed off us, I'd hear her indomitably yelling and bellowing at the elements that that's where the cotton and the corn and 'taters grow. When the sun sank it became quite cold so we changed into dry clothes.

-oOo-

From Townsville our road led west to Charters Towers, Cloncurry, Mt. Isa and Camooweal whence the East-West Highway, built during the war, ran to Tennant Creek in the Northern Territory. If we wished to go to Darwin, that was the way we had to go. However, we were in love with Queensland, especially Northern Queensland. The road went north 230 miles to Cairns and another 51 to Mossman where it petered out. The Great Barrier Reef and more islands ran parallel to the shore and behind Cairns there was a large hinterland of forests and lakes. It was all very tempting. We decided to spend a month going to Cairns and back.

Once more we had to sort our clothes, some to go with us, the rest to stay in Townsville to await our return. I was packed by noon but Shirl was sitting on the floor surrounded by piles of clothes and clutter, writing names in her indispensable address book. People were always giving us addresses of their friends and relations along our route or asking us to send them a postcard from Darwin. The list was growing ever longer. Finally at 1 o'clock she started sorting and packing and by three she was ready. We never managed to have an early start.

We rode ten miles out and when it started to get dark we asked the station-master at Derragun siding if we could camp in one of the workmen's huts. He said he could do better than that and took us to a stationary carriage which was fitted out for the convenience of flying gangers. It contained two beds, a table and lamp and he fetched us a bucket of water. We collapsed into bed.

In the morning we decided it was time to worm little Pete. He loathed worm syrup and we had a hectic, hilarious struggle trying to get it down. We tried tying his legs together but he'd roll and spill the sticky mess all over him and us. Eventually we got a teaspoonful down.

At Leichhardt River we waded and introduced Pete to swimming. He loved it and we couldn't get him out. His only previous experience had been at beaches and he didn't take to salt water.

A truck took us to Ingham. It was a rough ride bumping over rocky creek beds, potholes and desperately trying to hold Pete on. The bitumen surface had come to an end. It was very hot and my legs were sunburnt. Arriving in Ingham at 3 o'clock, we climbed down stiffly from the truck, dusty and sore. We really looked as though we'd ridden all the way. Unfortunately a lot of people saw us limp off the truck!

Ingham was an amazing town. Sugar was virtually the only source of income and 85% of its residents were Italians or other migrants. We were told that, prior to the war, one would never hear a word of English spoken there. I could believe it as, on closer acquaintance with the town, we found very few of the residents could speak English. Election posters were on the walls... '*Il nostro amico* – Bob Jones'. We tried to sell our books in the town but it was very difficult because of the language problem. I racked my brains for an Italian translation but could only come up with '*Io ho un libro*' which was obvious anyway as I was thrusting the inoffensive volume under their noses. We did sell a *Dairy Farming* to an Australian milkman and were promptly invited to stay at his farm.

Next stop was at a saddler. Little Pete's pads were wearing out and we asked about the possibility of making him some boots. The man was very kind and insisted on making him a set for nothing. He traced around Pete's paws and then cut out shapes from some soft leather. A few hours later we returned to collect them and fitted them on Pete. They were about three inches high and laced up the back of each leg. Pete wasn't sure about them at all. He went flip-flop in them and, going down steps, he couldn't get a grip and just slithered. Thereafter he became very famous. Everyone who saw him remembered the little dog in boots.

The milkman, Mr. Fraser, picked us up and loaded our gear onto the back of his truck which was already crowded with milk cans and children. He lived six miles out at a hamlet called Trebonne in a quaint, square, two-storied box of a house (rare in Queensland where most houses were built on stilts) standing alone in a field edged by acres of sugarcane. His wife was a gaunt, tanned woman with a baby attached to her breast. We hardly ever saw her without that baby and never got used to the sight of her unconcernedly feeding it wherever she happened to be when it was hungry. There were seven children in all and despite the crowd Mrs. Fraser made us very welcome. We were lent horses to ride around the district, a wide plain mainly devoted to sugar cane and ringed with blue mountains.

We were asked to speak to the children at the Trebonne State School. I had to be careful talking about places they wouldn't know or using big words, particularly as there were only about three Australian children. The rest were Italian, Sicilian, Spanish, Finnish and Chinese. Some didn't have any English. I gave the first half of the talk and when Shirl continued, a funny little Australian girl put up her hand when Shirl mentioned a certain town and said: 'Please Miss Duncan, I've got an uncle living there.'

'Oh have you? Well, isn't that nice,' Shirl said and resumed.

A minute later: 'Please Miss, I've got an uncle living there too, at least I'm not sure whether he's an uncle or a half uncle but he lives there.'

'Is that so! Well, what do you know! An uncle, eh?' Shirl enthused feebly.

Afterwards we talked to the teacher, a pleasant girl called Erin who boarded at the local hotel. She told us about the wonderful Italian meals cooked there by the proprietors, Delina and August Rotunda. My mouth watered. I love Italian food. We rode to the hotel and asked if we could buy a dinner there that evening. Delina asked what we'd like and I said minestrone, piles of spaghetti and anything else she liked.

In the afternoon we had addressed the local Methodist Ladies Guild and been plied with a huge afternoon tea including cream cakes, not common in Queensland, so by evening the edge was off my appetite.

At the hotel Erin said Delina had been cooking all afternoon and we must eat everything or she'd be insulted. With misgivings we sat down to bowls of soup followed by spaghetti and meat balls. It was delicious but then she brought plates of fresh fried fish and dried salt fish with salad. I had difficulty in getting through it. I didn't like the salt fish so managed to leave that. Then came stewed apple which was a relief after so much rich food. The whole meal was wonderful and Delina refused payment.

We heard of a truck going all the way to Atherton. We only wanted to go to Tully but climbed on the truck in the main street and sailed out of the town in full view of the large Saturday morning crowd of shoppers. It was a pleasant drive through canefields and we lazed on piles of bedding on the back of the truck. Then we ascended Cardwell Range. From the top there was a magnificent view of Hinchinbrook Island and Channel with smaller islands dotted here and there.

We reached Cardwell at noon and the truck drivers shouted us a wonderful fish dinner – barramundi, that peerless tropical fish. While we were eating, the Cairns mail train pulled in at the station opposite. A boy rang a bell outside the café to attract passengers to the fish dinner and swarms of them came over, ate and returned to the train. However, one chap was still talking to the jovial Greek proprietress, Mrs. Tringas, when the train slowly edged away. With a wild yell, he leapt out of the shop, over the stile, onto the platform and into the last carriage. Only in a Queensland train could that be done!

We set off again and drove through wide, open plains, whizzing along until we reached a little place called Euramo, seven miles from Tully. We had the addresses of three properties all owned by people called Henry so we tried to ring them to see if we could come and see them before going on to Tully. However, the George Henrys from *Cowley* weren't on the phone nor was Mrs. Brice Henry of *Riversdale* so we rang Miss Elizabeth Henry of *Bellenden Plains*. At first she just made polite conversation despite Shirl's efforts to bring the talk round to the subject of a visit.

At last she said 'I'd like to have you out for a while only the house is in a shambles. There is a carpenter here renovating.'

Shirl leapt at that and assured her we were used to roughing it and that we'd be out on Monday, goodbye!

We found our truck drivers who were improving the shining hour in a hotel and they produced yet another Henry – Bill, brother of George, son of Mrs. Brice and nephew of Miss Elizabeth. He said he'd run us round to his place, from where we could go and stay with his mother at *Riversdale* over the weekend. We waited at Bill's house for his mother to arrive but she didn't come. Instead, his brother George came and decided we should go home with him so we drove seven miles to *Cowley* through lovely bush country.

We passed *Riversdale*. 'Gee,' said Shirl, 'I wish we were staying there. Just look at those beaut horses.'

George had told us that at *Cowley* he raised bananas, timber and pineapples. No horses.

The sun had gone down by now and we saw myriad fireflies flickering in the trees. Lucille Quinlan again…

> *But now at last the fireflies with lights all lit,*
> *From croton-bush to palm tree delicately flit …*

We didn't reach the house until after dark and felt reluctant to land in on Mrs. George without warning. She was most welcoming however and whistled up some tea for us in no time. George produced a plate of their own bananas and we ate six straight off, leaving a heap of skins.

The next day was brilliant and hot despite our proximity to Tully where it is said to rain 366 days of the year. George said he'd take us to see flying foxes sleeping in the trees of the forest, so we walked across the cultivated land where he had planted bananas, pineapples and oranges and he pointed out many interesting things…the pumpkin beetle, a wild sort of spinach that is delicious to eat, the quandong trees whose hard, knobbly fruits are made into necklaces and Chinese Checkers pieces and the prickly fig which is widespread because birds drop the seeds. Then we went through a banana plantation and saw how the fruit grows out from the long tassel-like flower. We sampled some ripe ones then struck into the dense forest, George cutting his way with a cane knife. What a wonderful place! There were no gums to speak of, mostly palms, the pinhead type which George said was edible. He found a fallen palm and cut off a foot of tender green shoot just under the umbrella of fronds. The inside of this is soft and is wonderful in a salad. When cooked it tastes like cabbage. Then we saw the flying foxes or fruit bats hanging upside down in clusters at the top of the palms. They looked like fruits. Suddenly one became alarmed and took off. One by one the others peeled off and swooped away to another tree with a beating of wings like a great wind.

> *And see across the pale sky, dark shapes swoop –*
> *The flying foxes, leather-winged, the silent troop!*
> *Close your ears, my tender one – in the mango tall*
> *The greedy ones are fighting now with bark and squall!*

On returning to the house, one of the aboriginal workers, Joe, and a German from another farm, Bill, had the big drag-net ready to go fishing. We climbed into the dinghy with them and pushed out onto the river. Mrs. Henry restrained Pete from leaping in and following us and we were just congratulating ourselves on getting away when we saw a little head with two great ears coming downstream towards us. We encouraged him and the brave little dog swam over a hundred yards to the sandbank where he beached. Bill rowed in a great semicircle unloading the net as he went until he reached the sandbank again. Then the men pulled the net in. Twice they caught nothing but the third attempt produced thirteen black bream. We waded back upstream as it was shallow and too hard to row with a load of people. Then the fish had to be cleaned. We were anxious to learn everything so copied George, step by step. Mrs. Henry cooked the fish and they were delicious.

Monday morning and George was to drive us to Miss Henry at *Bellenden Plains*. We were excited because we had seen little Pete cock his leg for the first time. He had also learned to shovel dirt with his hindlegs after defecating. He was so pleased with himself that he did it without waiting for an opportunity and wherever he happened to be.

We arrived at *Bellenden* late Monday afternoon. The homestead was screened by a lot of trees and flowering shrubs. Miss Henry came out to meet us. She was a small, plump old lady – over seventy but looked fifty – dressed in a khaki shirt and corduroy riding breeches, boots and leggings. She had a cheery little face like a rosy apple, wrinkled a little, with eyes that screwed right up when she smiled. Her brown hair was worn in a bun at the back. She welcomed us warmly and apologized again for the mess the house was in. It certainly was! Apparently the whole house was falling to pieces and the carpenter was laying a new stump foundation and new flooring. Every room was piled with furniture and junk that had been moved out of other rooms. In the large living room there were two pianos, each groaning beneath stacks of books bereft of bookshelves. The table was invisible under stacked furniture, clothes and odds and ends. There was just enough space to walk through the room by means of a narrow passageway between the furniture. In this room was a dressing table with a mirror which she said we could use. Leading off the room was the verandah where we were to sleep. There was one bed with a net and a mattress on the floor. Half the planks on the verandah were ripped up and we had to step gingerly over great gaps.

For afternoon tea she had made some puftaloons...scones in the pan...very light and delicious with syrup or honey, and then she said we could get some horses and help bring in the cattle. Shirl and I looked at each other with wild glee. At last! We had always yearned for an invitation to a Station... 'Ride our horses! Eat our cream!' We raced to change into slacks and shoes and went out to where the two aboriginal lads, Charlie and Leslie, were saddling the horses. I am always apprehensive with a strange horse so asked for a quiet one. We walked them through the gate into the large paddock where the cattle were scattered. Miss Henry told us what to do and we separated to herd different groups. My horse had a most uncomfortable canter but I rounded up half a dozen beasts. Miss Henry then told me to go right over to the other side and look amongst the trees for more. To do this I had to either cross a muddy swamp or else a narrow creek. My horse refused to do either. He just didn't like to get his hooves wet! I kicked and urged him for fifteen minutes by which time all the cattle had been rounded up so we walked quietly behind them back to the yards. There, in the confusion that ensued getting them through the gate, one young steer got away. I was the only person near so I spurred after it. At least I spurred the rotten horse but it wouldn't go. Meanwhile the steer was trotting happily back to its hunting ground. I cursed and kicked but the horse wouldn't move till, all at once, it gave a leap and started to trot. We came to the creek again. The steer leapt nimbly across but of course the horse stalled.

'Here we go again!' I thought and rode along the edge looking for an easier place to ford. By a fluke we managed to cross and then the horse broke into a canter towards the steer which was standing lost in the middle of the plain.

'Now I must head it off. Looks easy enough. Just as well because it's nearly dark.'

Just then the steer wheeled and headed into a belt of trees and I had to rein in before I crashed into branches. I could have wept. Shirl called to me.

'Come and help me!' I yelled.

'Miss Henry says to leave it!'

I didn't like admitting defeat but it was nearly dark so I turned around and had to find the easy place to ford the stream. I felt very ashamed and incompetent but Miss Henry said nothing.

We sat down to dinner and she warned us that life there was very simple and we'd just have to rough it. 'We live on nothing but salt beef which might prove monotonous to a city dweller.'

'Not at all,' I said enthusiastically, thinking of my mother's delicious corned beef. 'I love salt beef.'

But when she produced the meat it was scrawny and brown, not juicy and red. I cut off a piece and put it in my mouth and then cast a horrified glance at Shirl. It was like string and salty as brine. Shirl was also looking desperate and consuming quantities of tomato and spring onions to alleviate the taste. After that we had tinned peaches which were as welcome as manna to the Israelites.

'Now that you're here,' said Miss Henry at the end of the meal, 'you can help with the mustering tomorrow morning.'

Feeling rather uneasy, I said: 'Er....what time in the morning? When do you get up?'

She hedged a bit and said 'Oh, fairly early.'

'How early?'

'Well, I usually start at 4.30 but there's no need for you to get up till a quarter to six.'

A quarter to six! Shirl and I exchanged agonized glances. When would we get our writing done? Diary and letters were so far behind but we should have to go to bed early each night in order to get enough sleep.

Miss Henry woke us next morning. 'Peep o' day!' she called brightly. It wasn't even light! We groped around, dressed by lamplight and sat down to breakfast feeling ghastly.

'This is the nicest time of the day, don't you think?' burbled Miss Henry.

At 7.30 the boys brought our horses and we mounted. Shirl and Miss Henry got away before me and I was just rounding the corner when I saw Leslie riding back towards me with a broad grin on his face. Looking ahead, I saw Shirl standing beside her horse. Surely she hadn't fallen off? I asked Leslie what was the joke.

'Miss Henry's horse bolted and threw her,' he said.

I trotted on to join Shirl and was horrified to see Miss Henry sitting on the grass with blood from her mouth to left ear, her jodhpurs ripped on her left thigh and the flesh underneath raked with cruel gashes from the barbed wire fence. She was badly shaken and said she wanted to sit down for a minute to recover. Then she said she'd go in and clean up.

We mounted again, weeded out the calves from the herd and drove them to the yards. I thought I'd better go and see Miss Henry. I found her lying on the bed having made no effort to undress or wash. She wanted to be getting about but I said she had a bad case of shock and had better rest. Her mind was blank. She couldn't remember who we were, what she'd been doing with the cattle, how she got on the horse, how she got off it! I washed her face and arms and smoothed some Johnson's cream into the grazes. Then I tried to get her to take off her breeches. She was too weak to move for a long time but finally got them off. I washed her thigh gashes, one of which was quite deep with a bit of flesh hanging out. I called Shirl and suggested it should be stitched and that she should have an anti-tetanus injection. She agreed and then we had to convince the old lady. She realized that the barbed wire was dangerous and after further argument agreed to let us ring the hospital. It took half an hour to get the exchange who put us through to the hospital. They said to bring her at half past ten. We rang for an ambulance to come at ten.

It was only half past eight. It had been a long day. I found some brandy and gave Miss Henry a swig. Shirl bandaged the leg and we let the old lady sleep.

Back in the yard the men were branding, earmarking and castrating the calves. It seemed barbarically cruel to us, all the cutting being done with a pocket knife!

At ten o'clock we dressed Miss Henry. 'A dress would be easier than trousers,' I suggested.

'I don't have any dresses,' she said, so with great difficulty we threaded her legs into the jodhpurs.

The carpenter had driven over to get her sister, Mrs. Sparvell, from her home two miles away. She returned with him and went to Tully with Miss Henry in the ambulance.

'Well girls,' said Miss Henry weakly as we bade her goodbye, 'I leave you to CARRY ON!'

As the ambulance disappeared, we looked at each other with glee. Only the day before we had been saying how good it would be for us to get a job as cook on a Station and learn the hard way. Now we were in sole charge! We pranced into the kitchen and began to plan lunch.

There was no salt beef cooked and we were stumped. Shirl decided to make some puftaloons. I rummaged through a cupboard and found a tin of tomato soup which I made up. Shirl's puftaloons were not like Miss Henry's. I called them leatherjackets. We wouldn't have worried much about food ourselves but there were the two station hands to feed. After we'd given them lunch we heard them giggling and felt sure they were laughing at our attempts to cook.

By the time we had washed up it was time to make the stockmen and the carpenter afternoon tea. The fire was out and the water luke-warm. We brewed some vile tea, slopped it into cups and told the men to come and have their tea before it got cold. Then we made ourselves scarce!

We saddled two horses and went for a ride. Shirl was to have the horse that threw Miss Henry but when she got on, it started to bolt with her. Then Leslie got on and it bolted with him. Something must have upset it. On inspection, a sharp grass seed was found under the saddle. So Shirl took the little grey-faced horse I'd had that morning and I had the slow stubborn one I had the day before. Shirl's went very well but mine just trotted. Horses sense incompetency! Still it was very pleasant. We came home at half past five and started to prepare dinner.

We decided to have fried salt beef (Shirl's idea), boiled potatoes in jackets and fried onions (my suggestion) followed by banana custard. It took us just on two hours to cook everything and I've never had such a hilarious time. Shirl's hunks of meat were hard like pellets and when dropped on the plate gave a metallic clang! It was impossible to chew them, they were so hard and dry and stringy. So we decided to make a gravy to moisten them and I added sliced tomatoes. The flour was self-raising and made little lumps of dough in the gravy. We were both dashing around the kitchen like wild things, straining to see through the smoke over the stove, shifting lamps to better advantage, washing up pots and crockery in order to use them again, dashing out to the tank for more water, making up powdered milk for the custard, slicing bananas, making a pot of tea for the men, cutting bread and setting the table. At last we set the steaming plates proudly in front of the aborigines then sat down inside for our meal. I have never tasted such fine food apart from the meat. The onions and potatoes and gravy were wonderful. And the banana custard! But still the men laughed! We began to suspect that they had never had it so good and were laughing at our efforts to please them. I made a bran loaf, the wonderful quick and easy wartime bread, and we had that for supper.

Miss Henry had told Charlie and Leslie not to do any mustering till she returned but to help the carpenter around the house. Consequently we could all sleep in next morning. We told the men to get their own breakfast as we wouldn't be up and fell into bed exhausted.

After sleeping in till nine, we wandered into the kitchen and were just wondering what we could possibly make for lunch when Mrs. Sparvell, Miss Henry's sister, arrived and announced that she'd come to stay and run the place as Miss Henry would be in hospital for a few days. We were glad on the whole but disappointed we couldn't do more cooking. Mrs. Sparvell was very pleasant, about 70 years old, slow-speaking with a merry wrinkled face like her sister. She immediately started organizing the house, cleaning and tidying the filthy cupboards, unearthing mouldering remains of food from dark recesses, washing up grimy pots and generally bringing order to the kitchen. She showed us the proper way to prepare the salt beef…it had to be soaked for hours to get rid of the salt…and put some on for lunch. When I came to lift it out of the cauldron later, I saw neat piles of little maggots, just laid. Ugh! That settled it, no more salt beef for me.

In the afternoon Mrs. Sparvell said she was walking over to her house and we said we'd ride with her. We would ride several hundred yards ahead and then come back to her. The track was very pretty, winding through trees with soft lawn-like grass under them. In one place it wound through a belt of dense forest, palms and vines, then into another clearing, over a creek then around by a strip of forest where an avenue had been cut to erect a fence. We rode to the end of it. It was like a cathedral, a thick palm grove with straight clean trunks and cabbage-tree tops. Everything was deathly quiet. Not suspecting our presence, a cassowary stalked out from the trees in front of us.

A little further on we crossed a creek and there was *Woolkoo*, Mrs. Sparvell's house. She showed us her sulky and buckboard then took us into the 'house', only a corrugated iron two-room shack. Everything was in a mess here too as she'd been called away suddenly by her sister's accident.

I asked where the lavatory was. 'Oh,' she said, 'there isn't one. It blew down in the cyclone!'

When I looked blank she said: 'Like the Israelites, I bury all – er – refuse,' and she indicated a hoe leaning against the wall. She then produced a chamber pot, laid some paper in it, put it on a box in a hessian-screened shed (which was the bathroom) and invited me to enter. Also in the room were two funny sitz baths, the first I'd ever seen.

Back in the sitting room she told us of her travels. Just before the outbreak of the 1st World War she set out for Germany but while in the Indian Ocean, war was declared and the German ship she was on evaded British and French ships and sought refuge in Mozambique. From there she went to Africa and got a job as a governess for over a year before proceeding to London where she worked as a VAD at a military hospital.

She dragged out boxes of old photos to show us, family portraits, pictures of *Bellenden* in its prime – a beautiful homestead and garden. There was a photo of her and her sister Elizabeth in their youth, both dressed as nurses. I asked her why her sister had never married. Apparently she was engaged to an officer in Rabaul where she was stationed at a hospital. After she returned to Australia, she received a letter saying that he was dead. It was a dreadful tragedy and she was so beautiful.

Back at Bellenden, we decided we should move on to Tully. Mrs. Sparvell was holding the fort and Miss Henry would be home in a few days. We packed our haversacks, rolled our sleeping bags and said goodbye to lovely chaotic Bellenden, kindly Mrs. Sparvell, Leslie, Charlie and Mr. Smith the carpenter, the horses, the cattle and the salt beef and headed north.

Chapter 16

TABLELAND

We saw Tully from a distance. It was overshadowed by a large black cloud. It was raining of course. The annual rainfall there is 4546mm (179 inches or 15 feet!) the highest in Australia. By the time we arrived in the town the rain had abated. The main street was full of Saturday shoppers from the surrounding district. We caused a minor sensation as our notoriety had spread ahead of us through the newspapers.

We went to Mullins Hotel to see Miss Henry who had been discharged from hospital and had a long talk with her. She was very sorry we were leaving and pressed us to come and spend a few weeks on our way back. She expressed her appreciation of our help after her accident and tried to give us some money which we refused.

We were still virtually living on icecream but now it was supplemented by wonderful tropical fruits. Four scoops of icecream on a dinner plate would be topped with sliced banana, papaw, mango or passion fruit and a mandarin or pineapple sauce. Now we were introduced to grenadilla, the most wonderful fruit, as large as a papaw and filled with delicious pulp like passionfruit. One of our hostesses gave us grenadilla pie.

We were staying in the kindergarten room of a church which was situated on the side of a mountain. On Sunday afternoon I was playing the organ in the church when the Finnish community of the district began to arrive for their service. It was conducted in English but the congregation sang Finnish hymns. What a peculiar language! There was no similarity to any other European languages which I knew and I learned that it is related to eastern European ones. We were singing the songs soon, the pronunciation being quite easy.

We rode down into the town to see the Innisfail-Tully rugby and basketball matches. The ground was terrifically muddy. The girls played basketball in bare feet and slid everywhere! Their uniforms were mud-spattered and soaked! No one seemed put out and I guess this was normal for Tully.

Dunk Island lies off Tully and we met Gerry Caught, the owner of the resort, and told him that we were very keen to see Dunk Island but couldn't afford it unless he had jobs for us over there. He said it was a slack season and he had enough staff. He was very pleasant though and was interested in our trip. At last he said: 'You know, I'm tempted to take you back and show you the island.' We were ecstatic. Just then an extremely handsome bearded man came along and was introduced as Ted. He was part of the Dunk Island establishment too. Our spirits rose!

Dunk Island, or Coonanglebah – the far more attractive aboriginal name – was the home of E J. Banfield, Australia's Thoreau, for twenty-five years. Although English by birth, his family emigrated to Australia in 1854 when he was only two years old. His father founded a newspaper in Maryborough, Victoria, then ran a paper in Ararat where the young Edmund started a career in journalism. He later worked on the Townsville *Daily Bulletin* until 1897 when, at the age of only forty-five, diagnosed as tubercular and in a state of exhaustion brought on by the stress of his newspaper work, he decided to put civilization behind him and make a new life on Dunk Island with his wife. Nowadays we would say that he had decided to quit the rat race. It must have been quite unusual in 1897.

He embraced island life, entranced by the solitude of his wilderness. He continued to write articles for the Townsville newspaper for the rest of his life and in 1908 his first book, *Confessions of a Beachcomber*, was published. His subsequent writings appeared under the pseudonym The Beachcomber. *My Tropic Isle* appeared in 1911 followed by *Tropic Days* in 1918. *Last leaves from Dunk Island* was published posthumously in 1925. His collected writings make fascinating reading although his purple prose is rather dated these days.

Unlike Thoreau who believed in simplifying one's life to the extreme, Banfield was a practician. He has been likened more aptly to Gilbert White, the father of British ornithology. Alec Chisholm wrote of him: 'His taste for natural history was unforced and sincere…He accumulated a mass of valuable observations including several discoveries new to science.' He must have been one of the earliest conservationists.

-oOo-

We left Tully on a big truck driven by Ted and stopped at Lower Tully to pick up some goods. After we'd gone a mile further we discovered Pete was missing. He must have jumped off at Lower Tully. We turned back and retrieved him. This was unfortunate as Gerry was rushing to catch the tide at the Hull river mouth. We boarded the launch *Starlight* and headed for the sea. At the mouth of the river was a sand bar to be crossed. The tide was running out fast and we became stuck in the sand. For two and half hours we lay aground despite efforts by Gerry and Ted who jumped into the water and tried to pull us off. It was embarrassing as we felt responsible for the delay.

Once in the open sea we passed a few small islands which were leased by artists who came here to escape southern winters and to paint. Approaching Dunk we hugged the coast, rounded the sand-spit and headed towards the settlement on the edge of the bay. We pulled in to the first jetty to load a drum of petrol. Two men were there, one elderly.

'The Major and his nephew,' Ted explained.

We chugged away and headed for the second jetty which is right at the settlement. It looked very attractive. There were no buildings visible, just a lush green grove of palm trees. We had let Pete off at the first jetty and he went bounding along the beach behind the Major. We felt rather piqued by his perfidy and, just to watch his reaction, whistled him. He stopped dead, spun around and headed for the water to come to us. The Major turned too, waved his cane and yelled something at us. He seemed very excited. We kept shouting encouragingly at Pete who by now was leaping about in the shallows. As we drew nearer we could hear the Major bellowing in a very irascible pukka English voice: 'You're not going to call that dog into the wortah are you! Don't you know the place is thick with sharks, you silly girl! If people don't know how to look after their animals, they don't deserve to have them!'

We were amazed at his vehemence as Pete had no intention of coming further out, he hated sea water. We looked contrite although I was inwardly convulsed with laughter. The Major stormed off very red of face. Ted was laughing softly and said: 'He's not a bad old stick. He's usually very nice.'

We were taken to a delightful chalet comprising two rooms and a bathroom. We had exclusive use of it as there were few guests and after unpacking we walked through a wonderful avenue of coconut palms and up some steps to the main house. Gerry introduced us to Mr. Holmes, a grey-haired man of about fifty who, on hearing who we were, rose from his chair and said: 'Bai Jove, eh! Rading round Orstralyah?'

I cast an amused glance at Shirl. Another one! He was exactly the caricature of an Englishman and sounded like Nigel Bruce the film actor. When we went to the dining room for tea we met Philip, the Major's nephew, looking very fresh and English with blue eyes and blond hair. As we were talking, a 'pillar of the British nation' in the form of Major Somerset stalked into the room in a dignified way. He was dressed in flannels, brown sports coat and an open-necked shirt with a khaki cravat neatly folded around his neck. He was also in his fifties, handsome for his age, blue eyes like his nephew, tanned face, iron-grey hair thinning a little at the temples and a proud nose. I mentally christened him Colonel Blimp. His mask of aloofness didn't drop as he said 'How do you do!' stiffly. We sat down to eat. They were the only other guests. I made polite conversation with the Major, smoothing his ruffled feathers, passing him what he wanted and being as polite as I knew how. Except for once when the conversation veered dangerously towards Pete and the sharks, we chatted amiably. It was the most entertaining meal. These Englishmen with their terrific accents and quiet, devastating humour kept me inwardly bubbling with merriment. I think they were the first Englishmen I had ever met.

The Major and his nephew had left England, thus missing the winter and short rations, and gone to South Africa. After travelling there for some time they came to Australia with the idea of settling. Obviously not sure what to do, they were now planning to go on to America and probably home!

The Major spoke quite nicely actually. It was Mr. Holmes who was so amusing. He'd tell funny stories and chortle, saying: 'Ho ho ho, good, isn't it! Ho ho, very good!'

The Major asked Gerry when he could take them out to the Reef and the answer was 'Tomorrow.' We tried to look unconcerned as we didn't expect to go but we were invited so we went out with Ted to help him net some fish for bait. There would be fishing in the deep water around the Reef. We sorted the big drag-net, rowed around in a circle unloading the net then pulled it in. No fish. We spread the net again, this time leaving a wide gap for fish to get in and left it for the night.

In the morning we helped cut stacks of sandwiches to take on the boat. Two women artists from another house joined the party. As soon as we left the bay the launch began to roll and plunge. We were lying on top of the cabin and had to hang on grimly to avoid rolling off. Also on the roof of the cabin was a great coil of hard, thick rope. During one sudden lurch I heard a heavy thud and found the rope had disappeared. I peered over the edge of the cabin and saw the Major tenderly rubbing his head. He must have had an awful wallop!

After three hours we saw in the distance the first sign of the Reef...a large yellow sand cay on the horizon. A little later we picked out the serrated edge of the sea where the Pacific waves were breaking over the exposed reefs. Most people who come north to see the Great Barrier Reef do not realize that the resorts on the numerous islands off the coast are nowhere near the Reef. Only two island resorts are actually on it, Heron Island way down south off Gladstone and Green Island off Cairns. If you want to see the Reef anywhere else you have to travel for up to four hours in a launch.

As we approached the broken water we could see the shelving bottom, the water was so clear. Gerry tried to land us on the cay but he couldn't thread his way through the surrounding coral so we anchored off it and had our lunch. I saw a sea snake (very venomous), a school of flying fish leaping in and out of the water with dazzling precision and a slender fish skittering along the surface of the water on its tail for a considerable distance. Shoals of tiny fluorescent fish swirled in formation.

I asked the Major what had happened about the coil of rope, had someone pulled it down or had it fallen?

'It *fell* on me...most painful too...and all Mr. Holmes did was to laugh uproariously and tell me how the same thing happened to him once. I don't understand why it is that whenever one is injured, other people feel constrained to tell one about similar misfortunes!'

The anchor was pulled up and we cruised away from the cay to a dark patch of reef. We were all dying to get out and fossick but Gerry hadn't brought the dinghy and couldn't get in close enough with the launch. Tempers were becoming frayed as we all shouted instructions on steering to Gerry who couldn't see the perilous reefs from his post in the cabin.

'Well now, will this do? Would you like to get off here?'

'Don't be ridiculous Gerry! It's fully fifty feet deep here!'

The water was so clear you could swear it was only a foot deep. I was lying on my stomach looking over the side of the boat near the prow and saw the most wonderful sight. Everyone else was at the back of the launch as we backed out through the reefs and consequently the water near the prow was still instead of ruffled when one is going forward. Through the pale green water I saw walls and battlements of coral and another beetling crag near it…a veritable underwater city. I yearned to dive down and explore it. Another fifteen years and we might have had snorkels or scuba tanks for diving.

Clear of the reef we anchored for fishing. Some fish for bait had been caught in the net and for nearly an hour we doggedly held our lines but caught nothing. On the way back Mr. Holmes was trawling and caught a magnificent kingfish, that most delicious tropical fish, five or six feet long with its satin-smooth skin gleaming like mother-of-pearl, blue and turquoise lights glinting.

Back on Dunk we tried to earn our keep by helping Gerry. He had masses of household linen to be name-stamped, bed and table linen, curtains, cushion covers and towels. After several hours we broke off to see a bit of the island. We went to the beach first where the cook, Mrs. Stannard, was collecting oysters for tea. She told us where we could find Banfield's grave. On his tombstone were Thoreau's famous lines: *'If a man does not keep pace with his companions, perhaps it is because he hears a different drummer. Let him step to the music which he hears.'* We saw the original homestead which was now used as a store room then we ploughed through thick vegetation, breaking numerous giant cartwheel spiderwebs, to find the suspension bridge over the creek. A gorge dropped away beneath it. Little Pete was scared to go across as we were making the frail bridge bounce and sway.

We had to leave next morning and said goodbye to the Major and Mr. Holmes with genuine regret, returning to Tully in a heavy rain storm, of course.

-oOo-

Next day we travelled to Innisfail. We were now in the heart of the Queensland sugar country. Our brief introduction to sugar back in the Northern Rivers district of New South Wales and again in Bundaberg had prepared us for the extensive sweep of canefields for 240 miles from Ingham to Cairns. Fields of the freshest green cane flanked the roads and at night the darkness was illuminated by cane fires which are purposely lit to strip the cane of its trash and clear out venomous snakes which hide among the canes. This makes it easier for the cane cutters who come each season to work the fields. There were several sugar crushing mills in the area but the Herbert River was insignificant compared with the lordly Clarence in New South Wales and I missed the barges floating downstream. Instead, there were little trains busily carrying loads of blackened cane to the mills. The air was heavy with the cloying smell of molasses.

In 1935 a giant South American toad *(Bufo marinus)* was introduced to control the grey-back beetle which in its larval stage did tremendous damage to sugar cane. Unfortunately the toad couldn't reach the beetles which burrowed into the cane several feet above ground. Instead of destroying the beetles, the toad was an ecological disaster, devouring bees by the hundred and eventually spreading from North Queensland west to the Territory and south towards New South Wales. Six to eight inches long, the cane toads were most frequently seen squashed by traffic on the Queensland roads.

It was always reckoned that white men couldn't cope with the hard, physical labour of cane cutting in the extreme heat of Northern Queensland and at first indentured labour was brought from islands of the Pacific, often by 'blackbirders' who brought the Kanakas on board their ships under duress. With the passing of the Polynesian Labourers Act of 1868 this iniquitous system was controlled and by 1904 the practice was abolished. Any remaining Kanakas were deported after 1906. To fill the need, Italian workers were brought in by the shipload with the result we had seen of Ingham being almost completely Italian. Eventually tough Australians became cane cutters too. Years later Ray Lawler wrote the highly successful play *Summer of the Seventeenth Doll* about cane cutters in Northern Queensland.

In Innisfail we spent most of the afternoon looking for a home. As it was a large town, all the halls had functions in them and would be occupied during the week. With great relief we finally found the C.W.A. hall, the comfortable headquarters of the Country Women's Association. Formed in New South Wales in 1922, the C.W.A. aimed to improve the welfare and conditions of women and children. Education, maternity support, instruction in first aid, hospital visiting and children's hostels were all matters they promoted. In most country towns there were rooms or even little cottages for which we were to be increasingly grateful.

A pleasant woman reporter on the *Sunday Australian* took our story but when the newspaper appeared I was amused and Shirl was horrified at the bold heading:

WOMEN CYCLISTS FIND MALES DISTRUST THEM.

'I'm not sending that back to Mum!' she said.

The article recounted how nice men were shy of asking us to dance.

Every day was filled with business and sightseeing. We placed several orders for books. Returning to the C.W.A. one afternoon we were shocked to find little Pete missing. We had left him there while we did the rounds of the shops and somehow he had got out. Frantically we hopped on our bikes and for three hours searched the district, asking everyone we met and even stopping cars to ask drivers if they had seen him. Night fell and we returned to the hall. Crushed with despair, we were writing our diaries when, ever so faintly, we heard barking. We leapt on our bikes and pedalled away in the direction of the sound. Crossing a bridge to the other side of the river, we saw an animated bundle of hair which launched itself at us and, dropping our bikes, we hugged him and rolled on the grass in joy. With great relief I went to bed with Pete curled comfortably on my feet.

-oOo-

25th May:

Wen, oh when are you coming home? The dahlias have bloomed and faded; the cannas have been cut out; the fish pond has been cleaned; the large poplar has lost its leaves; the chrysanthemums are blooming; the flower plots have been dug over; the spiteful cat has been delivered of kittens. So you see, if you do not return soon, the old College may not be recognizable; even the Principal may have retired!

Much love dear girl. Come and see us soon.

Your aged parent,

A. J.

-oOo-

From Innisfail it was a straight run of 68 miles north on the Bruce Highway to Cairns but we were never ones for the direct route. We chose instead to strike inland to the Tablelands, the beautiful region of mountains, lakes and rain forest. A truck helped us up over the foothills of Mt. Bartle Frère which at 5250 feet dominates the landscape and we headed for Yungaburra. We passed the extinct volcano on our right which is reputed to be the best example of a crater in the southern hemisphere. Inside it was covered with swampy grass.

It was now cold and raining. Forewarned, I had sent an urgent request to my mother for woollen socks and an extra jumper. We arrived wet through and cold at the house of a kind farmer's wife who offered us a bed for the night. While I was unpacking my haversack Shirl went off to find the lavatory. Ten minutes later she returned, closed the door behind her with a conspiratorial air, her face contorted with disbelief, and proceeded to tell me about the lavatory. It was situated in an outhouse, but under the hole was no pit or receptacle, merely a drain running out to some unknown destination. That served to dispose of liquid but for solids one had to spread some newspaper in the drain and when finished, wrap up the faeces in the newspaper and carry the little parcel across the yard to an incinerator. This, in steady rain!

A few days later we rode along a muddy road through wonderful tropical jungle until we reached Lake Eacham. It looked silver grey in the mist. I didn't think it was as beautiful as Lake St. Clair in Tasmania or the

Leg of Mutton Lake at Mr. Gambier. We walked along a track looking for
the Fig Tree Arch. It consists of three trees entwined and meeting over the
road, the whole inextricably suffocated by strangler fig. Another notable
sight was the Curtain Fig Tree. The original tree had half fallen and was
dead, the strangler fig alone being visible. A curtain of thin, hairlike roots
had grown down from the vine and taken root in the ground, thickening into
a wall. It was a colossal edifice. I started to climb it vertically, using
horizontal shoots as rungs but only managed to ascend six feet. Shirl found
an easier way. She started at its lowest end and climbed easily up the slope
to a point fifty feet high. I followed her with my heart in my mouth The last
third of the ascent had few toeholds, the wood was wet and a slip might mean
death. However, there was always another little cranny further on and soon
I joined Shirl on her lofty perch.

Continuing on to Lake Barrine, we stopped to see the giant red cedar
on the edge of the forest. It was reputed to be 2000 years old and was 160
feet high. Lake Barrine was more beautiful than Eacham and was obviously
the classier resort. At the Guest House we encountered the most uncooperative and cold woman. No, there wasn't a shed or hut or room where
we could camp; no, she couldn't think of any place in the district; no, she
couldn't sell us any butter. We were stumped. We didn't know where to go
for the night. A short distance away was the little school. The teacher lived
there himself but said we could camp under the house if we wished. He told
us of a farm a mile down the road where we might get butter. The farmer's
wife was in the middle of milking, aided by her four children all under ten.
She gave us some freshly made butter, a bottle of cream and a drink of fresh
milk. Unfortunately Shirl sickened me by saying: 'Isn't it awful to think that
an hour ago this was in the cow!'

We started to walk around the lake, a distance of about four miles.
Pete was with us, bounding along chasing wallabies and fetching sticks.
About two-thirds of the way round, the path was blocked by palm fronds and
tangled lawyer vine. Known to botanists as a prickly climbing palm, no
jungle is complete without the lawyer. It can envelop you in a network of
slender armed shoots, bristling with spines and can grow to a prodigious
length, twisting and turning to clasp with its aerial fingers every support until
it eventually surmounts the tallest tree. It can produce lengths of cane as
long as 500 feet. It weaves and entangles the vegetation of the jungle, links
huge trees together and thus forms compact masses of vegetation virtually
impossible to penetrate. The long leaves and the main rib carry sharp curved

spines sometimes three inches long and, once entangled, the unfortunate walker is held fast.

We couldn't face the prospect of retracing our steps all that way so decided to bypass the blockage by hacking through the jungle. There was a slight gully on the left, no dense undergrowth but just plants, a fallen log or two and lawyer cane. Shirl plunged down the slope and suddenly shrieked in anguish. The right side of her leg and arm had touched a stinging tree. This tree is quite common in rain forest and can cause poisoning, acute pain and sometimes blindness and paralysis. Shirl was in agony. I told her not to move and descended, sheath knife in hand. I cut off several stalks of the lily-like plant growing nearby and applied the juice to her stings. Then I cut away all the stinging trees and cleared a way through to the top path again. In so doing a piece of stinging leaf touched my ankle and a stab of pain shot through my foot. Greatly moaning, we continued along the path. Then Pete appeared and seemed to be grovelling at our feet. He must have been stung too as he was making convulsive movements with his right fore and hind legs and making little whining noises of distress. It was pitiful to see him writhing in pain. He couldn't walk and we had to carry him all the way back to the house. My, he was heavy! Back at the house, we applied more juice of the conjevoi lily to our limbs and Pete's paws.

Returning to Lake Eacham we kept meeting people in white tourist cars who would stop and take our photo. Then a car pulling a caravan stopped. It was the Fletchers whom we'd met at Miriam Vale months before.

At Lake Eacham guest house, Mr. and Mrs. Martin made us welcome and asked us to stay. I was aware of a sore spot on the upper lobe of my left ear. It felt like the head of a pimple but Shirl looked and proclaimed it to be a tick! Mr. Martin anointed it with kerosene and removed it with tweezers.

I was sitting in our bedroom writing letters when Shirl rushed in like a whirlwind and said 'Sailors!', pushed a comb through her hair and tore out! I sauntered into the kitchen and Mrs. Martin said: 'You've just missed some handsome young sailors.'

'Oh,' I said casually.

I knew they'd gone to look at the lake and would be back! I helped her to prepare afternoon tea for them. Shirl and I were industriously flitting in and out with sugar basins and milk jugs, painfully conscious of our Navy

Disposal bell-bottomed slacks and dirty shirts and shoes. I had my hair piled up and looked fairly presentable. Mrs. Martin told them who we were and we struck up a conversation. They were young and attractive and were based on two small ships in Cairns.

Just prior to their arrival Shirl and I had been arguing about staying on longer at the lake. I wanted to push on to Cairns. She wanted to stay. Nothing had been decided but now Shirl whispered hoarsely in my ear: 'If they're going to be in Cairns at the weekend, we'll leave tomorrow!'

It turned out they would be and they gave us contacts at the Strand Hotel. They were laughing amongst themselves and I suspected that the names they gave us were their own.

They left and Mr. and Mrs. Martin drove off to Yungaburra taking a telegram to send to Malvern Star in Cairns saying we should be arriving on Saturday morning. Left on our own Shirl and I walked around the lake and then, feeling greatly daring and knowing there was no one in the vicinity, swam nude in the lake. It was very cold but bracing and the freedom of being without clothes was wonderful.

Our last excursion was to accompany some timber hauliers out into the bush. We'd planned to catch the afternoon gate on the Gillies Highway which is so narrow and tortuous that the down traffic and up traffic take turns. We were assured we'd be back in time so set off with a small, active Italian called Franco on his large truck, leaving Pete with the Martins. We drove through the bush until we reached the clearing where several large logs were lying. When I facetiously asked Franco if he'd like me to lend a hand, he thrust an axe in my hand and told me to ringbark one of the massive logs. He showed me how to cut a strip right round it and then bash with the butt of the axe so that the bark flew off. It was very hard work. Then they proceeded to haul the logs alongside and heave them onto the truck by means of chains pulled by a tractor. Franco was very competent and had loaded six huge logs sixteen feet long inside an hour.

Returning to Lake Eacham we met Mrs. Martin who was distraught. She told us that an hour after we'd left she'd let Pete off his chain and he'd immediately streaked along the road and hadn't been seen since! After being lost in Innisfail I guess he thought he had to find us. Once more we set off, riding like mad women and calling every few yards. We rode to Barrine and Yungaburra and finally back to Eacham with no luck. We found the Martins had gone out and as we were walking around whistling and calling, we heard barking from the garage. Obviously he had come home and the Martins had shut him safely in.

Shirl said grimly: 'We've got to punish him Wen. He can't be running off all the time.' As I hesitated she said: 'Come on, we've got to teach him a lesson.'

We stripped switches from a tree and started to belabour him. It was the first time we had ever struck him with a stick. It upset me horribly. I was crying as I beat him and finally threw the stick away. Pete was cowering miserably and whining as he used to when a pup. At last he wrenched himself free and tore away. We felt dreadful. After a short while he returned and we allowed him one pat.

It was now too late to catch the afternoon gate to Gordonvale so we stayed one more night and got up at six next morning. A very thick mist was lying on the hills. Just before we left, Mrs. Martin rushed out with bags of mandarins for us. We said goodbye and set off at seven o'clock, our earliest start ever.

It was mostly uphill for three miles to the top gate. My watch said 7.45 but it must have been slow as the gate clock read 8am. The gate keeper said he shouldn't let us through as the down traffic ended at 8.00 but he let us go, warning us the up traffic would be coming at 9am. He was just going down himself by truck so he took Pete and our gear. Unencumbered we set off. The first two miles were up hill and we had to walk but just as we passed a notice reading '10 miles to bottom gate' the road dipped down. From there to the bottom was one glorious downhill ride, 750 curves and dropping 2,000 feet. Shirl was ahead of me but I came on her where the trees thinned out giving the first magnificent panorama of the lush valley below. She was taking a photo and I sped onward. Our bikes were very easy to manage having no loads and I just swooped along, rarely braking. A car has to slow down to take a sharp bend but one has only to lean on a bike's handlebars to turn quickly. The mile posts were whizzing by, one every three or four minutes. I arrived at the bottom gate at 8.50am and was tying my gear onto the bike when Shirl flew in with two minutes to spare, wounded. She'd skidded in some gravel and grazed her elbow. We cleaned the wound and set off again.

At Gordonvale we tried to get the postmark and failed. We had noticed recently that all the Post Offices we visited had been circularized

▲ Setting off

▲ Skiing at Mt. Kosciusko

▲ We reach Sydney

▲ We invest in sheath knives

▲ Jacaranda Festival, Grafton

▲ Relaxing at Coolangatta, Queensland

▲ Hiking at "Green Mountains," Lamington

▲ Wendy with friend at Lone Pine Sanctuary, Brisbane

▲ We meet the English Test Cricketers
l. to r. Major Howard (Manager), Wendy, Pollard, Shirley, Ikin, Washbrook

▲ Peter's Box

▲ Abbreviated skirts at Hervey Bay

▲ Thirsty Peter

▲ Australia Day Procession, Mackay

▲ Bombed building, Darwin

▲ Glamour image, Perth

▲ Weebabbie Cave, Nullabor

▲ Paddle Boat, Murray river.

▲ New look clothes, Geelong

▲ Peter becomes a member of the Tailwaggers Club

▲ End of journey, Melbourne

forbidding the giving of postmarks!

The heat was now so fierce that we got a lift to the outskirts of Cairns. In a café I rang the manager of Malvern Star to say we were almost there. On arrival at the shop we found a reporter and also the local Peters Ice Cream manager who told us the Bluebird Café was standing by to supply our needs!

Chapter 17

ROMANCE IN THE TROPICS

We loved Cairns from the start. It was a clean, modern town with wide streets and plenty of trees. The bane of most Australian towns is the dearth of greenery. The sea was nearby, although for beaches one had to go further north, but offshore were islands and beyond them the Great Barrier Reef. Behind was the Atherton Tableland if one wanted to escape the heat. It was now exactly four weeks since we'd left Townsville and we'd thought the whole detour would take only a month. We weren't anxious to return to Townsville, we had no deadlines to meet, Cairns was perfectly lovely and the Navy was in port!

We slept the first night at the back of the Malvern Star shop and spent the next day looking for a home. The brisk manageress of a YWCA hostel said she had just the thing for us, single bedrooms for only 45/- a week. What a laugh! We tried some disused Army huts which were derelict and stank but then we heard about the Naval Depot which had dozens of unused huts. A very sympathetic caretaker called Rex, who said he knew Shirl's father, got permission for us to use one consisting of several rooms, end to end, with a lavatory and washbasin. Hot showers were in an adjoining hut. He swept it for us and brought two mattresses, two chairs and a hammer and nails to facilitate the erection of our mosquito nets.

We were right in our supposition. The names we had been given at Lake Eacham were the naval officers' own and we soon learned that they spent each evening at the nearby Strand Hotel. One evening there was a new face. I was immediately attracted to him as he was quiet and thoughtful, looked like Rupert Brooke although his hair was dark brown and his eyes a deep blue. It transpired he was just getting over an unhappy love affair and consequently didn't socialize as much as his fellow officers. His name was Ross. He commanded a GPV, General Purpose Vessel, and Bill, who attached himself to Shirl, was on another. The two ships were based in Cairns and occasionally went to sea to destroy mines which were still appearing. Hardly an evening went by without our going to the pictures with the boys or sitting in the Strand listening to the pianist. The latter was very competent and also had a line of amusing songs which he sang – *The farmer's boy, The body in the bag* and *I'm a big boy now.* I had by now made an arrangement to play the piano each evening at the Pacific Hotel for which both Shirl and I were given our dinners and I received £2 a week.

There was great excitement in Cairns. The Governor of Queensland, Sir John Laverack, was to arrive two days later and there were to be several functions including a select Diggers Ball. We heard that we might be invited to it. We were ecstatic but we would need partners and what would we wear? It was to be a formal affair and even my case of good clothes left behind in Townsville did not contain an evening dress. We knew one family in Cairns, the Fogartys from the brewery. Their daughter, Daphne, told us to come around and see if any of her clothes would suit us. She was petite and it was highly unlikely that any of her dresses would fit us. Shirl found an attractive pale blue cloque dress which she tried on. Alas, the side placket wouldn't close. Daphne produced a royal blue jacket with white appliquéd leaves which neatly covered the gap so Shirl was well pleased. I despaired of finding anything. There was a white taffeta underskirt which looked good enough to be worn by itself, but not having any evening blouses, I seized on the idea of wearing my yellow floral dress tucked into the skirt with a royal blue cummerbund around my waist. It looked pretty good. But what were we to do for shoes? Daphne's feet were far smaller than ours. We had only our clod-hopper casual shoes with wedge heels and our brown leather strap sandals. I looked speculatively at my sandals. If only they were white!

'Let's make our sandals white!' I said to Shirl.

We asked for white adhesive tape and stuck it around the edge of the sole of our battered sandals. When that ran out, we got white cloth tape and stuck it with Tarzan's Grip across the straps. I was so excited! They looked marvellous! One could have imagined they were dainty white dancing slippers except for the rusty buckles on the ankle straps.

'We'll have to mince along so as to keep them hidden.'

Encouraged by having found decent clothes, we asked Ross and Bill to come as our partners. Off we went to the Ball. Cinderella could not have been more excited. I wore white and yellow frangipani in my hair and the heavy scent of the flower always reminds me of Cairns. Two of the other officers came too and with their partners we formed a happy group. The men were in their white, high-necked uniforms with gold buttons or white shirts, black trousers and cummerbunds. Shirl and I exulted at having overcome adversity although it was amusing to watch other women dancing by. Their eyes would travel down my body, appraising my dress and then their eyes would widen with horror as they saw my feet. Over the course of the evening the tape was rather worse for wear and I was tripping over loose bits trailing along the floor.

I was finding Ross increasingly compatible. He came from Melbourne and mentioned his time at Melbourne High School. I was surprised as I'd expected he'd gone to a Public School (that is, a private school).

'Did you ever meet my brother Phil? He taught there.'

'Not 'Percy' Law! Good heavens! He also taught me at Elwood.'

He started a flood of reminiscences.

'Phil Law, eh!* Gee, he was the first man who ever made any impression on me! He was terrific. It was he who started me along the lines of free thinking….and I'll never forget the lecture he gave us on evolution. He used to play the sax and piano, didn't he? First teacher I'd met who could play a musical instrument. Impressed me very much! Wonderful athlete too!'

I felt very proud and thought I must tell Phil.

Ross invited me to see his ship. He was 26 which I thought old for a male companion but young to command a naval ship. He showed me around the tiny bridge and his minute cabin, measuring six by eight feet, in which he ate, slept, dressed and worked. Over his bunk was a shelf filled with books including several anthologies of poetry. My heart leapt. There was also a thick tome on World Religions. I looked at it with interest. Flicking through the pages I saw a large section on Buddhism, another large one on Islam, on Judaism, on Hinduism. Where was Christianity? I finally found a small chapter on Christianity at the back of the book. That was the moment when the scales dropped from my eyes and a window opened on the world.

That evening while walking along the street I happened to say in the course of conversation:

> What is this life if full of care
> We have no time to stand and stare.

Ross continued the poem.

'Do you like poetry?' I asked. 'I noticed several books in your cabin today.'

'I love it!' he said fervently.

*Dr. Phillip Law, AC, CBE, probably the most experienced Antarctic explorer of the 20th century.

His favourite poets were Keats, Shelley and Milton. I told him I liked Yeats, Tennyson and Keats, then told him about the Australian School. He had never read any of the new poets although, I discovered, Rex Ingamells was his cousin. I wished I had my favourite volume *New Song in an Old Land* with me and told him I would lend it to him.

Most evenings we strolled along the Esplanade deep in conversation. He told me he had no one to talk with. He couldn't mix with his crew and his only other officer wasn't intellectual. I enjoyed talking with him too. Keith, my long-standing boy friend in Melbourne whom I'd known since I was fifteen, did not like poetry and, apart from the young man I'd been attracted to in Mackay, I never met men with 'soul'. My mind was in a turmoil of wild jubilation.

We woke up one morning to find Pete staggering around, his hind legs gone. We knew that this was a symptom of tick bite and feverishly examined him to find one, with no success.

'We'll have to take him to a vet,' said Shirl in anguish.

Dressing hurriedly, we rode out to make enquiries then, perching the little dog on a front carrier, went to the vet's surgery. He went over him thoroughly as we had done and then, separating his claws, found a great bloated tick almost concealed under a fold of skin. He gave him an injection and we took him home, greatly relieved. After that, every night before we went to bed, no matter how tired we were, we examined him meticulously, even looking in the crevices under his paws.

Cairns was rich in the number of offshore islands. Shirl and I wanted to see as many as possible. We learned that a launch was going across to Green Island, sixteen miles off Cairns and actually situated on the Great Barrier Reef, so we packed a small haversack and raced to the wharf. We had just boarded the *Merinda* when a man said: 'You can't take that dog to Green Island! It's a nature reserve.'

Shirl thought of asking Bill to mind Pete for the weekend. She leapt off the jetty, tore across the sand, over another jetty, up a breakwater and onto another wharf where the GPVs were moored. Bill agreed to mind Pete and she rushed back to the *Merinda* just in time.

From the sea we had a lovely view of Cairns. It was very beautiful with mountains ringing it, clustered white houses and blue sea. Half way across a huge sail was raised and we belted along. I thought of some lines in my Mackay poem:

> *Blue tropic seas,*
> *A swaying mast, a stiffening breeze,*
> *White sails, salt tang, brown decks aheap*
> *With silver harvest of the deep.*

On arrival all the passengers rushed off to have lunch but we decided to make the most of the reef while it was exposed at low tide. We put on our thick shoes, got sticks and headed for the brown expanse. Alas, most of the coral was quite soft and gave way beneath our weight. I was scared of being thus precipitated into a giant clam or of standing on a venomous stone fish and didn't enjoy it at all. Ecology wasn't a common concept then and I blush to admit we collected not only many varieties of shells (trochus, spider shells and those shaped like an ear) but also coral, brilliant ultramarine starfish six inches across, and even giant clams with their colourful mantles. I was very thrilled to find my first spotted cowrie. Usually invisible because of its grey mantle, I saw a couple of spots showing and dived to get it. We hid our treasures in the sand and returned next day to stow them in our sleeping bags. We had been learning a lot about shells and knew that the ones which are found on beaches are dead and lustreless. Only shells collected live retain their colour.

We loaded our heavily-weighted gear onto the *Merinda* for the homeward journey next day and as soon as we set off ran into bad weather – high seas, driving rain and wind. After half an hour nearly everyone was sick including Shirl. The side of the boat was lined with miserable bodies leaning over the water. As soon as we had rounded Cape Grafton we were sheltered and the sea abated. We carried our trophies into the hut and set up an exhibition in the adjoining room to the one where we slept. As the week progressed the shells and the animals inside them began to stink and we moved them into another room and then another more distant. Finally we packed them up and posted them back to our mothers and when I finally returned to Melbourne I donated mine to the Victorian museum. We were told subsequently that to get rid of the organisms inside, one should bury the shells and let the ants get to work.

One day Shirl and I and several of the naval officers went out on an RAAF air-sea rescue launch for six hours. Cairns looked even more beautiful from the sea. We went to a lonely beach several hours distant where an old mine had been washed up. The RAAF men blew it up and then we sailed to Fitzroy Island off Cape Grafton. There we were driven by the lighthouse keeper in a jeep up an incredibly steep mountain on a non-existent road to his eyrie on the summit. From there I had the most splendid view. Everything was an intense blue – the sea all around, islands here and there, capes and mountains, cloudless blue sky, sun pouring down and Ross's eyes as blue as them all.

Another day we were taken out to Michaelmas Cay, a flat sandy island absolutely covered with thousands of sooty tern nests and eggs. It was almost impossible to walk between the eggs and the hatchlings and the air was full of the deafening cries of hundreds of wheeling adult birds.

There were so many things to do in Cairns. Our days were filled with business, book selling (besides our original books we now had a line of glossy American magazines for which we took orders), visiting shops for advertising, having Press and radio interviews, speaking to groups of school children and country women. In the evening I had my piano playing at the Pacific Hotel and then there'd be pictures with Ross and Bill. Besides all that, there was sight-seeing. We were taken on a drive to Barron Waters, a delightful spot on the Barron River, then on to Yorkey's Knob beach. Another day we had a trip to Kuranda on the Atherton Tablelands. It was a wonderful drive up the Kuranda Highway which winds up the mountain behind Cairns affording a panoramic view of the sea, Green Island, Cairns valley, the Barron River and chequered canefields.

In between times we kept our eyes open for ships and luggers going north to Thursday Island at the tip of Cape York. There was a steady stream of ships coming and going and if we heard of a likely one we'd dash and plead our cause with the Captain, with no success. We met Captain Ray Parer who was sailing to New Guinea but couldn't take us. When we told Bill, he asked if we realized how famous Parer was. We didn't so he told us he was the sole surviving member of the flying pioneers – Ross and Keith Smith, Bert Hinkler and Kingsford Smith. Parer had made the first single-engined flight with another man from England to Australia in 1920 and the first solo flight from England to Australia in 1928.

Evenings in the Strand lounge were usually hilarious. Our naval friends, Ross, Bill, Dick and Les, were very amusing company, Dick and Les in particular keeping us simmering with mirth. Les commanded the second GPV and Dick was the son of Hal Gye, the illustrator of the Australian classic, *Songs of a Sentimental Bloke* by C. J. Dennis. He was always being picked on for wearing borrowed plumage although they all seemed to use each other's clothing. Dick would wear Ross's safari jacket, Ross had Les's belt buckle and Dick's buttons. They always looked great though, either wearing tropical khaki uniforms with gold buttons and insignia, or perhaps civvies. Shirl and I, expecting to take only a month on our detour to Cairns, had only two dresses each which we alternated for three months. I had the yellow floral and a pink and white cotton. In the evening I'd say to Shirl: 'I think that tonight I'll wear my pink dress for a change.'

'Oh, that'll be nice Wen. I think I'll wear my blue.'

The boys were great beer drinkers. Shirl and I didn't like beer. We weren't puritans but just for fun used to adjure them earnestly to *'leave the liquor alone, boys, leave the liquor alone! A man full of malt isn't worth his salt, so leave the liquor alone!'* For their part, they couldn't understand our addiction to icecream, Ross in particular looking pained when I ordered a dinner plate full of icecream and fruit. It was a nourishing meal for us. We had only one proper meal a day.

One night there were three women who had been drinking steadily in the Strand lounge. The tall dark one in black had gone upstairs. Alan the pianist was playing *Old Black Joe* when suddenly we heard a powerful soprano voice; the woman was slowly descending the stairs singing to the audience in the lounge. She reached the landing and, leaning over the banisters, threw wide her arms and declaimed loudly that she was coming, though her head was bending low. We stared amazed...it looked like grand opera. Then she came over and serenaded Les who, ever gallant, gazed up into her eyes with dog-like devotion. Meanwhile Dick and the other ageing debutante were playing imaginary violins to each other from opposite sides of the room. Alan the pianist was in good form and singing all his comic songs but the star of the evening was a very fat man who waddled up to the piano with a beaming face and started to bleat shrilly. He thought he could sing Al Jolson songs and gave us *Mammy, Sonny Boy* and *I'm in love.* Everyone was too stunned to laugh at first but towards the end, we were all convulsed. We clapped wildly and he beamed all the more. Then his friend came forward. He was tall, well-built, handsome and tanned in an immaculate tropical suit. He crooned softly into a glass jug, producing a sound mid-way between Sinatra and Mary calling the cattle home. All in all, it was a great night.

We took a few days break to go north to Port Douglas and Mossman.

It was very pleasant riding. The road was flat, we had light packs and it was sunny and warm with a tailwind. On the second day we got a lift with a man who was delivering fruit and vegetables to places between Cairns and Mossman. He said he'd be stopping at Port Douglas for a few hours fishing but then could take us on to Mossman. He invited us to ride in the cabin but we wanted a wide view of the Cook's Highway so climbed on the back. The drive through the bush was delightful. After passing the old toll gate we plunged down a long hill to sea level. From there the road curved along the coast, clinging to the side of the hills. It reminded me of the Great Ocean Road and Lorne in southern Victoria except that long stretches of road were flanked by avenues of frangipani and poinciana. At Hartley's Creek we made a stop and the owner of the refreshment rooms welcomed us with a cold drink then took us to see his three caged crocodiles. One was a big brute about twenty feet long. The others were babies but just as vicious. They snapped and barked and flicked their deadly tails when he poked them. In the wild, one lash of a powerful tail can knock a large animal into the river. The crocodile then carries it down to the bottom and stashes it in its larder to decompose a bit before eating it. We always kept a sharp eye on little Pete whenever we stopped by a river.

Further on we branched off the main road, cut through some scrub and emerged on the wide, four-mile long Port Douglas beach. The sand was so firm that it was used as a landing strip during the war and now cars drove along it regularly. We whizzed along it, our truck's tyres hardly marking the sand, and reached the headland of Port Douglas.

Our driver said we must meet a young couple from Melbourne and drove us up a steep road till we were on top of the headland. Julie Middleton came out to get her vegetables and showed us the little café she and her husband Peter were building. They had a superb site overlooking the ocean, river, mountains, sweeping beaches and Low Islets nine miles offshore.

Besides a kitchen, the Middletons had built a few terraces with tables and striped umbrellas. Julie offered us lunch while our driver went off fishing so we helped her prepare a great dish of prawns and salad. She was from New Zealand and had been a WAAAF. Peter was an Englishman, ex RAF. They had come up from Melbourne to carve out a new lifestyle in the tropics. I envied them their beautiful situation. While we were having our lunch a man called to leave Census forms for the next day. We didn't know where we'd be then so he told us to fill them out now.

We said goodbye to the charming Middletons and ran down the hillside to the township. There was virtually nothing there so there seemed no point in staying. When our driver returned from his fishing we jumped on his truck again and quickly covered the ten remaining miles to Mossman. It was very little larger than Port Douglas. The main topic of conversation in the town was the screening of the supposedly shocking film *The Wicked Lady* with Margaret Lockwood. Apparently the local Catholic church had forbidden its congregation to see it.

The Cook Highway terminated at Mossman. From there a rough track led sixty-six miles to Cooktown but there was not much chance of getting a lift there and we had no intention of subjecting our bikes or our bodies to such a grim journey. Besides I was longing to return to Cairns. We should have plenty more opportunity to see the outback on our journey west from Townsville.

Just as we were making plans to leave Cairns, however, we learned that the Aerial Ambulance was to make a flight into the centre of Cape York Peninsula to visit the famous Walsh River picnic race meeting. We had heard about this function which took place once a year and was the big social occasion for all the outback people living and working on the huge cattle stations. The pilot said he could fit us in the plane with minimal baggage and no dog. Rex, our friendly caretaker, agreed to mind Pete and with tremendous jubilation we each packed a small sack and took off.

From the air Cairns looked wonderful. There was the neat town with its white buildings backed by the Tablelands with their rain forests and lakes. Offshore was the deep blue sea, a scattering of islands and way beyond, the dark shadow of the Reef. We climbed until we were above the clouds then headed west. After about an hour and a half we descended through the clouds. The pilot pointed out the rough race course cut out of surrounding bush near an almost dried-up watercourse then landed at Wrotham Park Station. The station hands rushed out to meet us, unloaded gear and stretchers from the plane and loaded everyone and everything onto a beaten-up old truck. We set off along an appalling bush track, jolting and shaking until we reached the race track.

A large encampment had been set up nearby. Each station had its own cluster of tents, one for the station owner and his wife, one for the unmarried girls, one for the bachelors, one for the jackeroos and other station hands. We were welcomed and shown to the girls' tent where we unpacked and unrolled our sleeping bags on groundsheets. It was a Saturday and there was to be a dance that night. In fact there was a dance every night, usually lasting to the small hours.

As for the races there was a slight snag. Many of the horses had got away and gone bush. We were aghast.

'What about the race meeting?' I asked.

'Don't worry! We've sent some black trackers after them. They'll get 'em back.'

There was a large aboriginal camp a little way down the river. Aborigines are superb trackers and are used by the Queensland police in their criminal investigations. From the time they are children they learn the ways of the bush. They are expert horsemen, usually forming the work force of most Stations, and when tracking can ride at a canter while bending low from the saddle to look for traces of anyone passing by. They will see the faintest imprint of a foot or a broken twig on a tree. There was no doubt that the horses would soon be brought back. Sure enough the trackers returned later that day with the missing horses.

In the meantime other diversions were held. Shirl entered the ladies flat race. She had been a champion athlete at school and I expected her to win but she came in second. She hadn't run competitively since leaving school and perhaps had been eating too much icecream!

At the dance that night we had a wonderful time as there were so many men and few women. We danced non-stop until fatigue set in at about one o'clock.

The next morning I woke, aware of movement in the tent. I peered cautiously out of my bag and saw the other women in the tent dressed in attractive frocks, stockings, shoes and hats! Perplexed, I nudged Shirl and when she opened a bleary eye indicated the other women, raised my eyebrows and mouthed 'Church?' She looked puzzled too. There couldn't be a church service surely.

I sat up. 'Where are you going?' I asked.

'To the races!' said one and, checking her reflection in the mirror, swept out of the tent and with the others took up her position at a rough sapling fence fifty yards away.

I felt it was all very sad. This was their only social event of the year, the only occasion when they could meet other people and especially other men. They wore glamorous new clothes for their 'once a year' occasion and chatted vivaciously to the other Station folk. Shirl and I dressed as usual in shorts, shirts, sandals and bush hats.

I looked around with interest. The ground was bare and dusty. Bookmakers had set up their stalls around the course and were yelling the odds. Stockmen and jackeroos in their moleskins, check shirts and bush hats were strolling around, eyeing the girls. Some wore spurs on their high boots. Aboriginal Station hands and their women mingled with the crowd. Station owners had set up tables and chairs under umbrellas where they could relax in the shade. The climate here was quite different from Cairns with its frequent rain. West of the Great Divide the air was much drier and any grass was brown.

I am not usually fond of horse racing but this was different. The riders were either sons or employees of the Station owners and competition between the various large properties was intense. There were even races for the aborigines for which there was great enthusiasm. With caution I put modest sums of a shilling on any horse which I fancied but never seemed to back the right one. I was glad when lunch time arrived and we followed the crowd into the large shed where huge meals were being served. We did justice to the fare as we had had no breakfast.

One afternoon some jackeroos asked if we'd like to come with them on a truck to get some fresh beef.

'Where?' I asked. There were obviously no shops anywhere near.

'Come and see,' he replied.

We drove out across the surrounding trackless country, bumping over rough, tussocky brown grass until we saw in the distance a herd of bullocks. My heart sank. Surely they weren't going to......

The truck stopped near the beasts, the men conferred amongst themselves, got down from the truck and took their rifles from the back. They chose one beast which stood watching us calmly. I couldn't bear to look. Suddenly there was a loud report and I cautiously opened my eyes to see the animal lying on the ground, killed with one bullet. The carcase was manhandled onto a rough sledge made of eucalyptus branches and dragged back to the camp. The experience didn't spoil my enjoyment of luscious fresh steak that night when we had a barbecue in the dry part of the river bed. The aborigines in their camp were also celebrating. We could hear the chanting and clacking of boomerangs which accompanied their corroboree.

A group of stockmen gathered around a fire in the river bed, relaxing and smoking after their meal, telling jokes and yarning. I was interested to hear that they were familiar with many bush ballads, poems and songs which city-bred people thought corny and far-fetched but which were meat and drink to them.

'Give us *Clancy*!' begged one.

'No, let's hear *Around the Boree Log*', said another.

Banjo Paterson, Lawson, Kendall and the other bush poets knew their readers and the readers were well-acquainted with their work.

On the last day they announced a ladies' race. Shirl immediately volunteered. I wasn't experienced enough to ride a mettlesome grass-fed racehorse. Shirl wasn't so experienced but was quite fearless. Only two other girls entered the race. As they started, Shirl's horse sprang forward and streaked ahead of the others. Crouched low, she hung on as her horse galloped around the track. I was cheering her loudly but near the end the other two horses shot past her. Obviously the riders were canny and had been conserving their mounts' strength for a final burst of speed. However, Shirl upheld Melbourne's honour and received much praise being a city girl.

On the last night the dance was energetic and went on till dawn. Plentiful supplies of beer kept the men happy and some food was rustled up to restore flagging dancers. I slunk off to bed around two o'clock but many stayed on, whooping, singing and playing practical jokes on unsuspecting campers.

A strange stillness enveloped the camp next morning. Many families had already departed, other people were sleeping late. The Aerial Ambulance pilot apologetically told us he wouldn't be able to take us back as one of the gins from the aboriginal camp had been bashed on the head with an axe and needed hospital treatment. Shirl and I pulled out our map and considered the situation. We were right in the middle of Cape York, the nearest town of any size was Chillagoe, about fifty miles away, but how would we get there? As usual, fortune smiled on us and we got a lift with a family. From Chillagoe a railway line led back to our beloved Cairns where we had a vociferous welcome from little Pete and I was reunited with Ross.

In the ensuing days he declared his love for me. I was deeply attracted to him, mentally and physically, but was I in love or was it tropical magic? When I was in Melbourne I thought I was in love with Keith, but now? As my sister Marj wrote in answer to a letter I sent about my dilemma: 'Blessed propinquity is the thing!' Anyway, we should be leaving Cairns very soon and it might be another year before I returned to Melbourne. Ross would be out of the Navy by then and we would both have a more normal life style. My head had always ruled my heart so I postponed any decision. When I finally left Cairns we kept up a constant correspondence and Ross phoned me nearly every night for the duration of the trip. Fortunately he got a serviceman's concessions for his phone calls!

Chapter 18

OAK PARK PICNIC RACES

Eventually we had to leave Cairns. We had been away from Townsville for three months instead of one. Mr. Nabbs visited Cairns and was obviously wondering why we were dallying in North Queensland and we were dreading the Peters Icecream reaction to the huge bill we had amassed. However, one night in the Strand lounge, a man rushed up and wrung our hands. It was the Peters manager in Townsville. He took us to his table and introduced us to the Brisbane Sales Manager and two other executives.

'You'd better be prepared for the shock of the ice cream account when it arrives,' I said.

The Brisbane manager roared with laughter. 'Don't mind us! Just go on eating it!'

We intended to. It had been beautiful winter while we had been in North Queensland but from now on it would be blazing summer.

We took all our gear on the little train to Kuranda as we had already been driven up the mountain road. Now we were able to concentrate on the unfolding panorama of one of the most spectacular views in Australia. It was a lovely, sunny morning and the Barron valley was spread out below us. Chequered fields and wrinkled blue mountains led the eye out to the blue sea beyond. At one point the little train passed under a small waterfall and we pulled our heads back into the carriage. Every year Kuranda won a competition for the most beautiful railway station in Queensland. Its station building had hanging baskets of colourful flowers and ferns, tubs of a dozen varieties of croton stood along the platform and flower beds were ablaze with coleus, poinsettia and flowering shrubs.

We had arranged to see over the great Hydro-electric scheme and, on arriving at the Barron Gorge, we caught the flying fox which travelled on a cable across to the other side. The great gorge dropped away beneath us. On the other side we set off with a guide along a forest track till we reached the scenic railway which plunges down the side of the gorge. Our guide rang a bell and soon the little carriage appeared over the lip of the bank. It was a very rough affair, mainly used for carrying men and materials down to the works. We hopped in and while on level ground were nearly lying on our backs so that after tipping over the edge and going down the side, we were sitting in a vertical position. What a thrill! The gorge was magnificent, even with little water in it. It would be an awesome sight when the river is in flood. Leaving the carriage we entered a cave and followed a passage until we entered a big room full of machinery. I am not technically-minded but it was all most impressive.

Rain in Kuranda sent us on to Mareeba which is in a dry belt and rarely gets rain. Consequently it is the centre of tobacco farming. By contrast Atherton, twenty miles further on, is perpetually wet. It rained steadily for three days and was almost as bad as Mackay in the Wet. Maize and peanuts were staple products in Atherton but the rain continued to fall in a deluge. We were hurrying to get to Townsville within eight days as we'd heard of a ship going to Thursday Island and wanted to ask the Captain for a passage. If he wouldn't take us, we'd head west. We were beginning to get reports of another picnic race meeting at a place called Oak Park, north of Hughenden. That would be fun.

Travelling back to Townsville, we stopped at Millaa Millaa to visit the renowned Kjellberg Clinic tucked away in the hills. Way ahead of his time, Mr. Kjellberg worked miraculous cures with massage and spinal manipulation. Who should be there as well but the Fletchers whom we'd met nine months earlier at Miriamvale and six months later at Lake Eacham.

We called at *Bellenden Plains* where Miss Henry was running her station again after her accident. We managed to get away without having to eat any salt beef. And so we returned to Townsville. So much for schedules! We had now been on the road for sixteen months and still hadn't reached Darwin.

The trip to Thursday Island didn't eventuate so we turned west from Townsville and set off along the road to Charters Towers. It was late August and there was a very cold headwind. The road was corrugated. Along came a truck and picked us up. I kept looking for the so-called Tors or Towers, hills overlooking the city but couldn't see anything remotely resembling an ant hill. All was flat. Then I found that my bike chain had broken in two. We arrived on the outskirts of Charters Towers, loaded up our bikes and set off for the main street. I had to walk, pushing my disabled bike. The air was raw. As we passed houses I smelt the heavy scent of orange blossom, a lasting impression of Charters Towers.

We met the Mayor who ran a newsagency and he said we could sleep in the Town Hall over the weekend but must move after that. After a miserably cold night, the sun came up and it became quite warm but the westerly cut like a knife. We went to explore the town but no cafés were open and of course no shops as it was Sunday. We had a contact at one hotel and the proprietress was very kind and asked us to 'drop in any time' but didn't specify a date or ask us to a meal. We felt very depressed. I said to Shirl: 'No friends, no warmth, no sleep, no food, no cash, no bike and no Ross. Is life worth living?'

Fate relented and we found another home in the Workers' Club. While talking to the Malvern Star manager who was fixing my chain, I discovered that Pete's collar was missing. We had bought a new one in Cairns and took the precaution of fixing on it a metal plate with his name engraved on it in case he should get lost again. The engraving had cost four shillings, a large sum, but we couldn't risk losing him. There was great consternation at losing the collar. There was no way it could have fallen off so it must have been taken. We advertised in the *Northern Miner* and an apologetic mother returned the collar. She had discovered it at home and shamefacedly brought it back. Her young son had obviously thought it a good souvenir.

The next day was my 21st birthday. We were woken early by a knocking on the door. In a fog of sleep, I pulled on some clothes and opened it. There was a spry, energetic elderly man with a cloth cap. It was Ernie Old, the veteran 72-year-old cyclist who was making his way in a clockwise direction around Australia. We kept hearing about him and expected to meet him somewhere on the East-West road. Studying our map with us, he warned us about the state of the road and advised us to go by train at least as far as Hughenden as he doubted if we'd make it on the 167 miles of rough road. We had some publicity photos taken with him and he departed on the long ride to Townsville. I think he was in the habit of getting lifts too!

Ernie Old wasn't the first man to do marathon cycle trips. At the beginning of the 20th century Francis Birtle rode around Australia twice and crossed the continent seven times by bike. In 1912 he wrote about the poor conditions in which the aborigines lived.

I went to the Post Office and got a sheaf of telegrams including one from the Post Office staff! I began to feel more cheerful and by evening I began to suspect that something was going to happen later. I pumped Shirl for details but she wasn't forthcoming   Sure enough there was a party turned on for me. There were about fifteen teenage youths and girls who had decorated the hall and organized adolescent games like Winks and Forfeits before a large supper was served. It was all very jolly and it was more fun than having a solitary night at home. A phone call from Ross completed my day.

Charters Towers is on the edge of the great western plain and the nights were bitterly cold. One evening at sunset I climbed up to look out an upper window in the kitchenette and was immediately consumed by a feeling of boundless space. There was nothing to be seen but flat plain extending westwards. I felt that there was nothing between me and the West Australian coast two thousand miles away. Gone was the Great Dividing Range. There would be no more hills until Central Australia.

The road to Hughenden was indeed terrible as Ernie Old had said. We got a lift on a truck, bumping over stones and potholes for fifteen miles to Southern Cross where there was a railway siding. At 3.30pm the mail train came through. We asked the guard for a lift. He agreed so we 'jumped the rattler', bundling our stuff into his van and covering the hundred miles to Hughenden. It was a trying journey as the van was full of boxes of day-old chicks and Pete kept worrying them. I don't suppose he'd ever seen chicks. I couldn't sleep as I had to keep an eye on him. We arrived at Hughenden after seven hours and sneaked out behind a line of goods trucks. It was too late to knock up the church people, the manageress of the theatre wouldn't let us sleep there so the Police Sergeant let us use his station verandah.

We were woken next morning by flocks of screaming white cockatoos and the ringing of church bells. Our priority now was to find someone who would take us to the Oak Park Race Meeting. We met Mr. Best, the local barber and bookmaker who said he and his wife could take us. We were jubilant. We had loved the Walsh River meeting and this one was even more famous.

Hughenden atoned for Charters Towers and we were overwhelmed by hospitality. While passing the railway station one day we saw a lot of schoolgirls leaving a stationary carriage marked 'Department of Public Instruction – Travelling Domestic Science School'. We investigated and met a charming woman, Miss Ransome, who lived in her own private carriage and travelled up and down the line staying eight weeks in each town, teaching girls cooking and dressmaking. The schoolroom carriage was fitted with a wood stove, cupboards of crockery and saucepans, tables, a blackboard, stainless steel sink and two sewing machines. Her quarters had a bunk, basin, mirror, wardrobe, chair and a portable bath with a shower. We learned that there was also a mobile Baby Clinic.

The next day we were to drive 140 miles to Oak Park. I had awoken feeling nauseated and soon after was sick. There was no food in my stomach and I vomited only bile but felt slightly better. I felt very weak but had to sort out things to leave behind and things to take. We left our bikes at the Police Station and went to the Bests'. The back of their truck was full of camping equipment but we climbed up on top of it all and set off. Crossing the wide, dry bed of the Flinders River we drove along a fairly good dirt road. It was a hot day but there was a fresh breeze. I donned a headscarf to protect my hair from the dust.

After a while we picked up a stockman then an aborigine called Caesar. Somehow they fitted on the back of the truck too. After 75 miles we made a stop. The others had sandwiches and a soft drink but I'd been sick again and couldn't look at food. The unwieldy truck began to lurch a lot, shaking up my poor stomach and making the trip miserable. By now it was extremely hot, dusty and bumpy and Pete was crawling all over me and scratching my bare legs. The journey seemed interminable. At last we turned off the main road onto the rough Oak Park track for the last 28 miles. The surface was execrable and we were thrown about like peas for 2½ hours. I wanted to die. My stomach protested at each jolt. At last we reached Blackbrae Station and went into the cool garden. Shirl and Mrs. Best wolfed mulberries but I couldn't look at them. I picked some oranges to take with me.

At half past five we reached the camp. There was a large number of tents along the Copperfield River (dried up except for a couple of waterholes), a dance hall, a dining tent and kitchen and a number of amusement booths, stalls and sideshows. We had arrived two days early as Mr. Best wanted to set up his stalls. I went to sleep in the shade while he erected his tent. We hadn't known what to do about sleeping and eating but the Bests had brought two stretchers for us. When I awoke we set up our stretchers next to their tent in the open, hung out our frocks on convenient branches, had a wash and unrolled our sleeping bags. To our astonishment a car and caravan drove up and parked next to us. It was the Fletchers again.

Mr. Best told us that we should eat with them and, in return, we could help him run a stall of toilet requisites while he cut men's hair. He even said we could cut women's hair if there were any customers. Shirl and

I always cut each other's hair but I don't think I would've been brave enough to do a paying customer.

As at Walsh River, all the properties had separate encampments - Oak Park Station, Blackbrae, Cheviot Hills and so on, with tents for their families, employees and guests. We were outsiders from Hughenden and were snubbed consistently by several of the families. All the stations within miles were owned by relatives. There were four main families – Nimmo, Lethbridge, Collins and Murphy. Everyone seemed to be related. Consequently there was a tight, smug little aristocracy which governed its penny kingdom with contempt for the outsider. One Nimmo woman said to me: 'You'll find things are different on these Stations. Our stockmen are treated as our equals...(Gee, I thought, how wonderful!) ...at race meetings,' she finished.

Around a thousand people attended the meeting, coming from as far as Cairns and Normanton in the Gulf country. A caterer was engaged to feed the multitude and a vast quantity of food and drink was consumed.

After our long and tiring day we turned in although it was almost as light as day. There was a nearly full moon and masses of stars, a hundred times brighter in the bush than they appear in a city.

I awoke at eight, the hot morning sun making me sweat. It was very funny getting up at our late hour each morning. All the other campers would be up and about very early and we would be trying to get out of our sleeping bags and into blouses and shorts.

I had a slice of toast and honey for breakfast. My nausea had gone and I was very hungry. It must have been the Hughenden water which had upset me. We helped Mr. Best set out the goods on his stall and for the next two days sold visiting stockmen toothpaste, shaving cream, boot polish, combs, cigarette lighters and torches. The amusements were in full swing and over a loudspeaker corny hillbilly music was being churned out until I thought I'd scream.

In the afternoon I heard that the piano had arrived and I dashed over to the dance hall. It was a good piano and I played for ages. Then a crowd of young station folk arrived to decorate the hall for the dance and I had fun sitting on a hessian bag while they dragged it and me around the sawdusty floor to polish it. Most of them were Nimmos from Oak Park and Blackbrae.

My stretcher had collapsed under me during the night and a helpful man showed me how I'd assembled it all wrong. He fixed it as steady as a rock. I prepared for the night's festivities. I cleaned my shoes, carted hot water from the kitchen to fill the can in the shower booth and then had a wonderful hot shower. After a light tea I went to have a ride on the flying horses and, horror, saw a girl wearing my blue floral dress I'd bought in Atherton. I had a chat with her and arranged not to synchronise! She was one of the Station crowd and doubtless had several others to wear whereas I had only three!

One of the Nimmos came and asked me if I'd start the dance. I started playing and people came drifting in until we had a large crowd. I played for three dances and then a girl came up and asked if I were tired. I wasn't but I let her play for the Barn Dance. She made a frightful hash of it, everyone was out of step. Then she started playing a circular waltz. It went on and on until we were all dropping with fatigue. When she was about to play another old time number I protested. She didn't know any modern dance songs so I played a foxtrot and continued through the evening. Near the end a man came up and thrust a small bundle of cash into my hand. The public had subscribed! I was very thrilled. I'd worked for three hours instead of dancing.

The races were not starting till the next day and people were doing the rounds of the stalls and rides. Dartboards, coin games and coconut shies vied with hawkers selling anything from clothing to knick-knacks. One of these attracted customers by calling out 'I'm here to sell.' Money was flowing like wine so we tried to think of a way of earning some. Shirl suggested a guessing game like the number of peas in a bottle or the weight of a cake. We couldn't find any peas but I thought we could use strands of horse hair – which was in keeping with a race meeting. We found an unsuspecting animal and surreptitiously removed several hairs from its tail with nail scissors. We put the coil of hair in a bottle and set out to find clients. We charged one shilling to enter the game and the prize was to be a year's subscription to *National Geographic*, one of our fine American magazines.

Mr. Best was raffling a canteen of cutlery so we sold four-shilling tickets for that. Then we discovered that one of the cooks at Lyndhurst Station decorated bullocks' hooves. He polished them beautifully, bound the edges with thongs and then did designs in pokerwork on them. They were most unusual and attractive. He gave us one to raffle. These enterprises proved quite popular (we made over £5 each during our five days) and we were just starting to go the rounds of the tents when a woman from Cardington came up and asked if we'd like to go to Oak Park homestead with her. I loved visiting homesteads on these huge Stations. They were usually gracious homes, beautifully furnished with every comfort. We stopped first at the Werrington camp for morning tea with one of the Lethbridge clan and then drove five miles to Oak Park. In front of the house was a riotously coloured flower garden of bonfire salvia, larkspur, nasturtiums and herbaceous border plants. At the back was a garden with a wide variety of healthy, luxuriant vegetables. A plenitude of water made the whole area an oasis compared with the dry scrubby countryside nearby. The house was cool, partly slab-built with large fireplaces. It was shaded by huge mulberry trees laden with fruit and we gorged ourselves on them. We were driven further on to see the actual oaks, a great tract of casuarinas or she-oaks from which the property took its name.

The long-awaited races started the next day. Mr. Best now had to be bookmaker so we minded his toiletries stall and sold his raffle tickets. I stayed there all morning, Shirl dashing away now and then to sell the horsehair competition. I sold 7/6d worth of goods to a young jackeroo who had only come in to buy one of our raffle tickets. Then I lured a couple of partly drunk men in. I had a brainwave and sold them a tin of shoe polish with an offer to clean their very dusty boots right on the spot. One offered me two shillings to clean his. Shirl reappeared and chivvied the second man. We both started polishing energetically and collected our reward.

Every now and then a pack of horses would thunder around the track and we'd rush to look. I saw two riderless horses. One jockey broke his ankle when he fell but otherwise the races were uneventful.

At noon we packed all the goods away and had lunch. I changed my shorts for a skirt and blouse but refused to wear shoes so just washed my feet and wore sandals. We went to the racecourse fairly early and spent a profitable hour selling our three raffles but when the crowds started arriving, we felt rather embarrassed and stopped. We were getting snubs from the smartly-dressed Station families and regretted the fact that we wore no shoes or good dresses. We looked horribly hick in sandals and bush hats.

By mid-afternoon the sun was beating down and I craved sleep. We returned to the camp, grabbed our groundsheets, crossed the river bed and walked downstream a short distance to a cluster of shady trees. There we lay down to sleep. Alas! Ants swarmed over our legs and arms. I rolled myself in my groundsheet and roasted. After half an hour I gave up. Shirl fetched her stretcher and tried to sleep but I stayed at the camp.

Mrs. Best called me for tea – delicious grilled steak. Shirl returned at seven after an unsuccessful attempt to sleep. The ants had merely swarmed up the legs of her stretcher. I had got the remnants of a joint from the kitchen for Pete. It still had lots of meat on it so Shirl tucked into it as she'd missed her tea.

That night the dance went on until dawn. There was now a professional band but they packed up at three and I was dragooned into playing the piano. I played songs like *Good morning* and *Three o'clock in the morning* but by four o'clock I wilted and went to bed.

Saturday was the last day. Mr. Best didn't open his stall so we decided to go to the races in the morning and sleep all afternoon in preparation for the final night's revelry. In our best frocks and shoes we didn't feel so embarrassed alongside the elegant women. I enjoyed this morning very much. After losing a few cheap bets, I got a tip from one of the Station girls and backed Tessie for a win then put two shillings on Patch for a place at even money. What a finish it was! Tessie came in first and Patch third. I won thirteen shillings, my first win! After lunch we slept by the river all afternoon. Ants still swarmed up the stretcher legs but I climbed into my sleeping bag and, although roasting, slept.

In the evening we measured our horsehair. It was 79 feet 8 inches. One man thought he'd got closest with a guess of 79 feet but there was no record of it in our notebook. An old man had guessed 80 inches so we awarded him the prize. Then we drew the winning tickets for the canteen of cutlery and the bullock's hoof. An old gin, Nelly Connelly, won the hoof. Shirl offered her ten shillings for it and I offered eleven. The old aborigine's eyes gleamed happily at the prospect of money. Shirl and I were quarrelling over who was to have the hoof when Mr. Best said he'd give the old girl fourteen shillings and Shirl and I could toss for it. I was reluctant as well I might be. As usual, Shirl won the toss. A friend from Lyndhurst Station said he'd ask the cook for another one for me.

That evening for the final night's dance, I bathed and put on my new blue dress. 'Dance till dawn' was the order and most of the women were wearing full-length evening dresses. We enjoyed ourselves. There were always plenty of partners at race meeting dances! Prizes were presented to the race winners in the dining tent and somehow everyone crammed into it. By 4am I was very weary so I went back to camp and slept. Shirl carried on and at 6am, when the dancing finished, all the crowd paraded around the camp, banging tins, singing and pulling people out of bed.

The Bests packed up and returned to Hughenden next day but we had been invited to stay with one branch of the Lethbridge family at Warwombie Station 26 miles outside Hughenden. Our gear was taken on to Warwombie by Mrs. Lethbridge's sister and we got a lift there next day in a single-seater tourer. Unencumbered by luggage we were able to fit in the dickey seat with little Pete but it was quite cold in the wind and we huddled down behind the roof and tried to sleep. We drove to the main road via Cheviot Hills instead of Blackbrae and dropped another passenger there. We were then able to ride in the front seat next to the driver but we were both very sleepy and not much company for him.

We arrived at Warwombie at 4 o'clock just in time for iced milk and lemon butter tarts. Sugar rationing had just been discontinued. I wondered that it had ever been imposed with eight hundred miles of sugar plantations in Queensland.

Shirl discovered to her consternation that she'd lost her wallet. The last time she remembered having it was when she had her photo taken on top of one of the large magnetic anthills at Oak Park. There was no way she could describe the location to anyone even if she could have contacted somebody. Hundreds of these great anthills are dotted across the plains. They tend to be built several feet high in a north-south line with thin, flat walls and are useful for navigating in the outback.

Warwombie homestead was as charming as others we had seen. There were large, airy rooms and verandahs around the front. An old kitchen and an open-air dining room were at the back. A cool green fernery was at the side and a colourful garden all around.

I was impressed with the Lethbridges. They seemed more democratic than some of the squattocracy. Their stockman ate with the family and had a room in the house. He even called Mr.Lethbridge George. For two days we did nothing but catch up on sleep, write our diaries and many letters and eat wonderful meals with cream thrice daily. We washed our filthy hair in soft rain water from the tank next to the house. All the dust of Oak Park, acres of it, was in our hair. Every day we listened with Madge

Lethbridge to the next episode of *The Lawsons* on the wireless. This was a long-running serial about country people and was followed avidly by every woman in the outback. Mr. Lethbridge and Bob the stockman were out mustering all day so there were no horses for us to ride.

At last Mr. Lethbridge drove us back to Hughenden, installed us and our haversacks in the church hall and we collected our bikes and surplus gear from the Police Station.

Chapter 19

BEYOND THE BLACK STUMP

The minister of the church had to go to Richmond so he agreed to take us the 104 miles in his utility truck. The main road was merely a straggling track meandering out of the town. My bike was leaning against the side of the truck and on the carrier were tied the two bundles I'd left behind in Hughenden. About thirty miles out, I looked behind and they were gone. The rough road had jolted them off the bike and off the truck. It was bad news. There was my bag of newsagents' books and my sleeping bag cover full of surplus gear which I didn't take to Oak Park – music, poetry books, bike pump, water bottle and other bulky items. We drove back about eight miles with no sign of them so asked a woman in an isolated house to stop other traffic and to forward my stuff to Hughenden Police. Shirl had bought some leather to make another wallet but how could I replace my belongings?

Now we were traversing the great downs, flat, grassy, treeless country. 'Wonderful cattle country!' the cattle men would tell us but it looked dead to me! It was actually quite pretty with no harsh and glaring colours as I'd expected but pale blue sky, soft brown grass (or grey that looked a misty blue, like little Pete) and deep red dirt road.

Then the truck had a blow-out! Out jack, up car, off wheel, on spare, down car, away jack and on we went. We reached Richmond at noon. It was flat, dry and hot with only one street, two hotels, two stores and two cafés. While doing our business we saw a lot of cars and utility trucks outside the Royal Hotel. There were several well-dressed women who had come to town to attend Country Club and Country Women's Association meetings. We made feverish enquiries about lifts to Julia Creek or Cloncurry but had no luck. They were fairly local people. We resigned ourselves to staying in Richmond for the night and found a home at the church hall. It was filthy! There had been heavy rains ten days previously and a herd of goats had cut up the ground outside so that people coming to a dance in the hall had tramped in inches of sticky black mud. The black soil roads in this area need only an inch of rain to turn them into bogs. Cattle walking through them acquire hooves six inches high and car wheels can't turn for the quantity of mud which adheres to them.

The proprietress of one of the hotels said her utility truck could take us to Julia Creek next morning. Brilliant! We got up at 7am, packed rapidly and set off at nine. It was a terribly hot, dusty trip for 103 miles through dry and grassy plains but again the soft colours offered some respite from the glaring sun. In Julia Creek a man said he could take us 70 miles on the way to Cloncurry. As the total distance was only 92 and the railway line ran parallel to the road we accepted with enthusiasm and set off at 9.30am next day on the back of his roadworks truck. It was going to McKinlay. One of the men said he'd ride outside as it was cooler so Shirl took Pete into the cabin. The country at first was flat with arid soil and no blade of grass but soon it reverted to the usual grassy downs. It was a very hot day and my legs became burnt on one side. I asked the man, Mr. Galliano, where was the railway line which, according to my map, ran alongside the road. He blithely said: 'We're nowhere near the railway. We've turned off that road but you'll be able to get a lift much more easily at McKinlay because it's on the main North Western Highway from Winton and Longreach. No one ever uses the Julia Creek to Cloncurry road.' I whipped out my map and behold, McKinlay....seventy miles south-west of Julia Creek and still practically as far from Cloncurry after three hours gruelling journey. I felt sick with despair. I had hoped to reach Cloncurry by lunchtime.

'If you can't get a lift, come back to Julia Creek with us at two o'clock!' said Mr. Galliano happily. Ha! A day wasted spent tearing around the sizzling plains!

McKinlay was a tiny place with only two hotels and no cafés. There was nothing to eat and we felt hot, dusty and unhappy. Despite visiting the hotels on business we couldn't afford a meal and had no offers of refreshment or hospitality. Then we heard that a utility truck had left Kynuna Station en route to Cloncurry and might be able to take us. It was heavily loaded so we decided to send our bikes on by rail and were able to fit on the utility when it arrived. It already contained the Station manager, his son and two inspectors of the Scottish Australian Company which owned lots of properties in these parts. We had a speedy trip through delightful country. It was now very green and grassy with occasional belts of trees and numerous dry creek beds. It made a change from the plains. When we were near Cloncurry, lots of funny little hills appeared, all very green. I saw several wallaroos hopping about and even emus.

Cloncurry impressed us from the beginning. It was a very big town with lots of hotels, always our criterion in judging a town. Hotels meant a chance to earn money! We pulled up outside the Post Office Hotel and the men on the truck invited us inside to have a drink. To our horror we saw a group of Qantas pilots, some New Zealand Air Force officers who were returning from England, a few Englishmen and lots of elegant women. We felt like tramps!

I remembered Cloncurry as a name on a board game I had as a child. It depicted a map showing the stopping places for the Centenary Air Race from London to Melbourne in 1934. In the final stages the planes had to stop at Batavia, Surabaya, Darwin and Cloncurry. Because of its situation near the western border of Queensland, Cloncurry had always been an important landing strip for planes.

It was also the base of the first Flying Doctor Service. The Rev. John Flynn was a Presbyterian minister who from an early age had been fascinated by the vast empty spaces in the centre of Australia. In the same area you could comfortably fit France, Spain and the British Isles. In this huge stretch of country covering many thousands of square miles there were only 50,000 white Australians. In 1911 Flynn started to travel extensively through the Northern Territory and Central Australia and began to report to newspapers on the problems and hardships the people of the outback had to face. With the aid of public subscriptions he was able to found the Australian Inland Mission. He was a familiar figure among the cattlemen, drovers and boundary riders. He rode camels and mixed with other camel drivers. He carried his swag through the desert. Apart from the isolation and loneliness of the people, the main problem was the lack of adequate communication and medical assistance. There were no telephones or cars and often patients had to be carried strapped on an ironing board to the nearest telegraph station. Flynn dreamt of a chain of nursing homes at intervals of three hundred miles throughout the outback. But nursing homes didn't solve the problem of communication.

By 1920 radio had made great progress but Flynn needed a Transmitting Receiving Set so moderately-priced that an outback settler could buy it and so simple that he and his family could operate it. Fate led Flynn to Alfred Traeger, a young engineer interested in radio. Traeger collaborated with Flynn and, after three years of continuous work and innumerable discouragements, finally developed his now famous pedal transmitter-receiver in 1926 which proved to be the answer to Flynn's problem. These small sets were distributed to people in the outback as well as medicine chests containing various stock remedies numbered for simple dispensing.

Even with bush nursing homes being built and a pedal wireless there were still far too many people who could never reach the nearest hospital. Since the First World War aviation had been developing and Flynn realized this was the answer. The first doctor, Dr. L. Welch, was based at Cloncurry where Qantas Airways (Queensland and Northern Territory Aerial Services) had an airmail centre. They were prepared to help by having a suitable plane and pilot available, night and day, at a reasonable charge. A 50 watt transmitter was installed in the vestry of the Presbyterian church. Then the Stations had to clear modest landing strips for the plane to land.

The first flight was made in 1928 to Julia Creek. By 1934 the service had been extended to Western Australia then Victoria, New South Wales and South Australia. Eventually there were twelve Flying Doctor bases dotted across Australia. Flynn died in 1951, just before the first broadcast from the School of the Air, an offshoot of the pedal wireless network and another reason we must thank John Flynn. His grave is four miles outside Alice Springs but his living monument is the Royal Flying Doctor Service.

We met one of the Flying Doctors and asked if there were any prospect of flying to Normanton on the Gulf of Carpentaria. He had no flights in prospect. Shirl was keen to make a trip to Normanton. I wanted to see the Gulf country too but was becoming anxious about timing. My brother Peter was arriving home from Borneo on long leave from the Shell oilfields in Brunei. We had always expected to be home by Christmas. It was now September and we still had to go to Darwin and down to Adelaide before returning to Melbourne. Every day was important now.

The minister of the church where we were camping said he knew a man who could take us to Normanton.

'He's taking three black kiddies who are staying with me back to their home. They've been at the Bush Children's holiday camp in Townsville.'

We didn't leave till 8pm the following night. The big truck was laden with large petrol drums and the three aboriginal children, Laura, Alan and Anzac, were ensconced on the top of the drums and we fitted in where we could. We spread our sleeping bags and other padding and composed ourselves to sleep. What a joke! There was a brilliant moon and its light shone in my eyes. (I thought of Miss Farrell's dire warnings!) Little Pete was tied to a spare tyre on top of the drums and his rope was long enough to permit his walking over my face and licking the children's faces so that they awoke screaming and had to be pacified. I had tied myself to the tyre to stop myself from rolling off on the bumpy ride but the rope around my waist prevented my zipping up my bag and I froze. My hips were blue with the rough massage of the petrol drums as the truck lurched and leapt over the bumpy track and in the morning my right eye was swollen due to the unerring accuracy of Laura's shod foot as it shot out once after a bad jolt. Dawn found us a tired and irritable crew. I consoled myself with the thought that we were due to arrive in Normanton at dusk. After a day of merciless sun pouring down (even though we huddled under ineffectual awnings of mosquito net), dusk found us still 93 miles away. We'd been averaging only eight to ten miles an hour.

After another bumpy, sleepless night we arrived in Normanton at 9am. Good Lord, what a place! I felt as though I'd driven into a Wild West frontier town in an American film. There were a couple of hotels, a very wide red gravel main street – the sort it took minutes to cross, tin houses, windmills, flocks of goats sitting in the middle of the road or on house verandahs, cattlemen in Stetsons and spurs lounging at the hotel bar and aborigines wandering around.

The best thing in Normanton was the bore and the bore bath. Next to the School of Arts where we camped was an artesian bore spouting boiling water continuously. It had been flowing for fifty years, came from 6,000 feet down and was very rich in sulphur and other minerals, reputedly helpful for rheumatism. It flowed in a narrow winding stream across a paddock. A tin shed had been built over it and the stream flowed through the shed, filling a shallow bath about twelve feet by four and one foot deep. By this time it had cooled sufficiently to permit a bath. We couldn't wait to try it and thereafter, at the end of each blistering day, we went to bathe in the lovely warm water and then sat on the edge and washed our clothes. It was so easy as the constant flow obviated the need for changes of rinsing water and washed the soapy water away instantly. If I got hot again after scrubbing the stubborn garments, I'd just jump in again. Last of all we washed little Pete. Whether it was the minerals or the relief from the daily heat but he used to go mad after his bath, dashing around the surrounding paddock, jumping and rolling.

We learned that local housewives filled kerosene tins with water from the bore to do their washing and even used the boiling water for cooking. We tried shoving some potatoes in to cook but it took too long so Shirl built a little fire and boiled the potatoes in a small tin – the only time we ever cooked!

Another fun thing was to light the gas which emerged with the water. A man told me that the flame would spread along the channel and into the bath house to frighten bathers! We weren't successful in getting it to light.

We were hard pressed to find food that we could afford in Normanton and if it hadn't been for the hospitality of several residents we would have gone hungry. One afternoon as we were dozing on the wide shady balcony of our temporary home in the main street, Mr. McInerney, the Scottish white-haired Station owner staying at the Hotel National came across and invited us to dinner. Over a delicious meal he told us his father had been an Ambassador to the U.S. and he and his siblings had been born in different countries. He ran away from boarding school at fifteen and roamed the world. He had lived here for seventeen years and had never fallen in love or married. I was aghast at the idea of anyone living in Normanton for seventeen years, but it hadn't always been a sleepy settlement. At one time it caught the backwash of the gold rush at Croydon, 94 miles away, and had a population of 7,000.

Another afternoon as I was writing letters on the balcony, Flo Rosan passed by below and invited us to a meal. She was one of two missionaries who cared for the local aborigines and was full of interesting stories. We welcomed the idea of another chat so we went for a bath in the bore at four o'clock. We'd never been so early before and the water was unbearably hot. It took me ages to get my feet in then I sat on the side trying to get used to the temperature. It was no use. I just had to wash standing up and scoop water to rinse off the soap. It was too hot to wash Pete of course.

After dressing in clean clothes we walked to Miss Rosan's house. We sat on the verandah as the day cooled and she brought out a box of curios – spearheads and an actual death bone as used by the natives for 'pointing the bone'. It was about six inches long, white and skewer-like. If an aborigine knows that someone has pointed the bone at him, he will just sicken and die. Mind over matter? We heard of cases where the person did not know the bone had been pointed yet still he died.

Miss Rosan entertained us again with fascinating stories about her dusky charges. There was Malcolm proudly singing hymns from his 'hymn book'....actually a Gospel of St. Luke; Nipper, a snowy-haired old man who sent off for some hair dye from the town and emerged with flaming red hair; loyal wife Polly who, on Victory night when the church bell was rung by revellers, dashed to church in her best clothes; young Mary Ann and Cedric's marriage and the birth of their baby; Mina's baby who was born 'wrong way round' so the old gins pushed it back, turned it round and 'him come out right way', and funerals in the Wet when graves were full of water.

Aborigines live tribally under a system of communal ownership and they attach no importance to having a lot of possessions. A man has a tribal duty to share what he has with his relatives. They have no idea of the concept of personal property. Equality and sharing are the twin pillars of their life. Leading nomadic lives, they believe that in the Dreamtime, heaven, earth and the people were created as three different parts of the same thing that should never be divided. Because people were created for the land, they could not survive without it. Without land they feel separated from their life source, from their spirit.

We had met Dr. Boydell at the local hospital and when I thought we were about to leave Normanton I rang him and asked if we could come to the pedal wireless session that night. As we arrived he was just giving instructions to someone on Mornington Island about a patient there. As we listened, we heard a long and boring conversation between two cattle station owners, then at eight o'clock we heard a woman calling in various stations. Every Sunday night after the business was completed, a concert was held, each station supplying an item and one station acting as host or compère. We heard a woman singing, a nursing sister from Dunbar playing a mandolin, a man told a joke and Dr. Boydell whistled a song for them. That was difficult as he still had to pedal to maintain power. Then he introduced us to his far-flung audience. We told the people about our trip so far and our future plans and then came the questions! We were kept busy answering them until Dr. Boydell brought the session to a close.

We had learnt that a truck would be leaving for Cloncurry after lunch next day so we were ready on time. We should have known by now that time is very elastic in the outback. Our driver was loading some furniture and had a few other calls to make so it was four o'clock before we got away. He told us he was returning by a different route and would be staying the night at Talawanta Station, setting off early the following morning and reaching Cloncurry in the evening. We called at Inverleigh Station and were invited to eat. The owner, an old greyhaired man called Malone, was very hospitable. It was a lovely homestead, comfortable, tastefully furnished, cool and with a beautiful garden. After dinner we sat on the fly-screened verandah and talked. Mr. Malone had been there for twenty-one years. He served in the British and Indian army during the First World War, guarding a pass in Tibet.

We left Inverleigh in the dark and at 11pm reached Neumeyer Plains before going on to Talawanta. The owner, Mrs. May, was rather put out by the arrival of two girls and apologetically offered us a room with some beds lacking linen. We were so exhausted we were grateful for these and crawled into our bags, asleep already.

Next morning Mrs. May was more friendly. After all, the arrival of two unexpected guests in the middle of the night is not conducive to good humour. Her husband was out droving so she was glad of some female company.

Setting off at 9am I was optimistic about reaching Cloncurry by evening if we maintained a speed of 20mph. Then something went wrong with the carburettor and we had several long halts. At last we rolled on. There were dozens of gates for me to open and shut – I was on the window side – and I was longing to sleep. Hot buttered pumpkin scones at Donor's Hill were welcome mid-morning and by lunch we reached Cowan Downs where Mrs. Reagan, an elderly woman, greeted us. She was dressed in an immaculate white drill slack suit with silver buttons and her very brown face contrasted with her attire and her snowy hair worn in a bun. At Wurung Shirl and I changed seats and I sank gratefully into slumber. We reached Canobie at 7pm, had a wash and a hot meal then set off on the last lap at 8.30pm. From Canobie on, Shirl slept too and our poor driver had to open the gates, drive through, then close them again. (I remembered the old joke about the driver who offered a swagman a lift. 'No thanks, you can open your own bloody gates!') We finally crawled into Cloncurry at 2.25am.

Next day we reclaimed our bikes which had been sent on from Julia Creek. My lost bundles had also been forwarded by Hughenden police. While I was collecting them from the railway station I saw the Maternal and Child Welfare carriage standing at a side platform. This was what the Domestic Science teachers had told us about. We met the two very pleasant nurses, Sisters Harrison and Waugh. They had a lovely carriage, bigger and better than the Domestic Science one. Their comfortable quarters were adjacent to the Clinic room. We saw them at work as mothers brought in their babies from time to time. They told us they were going on to Dajarra next day and offered to take us as far as Duchess in their carriage. At least, we asked and they agreed! In the meantime we kept enquiring for trucks going to Mt. Isa. Back in the town I asked the Flying Doctor pilot if they were going anywhere interesting.

'We set off for Weipa Mission this morning,' he said, 'but had to turn back because of bad weather.'

Weipa Mission! Almost to the top of Cape York! However, we had a frigid reaction from the woman doctor whom we asked so resigned ourselves to going with the Baby Clinic carriage.

We tracked down the Stock Inspector. Little Pete had to have a clean bill of health before crossing the State border into the Northern Territory. He examined the little dog, found nothing wrong, sprayed him with DDT and issued a permit.

We boarded the Baby Clinic carriage next morning and had an enjoyable trip to Duchess, chatting while the Sisters sewed and knitted. The countryside was very pleasant, green and hilly with lovely rocky bluffs and orange coloured cliffs like Namatjira's paintings of the Centre.

Duchess was the proverbial one horse town only without the horse. We got its postmark, sold a Hotel and Café News and then were ready to leave. We met the guard of the mail train and asked if we could 'jump the rattler' in his van. The young man was very conscientious though and wouldn't give us permission.

'However,' he said, 'if you like to take a chance on there being no inspector on the train, you can hop in one of the carriages.'

We put Pete and the bikes in the guard's van and got in a back carriage. Opposite me was sitting a fair-haired chap about thirty whose accent proclaimed him German. He said he'd been in India at the beginning of the war and had been taken prisoner there. I asked if he'd been interned in Australia as I knew a man who'd been taken prisoner in Persia and been interned at Tatura camp. He said he'd been at Tatura too. I mentioned Karl Frisch's name and be became very excited. He'd been Karl's room-mate for six years! What an incredibly small world!

Mid-afternoon we arrived at Mt. Isa, the terminus of the 676 mile track from Townsville. My German friend said we needn't worry about not having a ticket as an inspector collected all the tickets before Duchess so we hopped off brazenly. We got Pete out of the dog box but a porter asked us for our bike tickets. We didn't have any of course so he told us to fix it up at the office. We wheeled the bikes away out of the crowd, packed up then rode into town.

I was excited by my first sight of the large American complex, the sprawling mine with its clustered houses and the gaunt hills encircling the valley. Mt. Isa was the world's largest producer of lead and silver which all came from one mine and the settlement consisted of two separate areas, the town and the mine. The whole population depended on the mine, people working either for it or in ancillary services. This was my first experience of a Company town.

We strolled along the main street looking at the shops and found a modern café selling Peters icecream but the owner was surly and resented giving us the icecream so we had to buy some. At the Post Office, despite the fact it was Sunday, we managed to get our mail from the Poste Restante. We started to ride to the mine but half-way my bike came to a standstill with a horrible clanking noise and a hiss of escaping air. I looked at the front wheel and saw that the same thing had happened as a year before in New South Wales. The rod connecting the mudguard to the hub had broken, whizzed round, buckled the wheel and severed the tyre! I felt crushed. I propped my bike at the side of the road and we got a lift to the mine. We enquired about accommodation and were told to contact Mr. Witcombe, the Community Officer, who would fix us up. We found his house and his pretty wife opened the door. She invited us in and introduced us to another woman with whom she'd been playing tennis. She was Mrs. Kruttschnitt, wife of the Chairman of Directors of the Mine! Soon afterwards Mr. Witcombe and Mr. Kruttschnitt arrived – they'd been playing bowls – and Mr. Witcombe said we could have a room in the nurses' quarters behind the former hospital. As the Kruttschnitts were leaving they invited us to their home that night, together with three young airmen who were staying in the guest house next door while making a photographic survey of Mt. Isa. Mr. Witcombe got them to pick up our bikes and drive us and our gear to our quarters. They were luxurious with linen, blankets, towels, lots of wardrobe space and plenty of showers. Mt. Isa had suddenly become more pleasant.

Mr. Kruttschnitt picked us up later in a magnificent new Pontiac and drove us to his home which would not have been out of place in one of our *American Home* magazines. The front door opened into a large sitting room with a baby grand piano in the corner, period furniture and attractive prints on the walls. A flight of stairs led to a cool sitting room underground where there were deep lounge chairs, tapestries, carved teak tables with brass tops, rich Persian rugs scattered on the polished floor, Balinese masks, *batik* hangings on the walls and gay, fringed curtains. We all sat around talking and drinking (I was introduced to iced fresh lime). Mr. Kruttschnitt had a dry sense of humour and was very entertaining. His wife had worked as a typist in the mine office and had married her boss. He, of course, was an American and told us various anecdotes about other mines in the area. He once hosted a dinner party on the four hundred foot level of a mine. There was a full three-course hot dinner with wines and all the trimmings while musicians played soft music in the background. He also told us of the superstition about women going underground. They never allowed them to do so here. Shirl and I were very disappointed.

Despite the interesting stories I was drooping with fatigue. (I had to remind myself I'd been in Cloncurry that morning!) I kept shutting my eyes and doing eye exercises to keep awake. I thought supper would revive me but although we went out to the kitchen to look at some cunning American gadgets, the food didn't arrive. It was a lovely big kitchen and an attractive young woman was working there with her husband. Newly-wed, they had lived all their lives as foster brother and sister then fell in love and ran away to get married. They were now afraid to tell their foster parents.

At eleven, Mrs. Kruttschnitt said something about supper. Shirl and I leapt into action for something to do. We handed around food, delicious sandwiches and a sponge then the talk resumed. At last Mrs. Witcombe made a move and said it was midnight. Everyone sat up and seemed surprised it was so late. Polite remarks, goodbyes and we were driven home.

We had a busy week, business interspersed with plentiful hospitality. In the town we met a Methodist minister, the Rev. Lanham, a jovial man with a most attractive wife and a small plane which he flew to outlying areas in his vast parish. They were very interested in our trip and we in his numerous flights to unusual places. We were hoping he would take us for a flight to Mornington Island in the Gulf of Carpentaria but he didn't offer.

My bike was mended and we started making enquiries about traffic on the East-West road, the splendid bitumen road built by the army during the war. It ran from Mt. Isa west to Tennant Creek in the Northern Territory, whence the North-South road, a similar war-time construction, led straight to Darwin. I had a most frustrating time. I asked about Lyons, Campbell, Freckleman and Peak trucks but they'd either just gone or weren't going or couldn't take us. I heard of a man called Farlow and found him at a hotel. He patted my shoulder in fatherly fashion and said how sorry he was, he was leaving this afternoon but couldn't take us, two other passengers were in a hurry to get to Darwin, goodbye. He walked off leaving me fuming. His truck was empty. I was terribly disappointed as he was our only solid hope. I was straggling homewards when a woman called out 'Good morning!' to me. I poured out my troubles and she said: 'Bill Armbrust should be leaving for Darwin today. He's a friend of mine. Let's go and look for him.'

We found him and his friend Phil at the Argent Hotel and I pleaded with him to take us, even as far as Camooweal (136 miles) or Tennant Creek. He said he had a very big load but agreed. Joy! I rang Shirl and told her to pack pronto! I rushed around saying goodbyes, and raced home. We packed and cleaned the room. I changed into slacks and a khaki shirt. We had to get our cases of good clothes into town too so I tied mine on the front carrier and put the rest of my gear on the back. It was a terrifically unwieldy load and I had to walk. On reaching the Mine-Town road I stopped a car and asked the driver to take my suitcase to the Argent Hotel. Then I was able to ride.

We found the Armbrust truck over at the goods shed where it was still being loaded. It did have a towering load. Somehow space was found for our bikes and everything was covered with a tarpaulin. Shirl, Pete and I clambered high up on top of the load and we set off at 6pm.

NORTHERN TERRITORY

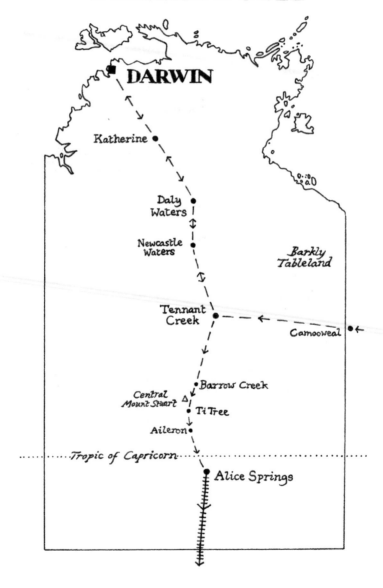

DARWIN

Katherine

Daly Waters

Newcastle Waters

Barkly Tableland

Tennant Creek

Camooweal

Barrow Creek

Central Mount Stuart

Ti Tree

Aileron

Tropic of Capricorn

Alice Springs

Chapter 20

WHERE THE SPINIFEX GROWS

The range shut out the sun fairly soon and darkness fell. We sped along the wonderful bitumen road and when the wind became too cold, we crawled into our sleeping bags. After an hour the truck stopped and soon we heard a crackling sound. The men had lit several clumps of spinifex, mounds of spiny, spiky grass, and a terrific blaze was raging. The heat was intense.

'Just to keep us warm!' said Bill.

We were now travelling across the Barkly Tableland and the air was very cold (the altitude was almost a thousand feet). We stopped every hour to light a fire in order to thaw out. The men kept asking us to go down and sit in the cabin to talk to the driver while the other slept. We were very cosy on top and didn't really want to but we compromised, one of us going below while the other stayed on top and slept. I took first shift and entertained the men by singing their requests. I nicknamed Bill 'Shakespeare' as, surprisingly, he could quote yards of poetry. He had an apt quotation to suit any occasion or subject. He recited *The Highwayman*, one of my favourites, with occasional prompting from me.

Shirl took over from me and I climbed into my bag and dozed, waking to stare sleepily at the 'Weal' – Camooweal – as we passed through. It did not look very impressive. Eight miles further on we reached the border of the Northern Territory. This was a significant boundary so we asked Bill to stop and clambered down to pose for a photo under the signpost in the headlights of the truck. Then we drove on another fifty miles and stopped somewhere on Rankine Downs. I slept on top of the truck, Shirl stretched out in the cabin and the men lay on the ground. Bill discovered he'd lost his swag and had to share Phil's blanket.

After a very cold night I woke at daylight and got up at sunrise. The men made a fire and cooked tinned sausages and tea. We didn't want anything so went for a walk to find some cover for calls of nature. Rankine Downs hadn't much in the way of trees, spinifex being the main vegetation. The men told us that there was one tree quite near the road. Approaching drivers saw it from miles away, they even became hypnotized by it and on approaching it, tended to leave the road and crash into it! It was a good story anyhow.

Walking around the flat terrain we found lots of beautiful ribbon stones, wonderful colours in a marble-smooth stone.

We continued our journey, Shirl and I lying on top. The sun was hot but the slipstream was very cool. During a long trip in high temperatures, drivers stop periodically to lower the pressure in their tyres. This lessens the possibility of blowouts.

Sometimes, to vary the monotony, the men stopped to have a pot shot at a plain turkey but didn't get anything. At noon we arrived at No. 4A Bore (Wonara Telegraph Station) and got the postmark. The young man in charge gave us glasses of fresh lime which we were beginning to realize was the Territory drink. Delicious! The men had rung ahead to Frewena Hotel and told them we'd be along for lunch in two hours. As we drove, they told us about the people who owned Frewena. The wife, they said, was a dried-up, brown Territorian such as we'd been expecting to find in these arid areas. She had run away from her husband with another chap a few years previously but had now returned. We were expecting a termagant but when we arrived at 3 o'clock found an attractive woman of about 35, very tanned in a slick sunsuit with a good figure. She was a capable type, as she would have to be, but not a shrew. We got the postmark there and sat down to a very welcome meal, a tasty vegetable soup made from a plain turkey and goat stock followed by cold meat (goat) and a huge garden salad. This was followed by bread and jam with lashings of goat's cream.

Bill had taken on extra passengers for the remaining 85 miles to Tennant Creek. Mrs. Connors and her two small children crowded into the cabin and Phil joined us on top.

We lumbered into Tennant Creek at 9pm. I was astonished at its size. What had been only a small dot on the map proved to be a good-sized township, harking back to Australia's last great gold rush in 1932. The story goes that a truck carrying building materials for the first pub in the area broke down several miles from the Creek and they decided to build the pub there rather than where the water was. The township sprang up around the pub and a good supply of water had always been a problem.

We had no idea where to go for the night so when the men had unloaded our gear we went to the Police Station. There was a man sleeping on the verandah who, on awakening, introduced himself as Sgt. McColl of Darwin Police, the celebrated policeman Bill had warned us about because of his wolfish tendencies. Fancy meeting him so soon! He conferred with the local Sergeant and they decided we could have the room belonging to another policeman who, when he returned, could unroll his swag on the verandah with McColl. I was tireder than I'd ever been. My eyes were sore from lack of sleep and the effects of sun and wind.

In the morning we learned that Sgt. McColl had left early for Darwin, taking our suitcases with him as promised. Bill Armbrust's truck had driven on during the night. We were just riding into town to start work when I stopped a big truck and asked where it was going.

'Gorrie. Past Larramah,' said the driver. His name was Geoff Kittle.

I didn't know where these were so asked if he could take us to Newcastle Waters, 175 miles further on.

'Yes,' he said, 'and I'll give you half an hour to get ready.'

I had a look at the map and found Larramah was 295 miles away, past Daly Waters and Birdum so decided to ask if we could go as far as Daly. Shirl wasn't keen.

'Why don't we have a day's rest and go to the pictures tonight. We'll be bound to get another lift tomorrow.'

I was amazed at the thought of turning down such a wonderful lift and wasting precious time. I was still obsessed with getting to Melbourne for Christmas. The matter was decided by a Police sergeant who advised us to go today as rain would probably blow up tomorrow so we dashed away to pack and loaded our gear on the empty trailer behind the truck.

Sixty-four miles out, we stopped at Banka Banka for lunch at a café. The woman who ran it came from Melbourne, had been there for eight months and didn't know a thing about the Territory. She was surprised to hear it rains from December to March!

Setting off again we drove through delightful country. There was no hot, dry desert as I'd expected but very green scrub, plenty of trees with great outcrops of red rock *à la* Namatjira. I was surprised to discover that from Tennant Creek up to Birdum, a distance of 213 miles, the road had an altitude of 800 feet, after which it gradually decreased. Darwin was 150 feet above the sea. No wonder the nights were cold!

We passed Churchill Rock which was right alongside the road. There was a slight resemblance to the great wartime leader, mainly due to a protuberance which looked like a cigar. Then we passed Lubra's Lookout, a magnificent pile of red rock jutting straight out of the ground, very craggy and wild. The truck stopped in the middle of nowhere and Don the co-driver climbed down to practise his revolver shooting on bottles and things at the side of the road. We asked for a go and I shot a beer bottle at 20 feet with my second shot. I was quite pleased as I hadn't used a gun since firing my brother Pete's Daisy airgun as a child.

At twilight there was a beautiful sunset and the countryside looked cool and dusky, calm and quiet. I started ruminating on a poem....*Night comes, an unexpected guest, in the land where the spinifex grows....*

We made a stop for food. I washed and put on my slacks and jumper as protection against myriad insects which swarmed around the headlights. We reached Newcastle Waters at 11pm. I was very surprised to find a township and not just a homestead. The men said they'd camp down by the creek but I thought that sounded too mosquitoey. We went to look at the hotel verandah and found a small room, enclosed by trellis, which looked better. It was very warm so we didn't get in our bags. I found I'd left my rope on the truck and couldn't erect my mosquito net, so fully dressed and with the net draped over a chair to get a bit of height, I crawled underneath and put my feet in my sleeping bag cover.

We were up at 7am as drivers start early before the heat descends. At one stage as we were bowling along the bitumen, we came on a plain turkey walking on the road. Geoff slowed down and with horror I saw Don, on the back of the truck, raise his revolver just as the ungainly bird tried to take off. The shot rang out and the turkey dropped. Shirl and I were sickened. We didn't need the bird for food and it was left dead or dying on the side of the road. What was the point?

We reached Daly Waters at noon. It was two miles off the main road but Geoff took us there. We bade them goodbye and went for a shower, the first for three days. I had lunch at the hotel, Shirl wasn't hungry, and over my meal I consulted an airways guide showing dates and fares of flights to Melbourne from Alice Springs. I was now seriously considering leaving Darwin, travelling by truck to Alice and flying on to Melbourne in order to be there when my brother Pete was home on furlough from Borneo. I found that the fares were not prohibitive and my family was going to contribute to the cost of the flight. I was greatly encouraged. The plan was that I should rejoin Shirl in Adelaide after she had made her way south from Darwin.

We had heard that a Lackman truck was going through to Mataranka. When it arrived we asked for a lift, loaded on the gear and set off, reaching Birdum at 5pm. It was a quaint place with only a hotel and a closed store but there were lovely poinciana and bougainvillea rioting over it. Almost 300 yards away was the railway, Birdum being the railhead of the small line which goes to Darwin. A couple of cottages and the Post Office were on the other side of it. Just then a rail trolley arrived containing Postmistress Dalton who invited us in to get the postmark. She pottered about showing us photos and warned us about Sgt. McColl! Everyone did.

We headed on for Larramah Telegraph Station and on arrival found a bit of a party in progress. The men on our truck leapt off and joined in. We groaned at the delay as we wanted to reach Mataranka...and bed! However we dragged ourselves into the building. The only personnel at the station were a middle-aged man, grey and fat, called Bob and Tony who was young and decidedly wolfish! They gave us the postmark and Tony asked me if there were anyone I'd like to phone. I said – my mother. One of our drivers said he'd pay. It was now 11 o'clock, 11.30 pm in Melbourne and I got Mum out of bed. She was delighted to hear me and know where I was. She wouldn't have been so happy had she known what was to happen at Larramah.

Shirl and I contemplated a change in our plans. Before reaching Mataranka we'd pass the Elsey graveyard with Maluka's grave. I had only recently read Mrs. Aeneas Gunn's Australian classic *We of the Never Never* so wanted to see Elsey Station and anything else connected with the story. If we went on with Lackman's truck we'd pass the graveyard in the dark.

Leaping Lena, the Territory's only train, came into Larramah while we were there and we inspected it. The driver invited us to hop on any time we wanted a lift so we thought we'd stay the night on the siding and catch the train to Mataranka in the morning.

When we told the Telegraph Station men they insisted we stay the night there.

'Use our beds!' they said. 'We can sleep on the verandah.'

We were terribly tired – we'd been up for 17 hours and the thought of real beds was more attractive than a hard siding.

Lackman's truck left and after a shower we prepared for bed. The men made up beds on the verandah. I didn't want to use their linen so spread my bag on the bed and, fully clothed, lay down with a blissful sigh.

A minute later the door at Shirl's end of the room opened and in sauntered Tony. He said she had his bed and he refused to sleep on the verandah. He sat on her bed and I could catch shreds of their conversation. I had every confidence in Shirl's ability to look after herself so composed myself to sleep. I was just slipping off when something touched my leg. I sat up and saw a big shape in striped pyjamas at the bedside. It was Bob, the dirty old wolf! Seeing Tony was still talking to Shirl he was chancing his luck too!

'What's the matter! What are you doing here?' I demanded.

He sat on the edge of the bed and said he wanted to talk. I said testily that I was terribly tired and just wanted to sleep.

'Well, you go right ahead, don't mind me,' he said.

'Not with you there. C'mon, off you go!'

He made no move other than to attempt to lie down. I pushed him away and with a supreme effort at self-control said calmly: 'Now what say we all go to our beds and get some sleep, h'm?'

Bob, seeing I wasn't co-operating, muttered something about making coffee and staggered out to the verandah. I was afraid to relax my vigilance but must have dozed off for I next woke feeling someone lie down beside me.

I sat up, mad as heck, and bellowed: 'What the devil's going on!' It was Bob again.

'Just lie down and go to sleep. Don't mind me.'

I was furious and started to clamber out.

'Look! Just make up your mind will you! If you want your bed you can have it and I'll sleep on the floor. Otherwise get the hell out of here and let me sleep! I've never been so tired in all my life and we've got a big day tomorrow!'

I was nearly howling with vexation. Bob said he'd go but first.....

'Give me a kiss goodnight! Just one! You've got plenty to spare! Come on!'

I pushed him and he stomped away. I was trembling with revulsion, fear and anger and started to weep when reaction set in.

The next morning the atmosphere was understandably very strained. We ate a quiet breakfast, said goodbye and caught Leaping Lena at 11am. Once Shirl and I were alone I was able to hear her story. She had had a tussle with Tony but having got rid of him had gone to sleep only to wake when Bob lay down beside her! Oh dear, the sex-starved men of the Territory!

Leaping Lena was meanwhile chugging through thickly wooded gum country and we arrived at Mataranka at 1pm. Like most of the settlements it consisted of a hotel, a police station cum Post Office and a store. The hotel proprietress was a pleasant woman. We asked for a wash and she offered us lunch as well as a bed for the night. We got talking to some young men who were demolishing an old army camp nearby and persuaded them to go and see the Elsey graveyard. They said we could go swimming afterwards so we got our bathers and set off in their utility truck. The graveyard was situated ten miles south. There was the Maluka's grave and that of Fizzer as well as other characters in the book or connected with Elsey Station. Then we drove to Mataranka homestead and along a track to the Springs. There was a small, thermal pool about five feet deep, constantly replenished from an underground source and the water was a pale blue and so clear I could see every grain of white sand on the bottom. The water was warm and tasted mineral. Shadows cast a black dappled shade and a black log under the water increased the mysterious appearance of black and blue fantasy.

Back at the hotel we settled down after dinner to write diary and letters but were diverted by two local identities, 'Cowboy' Collins and 'Nugget' Raymond, an old bearded prospector known throughout the Territory, who knew every inch of it and had many colourful stories

Next day Police Constable Holland drove us out to Elsey along a rough, sandy track. He was going to the Station to shoot lots of mangy dogs belonging to the aborigines. We were horrified. The aborigines are greatly attached to their dogs and in fact any dogs. They always made a big fuss of our Pete.

We reached Elsey Falls first and clambered down the hillside to the river valley. It was the loveliest place I'd ever seen – cool and green, thickly wooded like a fairytale forest and at the bottom of the hill was a stream so green that it looked like emerald honey – clear and translucent with sunlight streaking through it. Pandanus palms fringed the banks and the actual falls spilled over some rocks in the centre of the picture. We rambled along the bank, crossing from side to side on fallen logs. The stream was really a loop of the Roper River which we had sworn never to approach, due to its reputation as a breeding ground for crocodiles. Crocodiles, also, are very partial to dogs and we guarded little Pete vigilantly.

The river was at a very low level with only a few isolated pools here and there. Pete had a wonderful time leaping in and out of them. He loved water. We dived into the clear depths and swam lazily over to the Falls. I spied a rope hanging from a tree and rushed to it. I examined the landing area before trying it. There wasn't much depth of water but, by taking the rope as far back as possible and climbing some rocks, I could get more impetus and swing right out into the deeper water. Attached to the steel triangle at the bottom of the rope was a piece of thin wire for dragging the rope back up the rocks. Each time I dropped I'd catch the palm of my left hand on this wretched piece of wire and the last time I swung it ripped the skin off my left palm at the base of my third finger. It was very painful and there was blood everywhere. A flap of skin made it too painful to swim so I one-armed across the pool to the landing bank and Mr. Holland pulled me out.

We sat on towels in the truck and drove on to the Elsey Homestead. It wasn't the original building but it was the prettiest we'd seen. Built on the high bank of the Roper, terraced lawns and gardens sloped down to the water. The side of the house overlooking the river consisted of a wide, cool verandah, screened and cooled by dozens of ferns, creepers and trees growing outside. Bougainvillea swarmed up one side onto the roof and a frangipani tree, slender and delicate and covered with fragrant creamy blooms, made a spectacular contrast with a brilliantly flamboyant poinciana in full bloom.

-oOo-

We had reached Katherine with the aid of another truck. I was continually surprised by the size of settlements up the North-South road. Katherine had two hotels, a couple of shops and even an open-air theatre for films. Rain wasn't often a problem. If a performance were interrupted, customers were given pass-outs and came back next night.

We now had only 226 miles to cover before Darwin and I was becoming increasingly impatient. Darwin was our most northerly point, Ultima Thule. For eighteen months it had been our goal and we were both excited by its proximity. Besides, my brother would be passing through in the middle of October en route to Melbourne for his long furlough. I had to see him. Hence my plan to return secretly to Melbourne. Shirl and I were always disappearing into smoke for long periods of time. Our trip was so leisurely, we were not breaking records and newspapers would merely pick up the story when we reappeared.

To my great joy and Shirl's elation, a man in Katherine asked us to take his single-seater Austin car to Darwin for him. He had to go quickly by rail but wanted his car when he arrived. Shirl had got her driving licence two years previously in Melbourne but hadn't driven since then. She was wild with excitement and couldn't wait to get started. We went to see the car. I had some misgivings on seeing it. It had no doors and no roof. It did have a dickey seat although the handle for it was missing. There was also some vital part of the engine missing but the owner told us to contact his friend who would be able to fix everything. It all sounded very hit and miss but the owner leapt on the train heading north.

By next morning the car was ready to go. The missing part of the engine had been located, the dickey seat handle fitted and the tank filled with petrol. We strapped a bike on each running board, a network of ropes linking them, piled our gear into the dickey seat and perched little Pete on top of everything. Feeling very intrepid we climbed over the bike frames and sat on the front seat. The car lacked something else... an ignition key. Shirl had to use her thumb nail to switch on. The engine burst into life and with triumphant waves to the assembled onlookers, we headed out onto the bitumen.

Tentatively Shirl drove through Katherine, crossed the river and, now that she was more confident, inched her speed up to thirty. Her eyes glued to the road through the web of ropes, she hardly spoke and when, but rarely, we met another vehicle, she hugged the left verge. There was intermittent sun and rain. A light shower didn't bother us but when a leaden sky threatened a storm, we stopped and I burrowed in the dickey seat where I'd seen a tarpaulin. Dragging it out, we tied each front corner to the bike handlebars and wedged the back corners under our haversacks. As we set off again the canopy billowed and flapped above us like a spinnaker.

At the end of the first day we reached Adelaide River, the headquarters of the Australian and American armies during the war. We had safely covered 150 miles. To Shirl's chagrin, we met the owner of the car who had had business in the township and thought he'd wait for us. He said

he'd come on with us to Darwin next day. We were terribly disappointed as we'd hoped to drive into Darwin by ourselves. He revealed to Shirl that there were four gears. She had been using only three! Next day we somehow fitted him into the cramped space and drove the remaining 75 miles to Darwin.

What a beautiful city it was! With its tropical white buildings, wide streets with flowering shrubs and trees and the sun pouring down, Darwin was Australia's northern gateway. Most overseas flights landed there. The houses were very attractive, often built up on piles in the Queensland fashion with panels or even whole walls made of louvres which could be opened to let the breeze through. All had colourful gardens.

We were interested to see the cosmopolitan mix in the streets. Tanned urban Australian men dressed informally in shorts and short-sleeved, open-necked shirts; the women in fashionable cotton frocks. (Shorts had been banned for women both in and out of working hours in 1937!) There were aborigines and people of mixed blood from the many missions and Stations in the Territory; Chinese (some years later the Mayor of Darwin was a Chinese), buffalo and crocodile hunters in moleskins and high boots with bush hats on their heads, and a few travellers like us. The age of tourism had not yet begun, Arnhem Land was still empty except for its original inhabitants and Oenpelli Mission. There were no National Parks and no road trains thundering down to Alice Springs.

I was shocked to see the aftermath of the Japanese bombing on 19th February 1942, four days after the fall of Singapore. We weren't told the extent of the damage and fatalities during the war nor did we know that Wyndham, Broome and other northern ports had been bombed. Darwin had had only one minute's warning when 188 bombers flying at 14,000 feet appeared over the harbour in formation and commenced pattern-bombing at 10am. They were followed by dive-bombers and fighters which swept low and devastated the crowded harbour, airfield and city area. 243 people were killed, eight ships were sunk and installations wrecked. Four Kittyhawk fighters challenged the attackers but were greatly outnumbered. Another four planes on the ground were destroyed before they could take off. Civilian buildings including hospitals were badly damaged and Darwin was reckoned to be a ghost town from a military point of view. Many residents, fearing an imminent invasion, joined a rush to the south in any vehicles they could find.

By 1947 a considerable amount of reconstruction had taken place but I could still see scarred buildings, roofless with blackened rafters sticking up forlornly, and there were still sunken ships in the harbour.

We found a home in a lovely little flat which was part of the complex of the United Church. The minister, Rev. Grant, was very helpful and made sure we had everything we needed.

My mother had told me that my brother Peter would be passing through Darwin on his way home from Borneo on the very day we arrived, the 15th October. I thought how wonderful it would be to surprise him at the airport. However, in the pile of mail awaiting me was another letter from Mum giving a different date. How unhappy I was to receive news some days later that he had in fact landed in Darwin on the original date.

I sent a birthday telegram to Norman Banks, my boss at 3KZ, feeling very proud that its office of origin was Darwin. Many people had been sceptical about the possibility of our reaching our goal though not Mr. Banks.

It was now time to fulfil our promises to nearly a hundred people to 'send them a postcard from Darwin.' Shirl had kept the list and we sat down, night after night, writing brief letters to everyone. In 1946 a man had invented something called a Biro, a ballpoint pen, which contained its own small cartridge of ink. It was leakproof and could be carried in a pocket. By

1947 it was available in Australia and I was able to dispense with my bottle of ink and fountain pen.

We had just sent a postcard off to dear Mrs. O'Donnell who had housed us in Sydney, when we ran into her son Brian in Darwin's main street. We had last seen him in Cairns and were surprised to hear he'd dropped out of his medical course. Now here he was in Darwin with a girlfriend, preparing to fly overseas. We felt sorry for Mrs. O'Donnell who had been so proud of her clever son.

One day we had a flight with an Air Force plane to a remote airstrip down the western coast from Darwin where two lonely Leading Aircraftsmen of the 38th Squadron got the shock of their lives to see two attractive young women descending from the plane.

I played Chopin at a concert in aid of the Leprosarium and on other nights we had a busy social life at the Army Officers' Mess or dinners at the Darwin Hotel. We went on a picnic to Berry Springs, a local beauty spot, swinging on a rope over the river and dropping in.

The Botanic Gardens merited a visit. I was mentally transported back to beautiful North Queensland. Here were all the tropical plants which I loved...croton, frangipani, poinciana, cassia, hibiscus, poinsettia and acalypha.

But it was the end of October and my brother had already arrived in Melbourne. With renewed efforts I made the rounds of transport companies asking about trucks going south to Alice Springs. There was a more or less regular flow of traffic but some mightn't be going all the way to the Alice or they might be fully loaded. I finally found a driver to take me, two in fact – Colin and Mick – so I loaded my suitcase, haversack, sleeping bag and bike on the back, and after an emotional farewell to little Pete and Shirl, climbed into the cabin. We set off at 2pm.

Eighteen miles out we had a blowout. I sat for an hour while the men mended the tube with vulcanizer then drove back to get another tyre. They fixed the new tyre on, had something to eat and set off again at 9.30pm.

I sat upright in the cabin with Colin, desperately trying to sleep. I cannot sleep sitting up and ached to lay my head down but there was no space. Mick had flaked out on the back of the truck and I envied him. At dawn we stopped so Colin could sleep. I lay on the road but the flies were bothersome so I walked up and down until we set off again. That day we reached Katherine, Mataranka and Birdum where the men went to the hotel and stayed for four hours drinking! Dear Mrs. Dalton from the Post Office brought me chicken sandwiches and apples. We left at 9pm. Mick was out cold and Col was driving. I hoped he had his wits about him. He woke Mick at 4am to change over. Mick had a terrible hangover! The engine was conveniently playing up so we stopped till 6am and the men slept, then drove on through Elliot and reached Banka Banka for lunch.

I was strolling around in my khaki slacks, shirt and bush hat when an old man came up to me, tipped his hat and said: 'Excuse me Miss, would you be Miss Daphne Campbell?' I was greatly amused but had to disappoint the old cattleman. Daphne Campbell was the star of the successful Australian film *The Overlanders* and she had been similarly dressed.

In the middle of the second night, some distance after Tennant Creek, I opened my bleary eyes and saw in the blinding moonlight the Devil's Marbles by the side of the road. This was a group of massive boulders rounded into great balls by the effects of erosion. In the evening sunlight they glow as red as marbles. The aborigines say they were left behind by the Rainbow Serpent, that ubiquitous creature in their mythology.

We were nearing journey's end. After Wauchope and Barrow Creek we passed Central Mt. Stuart, the geographical centre of Australia, named for John McDouall Stuart who made the first crossing of Australia from south to north. On to Ti Tree and Aileron and then we passed the old Telegraph Station, the site of the original Alice Springs settlement. An early adventurer, W.Mills, discovered a waterhole in a dried up river bed and he named the river in honour of Charles Todd, the Superintendent of the Overland Telegraph project and the settlement which sprang up around it was named Alice Springs after Todd's wife.

In the afternoon we approached Alice Springs. We had covered 960 miles from Darwin in two days and three nights, driving almost non-stop with two drivers. I loved the wide, wide streets of Alice, its neat white houses and the feeling that time was standing still. The sun beat down and no one hurried. The Todd River is usually dry but very occasionally a rainstorm miles away will send water rushing down but it is gone almost as soon as it arrives, draining away in the surrounding dry terrain.

In November 1946 we had begun to hear rumours of a Government plan to build a rocket-testing range in South Australia, about 240 miles northwest of Adelaide. Already there was concern that the range could endanger aborigines living in the area.   By January 1947 plans were nevertheless being finalized for the project to be called the Long Range Guided Missiles Organisation.   By June the buildings and runway at Woomera were being built.   Woomera, in the South Australian desert, was chosen because it provided a 3,000 miles range over land and sea needed for the project.   Only Australia and Canada among British dominions offered relatively uninhabited sites and Australia was preferred because a Canadian site would have been permanently snow-covered, making it difficult to recover rockets after firing.

I spent only a few days in Alice waiting for my Qantas flight to Melbourne.   (Qantas had only recently been taken over by the Commonwealth.) I was looked after by some kind families, I met the real Daphne Campbell and bought my mother a beautiful opal brooch for £5, a great deal of money. I wish I'd had time to see the marvellous environs of Alice Springs, the dramatic gorges of the MacDonnell Ranges, Standley Chasm – a deep, narrow cleft in the bright red rocks which is barely wide enough to walk through, Simpson's Gap with its black-foot rock kangaroos and above all, the unbelievable colours of the so-called Dead Heart exemplified by the watercolours of Albert Namatjira. I should just have to come back and see them later.*

---

*Uluru (Ayer's Rock), the massive ironstone monolith thought to have been a meteor, was not then known to white Australians.

Chapter 21

MANNEQUINS AND VINEYARDS

Back in Melbourne I received a letter from Shirl. It contained startling news from Darwin. She had gone to bed one night with Pete under the bed as usual. She was suddenly awoken by his loud barking, peered through the mosquito net but could see nothing despite the brilliant moonlight illuminating the room. She felt uneasy but was dozing off when suddenly Pete started again, loud and vigorous, savage barks. This time she saw the outline of a big man in the doorway. She couldn't believe it.

She said: 'Who are you? What are you doing here?'

There was no reply but the large figure advanced. She let out the loudest, most piercing scream, hoping Rev. Grant would hear her. As soon as she yelled the man pounced on her, stooping over the bed and grasping her head through the net, trying to muffle her screams. She kept on wriggling and yelling, the pins fastening the net popped and it became wound around her body. The man then grabbed her throat and hissed: 'Shut up you little b.....or I'll kill you. How would you like to be killed?' She thought she was a goner and stopped screaming. Then she got a glimpse of his face and recognized him as a man we had met.

'It's you! What are you doing here?'

Then she heard footsteps racing across the adjacent tennis court, the man released his hold and she called out 'Is that you Mr. Grant?'

It was. He bounded up the back stairs just as the man rushed out of the flat and into the billiard room, slamming the door in Mr. Grant's face but not before he, too, recognized the man. Shirl, shaking all over and weeping with reaction, spent the rest of the night at the Grants' and the next day Sgt. McColl came and took statements. A black tracker examined the ground below the window where the man jumped out and found shoe marks.

A court case followed. The man was easily found at his work place but he denied everything. He even had scratches on his legs where he had scrambled through the window but he claimed they were made while loading crates of beer. Shirl was incensed when the judge fined him £10 for being unlawfully on the premises and only £5 for assaulting her! She was quite offended.

I was alarmed to read all this. We had never had any trouble in eighteen months. I always said that our innocence was our protection. Only at Larramah were we really importuned and we put that down to the men's isolation and lack of female company. One thing was abundantly clear. Although little Pete was a good watchdog, he was no good as a bodyguard.

Ross rang me most nights but on one occasion he was very subdued and said he had bad news. He could hardly speak but at last I learned what had happened. There had been a function in Cairns which all the naval men were attending. Ross left one man on watch on board his ship and the rest of the crew went ashore. That night there was a king tide and the water level at the wharf sank lower and lower. At its lowest point a projection from the ship became wedged under the pier and when the tide turned and the water level rose, the ship didn't. It foundered. There was to be an enquiry and probably a Court Martial. He was inconsolable. I didn't know what to say to make him feel better. What was there to say?

Some weeks later I flew to Sydney to be with him after his trial. In the evening papers was an account of how a naval officer had been relieved of the command of his ship and severely reprimanded. It was very sad but he was planning to leave the Navy anyway and find a career ashore. He wanted to be with me and kept stroking my ring finger and saying he wouldn't mind a finger in exchange for a ship. I was still undecided and couldn't give him the assurance he wanted. How could I ever be sure!

My indecision had not been helped by seeing Keith, my Melbourne boy friend, again. I had met him when I was fifteen and I had been faithful to him all through the war. I had last seen him when I returned to Melbourne for Sharpey's wedding. Now he was out of the Navy and training to be a teacher at my father's College. The old siren song of first love came back to haunt me and I felt myself falling under his spell again. Then Ross returned and I was torn. Oh for polyandry! Each had attributes which I loved and each had faults that I couldn't accept in a mate for life. What was I to do?

I was home when Princess Elizabeth married Philip Mountbatten and I listened to the broadcast service on a friend's wireless. We all thought Philip was so handsome.

The reason for my return to Melbourne was to spend a lot of time with my brother Pete. He was my favourite brother, we were inseparable as children and teenagers but he had been away in Borneo for two years and I had missed him dreadfully. Now I caught up with all his news. He told me wonderful stories about life in the tropics and made a great joke of coming down to breakfast on the hottest of days wearing jumpers and an overcoat. We played lots of music together and a momentous occasion was the 2nd Australian Jazz Convention held in the Collingwood Town Hall on the 30th December. Before he went to Borneo Pete had been playing trombone with Graeme Bell's Australian Jazz Band but someone had taken his place. He didn't participate in the Jazz Convention but three young men and I played *Basin Street Blues* and *Jada*. Dear old Pete was dashing around, putting a mike inside my piano then rushing to the back of the hall to check if I were audible. I played well and we had a good reception. I was the first woman to play in the annual Jazz Convention.

Another letter came from Shirl full of news about her visit to Alice Springs. Her trip south from Darwin had been easier than mine as she was able to sleep on the back of her truck. In Alice she'd been lucky enough to get a free flight with Connellan Airways to Hermannsburg Mission where Albert Namatjira and the other aboriginal artists lived. Albert was away at the time on a painting trip but she bought a painting by his son Oscar. It cost only three guineas whereas Albert's were beyond her reach.

From there she went to Palm Valley, fourteen miles distant, on a camel accompanied by a dear old aborigine with a white beard. (She left Pete behind in Alice with friends). The trip covered two days and they camped the night at the oasis with its lush green growth, water pools and abundant wild life. Here were the ancient cycads (Macrozamia palms) and other rare plants. She thought it was the most wonderful scenery she had seen in the Territory.

She had also been to the Hartz Range mica fields with the weekly mail truck and visited all the isolated mining settlements on the water-cart. Nearly all the workers there were Italian and they were very hospitable and gave her wonderful meals!

When she had arrived in Alice Springs she collected a swag of mail and a three-month old telegram reading 'Please advise Brian's where-abouts...Mother ill... very worried...Pat.' We had last seen Brian O'Donnell in Darwin when he was about to fly out to Europe. She couldn't help Pat.

Shirl was now keen to leave Alice and get to Adelaide where her boyfriend, now demobbed from the RAAF, was living. She planned to catch the Ghan, the famous train which ran from Alice to Adelaide. (There was no road to Adelaide). Afghan camel drivers and their beasts had been imported from Afghanistan in the 19th Century when the Overland Telegraph Line from Palmerston (later renamed Darwin) to Alice Springs was being built. The route followed was mainly that of John McDouall Stuart, the first explorer to cross the continent from south to north and back again. The huge job was completed and in use in 1872, only two years and 36,000 telegraph poles after the commencement. Work on the line in the searing heat of northern Australia had been arduous and the camels had been invaluable in carrying supplies and water over the long desolate stretches. Their descendants still roam the Centre today. When the railway from Adelaide to Alice Springs was completed in 1929 it was affectionately nicknamed the 'Ghan'. (The train now runs from Adelaide to Darwin.)

-oOo-

It was time for me to rejoin Shirl in Adelaide. Although our original plan had been to come home to Melbourne from Darwin and Adelaide (there being no road other than Madman's Track around the north-west coast), more and more people were saying to us: 'What! Not going to the West? That's almost half the country you'll be missing! You have to go to the West!'

We looked at our maps and considered the vast third of the continent which was Western Australia. Admittedly the settled areas were in the south-west corner and up the western coast for about 500 miles. Most of the interior was empty. Between Adelaide, the capital of South Australia and Perth, the capital of the West, lay the great expanse of the Nullarbor Plain. Were we going to ride across it twice? We should have to give it a lot of thought. In the meantime I had to rendezvous with Shirl in Adelaide.

I travelled overnight by train and at 9am reached a station where Shirl was waiting. I leapt off and rushed to meet her – and little Pete! I couldn't restrain myself and sat down on the platform while he leapt over me and covered me with licks. I was nearly weeping with joy and was the object of great amusement and interest to hordes of passengers.

Next day we made our official arrival in the city. The Malvern Star manager had loaded us, our packs, Peter and the bikes onto his car then driven out to the fringe of the city. It was a blistering hot day and we made him stop on the outskirts as we didn't want to ride too far. We loaded our bikes and rode back slowly to the city, shepherding Pete through the traffic. On arrival at the Malvern Star shop we were met by reporters from the *News*, the *Advertiser* and the Australian Broadcasting Commission. A crowd gathered. The manager wanted our bikes for a window display and lent us some awful old crocks.

Then it was back to work. We spent several days going round the shops for advertising purposes. At Myer's, sister establishment of the huge Melbourne emporium, the Advertising Manager was enthusiastic about a display window featuring sports wear and sent us to see the Secretary of the store who was also very keen and even broached the idea of our modelling sportswear in the Myer dining hall!

Walking on air we decided to treat ourselves to lunch at Allegro's Italian restaurant. While eating a wonderful meal of minestrone followed by a huge plate of spaghetti, I noticed a piano standing forlornly against the wall and started bantering with the waitress about the advantages of soothing music to aid relaxation during a meal.

'Don't tell me, tell the manager!' she said.

So I sought him, introduced myself and was just starting my spiel when he said: 'Well, how do you do! I was just saying to my wife this morning after reading about you in the paper that I wished I knew where you were so I could ask you to come in and give us some music.'

That took the wind out of my sails. I was amazed at my good fortune. After some discussion, it was agreed that I should play for 1½ hours each lunch time for five shillings a time, plus Shirl's and my dinner. Mr. Fabbro was no cheapskate. He told us to order whatever we wanted and not to worry about the price.

Bursting with elation, we left and went to see the Advertising Manager of Amscol Ice Cream which was the only make of ice cream sold in South Australia. We felt our luck couldn't last. As soon as we'd introduced ourselves, he said: 'Ah, you want to change the name of your dog!' He'd read all the blurb about Pete in the paper.

We explained the Peters set-up and he looked dubious when the financial aspect of the contract was mentioned. He had a word with his manager and returned apologetically saying they couldn't pay us anything but of course if we liked to have a pass for icecream they'd be only too glad to help. Well! We only wanted the icecream! He gave us two letters, showed us over the factory and sent us on our way with a large family brick each.

A pleasant grey-haired woman came up to us in Allegro's and introduced herself as Judy of Judy's Coffee Shop. She invited us to drop in for supper any time. What a friendly city!

By appointment we met a man known as the Walking Postman. For almost two hours he told us about his adventures in marathon walking. He had done two trips, Fremantle to Sydney and Brisbane to Adelaide. He seemed obsessed with the idea of doing something great rather than seeing the country.

Adelaide in those days was very sunny and unhurried, with lots of pubs and churches. A small city, we kept meeting people we knew. Quite often someone would come up and say 'Remember me?' There was a girl we'd met at Kosciusko and a man I'd danced with at the Larrakeah Ball in Darwin. One man who used to ask me to play *Für Elise* turned out to be an announcer at 5CL radio station where we had an interview.

One day a young Italian engaged me in conversation. After a while he looked at me with ardent eyes and said softly: *'Io vivo amare.'* I was nonplussed. I had only a basic smattering of Italian but remembered the word 'to eat'. *'Io vivo mangare,'* I replied.

One lunch time I was eating my meal at Allegro's after doing my stint at the piano. Shirl was late. What could be keeping her? She rushed in to explain her absence just as I was finishing. She had been coming into town and, passing the wide green parkland which surrounded the city on all sides, had seen a cow in labour. Her scientific interest aroused, she sat down on the grass to watch the birth of the calf, taking photos of each stage.

Ever since Shirl had been assaulted in Darwin we had discussed the question of self-defence. Pete was obviously not going to protect us. Shirl made enquiries about getting a gun and was told she would first have to get a permit so she went to the Police and must have presented a convincing case as she emerged with the essential piece of paper. Then she went to a gunsmith and appeared triumphantly with a revolver which we promptly named Ruby. It was a dear little silver thing more like a toy. She also had a box of 50 bullets, murderous hunks of lead.

There was another welcome addition. The manager of National Radio Corporation enthusiastically agreed to give us the innovative Walkabout Radio to take west. It must be remembered that this was ten years before transistor radios appeared. This was the first portable radio, slung on a shoulder strap, and it worked on batteries. It was quite heavy. The aerial was in the strap so if we were in a building we had to hang it on the back of a chair or on a hook. We took it away with us and had music as we walked through town. We called it Walter.

The highlight of our time in Adelaide was our appearance as mannequins at Myer's dining hall. The Fashion Manager sent us to the woman in charge of the ladies wear showroom who proceeded to bring various clothes. After a lot of trial and error four outfits for each of us were chosen. Suitable shoes were selected. The clothes were beautiful – shirts, tailored skirts, pedal pushers with a shirt and a sleeveless jacket to go over it, a woollen pinafore dress with a blouse underneath and a brushed wool jacket. The idea was versatility, mix and match garments.

The next day after finishing at Allegro's, we went to Myer's where we had our faces made up at the Cyclax Salon. Skin tonic, day lotion, rouge, powder, eyeshadow, mascara and lipstick were applied. Shirl even had anti-shine lotion and drops in her eyes to make them sparkle! The final result was startling. My lipstick was too dark for the light reds I was modelling so it had to be changed. A girl applied it with an orange stick and the outline was blurred and crooked so I wiped it off and did it myself.

Then we went up to the Apollo Hall and were briefed about walking. I was surprised by what we were told. I had always visualized mannequins drifting around looking beautiful, making graceful turns so that the dress could be seen from all angles. No, that was all wrong! One had to walk briskly, make a swish at each corner of the square and stride out again.

At 3 o'clock we dressed in our first outfits. An orchestra was playing lilting music. We waited in the wings and heard the band leader introduce us. After describing the clothes he signalled the band to strike up again, I stepped off the stage and turned right while Shirl went left. I felt rather tense and endeavoured to split my tight face into a smile. I walked briskly along the carpet which passed between the tables, did my turn and headed off along the side of the square. I was now able to see Shirl and my tension subsided as I was inwardly convulsed with laughter at the unusual sight of her doing her stuff. All the customers seemed approving; they smiled at us and said how nice we looked. We changed into successive outfits and all too soon it was finished. By now, I had completely relaxed and was enjoying it. We were told to return the next day.

The Hall was completely full next day and two professional mannequins were to model street frocks after us. It was very amusing as our dressers were having a private war with the two mannequins who, it appeared, had their noses put out of joint by our popularity! Jealous of our clumsy parading? We didn't care, we just laughed at their catty remarks. When we'd finished our circuits, we looked at them. They raced up and down the aisles, hanging on to their hats and seats of their skirts! I wonder the customers had time to look at the frocks.

After hearing my report on Melbourne, Shirl had become quite homesick and decided she'd go home for two weeks so, after she'd left by train, I decided to go and look at the Barossa Valley, which then made 80% of Australian wine. I'd read of the amazing little community of Nuriootpa whose fame had spread because of its experiment in community living. In 1936, the local hotel was bought by a number of citizens and soon the profits paid off the initial cost. Since then the first wing of a new hotel had been built. The profits had also helped build an Olympic swimming pool set in lawns and gardens, a free kindergarten and Centennial Memorial Park. It was planned to build a Civic Centre with a library and crèche. They had also secured musical instruments for the town band and provided a rehearsal room. There was a Community Co-op Store which belonged to the people and paid bonuses to all the members. The most important thing about Nuriootpa was the way all the people pitched in and helped with the work. The swimming pool and the kindergarten were built by voluntary labour, working bees which operated at weekends or at nights with the aid of car headlights. Nuriootpa is aboriginal for a meeting place and the townsfolk had made it a place where everybody worked together.

It sounded intriguing so I caught a late afternoon train with little Pete. It was a long trip but very interesting after Gawler. I was elated on seeing my first vineyards. They were so green! Then the famous wineries began to appear – Seppelts, Tintara, Gramps Orlando and Penfold. We passed Tanunda with its Château and reached Nuriootpa in the evening. I got all my baggage onto the platform and asked the stationmaster if he knew a kind family who would give me a wash. He directed me to the porter's house nearby – a Mr. Knispel. I knocked at the door and Mrs. Knispel opened it. I introduced myself and she welcomed me warmly. She showed me to the bathroom and when I had smartened up, invited me to stay and gave me some supper. I usually had no problem in remembering names but Knispel almost defeated me. I'd concentrate on remembering the K and N (the K was prounounced) but then I'd get the S and P the wrong way round and say Knipsel. They were a lovely family with whom I felt completely at home. They had three sons and a little daughter and they absolutely adored Pete.

Next day one of the sons rode out with me to look at the town. The first thing that impressed me was the row of shops on each side of the main street, each one bearing a German name – Schmidt, Reusch, Baecker, Hoffman, Saemler, Heutzenroeder. The Church was Lutheran.

I walked along the creek and was excited to see a large sculpture by William Ricketts, a visionary artist who worked in clay. He was deeply committed to the cause of the aborigines and their ancient culture. I had visited an exhibition of his work in Melbourne and bought two of his potboilers priced at thirty shillings each. One was a plaque depicting an aged tribal elder with a long beard swirling. The other was an ashtray showing a piccaninny's head sprouting from a tree stump. Both faces showed a haunting expression of disillusionment and alienation. The Nuriootpa sculpture showed bush animals and aborigines and the large piece had been mounted into a bank by the water. This was unusual and I feared for its safety but it was a wonderful way of bringing art to a rural community. Later, I saw three other fine Ricketts works in the town.

The Community hotel, the Vine Inn, was very pretty with lawns and flowers all around it. I met the Community live-wire, Mr. Reusch the chemist, who told me about the town. I learned that the Barossa valley had been settled by the first organized non-British immigrants in 1838. They were a group of Evangelical Lutheran Prussians, seeking a country which practised religious toleration as their own country was seeking to unite Lutherans and Calvinists which they thought would destroy their own fiercely independent communion. They had heard of the emigration schemes of George Fife Angas in England and two hundred of them took passage to South Australia. They were expected to make a significant contribution to the young colony, particularly in farming and wine-growing. Their industry and sobriety would make them ideal agricultural labourers. Now, over a century later, their descendants had established themselves and formed numerous settlements with a strong ethnic flavour. Many of them still spoke German, the women cooked intriguing German dishes, there was a Vintage Festival each year at which a Daughter of Bacchus was chosen as Queen and there were street processions with decorated German farm wagons and brass bands. It was all so un-Australian I was fascinated!

I stayed with the Knispels for several days, using their house as a base for exploring the other townships in the valley. There was a drama when Pete mauled one of their pet Angora rabbits when it got out of its cage. I guess it was the first rabbit he'd seen. It died later and I felt dreadful.

Mr. Reusch arranged for me to inspect Seppeltsfield winery. Every field was planted with vines and everything was delightfully green. Such a change from summer-parched paddocks in Australia! The winemaking process was explained by a guide and I sampled the product. All dry and sweet wines were made there, brandy at Château Tanunda and sparkling wines came from Seppelts' Great Western winery on the slopes of the Great Dividing Range in Victoria.

Tanunda had the only Skittles Club in Australia. I tried my hand at hurling the heavy bowls along the wooden alley in an effort to knock down the formation of pins at the far end. Was this a German import too?

The next day it was very hot again but the sun was replaced by a blustery west wind. I was contemplating riding to Angaston and it was a tail wind so I didn't mind but it was extremely humid and sticky. I set off at three o'clock but it was very slow going as Pete was tired and hot. I stopped twice to rest him but still reached Angaston by 4pm. I was continually surprised by the short distances. Usually Australian townships are from twenty to fifty miles apart but the Barossa Valley is so fertile that there is a village every two or three miles. So wonderful for biking! I was able to ride to Tanunda in the evening to go to the pictures. I was told there was no other district in Australia where such a lot of people got their living from the same industry in such a small area.

Angaston was built on hills whereas Nuriootpa was on the plains and in Angaston the vines had been almost replaced by orchards. I was invited to stay at the Angaston Hotel overnight. The owner of the Amscol café where I'd had some icecream offered to take me for a drive around the district in the evening. We drove past Yalumba winery and out into sheep country. There were lots of orchards. Everything seemed to grow there. What a pretty district the Barossa was with its green vines in summer, red vines in autumn, green pastures in winter and fruit blossoms in spring.

Mrs. Angas had invited me to visit her. She belonged to the present generation of the family which first settled the district and gave its name to the town. We drove into large grounds with splendid gardens and were greeted by an attractive slender woman whom I took to be about 35 but who turned out to be a grandmother. She was very gracious and friendly and took me inside the house to a luxurious lounge with a huge fireplace, walls lined with books, a few good original oil paintings and period furniture. The family owned a very large sheep run.

She told me that The Silent Stockman, one of the two surviving characters from Mrs. Gunn's book *We of the Never Never* was living in Angaston! I found him in a small cycle shop in the town. His name was Jack McLeod although his name was never used in the book. He was a very pleasant, friendly man and chatted about the Territory, the Elsey Station and Mrs. Gunn. She apparently was living in Hawthorn, a suburb of Melbourne, and he was going to visit her soon.

The whole valley was fascinating. In Tanunda especially, German was still spoken in most homes and services were held in German in one of the five Lutheran churches. German epitaphs and inscriptions predominated in the cemeteries (carved on marble headstones from Angaston quarries) and German food was eaten. It was interesting sampling the different dishes. Grated cucumber mixed with cream was a salad dish and dill cucumbers were popular. Every housewife made her own. Into an empty kerosene tin she laid vine leaves then a layer of whole young cucumbers topped with dill then more vine leaves and so on, repeating the layers and finishing off with vine leaves. Then she filled the tin with boiled water in which one cup of salt had been dissolved and two cups of vinegar. The whole was covered with a plate and weighted, leaving it for two weeks till it had fermented. One then plunged a hand into the rather slimy liquid, withdrew a cucumber and washed it. I quite liked the sour taste. Mrs. Knispel gave me a copy of the Barossa Cookery Book, a collection of recipes from the women in the valley. There were lots of strange concoctions including a German Cake, a large, flat, round cake of a yeast mixture covered with *streusel*, a crumbly topping. I was fascinated by all this foreign-ness and had to keep reminding myself I was in Australia.

I spent a week in the valley and then returned to Adelaide, picked up a lot of mail and then headed down to Victor Harbour for a few days. The weather turned cool and wet, not good for a beach resort, so I trained back to Adelaide, returning on the same day as Shirl.

Chapter 22

THE UNKNOWN WEST

Thursday, 26th February 1948:

We had received exciting news. After pursuing shipping agents for some time with little success, we were now told we could have berths for £10 each on the P & O liner *Stratheden* on its voyage to Perth. This was marvellous! At last we would sail on a ship and we wouldn't have to cross the Nullarbor twice. We hastily said our goodbyes, packed up, had our last meal at Allegro's and proceeded to Outer Harbour by train, all our luggage and bikes being booked through for nothing by friendly porters. It wasn't possible to take Pete on board so we left him with friends in Adelaide. They would put him on the train to Perth as soon as we arrived there.

With great excitement we boarded the beautiful gleaming liner and found our cabin, seven decks down on G Deck. It was a very comfortable inboard cabin with two berths.

The quay was packed with passengers from the *Strathaird* (recently arrived from London and bound for Sydney) and the *Stratheden* (Sydney to London). Later on we watched the *Strathaird* depart, almost concealed by a curtain of streamers, a delightful Australian custom. It looked so beautiful in the sunlight, the multi-coloured web of streamers connecting passengers on board and friends on the wharf stretching taut until finally breaking. For once I wasn't envious of the passengers nor filled with regret that I couldn't be sailing.

Back in our cabin I found a telegram and a box of flowers from Ross. There were delicate pink waterlilies, blue larkspurs and fern. I felt like a film star being farewelled with flowers.

There was no bath in our cabin. The bathroom was along the passage-way and one had to summon a steward and ask for a bath. The deck crew were all Lascars, southern Indians clad in blue tunics, white trousers, red turbans and sashes. They were so exotic I felt I was really sailing to England! The cabin and dining stewards wore white uniforms. A bath steward brought a baby's bath of hot fresh water because the water which came out of the enormous six-inch taps was salt. The bath filled in no time.

The baby's bath sat on a wooden support across the big bath and its water was used for washing and final rinsing.

We were allocated the second sitting for dinner and had to wait till eight o'clock. To my surprise there was only a set meal. There had been a wonderful menu on the *Nairana* across Bass Strait. Going to the lounge for our coffee afterwards, whom did I see but my Gershwin fan from Allegro's, the pleasant man who came in every day and asked me for *The man I love* and *Love walked right in*.

I slept in the top bunk and woke with the gentle throbbing of the engines and slight motion of the ship. We had sailed after I'd gone to bed. It must have been nearly daylight and I threw on a jacket and went on deck. It was very windy and cold. We were apparently just leaving St. Vincent's Gulf and Kangaroo Island was on the port bow. I went back to sleep until 6.30 when a cheery stewardess knocked on the door and announced she'd brought some tea. How utterly barbaric! I moaned surlily that I wanted none of it and tried to sleep again. It was not to be. Horrible little children whooped along the passages and blithe early-risers hailed each other jovially. I dug deep into my warm burrow, tried to forgive mankind and concentrated on thinking beautiful thoughts but was forced to crawl forth wearily at last.

Crossing the Great Australian Bight I felt distinctly uneasy. I had always thought I was a good sailor – in Queensland on launch trips I had never felt sick – but now I didn't fancy meals and had to keep telling myself I felt fine even though I had to continually rush up on deck to inhale fresh breezes. All that and sleeping too. With the weather freshening Shirl and I went to the cabin to get jumpers and thought we'd have a short nap. I climbed into my bunk and woke three hours later! To salve our consciences we had a vigorous game of deck tennis afterwards. In the evening there was a dance. It was fun trying to maintain an even keel when the tendency was for all the couples to pile up in a heap in one corner of the floor.

The next day I actually had some interest in food. We were approaching the south-western corner of Western Australia and had probably seen the last of the rough weather in the Bight. While I was playing the piano later Shirl had a game of draughts with two men who were on their way to 'Oireland'. I had seen them on deck, always dressed in black suits with open-necked shirts. One was young and slight, the other burly and coarse-featured. Perhaps he was a policeman? (The majority of Australian policemen were Irish.) Or was he a pugilist or a footballer? When I first saw them I thought: 'Gosh, what a pair of thugs!' I was amazed to learn they were priests. While playing draughts, the larger man spoke continuously in a soft melodious brogue, peppering his speech with blasphemies to contrast with his inevitable interjections of 'The Lord be praised!' Our delight was increased when, at one stage of the game, he leaned forward and said excitedly, 'Two to one the field!'

The sea was wonderful on this last day. It was like whipped ink garnished with crème de foam. The ship sent up mountains of water on each side as it forged through. It was a very angry sea, hissing and spitting as it crashed headlong into its own chasms. The wind was bitterly cold so we didn't spend much time on deck, unlike the be-rugged deckchair sitters who had been forming fours on each deck ever since leaving Adelaide. They never seemed to move although I suppose they ate occasionally. Every time I passed, there they were, the same cloth caps on the same men, kerchiefs on the women, rugs from toe to chin and heads lolling on shoulders in untroubled sleep.

'Perhaps they're scared they'll be sick if they leave the fresh air,' I said to Shirl.

'Maybe they just like sitting in deckchairs.'

It was a shame that just as we recovered our spirits, we arrived in Fremantle, the port of Perth, capital of Western Australia.

Western Australia is a vast State about one third of the whole area of Australia. With an area of 975,920 square miles, it is four times as big as France, ten times as big as the United Kingdom and very little smaller than India. It is the only State which stretches from the north coast to the south of the continent. Perth and Sydney are further from each other than London and Moscow. It has been said that there is not only a white race and a black race in Australia but two antagonistic white races, one of which lives in the eastern half of the continent and the other in the State of Western Australia!* Because of the daunting prospect of the immense Nullarbor Plain, few people from the eastern states bothered to travel to the west. Before leaving home, I had no idea of the magnitude of my country. Of course it looked big on the map but even great mileages didn't make an impact. I wonder if we would have thought twice before embarking on our mammoth odyssey if we had known how long it would take.

*'The Scarce Australians' – John Yeomans

Perth is most attractive. It's a pity it is so far from the Eastern States and has developed a Cinderella complex, rather like Northern Queensland, but what a beautiful city! Built on the banks of the Swan River, which is more like an inland sea than a river, water is very much a part of Perth's image. In the expensive suburbs of Nedlands and Dalkeith the road was flanked by the most wonderful houses and gardens I had ever seen. There were no fences or footpaths, just gardens and immaculate lawns bordering the road with lots of trees – great old gums and other tall species. Behind each house more garden extended to the edge of the river where the owner could moor his boat. On the broad expanse of the Swan River black swans floated serenely and snowy-sailed yachts skimmed across the water. Perth claims to be the sunniest capital in Australia and its residents are geared to outdoor living. Almost in the city is magnificent King's Park, an area of about a thousand acres of bushland which provides lungs for the city and in spring masses of colourful wildflowers.

There are beaches along the Indian Ocean coastline and a charming island called Rottnest which Perth residents visit at weekends. We joined them. The island is famous for its quokkas, little marsupials which the Dutch navigator Willem de Vlamingh, who landed there in 1696, mistook for rats. Hence the name he gave to the island….Rottnest. It was a rather intriguing little settlement of convict origin and looked like a fort with a mud-coloured wall stretching along the seafront, steps leading up to the streets behind.

There was great excitement in Perth when the prestigious Old Vic Company arrived for an Australian tour. We were hoping for a glimpse of Laurence Olivier and Vivien Leigh, the most famous British actors at that time, but we couldn't afford tickets. When the Company reached Melbourne, my sister Noel met one of the cast, John ('Pip') Barnard, son of the fine character actor Ivor Barnard, and subsequently married him.

We applied ourselves assiduously to our business. We hated having to stay in a city for several weeks but we had to earn money to carry on with the trip. Flushed with success from our experience at Myer's in Adelaide, we approached Foys for modelling. They agreed, a fee was decided, clothes selected and at noon the next day we dressed in our outfits (mine was a midriff beach suit with a thigh-length casual beach coat in red linen) and sauntered out into a deserted showroom! We were nonplussed. As there was no one to see us, we felt stupid strolling around between the counters and racks. A few casual shoppers came in during the lunch hour. We changed our outfits and between two and three o'clock a great horde of shopgirls and kitchen maids engulfed us!

The next day we cut it fine and arrived at noon with the floor supervisor panicking. People were waiting for us already. Three hectic hours passed. There had been more publicity by now and we were surrounded by crowds all the time. And whom should we meet but Ted, the attractive golden-bearded man from Dunk Island. He was clean-shaven now and working as a travelling salesman but said he wanted to go back to Dunk for the winter.

Having settled in Perth we told our friends in Adelaide to put Peter on the trans-continental train and then waited anxiously for his arrival. A few days later we went to the station to meet him. There were newspaper photographers there to record the great reunion. We found Pete in a little dog box at the rear of the train and had a vociferous welcome through the bars. He was barking very loudly and we were trying to find a man to unlock the box. We got him out at last and he went mad with excitement. He was terribly thirsty and *hungry*! I don't think he'd been fed for days. I bought a meat pie and some icecream on the platform and fed him. He wolfed it down. He was exhausted too and probably hadn't had much sleep.

We were staying with friends of my father. Our hosts had two irritable Scottish terriers, horrible yappy creatures which took an instant dislike to Pete. The feeling was mutual as all three dogs bristled whenever they sighted each other. I took Pete into the garden first thing one morning and on re-entering the house I saw the Scotties advancing from the dining room, Sandy in the lead, growling savagely. I realized the danger too late. Pete stopped, immobile as a statue while Sandy circled him growling ferociously. Then Sandy dived to the attack and a terrific fight ensued. Our hosts rushed in with sticks to beat off Pete and I was trying to separate them. In the fray Sandy bit my hand. I got Pete outside and walloped him and then discovered my hand was covered with blood. I eventually had to have it sutured at the hospital and have an anti-tetanus injection. My hostess thought Pete had bitten me and I hesitated to tell her it was her dog. After that, the situation was very tense in the house. I had to guard Pete from attack and accompany him everywhere. We felt it was time to leave Perth.

First we had to go to the Malvern Star factory to pick up our newly-geared bikes. The firm had decided it was ridiculous for us to be touring without gears. We went for a trial spin up and down a hill. It made riding on hills very easy but I didn't like having to use a hand brake. I had always had back-pedal brakes.

The south-west corner of Western Australia is fertile and close-knit with plenty of towns to break up the spaces. We decided on a short circuit of the south-west. Two weeks we estimated. It proved to be two months before we returned.

At Pinjarra, our first stop, we visited the Kingsley Fairbridge School. Its logo was a picture of a small child seated on a large horse. The school was founded to care for under-privileged children from Britain and turn them into good Australian citizens to fill our great empty spaces. (Although migrants never seemed to want to live in our great empty spaces but clustered in the five mainland capital cities.) There was an extensive complex of buildings, although at the time of our visit there were only a dozen children left but a post-war influx was expected. Pre-war there were about three hundred children at the School.

On the outskirts of Harvey we dismounted by the side of the road and had our long-deferred trial of Ruby the revolver. There had been no opportunity in Adelaide or Perth. It was very easy to shoot. There was no recoil or smoke. We took a few pot-shots at the trunks of trees but didn't want to waste the ammunition.

From Bunbury we visited Australind which was to have been the first settlement in the South-west. Marshal Waller Clifton came out from England in the 1830s as the representative of the West Australian Company to found a settlement. Australind's favourable position on the broad Leschenault Inlet seemed ideal. However it was discovered that the estuary was only about a foot deep except for a small navigable channel in the middle so all the plans for a prosperous city fell through. Now all that was there were a few farmhouses, a school and the original Church, the smallest in W.A. Looking more like a shed than a church, inside were a few pews, a tiny altar and an organ. On the wall was a memorial plaque to Marshall Clifton and, in a recess, his pedigree and the names of all his descendants here. We called on old Miss Clifton in the original homestead which the Cliftons built. There was a fascinating display of photographs and relics of the early days.

We passed through Collie with its coal mine and pretty Busselton with its poplars and willows crowding around a green rushy stream crossed by low bridges. Cattle Chosen, the original homestead of the Bussell family, was a quaint house built of whitewashed stone with steep roofs. Mrs. Vines, the present descendant, showed us into the sitting room, the only room open for inspection, which was kept exactly as it used to be. I would have liked to potter around this fascinating room for hours. Old books lined one wall and portraits and family groups were hung on others. Photo albums, fashion plates and some of Aunt Fanny's diaries lay on the table. A silk shawl was draped on a chair and a dress sword in its scabbard was on show together with a pair of duelling pistols. There was a glass case of shells including some beautiful nautiluses, a block of wood from Nelson's *Victory*, old illustrated papers, beautiful miniatures and lots of other relics.

From Busselton, we travelled to Margaret River Caves which, although I have seen many caves, remain my favourite. There was the Mammoth Cave where more than 10,000 marsupial bones had been found and then we descended 230 steps into the great crater which was very lovely and green with trees. A small opening in the rock face led to the second cave which was unusual in that there was a shallow lake spreading through it reflecting the stalactites, the whole lit unobtrusively. It was the loveliest cave I'd ever seen.

We met a young man there, ex-RAAF, who had flown his Tiger Moth down from Perth and offered us flights. Unfortunately the plane didn't have dual controls but the pilot said he'd give us a thrill and do some stunting. Shirl was wildly excited but I was quite nervous, hoping that the pilot was competent! I sat in the front cockpit and we climbed slowly to 2,000 feet. Then the nose went up and up, the strain was terrific and I clung to the cowling and gritted my teeth. The wind was whipping by so forcefully that I couldn't open my eyes and cowered behind the windscreen. Then suddenly everything was quiet and easy. Opening my eyes, I found we were cruising along upside down. I was amazed. There was no unpleasant sensation of blood rushing to my head or dizziness or a feeling of falling out. Then we started diving and spinning which weren't very enjoyable because the pressure was so great. The pilot asked if I'd like to fly through some cloud and headed into a huge bank of it. It was ghostly flying in nothingness and through nothingness towards nothingness. I started thinking that time had stopped and that we were just suspended there for all time and that the world had disappeared for ever....a rather frightening idea. Then I wondered what would happen if we collided with another aircraft and just as I was becoming worried, we shot out into the sunlight.

Leaving Busselton to return to Bunbury one evening we got a lift on a huge Vacuum Oil truck. We loaded the bikes alongside the great tank and tied Pete on a short rope. We then sat in the warm cabin and set off. Every now and then I looked back to check on Pete. Darkness fell and the next time I looked, I couldn't see him.

'Stop!' I screamed to the driver. I got out and raced back and found little Pete hanging by his neck on a foot of rope. I rushed to lift him up and heard him wheezing and bubbling for air. I felt weak and sick with worry but after he'd been let off the rope he ran about a bit and in a minute was fully recovered. I took him in the cabin then and nursed him. A little further along the road a man ran out into the road and stopped us. He'd been phoned by another farmer two miles back who'd seen a dog hanging from a passing truck and had asked this man to stop it. How considerate!

Passing through Donnybrook and Bridgetown we were in apple orchard country. Donnybrook had a cider factory which also canned tomato juice, apple juice, apples and plums. In Bridgetown we suffered dreadfully from cold. On the first night the temperature dropped to 34° Fahrenheit. We were staying in one of the little Country Women's Association cottages which seemed to be in every town in the South-west and despite the shelter could hardly sleep for cold. We kept a fire burning all through the next night and, rushing out to the shops in the morning, bought five yards of winceyette and a pattern for pyjamas. We cut out the pieces for pyjama pants and laboriously tacked them together, not having access to a sewing machine. Every morning, half of the seams were undone and had to be tacked again but at least we slept snug and warm.

At Bridgetown our social life improved. We were invited to a dance by the Younger Set. We weren't very optimistic and thought the crowd would be 'too young or too old'. However it was a wonderful evening. Everyone was very friendly and there was a visiting group of Apex Club delegates from the Eastern States. I hit on the idea of charging people sixpence to see Pete, proceeds to go to the group running the dance. I fetched Pete from our cottage and put him in the kitchen then canvassed everyone in the hall to come and see him. I even nabbed the policeman on duty outside the hall. It was very funny, especially as Pete kept wandering out into the dance hall where anyone could see him for nothing.

Amongst the visitors from the Eastern States was a man from our old school, two brothers Callinan from Colac who knew my brother Geoff, one from Benalla where my father was born and one from Geelong who remembered my father as an Inspector of schools. The Master of Ceremonies welcomed us in a speech and we responded welcoming the Apexians. Big Len Callinan stepped forward and in his Oxford drawl said: 'Right boys, let's give them our Eastern States greeting,' and all the men yelled 'HOO-rah! HOO-rah! HOO-rah!' It brought the house down although some of the locals were bewildered.

Then the M.C. came up and asked to be introduced to Bob Dyer.

'I'd love to meet him. You know, I heard him up in the Solomons when I was in the army. He was in a concert party and was wonderful.'

For a second I didn't understand then realized there was quite a likeness between Len Callinan and Bob Dyer, the famous comedian and variety show compère on the radio. Someone went off to fetch Len who carried off the pretence in an assured manner. Pressed to do an item for the crowd, Len strolled to the microphone, urbane and immaculate, and proceeded to organize a mass stunt.

'Now I want everyone to fall in, facing each other in two long lines. Now kneel down and salaam to each other, repeating after me:

> I know my heart,　　　('I know my heart')
> I know my mind,　　　('I know my mind')
> I know I stick out my behind.

A jolly night altogether.

It was during our tour of the south-west that our advertising skills were sharpened and we became proficient in the art of selling ourselves. Our 'free garment' enterprise was becoming very productive. We now carried a photographic block which we could give to the newspaper to accompany the blurb we wrote for drapers' shops. The only trouble was, with the towns being fairly close and their newspapers overlapping, we had to be careful not to use the same words. In Bunbury we were 'amazed' at the wide range available while at Collie we were 'impressed' by the great variety of good quality woollens. At Wagin we were 'genuinely surprised' at the very fine range of Ladies Wear. At each town we agreed that 'only the best quality garments can stand up to the hard wear of cycling so naturally we went to............to outfit for the rest of the trip.' Whereas in the early days we used to gather free gifts willy nilly, we gradually became more organized. I was collecting goods for my future married life (Ross was still ringing me every night) and I was sending home sheets, pillow-slips, table cloths, towels and lengths of material for lingerie and dresses. Shirl would just get anything which took her fancy. We decided we must be more disciplined and each made a list of Small Things and Big Things according to how much the shop's owner allowed us. Stockings, underwear, gloves, cosmetics, an umbrella, socklets, a blouse or hats appeared as Small Things. Shoes, sandals, a dressing gown, a raincoat, a dress or skirt all figured on the Big Things list. These all depended on whether we had enough clothing coupons although often the shop would give us the clothes anyway. Each week parcels were being mailed to our mothers and, at the end of the trip, I found myself in possession of a large trousseau.

Continuing down the South Western Highway we met a forester at Bridgetown who told us about the wonderful hardwood forests of jarrah and karri we were approaching and about Eastree, the very tall tree which was used as a firewatch post. The tallest tree in an area was chosen, a lumberjack went up it, lopping off lower branches and levelling the top so that a small cabin could be built there. Then an ascending staircase was made of spikes driven into the trunk in a spiral so that a warden could mount to his eyrie each day. As he told us this I felt an icy hand clutch my heart. I knew what would happen. Sure enough, Shirl turned to me, eyes wide with excitement, and said: 'Gee Wen, let's climb it!'

She was game for anything. I, on the other hand, always heard my mother's words: 'Before you do anything reckless, think of me!'

Before leaving Bridgetown we stocked up with apples. We each had about six dozen and ate our way doggedly through them in the following weeks.

On our way to the timber country we passed first of all through Manjimup. It was different from any other township I'd seen. There were buildings on only one side of the main street, the other side having a railway line and behind it the forest crowding. It gave me the impression that the town wasn't important. Manjimup's importance lay, not in its shops but its timber and I got the feeling that the forest contained great force; somewhere inside it was industry and riches and it was just by accident that in a small clearing a township had appeared.

That night we slept on the floor of a farmhouse sitting room. Pete was having a wonderful time with a bitch, the first he'd met to our knowledge. She was a pretty little fox terrier, very gentle. Pete was completely bewitched and followed her around, nose to tail, all evening. Even when we went to bed, he wouldn't come in. A clock kept us awake for hours striking the quarters then Pete started scratching to come in. We let him in and then the foxy started crying so in desperation I let her in too and they both made themselves comfortable on our feet.

Despite a fairly sleepless night we were out on the road early next morning. We stopped a truck going all the way to Pemberton. It dropped us just outside the town and we rode in. Most of the town lay at the foot of a ghastly hill and I careered down, madly trying to brake. At the Post Office we got the postmark in our books and shortly afterwards were reprimanded by the Postmaster! Collecting my mail I learned that my brother Phil had just returned from a voyage to the Antarctic on board HMAS *Wyatt Earp*. He was Chief Scientific Officer for the voyage, the intention of which was to survey the coast of Antarctica in George V Land to locate a site for a permanent scientific station. Extensive pack ice, however, prevented the ship reaching the Antarctic coast. Phil took measurements of cosmic rays in the far south before returning via Macquarie Island to Melbourne. He was now sporting a beard.

A man drove up in a utility truck and offered to drive us around the district. He took us first to the trout pools. It was the first time I'd ever seen a trout. There were some colossal fish, some almost three feet long and very thick. I tried to tickle them as they lay under the cress at the side of the pool. I couldn't understand why some men spent hundreds of pounds breeding fish to put into rivers so other men could catch them!

Then we drove to Eastree. I had been inwardly dreading this visit as I knew I should have to climb it and I was terrified. We arrived and there it loomed! It was so high that I felt giddy as my eyes travelled up the smooth trunk to its summit. Back in the 1930s small lookout platforms were built on trees but in 1946 the skill of the forest worker resulted in the construction of the world's highest fire control tower on Eastree, two hundred feet above the ground. Our driver said he had to get back to the town but would wait for us if we wanted to climb the tree. So we started.

Shirl went first. I had climbed about ten rungs when I decided to discard my slippery sandals. The steel rungs alternated with wooden ones which were wonderfully restful after the hard steel. Chicken wire stretched between each rung. My mouth was dry with fear and I mounted very slowly,

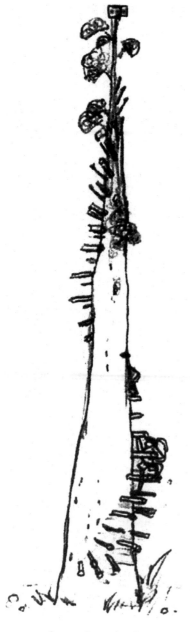

one step at a time, my eyes fixed in front or above me but never down. Our driver shouted encouragingly at intervals. After climbing interminably, I heard his cheerful shout: 'Keep on girls! You're a third of the way now!' My heart quailed at the thought of the colossal height still to be scaled. I seemed to be way above all the other trees even then. I kept climbing ('You're half way now!') and soon I heard Shirl's triumphant cry as she reached the top. After much more climbing I turned the last bend and pulled myself through a trapdoor in the floor of the cabin. I lay in a quivering heap of jelly as I drew breath and realized I was safe. After a few minutes I stood up to peer out of the window.

We were terrifically high! The car was a small mouse on the ground, we were far above all the other trees and on a clear day I believe we could have seen the ocean. There was a warden on duty, armed with a sector map, a telephone and binoculars.

By now I was crawling with fear again because the realization had dawned that somehow I would have to descend. No way was I going to stay up there for the rest of my natural life. Came the moment when I sat on the floor again, fished around with my foot through the trapdoor for the first rung and eased my body out. For some psychological reason it was better going down as I knew that each rung took me nearer the ground. What a relief to be safely down! Actually it was fairly safe as a second fence of rungs and wire was behind me so that I was climbing through a tunnel but there were still gaps at the side of the tunnel to fall through.

We saw several King Karris in the Valley of the Giants, some reaching 270 feet with girths of forty feet. Eastree could not compare with these but was a typical karri, rising in a majestic cylindrical taper from a girth of 24 feet at breast height to thirteen feet before its perfect symmetry was broken by the first branch. The karri trees were lovely, smooth-trunked and an orangey-pink in colour.

We now found ourselves down in the Up country. I collected the more interesting town names like Porongerup, Goowangerup, Yallingup, Cookernup, Kojonup, Dandalup, Quininup, Mandogalup, Quindalup, Wagerup, Minnimup, Boyanup and even Chinocup. Australian place names are intriguing. The aboriginal names are so mellifluous. I thought it was a pity that two of our States and the Territory were named after points of the compass and three had names associated with the British Empire. Tasmania was all right; that commemorated Abel Tasman the Dutch navigator, but why couldn't we have had aboriginal names for the other six States? The USA has Indian names for some of its States...Dakota, Mississippi, Missouri, Iowa, Tennessee. We could change Western Australia to Tambellup, South Australia could be Oodnadatta, Victoria would be Tallangatta, New South Wales Tibooburra and Queensland Cunnamulla. The Territory would be Borroloola. So much more interesting!

We passed through Walpole and Denmark and reached the beautiful town of Albany perched on its hills overlooking the panorama of King George Sound with its magnificent harbour of deep blue water. Because of the fear of French colonization, British settlement first took place on Christmas Day 1826, two years before the settlement at Swan River, later the site of Perth. Albany became an important coaling station for mail steamers going to England until the opening of Fremantle harbour at the turn of the 20th century.

The south-west had been enjoyable, apart from the cold and the frequent rain, but now it was time to return to Perth. We came back on the Great Southern Highway through Katanning, Wagin and Narrogin, passing the delightfully named Pootenup and Pallinup. In Wagin our advertising produced a gift of thirty shillings and I bought several items including a wool rug kit. It was a piece of hessian with a printed design of a Spanish galleon, its sails puffed out in the wind. We sometimes had spare time in the evenings or while sitting by the road.   My mother was a great handywoman, always busy with some craft and I found working my wool rug very relaxing. The trouble was, it became increasingly bulky over the following weeks and on one occasion while working it on the back of a truck, the ball of wool fell over the side and proceeded to unwind. I had to wind it in rapidly with the ball bobbing merrily a hundred yards behind and then spent half an hour rewinding it from the right end. A week later Shirl was imbued with zeal for some handwork and bought a tapestry. It amused us that we were both keen to do feminine housewifely things!

Near Narrogin was a town called Williams and I seized the opportunity to register my bike there. Bicycles in W.A. were registered and carried a small number plate, the number prefixed with two initials relating to a particular town. My Williams registered number had my initials, WL. Shirl couldn't find a town with her initials so registered her bike at Bunbury – BN.

We then travelled through Beverley and York before turning west to Perth. Now we were in the ING country. On the map I saw Goomalling, Quairading, Malebelling, Noggojering, Dulbelling, Morbinning, Balkaling, Badjaling, Popanyinning, Yilliminning, Minniging and Cumberning. Lovely!

Back at last in Perth we entered the big Australia Hotel to do some book selling and were amused by the murals in the foyer. There were large cartoons depicting each State. Australians enjoy mocking themselves. Victorians are known as Gum Suckers, New South Welshmen are Corn Stalks; Queenslanders are Banana Benders; South Australians are Crow Eaters and West Australians Sand Gropers. Tasmanians are Taswegians. Territorians are a race apart. The Northern Territory is not a State and the residents have resisted all attempts to make it one.

The owners of the Hotel were very hospitable and entertained us to meals, even inviting us to the theatre to hear a recital by Erna Berger the celebrated singer. We dressed in our best dresses, stockings and high-heeled shoes and went to the concert. The second half was spoiled for us as during conversation at interval it transpired the tickets cost 13/6d each and we were to pay for them! We had thought we were being taken as guests. Had we thought of asking beforehand we could have tactfully withdrawn from the outing but it was too late now. We could not afford such expense and worried through the rest of the programme how we could pay.

The state of our finances was grim. Despite the success of our advertising in the south-west, book sales had not been good. Frequently people asked how we financed our trip and we'd mention the books we sold but they weren't much use to anyone who didn't own a café or hotel or who wasn't a cattle farmer or pig breeder.

'Why don't you have something about your trip? We'd like to help you on your way,' they'd say.

More than a year before, the Malvern Star manager in Townsville had suggested we prepare a pamphlet but we had never got around to doing it. Perhaps now was the time. We already carried a photographic block with us so we sat down and wrote a blurb detailing our route and some of our activities. We got a quote from a printer for £5.5.0 and placed an order for two thousand pamphlets to be railed to Geraldton.

We now had our sights set on the northern coast of Western Australia. The bitumen road went only as far as Geraldton with an unsealed road going another 483 miles to Carnarvon. From there to Broome there was only a track and then Madman's Track straggled on to Darwin. Ships sometimes called at Port Hedland, Broome and Derby but there was no road traffic so Carnarvon was the limit of our horizon.

Chapter 23

WE BEGIN TO MAKE MONEY

We rode to South Perth in the dark at 5.30 one morning, our earliest start ever, and boarded a truck to New Norcia, a little piece of Spain dropped into Australia. Two Benedictine monks founded a Mission in 1845 to care for orphans and other deserving children. Other Spanish monks and nuns arrived and built up the Mission. There was now a large complex of buildings including a beautiful church and colleges for boys and girls, all of which were magnificently decorated with ecclesiastical paintings by one of the monks. There was also a school for half-caste aborigines. (One might just as well call them outcasts as they were rejected by both whites and blacks in their own communities.) There was a hostel for visitors and a monastery and nunnery. The name of Dom Moreno had been familiar to me as the composer of lots of sacred music and songs but I didn't know who he was until I went to New Norcia and found him there playing the organ. The whole establishment was self-supporting and even had its own vineyards and winery which produced its Benedictine wine.

On we went through Moora, Carnamah and Mingenew to Dongara with its delicious crayfish and its great sandhills which we slid down, then on along the coast to Geraldton with its distinctive, flat-topped hills and lovely surfing beach.

Our first errand was to the railway station to collect the large package of pamphlets. With great glee we each took a bundle of them and set off for the town. Within an hour we had each made £2, selling them for sixpence each and threepence to school children. At the pictures that night we sold more, each making £3.15.0 for the day! The next day we earned £3.10.0 and the following day at a football match made £2 each. We were elated! I was down to my last ten shillings and, with the prospect of our route passing through sparsely settled regions, this sudden infusion of ready cash was good news. Now every man, woman and child was a market, unlike the hotel proprietors who were only 2% of the population. Within three days we had sold a thousand pamphlets so hurriedly sent off an order for 3,000 more. This, too, was sold after three weeks so we ordered 10,000. This time we asked Malvern Star to pay for the printing in return for an advertisement on the back page. They said they would pay for only 2,000. When we received them we saw why. To our fury we discovered they had splashed their name through the whole text making it horribly commercial. They had changed what we had written and introduced whole paragraphs of statistics and unimportant data irrelevant to our trip. We straight away contacted the printer and told him to print another 5,000 without the Malvern Star additions.

ROUND AUSTRALIA

GIRL CYCLISTS

SHIRLEY DUNCAN, WENDY LAW,

and their dog, "PETER."

With our increased load we travelled for 483 miles to Carnarvon on a truck and huge semi-trailer containing two hundred rams. We didn't want to sit up in the cabin for the extremely long journey but couldn't see where else we could go.

'You can lie down on the tailboard,' said the driver cheerfully.

We were to leave at 2am so had dressed in our slacks, shirts and warm jumpers. We left our bikes in Geraldton as we wouldn't need them for a few days. The narrow tailboard was down, secured by two chains, and we clambered up and spread our sleeping bags on groundsheets. We tied Pete on securely and roped ourselves together before getting into our bags. The truck with its great load lumbered off.

We had an uncomfortable night. We were to the windward of the rams and they were very smelly. It was an extremely dusty road and when I awoke next morning, I shrieked on seeing Shirl although I quickly discovered I looked no different. We were both covered with thick red dust, our bags, our faces, our hair. Little Pete looked more like a dingo than a Queensland Blue. We stopped for breakfast of sausages, herrings and coffee with the men at a catchment shed and brushed ourselves down before driving on all day. We had no more meals and it was 6.15pm when we entered Carnarvon after the long trip.

Carnarvon is on the same latitude as Bundaberg in Queensland and is similarly endowed with a climate suitable for growing tropical fruits. We visited a Government Research Station where all sorts of varieties of fruit were being grown. We tasted papaws, oranges, pineapples and a wonderful 'pear' banana tasting like fruit salad. It was delicious but unfortunately it could not be marketed because its skin was too thin and therefore unsuitable for transporting.

The town was also a whaling port. Tides along this western coast are very high. (At Broome, 600 miles further north, low tides leave ships anchored at the jetty sitting on the sand without a drop of water around them!) We drove to see the very long jetty at Carnarvon and were told how the lighthouse keeper used a trolley with a sail to travel to the end of it. So did his wife when she took his lunch to him!

Surprisingly it was at Carnarvon that we first saw the New Look dresses introduced by couturier Christian Dior at the end of the war. Gone were the straight, skimpy skirts, the mannish padded shoulders. In came femininity....tiny waists, rounded shoulders and huge full skirts down to mid-calf. In our testimonial for Anne Collins, Carnarvon's leading draper, we wrote: 'Nowhere else during our tour of the North have we seen a finer collection of new season's frocks, including many with the fashionable New Look.'

The western coast is thick with names laden with history. Dirk Hartog Island was where the Dutch sea captain landed in 1616, the first European to set foot on Australia's west coast; Cape Inscription was where he set up a pewter marker; Dampier Archipelago was named for William Dampier, the Englishman who explored the area in 1699 and whose scathing reports of miserable conditions discouraged other explorers for many years. Roebuck Bay was named for his ship.

We returned to Geraldton from Carnarvon perched high on an immense load of bananas. At our height the air was sweet and clean and we escaped the red dust from the road. A Geraldton beauty salon offered us free hair-dos. I plucked up courage and had a curly-cut. Since I was fifteen, I'd had a long, smooth page-boy style but I had some curl in my hair and reckoned if it were cut in layers it would wave. I had never been brave enough to do it before but now I felt reckless. It worked! Now I had a short wavy style and it was so much easier to look after. Even when I was windblown it hardly looked any different.

We heard of a ship, the *Indian Trader*, which was in port. It was a cargo boat with Indian and English officers. They were going to India! We were wildly excited and asked if we could come. The Captain was very pleasant, even cooperative and suggested we stow away! He did not seem to be pulling our leg or were we just naïve? We made wild, extravagant plans to go to India. Over an excellent curry lunch on board we examined every aspect. What would we do on arrival there, what would we do with Pete? We even signed papers applying for passports and were about to wire home to Melbourne for a tax clearance.

A few days later doubts began to arise. India had been independent for only nine months, Gandhi had been assassinated four months previously and there was a lot of civil unrest. The country was still finding its feet. We mightn't be able to get work and food was scarce. Ross was in despair about the possibility of my sailing off to India. He wanted me to come home. We gave up the idea and turned south again.

We travelled down the inland road through dreary wheatbelt towns, each one looking exactly like the last – Mullewa, Morawa, Wubin, Dalwallinu and Wongan Hills to Northam. The weather was bitterly cold and we were woefully ill-equipped. In later years I used to ruminate on the reason Everest wasn't climbed until it was. Before nylon and other synthetic materials were invented, expeditions couldn't hope to cope with bad conditions. Canvas tents were too heavy to be carried by one man, rubber waterproofs were bulky as were woollen garments. It is hard to remember how cold we were before anoraks, wind-proof jackets and trousers and padded clothing were made.

We had each bought a pair of Long Johns, fleece-lined men's long underpants cuffed at the ankle, and a matching fleece-lined singlet with short sleeves. We could either sleep in these or wear the Long Johns under slacks and the singlet under thin dresses. Our winceyette pyjama pants were now reliable as we had managed to sew up the seams on a machine. Moreover we had made winceyette liners for our sleeping bags. It was just as well we had finally solved the problem of cold as we were about to face our severest test.

We turned east! To the east lay home. We had a marked psychological mood swing. It was now June 1948. We had been on the road for two and half years and had travelled nearly 10,000 miles. It would be nice to go home. Forty miles east of Northam we crossed Rabbit Proof Fence No. 2 and after another seventy, east of Merredin, crossed Rabbit Proof Fence No. 1. Fence No. 1 is 2,036 miles long and extends from a point near Hopetoun on the Great Australian Bight up to a point above Port Hedland on the Indian Ocean. It is believed to be the longest fence in the world, especially as it throws off a spur to the west north of Geraldton and another south (No.2) to a point near Albany. It was built at a cost of £250,000 and took five years to construct, finishing in 1907. This expensive project was necessary as rabbits were threatening Australia's pastoral industry. A few had been brought out with the First Fleet in 1788 but the real problem began when a Victorian grazier, Thomas Austin, let two dozen wild English rabbits loose on his property near Geelong in 1859. He intended them for sport or perhaps he was just fond of baked rabbit! Then the population explosion began. There were no natural predators of the rabbit in Australia and they increased prodigiously. A doe rabbit can produce three dozen offspring in a year. In 1906 92,000 crated rabbits were even shipped back to England! Such a desperate measure wouldn't have made a mark on the rabbit population and anyway, even though the graziers were in despair, there was a profitable hat industry which used the rabbit fur.

We reached Coolgardie which was founded during the 1892 Gold Rush. Over 15,000 lived there then and there were sixty shops, around thirty hotels and three breweries. Then even richer fields were discovered at Kalgoorlie, twenty-four miles away and the gold in Coolgardie eventually petered out. When we passed through, it was a ghost of its former self and the name was memorable only for the Coolgardie safe, an indispensable item in any home throughout the outback. This was a marvellous contrivance which kept milk, butter, meat and eggs cool and free from blowflies through the scorching summer. A tin safe with fine mesh walls had a trough of water around the top surface. From this hung four strips of flannel, one down each side. The evaporation of water from these four strips lowered the temperature inside the safe.

Kalgoorlie was a large city of 19,000 people all earning a living directly or indirectly from the Golden Mile. There were even trams. I thought it should have been called Hannan. Nearly everything else in the place was. Paddy Hannan was an Irish prospector who discovered the first gold there. With his two friends, Flannigan and O'Shea, plus a lot of Irish luck and quite a bit of shrewdness, Hannan explored the area slowly, looking at the waterholes and places away from the main wagon routes. The story goes that he and his friends were riding across the land when his horse kicked up a coloured stone. On further examination they found it to be a large nugget of gold. The great Gold Rush which ensued eclipsed that of Coolgardie the year before. Kalgoorlie has not forgotten Paddy Hannan. There is a fine bronze statue of the bearded prospector and his water-bag on a street corner and a lake, a street, a hotel and the local beer are all named after him.

The establishment of the goldfields depended on a good permanent water supply. The Gold Fields Water Supply Scheme involved laying 352 miles of thirty-inch pipe from a new weir at Mundaring, near Perth, to Kalgoorlie and Coolgardie. It was planned to pump six million gallons of water daily to the rich eastern goldfields. Its designer, Charles O'Connor, West Australia's engineer-in-chief, suffered persistent criticism of the project. We were told the story of how, on completion of the project, Kalgoorlie waited for the water to arrive. It did not come on the specified date and O'Connor shot himself. The next day the water arrived. It's a good story but I fear apocryphal. O'Connor shot himself the year before the water was turned on by Sir John Forrest in 1903.

We went looking for gold. We followed the water carts down the street as they watered the roadside trees, we scanned the gutters after rain. People fed us stories about how one could still pick up grains of gold along the Golden Mile. As recently as 1930 a young lad of seventeen called Jim Larcombe had dug up a slab of gold measuring 28 by 12 by 3 inches. It was the biggest nugget found in W.A., weighed 78 pounds and contained £5,500 worth of gold. Imagine! It was named the 'Golden Eagle' and set its discoverer up for life!

We went to see over the Great Boulder Mine. Perhaps we should now see some gold. We put on dustcoats and helmets and got into the cage with trepidation. It started descending and gradually gathered speed. The walls and lighted levels were flashing by in a flicker of light and shade. At the 2,800 feet level we got out, went through the draught doors and walked along corridors. We came on a group of men having morning tea and were invited to partake. One of the men was operating a complicated system of gears and levers which controlled a 'lift' to lower levels. We wanted to go right to the bottom so when the two men who were working down there came up, they offered to take us down. There was no cage on this contraption. It consisted of a kibble and a monkey. The kibble was a large sort of bucket (used for hauling up seeping water). It was suspended from the monkey, a square frame. Shirl stood on the edge of the kibble and held on to the chains. It looked very precarious but she could always step into the barrel if she felt herself slipping. I had to stand on the horizontal bar of the monkey and hold on to the upright bars with bottomless perdition yawning beneath me. It was very scary! However, we rocketed to the bottom, finishing the last twelve feet by ladder and a leap. We were now 3,000 feet down at the bottom of the Great Boulder mine. The two men were engaged in drilling and blasting the rock. Water was continually seeping and they worked knee deep in it. There was still not one speck, one glint or one twinkle of gold. We returned to the surface and trailed around the mill disconsolately for a couple of hours, inspecting the process of getting gold from tons of dirt and rock. What a depressing industry! I had always thought one would see the glitter of gold on the walls of the mine. It wasn't till we went to the gold room and saw them pouring their weekly batch of two ingots that we knew we weren't in a coal mine. They took a photo of us, each holding a heavy bar worth approximately £4,000. It seemed to me so futile to have thousands of men slaving to get this small amount of metal from the ground and then, as the miners bitterly complained, to have it all go back into the ground, in the vaults at Fort Knox.

On this day we were overjoyed to learn that meat and clothing rationing had been discontinued. Meat didn't bother us but our free garment enterprise often depended on whether we had sufficient coupons.

Once a fortnight was pay-day for the miners and the money flowed like wine for a few days in a riotous orgy of spending. Then everyone was broke for the rest of the fortnight. All the miners had beer and food accounts at their favourite hotel or café and paid their bills when they received their cheques. We did a roaring business selling our pamphlets at a shilling each.

Kalgoorlie – or Kal as it was affectionately known - had the reputation of being the most legally illegal place in Australia. The police were supposedly bribed to turn a blind eye to many things. Pubs were open at all hours and the local two-up school, three miles out of town and patronized every Sunday, was famous all over the country. Women and beer were not allowed on the premises but we thought we'd chance our luck and see what we could. We came to a paddock filled with cars. Dumping our bikes we walked across the intervening grass, keeping behind the cars, and had nearly reached the brushwood screen when a scout sitting in a car saw us and started blowing the horn in sharp bursts of warning. The game broke up, men streamed out of the shelter and the leader of the game strode up and told us to leave. We argued that if it were illegal, he shouldn't be there either and if it were legal, we were perfectly entitled to be there. He didn't appreciate our logic and said the game wouldn't continue until we had gone. I suppose if we'd been brave enough we could've just walked in brazenly but probably we would have been forcibly removed.

After a wonderful fortnight in Kalgoorlie – our social life really blossomed with two Balls, a wedding, a dance and a party in one week – and our funds considerably boosted, it was time to set off on the most daunting part of our journey, east to the W.A. border and then across the Nullarbor Plain. Despite sounding like an aboriginal name, Nullarbor simply comes from the Latin – no trees. There were almost 800 miles to be covered between Norseman and Ceduna, with only seven homesteads and seventeen catchment or underground tanks for water. In blazing summer it would have been impossible for us to carry enough water for each day's journey or to ride far enough in the heat. As it was winter, we hoped to make a station homestead every second night and to camp out of doors on the alternate nights.

SOUTH
AUSTRALIA

Chapter 24

THE GREAT AUSTRALIAN LONELINESS

On our last day in Kalgoorlie Shirl bounded into the hall and said there was a truck which could take us all the way to Eucla, 520 miles away on the West Australian border with South Australia. That would leave us only 324 to ride across the Nullarbor. What astonishing luck! We were greatly cheered and started sorting and packing. Our cases of good clothes had to be railed to Adelaide and parcels of free garments sent to Melbourne. I had finished my galleon rug and posted it home. We cleaned the RSL hall where we'd been camping, said goodbye to all the kind people who had helped us and rode out of town.

The truck came along at 2.30pm and we piled into the cabin with the driver, Rooney Havlin, and another man and soon passed through Coolgardie. I sent a silly telegram to Ross reading: 'Don't attempt this hazardous road potholes stumps' referring to the perfect bitumen road. At Widgiemooltha the men went into a hotel and stayed for one and half hours drinking beer with the publican and recalling their war experiences. We had soft drinks and practised darts. The next stop was at Higginsville where the other passenger left. It was a quaint mining canvas town, little more than a camp in the bush although a few converted army huts had replaced some tents. Trees grew thickly around the houses and a rough dirt track wandered through the settlement.

On the next stretch the road was fair but quite corrugated. We reached Norseman at dusk and camped in the CWA house. I sent another telegram: 'Surrounded by blacks no more food water eating Peter tomorrow.' That night I had my last call from Ross in Brisbane where he had been stationed since his court case. He was to fly home to Melbourne next morning.

When we woke it was a filthy day. A terrific gale was roaring through the streets bringing clouds of dust which stung our faces. Shirl's gears were giving trouble. They were too delicate for the rough handling our bikes received. I much preferred my original gear-free bike. We wired Malvern Star that we were leaving Western Australia.

The next stage was very pleasant through wooded country along a fairly good road with a few rough, rocky sections. I had managed to get a piece of hessian and designed another rug to use up all my odd bits of wool from the galleon rug. It was to have a dark brown background with coloured circles of different sizes across it.

We reached the sheep station at Balladonia as it was getting dark. We had been given the name of the owner's wife by her aunt and hoped to stay the night there but we weren't feeling very confident as there was a notice on the drive saying 'Balladonia Station. PRIVATE PROPERTY. Trespassers prosecuted.' We knocked at the door of the homestead and the husband opened it. We asked for his wife. He turned back into the room where we could see they were having tea. It was a bad time to arrive. His wife came out closing the door behind her. She didn't invite us in out of the icy gale, didn't enquire whether we'd eaten or would like a hot drink. We mentioned her aunt but there were still no kindly offers. Conversation petered and I asked could we see her paintings about which we'd heard. She led us to another room with walls adorned by numerous exquisite paintings. She specialized in amazingly accurate oil paintings of insects and animal life. In fact, her bugs and spiders, butterflies, caterpillars and lizards were so excellent that they were used for school text books. She bemoaned the fact that we could not see her work in the daylight. We agreed. She also wished we could see the solidly built homestead with fossil shells in its walls. We, too, wished we could. She told us how they used camels to carry their wool to Norseman or the coast until a couple of years previously when shortage of labour forced them to buy a truck.

At last we could postpone our departure no longer. She asked how far we were going that night. I looked vague and said 'To the next civilization, I suppose.'

'That's two hundred miles away!' she said. 'But there's a hut thirty-six miles further on. There's plenty of wood there. You'll be all right. Goodbye!'

We turned away disconsolately, clambered on Rooney's truck and drove on to the hut dog-tired. Along the road we stopped at a tank to refill our water containers and a beautiful fox trotted out of the scrub, fascinated by the headlights. It stood motionless some distance away, then went into the scrub and reappeared at another spot nearer us. It did this a few times until it was only about seven yards away, then Rooney shot it. I was upset but Shirl surprisingly argued that it would kill sheep otherwise. It had a beautiful pelt.

'Let's keep it and tan the skin,' said Shirl.

At another stop I was squatting in the undergrowth when I heard a tiny squeal of pain where Pete was sniffing amongst the bushes. I switched on my torch and saw a baby rabbit cowering under a bush, its neck broken. Pete's first kill! (Not counting Knispels' rabbit at Nuriootpa. This was in the wild.) Nimrod, Mighty Hunter! We took it with us and drove on to the hut which was next to an underground tank. We lit a fire and Rooney brought out his tuckerbox. We cooked some chops and tomato and fried bread. The little rabbit was too small to eat though we hacked off its hindlegs, cooked them and had a mouthful each! Rooney lent us a mattress and we spread our bags on it and went to sleep.

There was intermittent rain as we drove on at eight o'clock next morning. The country-side was pleasant with green grassy plains and sparse trees. There would have been a splendid view from Madura Pass except for cloud. We turned off the main road and descended a steep track into the coastal plain which runs along at the foot of the shelving Hampton Range all the way to Eucla. This detour brought us to Madura Station at lunch time and we were asked in by genial Scot Mr. Mackey. It was his birthday and Rooney had a bottle of Scotch to deliver. Mr. Mackey took to Rooney and before long they were drinking the whisky and some of Rooney's beer. Shirl and I made some toast and Bonox and sat by the fire doing our handwork. Time crept on and Rooney kept saying how we had to get to Eucla tonight but Mackey would pour him another glass. Shirl and I made more toast and Bonox for afternoon tea. We asked one of the aboriginal station hands to skin the fox. It looked such a pitiful creature without its lustrous hair. It looked rather as Pete might and that disturbed me.

We finally got away at 5.30pm, Rooney much befuddled and drowsy, so Shirl said she'd spell him at the wheel and drive to Eucla. She had never driven a truck before but I trusted her and slept. After Mundrabilla, sixty miles before Eucla, the road was very slippery after the day's intermittent rain and the truck slithered from side to side. Rooney woke in alarm and decided to drive the rest of the way. This road was part of what subsequently became known as Highway 1 and followed the east, south and west coasts from Cairns to Darwin – 7,664 miles long and one of the longest highways in the world. However, when we were there, it was still an unsealed dirt road which twelve points of rain made quite hazardous.

We reached the 'township' of Eucla at about nine o'clock. It was a deserted repeater station from the old telegraph line. There were three or four bluestone buildings plunged in darkness. We traipsed around looking for a sign of life and finally saw a gleam of light from a house. We raced to it, thankful for a sign of humanity, and a voice boomed out: 'That you girls?' It was the driver of a truck which had left before us from the catchment hut. He had arrived in the afternoon. The houses were all deserted except for one where a gang of roadworkers was camping. They asked us in to a room where a large fire was burning. Rooney introduced us to a giant, bald-headed young chap called Joe. He was very friendly and told us there was an empty room where we could sleep but to eat with him and Rooney and dive into his tucker. He then made us great steaming pannikins of coffee and we warmed ourselves. The walls of this room – and the others we explored – were completely covered with the names of people who had passed through. Not mere scribbling or vulgar graffiti which often deface buildings but interesting records of overland trips by car, truck, cycle, foot and camel. Ernie Old had passed this way, so had Jack Orr, another touring cyclist we kept hearing about. The Walking Postman had also stayed here. I wanted to read every inscription. I drew a picture of our bikes, wrote our names and then pasted one of our pamphlets on the wall. We sat talking with the men by the fire.

'Know of any trucks going across to Ceduna?' I asked.

'Hell no! There hasn't been anything through for a couple of months and since the petrol ration was cut again, there's not likely to be anything. You'd better start riding girls!'

The men laughed loudly and Shirl and I exchanged horrified glances. We borrowed Rooney's mattress again and turned in.

By the time we woke at 10 next morning all the men had gone to work. We made some breakfast in Joe's room, put on warm clothes and went to the hotel to call on the Simons family whose name we'd been given. Mrs. Simons was a small, dumpy woman with untidy hair and a complaining voice. She gave us a long recital of her grievances. She and her husband had had the hotel for seventeen years and were the only permanent residents of Eucla. She couldn't have had much custom as there was virtually no traffic on the road. The previous year she leased the hotel to some other people who made a mint of money from rackets (charging people in distress extortionate prices to drive them to Norseman and so on) and finally packed up their goods and half of Mrs. Simons's and drove back to Melbourne. Her husband had to go to Melbourne to try and get it all back. He managed to get a truck as compensation. The Simonses were now planning to reopen the hotel. They sent and received telegrams and I received one from my sister Noel saying our brother Phil was sailing from Sydney that day for Japan to continue the cosmic ray measurements begun in Antarctica. He wanted to take readings in equatorial waters. I sent a bon voyage telegram to him and another to Ross reading; 'Reached metropolis having hectic time theatres dances parties.' In Eucla!

After lunch Shirl and I rambled across the magnificent sandhills that sprawled along the sea. Little Pete was wonderful. He raced up and down the hills with unflagging energy. We walked out along the old jetty. The sea was fairly calm and we ceremoniously dipped our fingers and toes in the Southern Ocean water of the Great Australian Bight. The whole beach and the lonely atmosphere were strangely evocative.

We had promised to make dinner for the men that evening. We put a joint of beef in the camp oven with potatoes, onions and carrots and when the men returned they sat straight down to an appetizing dinner. It was followed by tinned pears and a watery custard. Our cooking had slightly improved since Queensland.

Mrs. Simons's son had offered to take us out to see Weebabbie Cave. Much of the Nullarbor Plain is honeycombed with subterranean caves, many unexplored, and this one was very accessible. The men lent us their heavy leather overcoats and the whole population of Eucla piled on to a truck and drove out into the night. It was very cold and we huddled in the back under blankets as we bumped across the plain. When we reached the location – it seemed to be in the middle of nowhere – I was astounded to see an immense gaping crater in the ground. This was the sink hole. We shed our topcoats, grabbed lanterns and swung over the precipitous side, hanging on to a rope. We descended carefully two hundred feet into the hole then scrambled over rough, loose stones till we came to the entrance of the cave. We climbed down a ladder, over more stones and entered a vast chamber. It was not a moist limestone cave so there were no stalactites. We clambered down another hundred feet and came to a placid lake extending a quarter of a mile in one direction and so amazingly clear that I could see the bottom even at a depth of twenty feet. The greatest depth was a hundred feet.

There was immense hilarity when Joe, being smart, pushed out from the bank on a flimsy raft which, becoming waterlogged, gently lowered him into the middle of the lake. He declared the water fine and several of us decided to swim. After all, not many people have swum three hundred feet beneath the Nullarbor! I shed my slacks leaving my pyjama pants and a man lent me a sleeveless jumper to wear on top. Some of the men stripped down to their underpants. I took a deep breath and dived in…and barely managed to come up again. The cold was so intense it paralysed my lungs. The water was slightly brackish. I climbed out quickly, put on my dry clothes and climbed up the slope to the sink hole where Shirl and a man were chipping away at fossils. They found some interesting ones of shells. The Nullarbor is supposed to have been an inland sea or perhaps the water from the Bight had originally covered the coastal area.

On the way home I was overcome with intense fatigue and was happy to doze all the way. On arrival the men lit the fire and Joe cooked damper and coffee. It was the first damper I had ever eaten and it was delicious, eaten hot with butter dripping. It is the bushman's bread used throughout the outback.

In the morning we packed up, made sandwiches and hard boiled eggs to take with us. Joe took us on his grader to the corner of the road where he had set some rabbit traps. One had been caught so he gave it to us and one of the men skinned it. Les, who was a Seventh Day Adventist and didn't work on Saturdays, said he'd drive us to the border. We stopped where the men were working at the Pass and said goodbye to them and to the delightful prospect of Eucla and its magnificent sandhills.

Ten miles on at the border with South Australia Les took our photo, insisting on the front of his truck being in it, then he said he'd take us a bit further, leaving us only about thirty to cover before reaching Koonalda Station. We expected to reach it in three hours. The road was now about fifteen to twenty miles inland but followed the shore of the Bight. The Cliffs of the Nullarbor, which had so impressed explorer Edward Eyre, plunged into the sea away on our right so we were no longer at sea level.

When we climbed down from the truck and watched it disappear over the western horizon, we were at last alone. Alone in the Great Australian Loneliness. Feeling very intrepid we leapt to saddle and pushed off with imaginary martial music in our ears. After fifty yards I stepped off gravely and looked at Shirl.

'Shirley,' I said, 'I'm tired!'

'I'm exhausted,' she said, 'and something's wrong with my back wheel. It won't run.'

There being no trees, we pushed our bikes off the road, through the scrub and leant them against a telegraph pole. Shirl unloaded her gear, upended the bike and dived into her haversack.

'Hope I've got a spanner,' she prayed and I fell about at the idea of the 'two intrepid girls' setting out to cross 800 miles of desert without a tool kit. Miraculously she found a spanner then proceeded to search for an elusive cone or something but wasn't very successful as our knowledge of the subject had hitherto been confined to the wafer variety, Peters brand. However, she looked most efficient and mechanical so I let her tinker about while I did my wool rug. Apparently her wheel was stiff as though the brake were being applied continuously but she was scared of messing up the Sturmey Archer mechanism and decided to let it go.

She packed up again and we were just setting off when she said: 'I'm hungry! Hang it all, it's lunch time. Let's eat!'

I was dubious as my native caution warned that we might need our food later but my resolve crumbled, as did the biscuit and stale bread sandwich I'd brought from Eucla. As I was eating, an uneasy thought sneaked into my mind.

'Shirl, what have we got in the way of food?'

'Chocolate, a bit of fruit and a tin of sardines. And the rabbit. We'll cook it tonight.'

'Any matches?' I asked.

Panic on her face. 'No,' she said bleakly.

I had a Shell strip map covering the route from Adelaide to Perth. It had instructions for the motorist but nothing for the cyclist. The vehicle should be in thorough mechanical order, it said, with at least two spare tyres and tubes. There should be a good tool kit, a stout jack, axe and spade and a piece of substantial fly wire to protect the radiator from grass seeds. The rear tyres should be partly deflated when driving through sand and when driving in hot weather over stony country. At least two gallons of water per head should be carried and sufficient food to last four or five days. The overlander was also advised to carry a first aid outfit and some brandy for emergencies such as the warding off of a chill. We were ill-equipped!

I rolled on the ground with mirth at the grisly humour of it all. No matches, no food, no bike repair material to speak of, four or five days travelling ahead of us and bikes so heavily laden that we could go no faster than six miles an hour. It was very hard work pushing.

In Kalgoorlie we'd had to make an important decision. We could either go by train across the Nullarbor to Port Augusta or go by road through Norseman, Eucla and the widely-separated homesteads to Ceduna. The latter would mean long stretches between water but we gaily envisaged trucks whizzing across as in the Territory. The scenery, although interesting and varied, would not include the real Nullarbor gibber plain which did not extend as far south as the coast but we were tempted to go by road as the train trip would always be available whereas this would be the only opportunity we'd have of crossing by road. Besides, we'd be the first girls to cycle alone across the vast, deserted area.

The point was, we had to make a decision before leaving Kalgoorlie as rail and road diverged after that and there would be no chance of changing our minds later. We chose to come by road expecting a steady stream of trucks to carry us, Pete and our gear. Now, with no traffic expected, we were faced with the prospect of carrying our heavy haversacks, our dog, our sleeping bags and groundsheets, our bulky portable radio and our package of over 2,000 pamphlets. The latter at least could have been sent by train had we known there'd be no trucks.

So there we were on our own, somewhere east of Eucla, alone on the edge of the Nullarbor. Time passed. So did telegraph poles but not one milepost. They ended at the border. We estimated our speed but as my watch wasn't working we didn't have a clue as to our position. There was no way of knowing just where we were on the strip map. Besides I had to read it backwards as we were travelling east not west. I knew that about five miles before Gurney's Koonalda Station we should come to a blowhole or a turn-off to one. I saw tyre marks turning off the road at several places but couldn't afford to explore them all. We plodded on, expecting to come to Gurney's at any minute. The road was dead straight. Darkness fell and with the aid of one flickering torch we kept our eyes glued on the road where some recent tyre marks showed faintly. We knew this car had been to Gurney's because the driver had told us they were expecting us so we watched for the tracks to turn left off the road.

Then we ran into several patches of bog. Our bikes stopped dead, the mudguards clogged with mud. We somehow found a stick and poked around in the dark with it, managing to dislodge most of the mud. We carried the stick after that and each time we came to another boggy patch, we dismounted and walked off the road and around it. For the first time in two years we'd Had the trip and wondered why we'd left home. We were absolutely exhausted, didn't know whether we'd passed Gurney's or how far ahead it was so we got off, dumped everything at the side of the road, cleared a spot under a little stunted spiky tree and crawled into bag on the spot. Low saltbush was all around. I felt a wee bit scared out on the plain with foxes and dingoes all around but oh, the blessed prospect of rest and sleep!

The stars blazed above us and seemed within grasp. My personal star, George, shone brilliantly and comfortingly above me. (We had each adopted a star after seeing a Van Heflin film where he had one. I chose the very bright one at the right-hand base of Triangulata and Shirl had one called Albert somewhere.) A tremendous silence surrounded us and I experienced the same sense of limitless space that I'd felt looking west from Charters Towers. In a straight line to the north there was nothing between us and Darwin, 1300 miles away. No settlements at all! Solitude! Only those who have crossed our great continent can appreciate the immense emptiness of it. Overpopulated nations looked greedily at our huge area and coveted its space. There were only seven and a half million inhabitants in a country only slightly smaller than China or the USA. This tiny population lived around the coast, mainly in the five mainland capitals. The interior, especially of Western Australia, South Australia and the Northern Territory, was almost empty.

It was an exceedingly cold night. Little Pete was wearing a jacket which Shirl had made out of an old bit of grey blanket but he was curled into a tight little ball, nestling against us for added warmth. My toes were icy all the time despite wearing socks and winceyette pyjama pants. I slept well although Shirl declared it the worst night she'd ever had and vowed never to sleep out again! Talk about 'the sands of the desert growing cold'! There was a white frost to make things worse and in the early hours a terrific icy gale sprang up and we cowered in our bags for ages, postponing the moment of arising. Then I discovered it was a tail wind and leapt up. We packed quickly and had a row of chocolate for breakfast.

I was determined to do something about a long-planned idea of erecting a sail. I folded my groundsheet to a rectangle, tied the left corners to the left handlebar and the right corners to the right bar. From the middle of the top edge I fastened a string which I held in my raised hand.

'Shirley,' I said, 'you are now about to witness the first experiment in sail-cycling.'

I pushed off but the darned thing wouldn't fill. I decided on a variation. With my head through the opening of the groundsheet/cape, I raised an arm at the side, making a sail which I hoped the wind would fill. My arm tired very quickly and the wind didn't really puff out the sail.

Setting off, we found that the strength of the wind was sufficient to blow us along at a good pace. We free-wheeled a lot of the way. What a contrast with our slow rate of travel the day before! About an hour later we saw Gurney's welcome sign. We turned up the side track to the homestead and ran into a solid wall of wind and dust. I fell off. I could hardly walk against it, let alone push my bike. We made slow progress along the quarter mile to the house but on reaching it were warmly welcomed by Mr. and Mrs. Roy Gurney, their five children and an older woman who was their teacher. We sat by the fire and rested. They told us it was half past noon. I realized we hadn't eaten anything but a sandwich and a little chocolate since the previous morning. Mrs. Gurney was just fixing lunch and it was assumed we would eat with them. We had a filling meal of two helpings of a warming stew, then home-made bread and jam. The bread tasted sour like rye bread. After lunch we wrote in their visitors' book, collected our membership sticker of the Gurney's Overland Club – East-West Road – which depicted an aborigine spanning the plain with his outstretched arms and Gurney's Station marked.

Mr. Gurney advised us against leaving as he expected rain very soon. The dirt road became a quagmire with very little rain and it would be no joke being stranded between Koonalda and Nullarbor Station, 65 miles away. However, we didn't want to waste the wonderful tail-wind and decided to push on to a shelter at the 25 miles mark. (Gundalabbie Tank). If rain threatened sooner there was a hut four miles away.

We bought bread, butter, jam, two tins of meat for Pete and some matches. Mrs. Gurney cooked our rabbit for us to take. We set off at 3.30pm and had a wonderful trip, flying along, free-wheeling a lot. Mr. Gurney had told me that there were twenty telegraph poles to the mile and I doggedly counted 540 of them. It was most accurate but drove me barmy. We reached the catchment tank as dusk was falling. We scoured the ground in a quarter mile radius for firewood. There was no timber or saltbush anywhere but we found a few small sticks, lit a fire and toasted some Eucla damper with a bit of the rabbit. We made our beds in the lee of an L-shaped wall which broke the force of the wind. Our fire was terribly smoky. My eyes ached unbearably and little Pete was in distress too. We got into our bags and soon were covered with a layer of fine dust.

A gale howled all night but by morning there was hardly any wind behind us. We packed up and filled our water bottles at the tank. I was aghast to find that the water from which I'd drunk in the dark had a rabbit in it. I could see an eye looking at me balefully. I thought it had tasted strange.

We set out on the remaining 36 miles to Nullarbor Station. Progress was as slow as on the first day. Shirl was carrying Pete on the back of her bike and I had the huge, heavy bundle of pamphlets. Mad as snakes! If anything had happened to our bikes, we would have been in big trouble. We seemed to be going uphill although, looking back, we appeared to be going downhill.

Before and after Gurney's Station there were four vermin fences at about 25 mile intervals. These had no connection with the great West Australian Rabbit Proof Fence but were our salvation. They crossed the road and were accompanied by the usual stock-proof metal grids. Although the grids were difficult to negotiate and Pete had to be carried across, the fences offered us the only chance of sitting or lying down for a rest. With no trees to rest our bikes against and no telegraph poles nearby after Koonalda (they diverged from the road to take a more direct route), we could not lay our bikes on the ground. They were so heavy that it took two of us to lift one and then there wouldn't be two of us to lift the other! At the vermin fences we could prop our bikes.

After twelve miles we reached Wigunda underground tank, the Chiller, and decided to have breakfast, two slices of sour bread and jam. The water here was foul too with dead rabbits and crows in it so we pushed on the ten miles to Mallabie catchment tank.

We were really in bad shape. Our speed was down to 5mph, we were resting after every mile (twenty poles) and our morale was very low. It was becoming painful to ride and we even walked as a change from riding. I was stiff and my thighs were chafed. I now had a sore knee which had been bashed when I fell on a cattle grid and my mind was dulled and numb from counting poles. In two days I counted 1500 of the darned things. We were horrified at the thought of the 87-mile stretch from Nullarbor Station to Colona which had to be done in the next two days before the mailman came in from Ceduna. If only the Station people would drive us out twenty miles the next day.

At last we topped a rise and saw a wonderful vision, a white house catching the slanting rays of the sun. It looked so close I thought my mileage estimates were wrong. However, we struck out with renewed vigour and found that it was still a long way off. After two miles we came to a track leading in. It was a rough track and I walked it. It must have been a mile long. Shirl reached the house first and by the time I came limping along, she had told Mrs. Beattie of my plight and of our general collapse. I couldn't have gone another step for sheer exhaustion.

Mrs. Beattie was wonderful. She took us inside where we had a hot wash. Then she showed us a room with a beautiful double bed made up with crisp white sheets and asked us to stay several days with them.

Mr. Beattie came in. He was a big, hearty, friendly man. We told him of our apprehension about the next lap, 87 miles to Colona Station, hoping for a helpful suggestion but he lamented that he wasn't Manager, otherwise he'd love to help us. However, he said he'd ring the Manager at Colona after tea.

We sat down to a wonderful meal – savoury stew and loads of feathery potato and onion, then two helpings of baked apples submerged in CREAM! To think our search for it should end on the Nullarbor! Mrs. Beattie said she couldn't live without a cow and always had lots of milk, butter and cream.

In the evenings the Beatties always chatted to their distant neighbours by phone. They had been told of our imminent arrival and had we failed to appear, a search would have been instigated. We phoned Simonses and Gurneys to tell them of our safe arrival.

I was feeling very drowsy and ready for bed but Mr. Beattie cheerfully built up the fire and said they were waiting to hear of our travels so we sat and drowsed in the warm room, my head dropping every minute. At last I turned in with a sybaritic stretch of enjoyment. Sheets, mattress, warmth! And joy….the Colona manager had said he had to come to White Wells Station, eight miles away, one day that week and, hearing of our plight, he offered to come on Wednesday and take us back to Colona to catch the mailman on Thursday. Everything had worked out perfectly!

Relaxing at Beatties, I agreed with Marco Polo's comment: 'An adventure is misery and discomfort relived in the safety of reminiscence.'

We rested for another day and a half, catching up on diary and being fed huge meals by Mrs. Beattie. There was a strong easterly blowing now and I thanked God we weren't having to ride into it. The country around Nullarbor Station was very bleak and bare. There were no trees, only low saltbush. I wondered how the sheep lived but Mrs. Beattie had told me that the succulent saltbush flourishes in dry country and provides food for both sheep and cattle.

At 3.50pm the next day the manager of Colona Station, Mr. Carn, arrived and loaded us onto his tiny utility truck which already was carrying two large kangaroo dogs. It was a very enjoyable drive through ever-changing scenery. It became a little hilly at one stage and then smoothed out into gentle grassy plains with plenty of shady trees. I realized we had left the Nullarbor behind. The road was still poor. Near White Wells Station the map warned there were 'roots in road, on rises, stone outcrops, pot holes and corrugations for short distances.' The afternoon sun gilded everything in a rosy glow. I love that time of day best, the colours are so soft yet shining.

At dusk we reached Colona. There was a very large, modern shearing shed on the road with shearers' barracks behind it. Half a mile behind these was the homestead. Mr. Carn unloaded our gear and showed us to a dear little one-roomed cottage with two beds in it. He said tea would be ready soon. (Mrs. Beattie had warned us of the housekeeper there and didn't think we'd get any food!) I wasn't hungry after our meals at Nullarbor but went to the house when a bell rang. We sat down at the table and a woman came in with the food. She was dumpy and slummocky with an old skirt, a V-necked man's knitted jumper on top (and nothing else!) and a scarf covering her head pirate-fashion. I smiled pleasantly and said 'Good evening!'

'How do you do!' she replied in level tones and disappeared.

She silently, almost contemptuously, served us with soup, stew and vegetables then announced defiantly: 'You can have jam tart or bread and jam. There's no sweet and no butter' and withdrew.

We praised her cooking and tried to be pleasant and no trouble. Mr. Carn, a middle-aged, white-haired gentle sort of man who had had his housekeeper for years chatted to us at the table and smoked his pipe.

I told the woman we loved animals and might we see her dogs? She grudgingly led us to the kitchen where an amazing sight met our eyes. Two dogs were tied to opposing legs of a table, four more lay on the floor about the room, two more bounded in the door and on the table were baskets containing a couple of kittens. She worked quietly amidst the uproar and kept up a continual chatter to her 'children'.

'Now come on Bruce, here's your bone. Sit down there! That's right precious. Curly! How dare you tease Fan! Come here this minute! Never you mind pet......'

We followed her out to the barn where several more hounds were bedded down for the night.

Just then the mailman arrived and we rushed to make arrangements for the next day. He was to leave at 6am! With the prospect of a 5.30 call, we went to bed.

When we left at six o'clock next morning there was a thick fog as well as darkness and it was very chilly. The mailman was Dick Miller and he detoured along a track to deliver and collect mail from small settlements. He stopped at Coorabie where his sister lived. She gave us a hot breakfast of fried eggs and vegetables on toast and we set off again, this time in the back of the van with the luggage as two more passengers had joined us. We drove through interesting country, scrub and farmlands, and finally crossed the inlet or salt lake to Fowler's Bay. It was beautiful with huge white sand-dunes like snow-covered hills. We got the postmark in the Post Office and had coffee and hot scones which the post mistress was serving to the early passengers! The last lap led through Bookabie, where we rejoined the main road, and on to Penong, Kowulka, Watraba, Charra and Athenna to Denial Bay and finally around the bay to Ceduna. This was the easternmost outpost of civilization. Our crossing of the Nullarbor was over.

My one regret was that with false hopes of a stream of traffic across the Plain, we had written in our pamphlet '....*with the help of a friendly truck, we safely covered the 800 miles of treeless desert.*'

At Penong the local policeman said the Adelaide *News* had been in touch with him continually, asking for news of us so in Ceduna we hunted out Mrs. Watson, the local reporter, and gave her our story. We were greatly amused to see the resultant article headlined 'Girls read Omar Khayyam's *Rubaiyat* on bike ride.' I don't know where they got that. We read *'Pig Breeding'* yes, but not Omar.

In Ceduna I received three telegrams, the customary one from Ross and an unexpected one from Mr. Gurney at Koonalda Station: 'Would you consider returning teach subsidised school commence September term.' I felt very flattered but had to send him my regretful refusal.

The third telegram was from my sister Noel telling me that both my parents were ill in hospital and to come home immediately.

Chapter 25

MURRAY COUNTRY

For several weeks I was in Melbourne. My father had pneumonia in one hospital, my mother had had exploratory surgery in another. Moreover, Ross had been diagnosed with tuberculosis and was in a Services hospital. It was a very traumatic time visiting three patients daily. Dad was cured with penicillin, one of the first patients in Melbourne to be given it. Mum came home and continued her convalescence there.

I was sorely troubled about Ross. I had decided not to marry him. I never felt sure of my feelings for him and continued to be attracted to other men. But how could I forsake him now that he was sick? My brother Phil said, 'Beware of unlucky people! Nothing goes right for them in life. Their houses burn down, their children die....' I was shocked by this. It sounded very calculating, the idea of going out to find someone to fall in love with, someone who was successful and blessed by fortune. Yet what he said niggled at me. Ross had not been fortunate. His ship had sunk and now he was ill and might be in hospital for two years. But how could I walk out on him now, when he needed me most?

-oOo-

It was now August 1948 and I travelled back to rejoin Shirl in Adelaide, beautiful sunny Adelaide. Mr. Fabro at Allegro's welcomed me back and I resumed my lunch time playing in the restaurant. We finally met Jack Orr, the touring cyclist who had been dogging our tyreprints for two years. He was a strange-looking man with a huge red beard almost to his waist, a mop of hair encased in a beret and a pair of bright blue eyes. He was very friendly and excited at finally meeting us. He gave us each an Adelaide-crested spoon. (This started another habit. Whenever we could afford it we bought a crested spoon in large towns.)

We were now staying at the Adelaide Teachers' College. The Principal was a friend of my father. Shirl and I wanted to get work at the Adelaide Show and spent a week going the rounds of firms wanting help with their Show exhibits. We contacted Cadbury, Nestlé and Amscol and were excited to be accepted by Cadbury until we heard that there would be no chocolate! We were to serve cups of Bournvita and Ovaltine *and* take our turn behind the scenes washing cups. We were issued with ghastly uniforms and told to start on Saturday. We went to the Show a few days earlier and went around other stalls asking for work. I landed a job at Savery's music pavilion playing the piano and Shirl got one selling tubular steel furniture. We went to Cadbury's stall and were delighted to find the girls standing around idly with nothing to do. I told the Manager we wouldn't dream of holding him to his promise as he had too many girls already!

I was on duty each night from seven till ten, playing on the beautiful 240 guinea pianos in the showroom. The first night it was amplified outside and people were flocking in so much that I had to stop after each item and make the crowd move on. After that, amplification was prohibited. I was paid 2/6d an hour. There was usually a group of young people around me asking for requests, the deadly *In the Mood* of course which I refused to play and a new song called *Baby, it's cold outside* which I didn't know.

Shirl related with amusement how a couple had looked at the tubular steel furniture she was selling. The surfaces were made of a new material called Laminex. It was a hard plastic, waterproof, scratch-proof. Ideal for kitchens, it was possible to cut and chop on Laminex. It was very functional if clinical. The husband was most impressed with it and to his wife's consternation wanted to replace his sitting room furniture with it. She was appalled! 'But I like our lounge suite!'

Shirl and I were bothered about leaving Pete at home each day and thought of a solution. We could exhibit him! Unfortunately the deadline for entries had passed and there wasn't a section for Queensland Blue Cattledogs anyway. The attendant in the Dog Pavilion said we should put him on display in a stall. So we took him in every day, put him in a compartment covered with notices saying who he was and he attracted a tremendous lot of attention. On the last night we took him in the Grand Parade. The attendant said he should just tag on the end of the line as he wasn't entered. All the other dogs were in their various classes behind placards denoting their breeds. We didn't have a notice and found ourselves on the end of the Dachshunds. As we walked around the arena, the commentator was giving a short history of the various dogs and their origin. We wondered what he would say when it was Pete's turn. He said, 'And now, last but not least, we have a most interesting dog and that is the whippet. A small greyhound, it is capable of phenomenal speed. It can attain a speed of thirty miles an hour over short distances. This is a most outstanding dog...' We howled with mirth and poor little Pete trotted along innocently under a mistaken identity! We had always been apprehensive about his ancestry but we asked one of the judges and he said Pete was a very good cattledog so we felt extremely proud.

On our last day in Adelaide I looked in the window of a tiny jewellery kiosk at the head of the stairs leading down to Allegro's and saw the most beautiful opal ring. I had seen marvellous opals in Alice Springs but here was *my* ring. The stone was quite small, set in a gold band, and the price was only £2. I had just received my pay from Allegro's so rushed in and bought it. Most fire opals have crimson red in them but this one had cyclamen. I loved purple shades and I'd never seen cyclamen in an opal. I was besotted with this ring and packed it carefully amongst my belongings.

In Adelaide Malvern Star made us a wonderful offer. They wanted us to ride their new design, the New Look bicycle. Christian Dior's New Look fashions were very much the thing at this time and so Malvern Star had designed a quite different bike. The ones they gave us were an attractive pastel red colour, like crushed strawberries, and had curved forks to the hubs.

I felt sad at losing my old bike which I'd had since I was ten so I asked if I could buy it back. I had a letter from 'Oppy' Opperman agreeing. I could buy it for £4.10.0 plus freight to Melbourne. It had cost only £4 twelve years earlier! We transferred our carriers to the new bikes and left the next day from the G.P.O. where reporters and photographers had gathered. A large crowd of people gave us a send-off.

We rode out to Gawler and then to my much-loved Barossa Valley again. Shirl was eager to see it. It was very green now but the vines were pruned low and bare as winter was just turning into spring but the fruit trees were covered in blossom. Once more we met interesting people there. There was the hospitable Marchant family in Gawler. Mr. Marchant constructed grottoes in his garden from concrete and embedded pieces of glass, shells and coloured stones in it. It looked weird but unusual. In Tanunda we met Mr. Riedel, an extremely clever man. An auctioneer by profession, he also did legal work. His hobby was making lamps, vases, table tops and other things from thin slices of a highly-coloured rock called damourite, mined from Mt. Pleasant near Williamstown, and he was proposing to market it as Dellite Ware. The lamps were particularly attractive, the light enhancing the marbled colours of the stone. He showed us his latest invention, a machine which could be operated by one man for taking roots and large stumps out of the ground. He had also devised an anti-weevil process for drying fruit but a man he talked to stole the formula and claimed the Commonwealth Government prize of £2,000. More importantly for us, he showed us how to squirt warmed liquid honey through our tyre valves with a bike pump. As he turned the wheel slowly, the honey coated the inside of the tube preventing leaking of air and perishing of the rubber. He said that we should only have to pump our tyres once a year or even less frequently. (It worked!)

On Sunday we went to the Lutheran church to hear a service in German. I followed the proceedings with difficulty despite the prayer book but sang the hymns lustily. Then the sermon commenced. Pastor Held was a dear old man with a soft, velvety voice like the actor H. B. Warner. He spoke slowly and distinctly but just when I'd be getting the sense of the discourse, an unknown word or phrase would confound me. It was all about Palestine and the Jews, Nebuchadnezzar's destruction of Jerusalem and Daniel. I couldn't see any connection!

A pleasant man called Tummel arranged with us to sell copies of the delightful Barossa Cookery Book.

We rode four miles to Nuriootpa to see the Knispels and were assailed by the heady, bad smell of fermented grapes from the Penfold winery. At a crystallized fruit factory at Angaston we came away with a huge pack of pears, peaches, apricots and raisins. We ate a lot but sent most of it home.

A kindly woman called Mrs. Gersch gave us breakfast. Hanging in her kitchen was a lovely illuminated motto reading:

Dieses Haus der Zier	(The ornament of this house
Ist Reinlichkeit.	Is cleanliness.
Dieses Haus die Ehr	The honour of this house
Gastfreundlichkeit.	Hospitality.
Dieses Haus der Segen	The blessing of this house
Ist Frömmlichkeit.	Is piety.
Dieses Haus das Glück	The fortune of this house
Ist Friedlichkeit.	Is peacefulness.)

Reluctantly leaving our German friends in the Barossa we headed north-east to the Murray. The source of this mighty river is in the Australian Alps. For most of its course it forms the border between Victoria and New South Wales before flowing into South Australia. Its European discoverer, Captain Sturt, named it in 1830 after an English river but it was important long before that in the Dreamtime of the aborigines.

The countryside was beautiful around Truro with fields of Salvation Jane, the lovely purple-flowered weed, standing out against green grass, brown soil and budding vines. Then the landscape became dry with gum trees and at Blanchetown we whizzed down a hill into the river gorge. Here the Murray was running south to its mouth on Lake Alexandrina. North of Blanchetown it made a right-angled turn and the paddle steamers headed east to Waikerie, Berri and Renmark. We rode down a very pretty avenue of willows and gums to the river and waited for the ferry to come from the other side. Pete, of course, was straight into the river for a swim. How he loved water!

At Waikerie vineyards and orange groves flanked the road, the bright fruit gleaming against the sombre olive green leaves. The perfume of the blossom, strong yet delicate, made me almost swoon with delight! A visit to an orange packing shed resulted in a load of marvellous oranges.

Many of the towns along the Murray had Community Hotels. We had seen the one at Nuriootpa earlier but now there were others at Barmera, Berri and Renmark.

Someone said a riverboat was coming and we raced to the landing. Riverboats had been operating on the Murray since 1853 and were an important means of transporting passengers and goods. The paddle steamer *Marian* was on its way to Morgan. I was rather surprised at her modest dimensions as tourist pamphlets painted rosy pictures of her sunny decks. We went on board and inspected her. We asked the Captain about the possibility of going to Mildura from Renmark with him, sleeping in the lounge or somewhere. He was quite agreeable and we arranged to see him in Renmark on his return.

We rode on in a leisurely fashion to Renmark listening to pleasant music from Walter, the Walkabout radio. A few miles outside the town we entered the 'approach', a lovely avenue of tall poplars and weeping willows. Renmark had lots of trees; each horizon had a serried line of trees along it, poplars, palms and others. As we rode into town we saw the Showboat *Trix* at the wharf. The paddle steamer *Gem* was also in and we hastily boarded her to ask about a passage to Mildura. It was going a day later than the *Marian* which would give us more time in Renmark. The Captain agreed and said the fare would be only 7/6d.

The Malvern Star manager took us to the newspaper office and then to meet the Mayor who invited us to attend the Civic Reception for the Governor of South Australia who was touring his territory. That would be fun but what would I wear? We started our round of the dress shops and I found a lovely yellow floral frock for £3 which I immediately bought. It was very New Look with a long flared skirt, cap sleeves and a pleated peplum. Peplums were all the rage and I felt I looked very fashionable. I decided to give my ring its first wearing.

We reached the Institute just as the Governor's party arrived. There were Sir Willoughby and Lady Norrie, Lady Norrie's niece and the Lady Mayoress, together with a young aide-de-camp who, we learned, was Captain the Viscount John Althorp*. An entertainment followed. A woman played a long piano piece then a stout woman sang *Land of Hope and Glory* (two verses and three choruses!). After that there were speeches by the Mayor and the Secretary of the Irrigation Trust. The Governor gave a friendly and amusing talk, mainly lampooning himself and his now-famous camel incident. (He was thrown off one at Maree!) Then the audience was invited to file past the official party and meet them. The Mayor introduced

*He later became the 8th Earl Spencer, father of Diana, Princess of Wales

us to them. Sir Willoughby and his wife were both acquainted with our doings and expressed pleasure at meeting us. Then we met the handsome young ADC. He looked foppish and very British Army from a distance but was pleasant to talk to. We were the centre of attention from then on. People were asking questions and Sir Willoughby kept dashing up when not shaking hands to put in his bit. The ADC said to call on them if ever in Adelaide again and Sir Willoughby himself delivered a personal invitation.

The next day the town was splashed with bright yellow posters advertising our stage appearance at the theatre that night. It was the first time we'd been posted.

An interesting thing happened when I went to the dentist to have some cavities filled. Having always been a highly nervous patient due to childhood traumas, I practically fell asleep as the dentist, Mr. Cock, was drilling. He had given me an intra-osseous injection, a process used in the 1890's which had fallen into disrepute through ignorance of the correct method. I would never have thought I would enjoy tooth-drilling.

In Renmark we met its famous aborigine, George Disher. He was about 68 and was brown rather than black. His mother was a full blood, his father a half-breed. He was well educated and spoke extraordinarily well with a fine command of language. He gave us each a sample of 'black fellow's writing', mirror writing which he had perfected. He wrote little verses in this writing and signed himself George Disher K.C.M.G. (Kindly call me George!)

At a packing shed we got bags of dried fruit and loaded up with Renmark's *Chowilla* navel oranges then raced to the railway freight shed and collected a new bundle of pamphlets. The *Gem* came in and tied up soon after. The Captain showed us to the fore-deck where we could dump our belongings, tie up Pete and sleep. When we returned to the wharf for our luggage we were met by a deputation consisting of the Mayor, the Lord Mayor of Adelaide, the Chairman of the Board of the State Bank and my wonderful dentist Mr. Cock! What a send-off! They helped us on board with our gear, and whether through the Mayor's intercession or not, our home was changed to the Music Saloon. To the astonishment of some passengers we dumped our huge pile of baggage on a table there. Then we sorted it and kept only what we needed, stowing the rest on the deck with Pete.

We cast off at 9.45pm. There was a gentle pulsing of the engine and a splashing of the paddle wheel. I was deadly tired and as soon as the passengers began to leave the lounge, we pulled the chairs into a barricade and laid the large cushions on the floor. I climbed into my bag and was asleep almost immediately.

Chapter 26

FULL CIRCLE

Thursday, 7th October 1948:

During the night we crossed the South Australia/Victoria border and were awakened early in the morning when the boat stopped to load wood. The crashing of the logs prevented any further sleep. The sun was shining and the river looked delightful so we dressed quickly and rushed to greet Pete and take him ashore. He was overjoyed and rushed from tree to tree. The landing place was on the New South Wales bank. He had never been to NSW so assiduously left his mark.

When the boat set off again I was sitting in the saloon writing when I felt in the pocket of my jeep jacket for my opal ring. I had put it there after the Governor's Reception. It wasn't there! I felt sick and tried to think where I'd been. The jacket had been hanging over a chair so I searched every inch of the room and questioned the cleaner. Shirl reminded me that I had flung the jacket over my shoulders when we dashed ashore. Despair seized me as it might be anywhere in a hundred yards of river bank where I had walked. I felt empty with a terrific heart-rending sense of loss. This surprised me as I had thought myself devoid of any deep feeling for anything. More and more I had felt during the trip, over months of having virtually no property, that all is fleeting, nothing matters. Now to find myself grieving over a worldly bauble was strange. I reported the loss to the Captain.

Our progress along the river was slow and infinitely relaxing. It seemed too slow to me at first but once adjusted to it, I enjoyed lying in the sun on deck and watching the yellow water and the giant river red gums on each bank, many of them 500 years old. Regent parrots flashed past as a streak of yellow with red beaks. Meals usually featured delicious Murray cod (a huge fish that can weigh as much as a man and live for a hundred years) and there'd be infrequent periods of activity when we approached a lock, everyone going ashore to watch the procedure of locking and flooding. Pete was able to go ashore again, this time on Victorian soil. Now he had been in every mainland State.

We reached Mildura the next morning. We paid the Captain our 7/6d fare and my last words to him were:

'Mark my words! Ill-luck will dog you if my opal's still on board!'

On its next trip the *Gem* had its funnel damaged while sailing under a low-hanging cable and on the following voyage it struck a snag near Cal Lal and sank. I am convinced my beautiful ring is at the bottom of the Murray.

Mildura was a clean, modern city with wide streets, good shops and attractive bungalows. It was the sort of place where we ran into people we had met the day before and after a few days we were no longer strangers. I decided I would like to live in such a town in the country although it did have some drawbacks. Only the main street was metalled! Side streets and footpaths were rutted, sticky, muddy morasses! I wondered the residents put up with them.

There was a University six miles out, an informal place consisting of dozens of Army huts grouped around several sports ovals. The students wore shorts, open-necked shirts and sandals. We soon made friends and joined in their social life.

As we were now back in Peters Icecream territory we wrote to Amscol thanking them for their generosity.

In the mail awaiting me was a letter from Mum telling of Jack Orr's visit to her. She, quite ignorant of his existence and unprepared, was rather staggered to see the dreadful bearded apparition at her door! There were also newspaper cuttings of a laboratory fire at the Natural Philosophy School at Melbourne University which had destroyed my brother Phil's records of the cosmic ray research he'd done in Antarctica and later his equatorial measurements on the way to Japan.

As Mildura was our first Victorian town, Shirl had to re-license Ruby. A constable at the Police Station advised her to take it to Swan Hill as the Superintendent was there. We sold the constables some pamphlets and 'autographed' them with our fingerprints and Pete's paw prints.

In 1886 Alfred Deakin, Victorian Minister for Public Works and Water Supply (and later Prime Minister of Australia) had visited California to examine irrigation systems. Droughts around the Murray in north-western Victoria and South Australia had convinced him that irrigation was needed.

He therefore invited the Californian brothers, William and George Chaffey, to set up an irrigation scheme at Mildura.

'We shall have a large and prosperous population obtaining its wealth from the surest possible means, delivered from the risks of natural rainfall,' he said.

He was right. The Chaffey brothers transformed the drought-stricken land into a vastly successful citrus growing area. Mildura and Renmark were now the premier producers of dried and citrus fruits. In Renmark we had visited Olivewood estate and seen the two original orange trees which were planted by the Chaffeys. From these all the others had been budded. The Chaffeys used to live in the picturesque old log cabin which was now a delightful home, beautifully furnished. Orange blossom filled the warm air with a heavy drowsiness and the whole atmosphere was lazy and peaceful.

At Rio Vista, the Chaffey homestead, we met old Mrs. Chaffey, the widow of one of the brothers. The house was very stately and large with extensive grounds around it. We went on to the Mildura Co-op packing sheds and saw oranges and lemons being processed for cordials and dried peel. I was shocked to learn that the crystallized cherries in mixed peel are only sugary chunks of dyed melon!

We had done a roaring trade with our pamphlets and had to order another consignment of 3,500. This time we added a Stop Press on the back page, giving details of our Murray wanderings and got the Co-op Fruit Company to pay for the printing in exchange for an advertisement.

Now that we were back in Victoria our thoughts were turning towards Melbourne and home but then we heard of a truck which could take us to Broken Hill, the Silver City, almost two hundred miles north in New South Wales. So back we went across the Murray again. It was a wonderful morning with clear skies, warm sun and fresh air. We drove to Wentworth through beautiful country – orange groves and vineyards – but after that passed desolate, dusty flat land with little vegetation, proof, if any were needed, of the benefits of irrigation. We called at Coombah Station for a drink around noon and afterwards came to a lot of parked cars and buses. An annual Masonic picnic was being held in the dry bed of a creek and separate groups of people were dotted all over the place. There were six charabancs and about fifty cars. Our driver was plied with beer and persuaded to spend the afternoon there in order to sample the excellent chops and sausages which would be available at 4 o'clock. We were not averse. I was starving and tucked into the barbecue with a great appetite. I fed Pete scraps. We had missed the butcher the day before and he was ravenous. Despite invitations from many hospitable people, we eventually got Joe, our driver, away and headed for Broken Hill, arriving after dark. We scouted around for a home. At the Church of England we learned that the curate was living in the hall due to a housing shortage! The Presbyterian parson sounded gloomy and said he'd have to consult his Board of Management. The Girl Guides never let their hall to *anyone*. The CWA room was at the back of a shop in town and the President would meet us in the morning. We went back to the Presbyterian church where the service was just coming to an end. We loitered in the lobby, wan and exhausted. Two men from the Board of Management stated sadly that it would be contravening the Health Regulations to sleep in the church hall. (Poppycock!) We were stunned by their refusal as it was too late to go elsewhere. However, a nice Yorkshire couple standing by invited us to their home. We had been up for seventeen hours and fell into bed.

The next day the President of the CWA gave us permission to use their room. We moved in and then started on our business. We did a few hotels and, after a few snags (I was told I couldn't be employed as I wasn't a member of a local Union!), I finally arranged to play the piano nightly at the Palace Hotel.

Next morning we tidied the room and put all our gear neatly behind some chairs along one wall as the kitchen was to be used for a business girls' luncheon. In the middle of the afternoon I went back to the room and found the door open and a couple of hatchet-faced women sitting there. I beamed brightly and went to fetch something from my haversack. I couldn't find it so wandered out to the kitchen. One of the women followed me and then the storm broke! In a frigid manner she abused me for leaving our belongings behind the seats. I apologized and said I thought the kitchen should be left clear.

'And so it should! Your things shouldn't be anywhere!' she screamed unreasonably. 'There were dresses hung in the kitchen, making the place look like a jumble sale. And wet washing too! You have no right to do washing and cooking!'

'We never cook,' I said.

'Well, you can't do washing here!' (I'd rinsed out my smalls.)

Just then Shirl arrived looking wary and the incensed woman started again.

'Our President would never have given you permission to stay here if she'd seen all these things. She said you were only going to sleep here...'

'So we do.'

'...not wash and cook...'

'We don't cook.'

'...and litter the room. We're proud of our room...'

'We didn't litter the room. We left it as neat as we could. Where else could we have put our gear?'

She could offer no suggestions. She had moved all our things and piled them in an unsightly heap at the curtain between lounge and kitchen. All our carefully ironed garments were flung carelessly on a chair, together with my wet washing. I was furious! She stomped off into the lounge and saw little Pete, peacefully sleeping under the table. The heavens fell!

The next day we came back and there was no Pete. We looked everywhere and finally found him out in the street. Shirl couldn't understand it as she'd left him locked in.

We arranged to visit the Royal Flying Doctor Base three miles outside Broken Hill. In the studio a man was transmitting telegrams and messages over the wireless network to Station people. At the conclusion of the session he did an informal interview with us for their benefit. They, in turn, asked us questions and wished us luck. We even spoke to one property up in Queensland near Cloncurry. I wanted to talk to a Station which had 8WL (my initials) as its call sign but they couldn't be contacted.

Back in Broken Hill we caught a bus to the Zinc Corporation. Broken Hill Proprietary had opened its silver and lead smelting works in 1886 and it was now an immense undertaking where huge mines were gouging out the world's largest silver-lead-zinc lode. We were told all about the process before visiting the crushing station, seeing the flotation process and finally the drying of the concentrates which were then transported to Port Pirie in South Australia. We saw the plate shop, the machine shop and foundry and then the handsome playing fields and courts, the indoor swimming pool and modern cafeteria. I asked about industrial disputes and was told there had been virtually none. The men didn't work under

Arbitration Awards. They settled differences by conferences between the owners and the workers.

That afternoon Shirl had a showdown with the CWA woman. The latter had come in again and opened fire with a remark about our abusing the room.

Shirl said fiercely, 'What have we done *now*!'

Apparently the woman had come to the room the night before and found Pete locked in. (It was she who had put him out.) Shirl reached the end of her patience.

'You just don't think of things from our point of view! You've been thinking of yourselves all the time! I hope the President isn't going to get into trouble because she did us a good turn. After all, your motto is: *I will be friend to all, the foe, the friendless.*'

That stumped her! The CWA's illuminated Promise was always framed on the wall of each hall and we knew it by heart. Shirl and I reflected later that if you stand up to bullies they deflate! Later on, the woman and a friend came to the room. They were both as sweet as pie and we actually sold them copies of the Barossa Cook Book!

We heard about another Race Meeting at Kimberley and went with a bus load of people. Paddy ('the Roarer') Newell, the bookmaker, was an audible member of the party. He was a funny man, loud-voiced, bluff and hearty. There was a full load of people so our gear and Pete were on top. It was just as well we'd left our bikes in Mildura. Soon we were bumping over the rough Mildura road. The dust began to seep in and I was glad I hadn't washed my hair. I did my wool rug as we bumped along and listened to the ribald chatter of Paddy and the other bookies. Most of the men soon needed the lavatory and they were all looking uneasy and checking their watches, hazarding guesses as to our probable time of arrival. After completely exhausting the subject, they would start on another topic. Then a plaintive voice would pipe up, 'Guess we've only got another fifty to go, don't you think?'

'Hell no! We've only done another ten. We're not doing more than twenty miles an hour.'

'Twenty! Don't be silly! We're doing thirty at least.' And so on.

Shirl and I were sitting on the back seat and getting all the bumps, bouncing six inches in the air sometimes. Suddenly I hit a hard object and crumpled up on Shirl's lap with a pain in my forehead and neck. I must have struck my forehead on the roof and my chin had scraped the metal end of the luggage rack. There was a nasty graze under my chin which hurt a lot and a bump over my left eye. I was the only casualty and everyone was very sympathetic. I felt miserable.

We arrived at the race course at 11.30am, to the relief of the men who made a speedy exodus. The course was similar to that at Oak Park, very rustic with a bough shelter, a secretary's office and tote, a bar, a tea stall and lavatories. It was extremely hot and we were glad to be wearing shorts although all the other women were in dresses. They were very friendly though and didn't ostracize us. We were asked to join one family for lunch and accepted gratefully. We had no food with us and had expected to buy stuff there. There was a splendid spread of cold chicken, ham and corned beef, cold pasties, hard-boiled eggs, bread and butter, lettuce and celery. Tarts and apple slice followed.

It was an ideal day, hot and cloudless with no wind. We discovered that the women always wore evening frocks to the dance so we hung ours out on a tree. (As we had needed evening dresses in Cairns and at the two previous picnic race meetings, we had asked our mothers to post us practical cotton long dresses.)

We had been discreetly selling pamphlets all afternoon and at one stage sold one to a jockey at the saddling enclosure. He put it in his skull cap and I said, 'That will be a lucky talisman to bear you to victory.'

'I hope so,' he said wryly.

'What are you riding?'

'Brownie,' he said.

'Good, we'll back it. Is it any good?'

'No, I don't think so,' he said.

We mingled with the crowd seeking hot tips and placed some modest bets of a shilling. While waiting for the horses to get away I suddenly remembered poor Brownie. Well, of course, she romped home. We were mad! We rushed up to the excited jockey and congratulated him.

After tea we climbed onto a truck that was going to the woolshed where the dance was to be held. It was plunged in darkness and men were running around fixing things. I felt dreadfully tired with a pounding headache so I lay down on the back seat of a car and slept until wakened by the start of the dance. We looked for our gear and found it on a truck half a mile away then entered the ladies' dressing room at the back of the hall. It had four beds in it, basins and mirrors. The walls were made of hessian and the floor was covered with it. We had a wash and donned our evening dresses. I had taken an aspirin and now felt very bright. The dance was in full swing and most of the men were merry, having been drinking all the afternoon. When we emerged we were besieged by men and had to book dances three in advance. While I was dancing with a pleasant young man, his friend came up behind him and playfully dealt him a blow on the neck which, however, served to crash our heads together. I got the impact on my nose and my head swam. The pain was intense and I asked my partner to lead me out. I sat on the steps outside and wept. Was I in the wars! My whole face was sore, one way or another.

Supper was served and I rallied! Savoury slices of sausage with gherkins and onions were devoured then plates and plates of cakes and sponges. I felt rather tired between midnight and 2am so after each dance I'd dash to the dressing room and lie down for five minutes until the next dance. Little Pete was trying to sleep on one of the beds too! I managed to keep fairly fresh and indeed felt better as the morning progressed. Outside the shed was a big fire where the billies were being boiled and sometimes we'd join the folk sitting round it, singing and telling stories. Paddy the Roarer was well to the fore doing the jig up and down by himself, still in his grey dustcoat and hat! Then he disappeared to sleep somewhere. All the cars and trucks outside had someone in them – drunks, tired dancers or lovers. At about 4am we had a second supper and then I took my aching head to bed.

-oOo-

Two days later we were back in Mildura and collected a huge consignment of pamphlets. I had gone to see one of the kind families who had befriended us and was chatting to them when Shirl dashed up, white of face, and shrieked: 'Quickly! The dog catcher's got Pete and won't give him back to me!'

I raced down the street with her and saw a grim-looking man tying a rope to Pete's collar and dragging him off with another dog. Pete wasn't at all bothered as the other dog was a co-operative bitch and he was intrigued! We panicked.

'You can't take Pete. He's our dog'

'He shouldn't be wandering around then!'

'He isn't, he's with us!'

'Well, he ought to be on a leash!'

'How can he be when we're riding bikes?'

'Well, you should leave him at home!'

'We haven't got a home!'

He dragged the hounds off to the City Council and we rushed and found a policeman. We were actually scared we'd incur a mighty fine for not having Pete registered. We'd originally had him registered in Queensland but as Mildura was our first Victorian town, we hadn't had time to see to it here. The policeman interceded for us and begged for mercy so the dog catcher released Pete on payment of 2/6d and we took him home.

Now the way was clear, heading south-east to Melbourne and home. We travelled through Ouyen to Swan Hill, still zigzagging to see as much of our home State as possible.

We dutifully went along to the Police Station to register Ruby. We were there for two hours and had a terrific tussle. A brute of an Inspector wouldn't authorise it. He refused Shirl permission for a pistol licence and wanted her to sign it away in order for it to be confiscated. She refused. She said she'd apply direct to Russell Street, the police headquarters in Melbourne. If they refused, then she'd send the gun to a friend in New Guinea. When the police confiscate a gun they don't compensate the owner. Her refusal put them on a spot as the only other course left to them was to prosecute her for having an illegal weapon. She finally cajoled them to wait for a couple of weeks before they started proceedings.

We left then for Kerang and Cohuna, a large town with a beautiful deep-flowing canal flanked with rushes and waterweeds down one side of the main street. My eyes were inflamed from the dusty road so I bathed them in the cool water. On the other side of the canal was Gunbower Creek, wide and deep with ghostly dead trees standing in it. In fact, a huge forest of these grimly beautiful trees stood rooted in swamp. I thought of *Chloe*, Song of the Swamp, one of my favourite songs. The place teemed with bird life and was a sanctuary.

Echuca was the only town we had visited twice. (We went there for a weekend break from the cannery at Kyabram two and half years earlier.) Billed at the theatre was *When the Kellys rode*. We thought it would be a sneak preview of the Harry Watt film which had just been made at Benalla so went to see it. Alas, it was the old original film probably made in the thirties and was hilarious. It was terribly dramatic with eye-rollings and arm-flingings and every action exaggerated like Pearl White. Very exciting too, as good as an American Western. Troopers and bushrangers were galloping around madly even though the sound track was the *Light Cavalry Overture*. The location being country the audience knew, there were lots of ejaculations such as 'The Murray's pretty low there!' as horses were being walked across it, and 'Gee! Strathbogie to Jerilderie in four hours! How'd yer be!'

Silver's Circus was in town! This was the circus we had seen two years earlier in Southport, Queensland. It was visiting Victoria for the first time. The acts were as good as ever and the performers were glad to see us again although the Russian bareback rider who had tried to teach Shirl some equestrian tricks was on holiday in Tasmania. (He was actually a Tasmanian!) We mentioned to one of the women that we had seen their advance agent in Kerang earlier in the week. He'd been with a gaudily-dressed woman and we were wondering if he were married. He was the attractive young man we'd met in Grafton two years before who had taught us to bow in the circus manner, bending gracefully like trees and using our hands to acknowledge the applause.

'Oh yes, that's his wife and he has two children, one about to start school.'

Shirl was outraged. He had wanted her to marry him and learn to do a trapeze act together. It was a good line anyway!

We had a phenomenal success in Bendigo. I had thought of it as a very conservative city and assumed it would be a hard nut to crack but we made the front page of the newspaper for five days running and there were other mentions and photos. We made one stage appearance and had some radio interviews. Dance Committees sought us to make appearances at their functions. Shirl heard from the Commissioner of Police refusing her a permit for her revolver but enabling her to dispose of it when she returned to Melbourne.

Our days were now fully occupied with business, giving our story to newspapers, seeking advertisers, selling books and pamphlets, giving talks to youth clubs, schools and churches. Victoria's towns and cities were more numerous than those in other States and a big city would necessitate our spending a week methodically covering all the shops. We were perpetually tired. After a busy day we still had to write letters and diary, thank you notes to people who had given us hospitality and advertising blurbs for our sponsors. We never got to bed before midnight, often after, so had to sleep in the next morning to get enough rest.

We entered a café one day but the owner was out. As we were leaving an old bearded man came in. He was the image of Edward VII but clad in a green shirt, old trousers and a well-worn hat. His beard was silver and his cheeks unshaven. His eyes were slightly red with the lids turning out. He asked had we had our dinner and if not to have some with him. We demurred but he pressed us. He had recognized us and said to himself: 'I'll go over and pay for the girls' tucker.'

We had steak followed by jelly and icecream while he talked about his life. He was 84 and had been a miner all his life. He came to Bendigo during the Gold Rush and struck it rich. He had been prospecting up in the Gulf Country (Croydon and Cloncurry) in the 19th century and made a seven-month trek to Western Australia 'following the ridge'. He was about to open another show and expected to make £1,000 a week. When he was thirty-seven he married an English girl, had ten children and now had a tribe of 'greats'. He was Mr. Johns and was caretaker of the Bendigo racecourse.

We drove to Castlemaine on a truck chassis! There was only the cabin connected to two wheels half way back and another pair of wheels right at the back. The axles were connected with the cabin by a long plank. Somehow we piled the bikes on and crouched on a small area of flooring. On arrival we went to the Methodist parsonage and met the Reverend and Mrs. Arnold. They said the hall would be in continual use for the next few days but invited us to use their spare room. It transpired that Mrs. Arnold was the niece of Ernie Old, the veteran cyclist whom we'd met in Charters Towers, and both she and her husband had lived in Geelong and knew my father. Mr. Arnold told us stories of his mission work in Papua with interesting accounts of black magic when the natives would deliberately cause sickness and even death.

Some kind people were driving us around the town showing us the sights. Pete was standing on the back seat next to me, his forepaws on the front seat, his tail erect as a mast as usual. Just under his anus was lying an inch-long white torpedo-shaped object. I looked at it, puzzled, then it made a slight movement. My gorge rose and I drew Shirl's attention to it.

'Quick! Remove it, it's alive!' I whispered. 'It's a platyhel, a flat worm!'

She looked horrified but, her scientific interest aroused, tore off a piece of paper, removed the object and placed the little twist of paper in her bag for further examination later. We tried to carry on an intelligent conversation with our hosts but five minutes later I looked at Pete again and saw another thing half out. My stomach squirmed and I gestured weakly to Shirl. The object came right out and, as Pete moved, it fell onto the seat. Shirl captured it and stowed it away. We were convulsed with horror and mirth and couldn't control our crimson faces. We managed to keep saying 'Yes…no…Ah…er…' I felt my skin crawling and longed to wash my hands free of contamination.

A little later the lady in front asked, 'Aren't you ever scared of catching something from Peter?'

This was the first time anyone had ever asked us that and today of all days!

'Oh no!' I said. 'Pete's perfectly healthy. Why, what could we catch?'

'Hydatids,' she replied. 'I'd never go near a dog or handle one.'

She then proceeded to tell us of a young girl who became infected after drinking from her puppy's saucer of milk. She became very sickly and delicate. We exchanged horrified glances. We always gave Pete his milk or icecream in our pannikins.

Back in town we rushed to a chemist and asked what to do. He gave us some capsules to give Pete and advised a dose of Epsom's Salts two hours later. He said the object would be part of a tapeworm. It didn't look like the tapeworm segments we'd studied at school. Shirl took out the specimen and it had changed completely. It had shrunk to a small square, more like a proglottis. It was very puzzling. We resolved to go to the next big hospital and have a test.

Once home we started the daunting task of giving Pete the medicine. After vainly hiding the capsule in his meat, Shirl managed to get one down by pushing it down his throat and clamping his jaws shut.

Passing through Clunes next day (my brother Phil had been a teacher at the Higher Elementary School there) we reached Ballarat and went straight to the hospital to have a test for hydatids. This involved two injections in the forearm, one of saline as a control and the other a Casone test. We waited for half an hour but neither of us had any reaction so we were allowed to go.

We were now in the heartland of Victoria's goldfields. Just on a century earlier gold had been discovered at Clunes, closely followed by the discovery that the field extended to Ballarat. Word went out that gold was available to any who had the tools to dig! Unlike the alluvial gold found in New South Wales, Ballarat gold was mostly embedded in a stratum of grey clay beneath the surface. It was not unknown for a digger to obtain eight pounds of gold in a day. Some found gold nuggets on the surface. When another field was discovered at Bendigo the towns of Melbourne and Geelong emptied of men. Ships in the harbour were deserted. Cottages were empty, business was at a standstill and even schools were closed. In one wet month the yield from the Victorian fields was ten tons!

Adventurers from all over the world landed in Australia in tens of thousands. Victoria's population doubled. New immigrants were warned that they would need great stamina. They must be prepared to work like a navvy, live in a 'gunyah' made of sticks and leaves, work under a burning sun and put up with flies during the day and fleas and mosquitoes at night.

It was hard to reconcile these images with the beautiful city which Ballarat had become in the 20th Century. Wide streets threaded rows of elegant buildings and plentiful planting of trees and flowers softened its outlines. We took Pete for a run around Lake Wendouree which was flanked by the Botanic Gardens. Beds of massed blooms gladdened the eye in all directions. Little Pete was more interested in chasing squirrels. Neither he nor we had ever seen them before. I enjoyed the sculptured busts of Australian Prime Ministers which formed an avenue through the gardens. Unfortunately the weather was cold and bleak with drizzling rain. I was not optimistic about an improvement as in Melbourne we rarely had any hot summer weather till after Christmas.

Although we were now just over a hundred miles from Melbourne we realized it would be silly to arrive during Christmas week as our publicity would fall flat. When all the holiday fever was over and news scarce we would burst in. Consequently we decided to detour to Ararat and then head south to Warrnambool in order to make a leisurely journey home through Terang, Camperdown and Geelong.

On leaving Ballarat we were caught in further rain and were sheltering under the Arch of Victory when a big animal transport truck stopped. The back cages were filthy with sheeps' mess but we put our bikes there, shut Pete in the dog box and crammed into the cabin. We reached Ararat in an hour and a half and liked it from the beginning. We were just setting off to look for a home when a Salvation Army man, Captain Rawlins, stopped and asked if we had anywhere to stay. He offered us mattresses and blankets in the hall of the Citadel. We were glad of the blankets as it was a bitterly cold night.

The obliging editor of the *Advertiser* newspaper offered to run off some personalized Christmas cards free. They featured our photograph and a seasonal message.

Now we were in the Western District and passing through towns whose names were familiar to me, mainly because of my brother Geoff who had been a teacher at rural schools throughout this area. I knew of Mortlake, Dunkeld and Portland. I had been born in Hamilton when my father was a District Inspector of Schools there. Warrnambool, an old whaling town was disappointing because of the weather. There was a terrific western gale, cold and strong, with lowering clouds. At our theatre appearance a woman interviewed us. We were apprehensive as, although women were fine on a radio programme, a stage appearance needed a more forceful personality. As usual, Peter saved the day. He knew what to expect by now. As soon as he heard applause he would run on and start rapidly chasing his tail to the vast enjoyment of the audience. On this occasion he slipped and fell during his gyrations and it brought the house down. A men's wear shop in the town had given us a miniature trilby hat which was used in their window dressing. I thought it would be wonderful for Pete!

We rode to Shelly Beach which was very rugged and rocky but the wind was whipping sand into my eyes and hair. We met a crowd of boys from the Legacy Club camp and arranged to give them a talk. These boys had come from all parts of the State. Some had never seen the sea, a film, a shower or a merry-go-round. They were pleasant kids and listened attentively to our talk and played with Pete. There was an embarrassing moment when Pete lay on the floor in front of everyone and started jerking. I had always been scared he'd do it on stage some night!

We made an appearance at a large sports meeting and did some discreet pamphlet selling, making £2 each. Next day, in the main street, Shirl was embarrassed when a young man from the chemist shop said, 'Well, I must say I'm disappointed in you. I didn't think you'd be hawking things around the town!'

In Colac we met some of the Apex Club men whom we'd encountered at the Bridgetown Convention in Western Australia. They threw a party for us and showed amusing films of the Bridgetown visit.

I had been looking forward to reaching Lorne. That was where Shirl and I and our other friend Sharpey had ridden on our first long bike trip in 1942. My brother Pete and I had also played music at the prestigious Cumberland Hotel over the Christmas and New Year period at the beginning of 1946. Lorne was idyllic. Built on low, wooded hills around Louttit Bay it had the indescribable atmosphere of a popular beach resort. White surf crashed into the curving sandy beach so it was a favourite resort for surfers and its lively social life attracted the young. Behind the town was bush country ideal for horse-riding. Further west along the Great Ocean Road were the superb Otway Ranges which impressed Kipling. I couldn't wait to see Lorne again.

On a very cold morning we rode into a dank and limp-looking Lorne. How disappointing! Even the holiday-makers seemed subdued by the weather. We were camped in a church hall when there was a knock at the outside door and Shirl came back and said, 'There's a funny little man with a beard asking for you!' Who could it be? I knew no one in Lorne. I went to the door and there was Archie (A.D.) Colquhoun, the famous artist of the Meldrum School, who had painted my portrait when I was fourteen. How exciting! He looked older and seemed to have shrunk since I last saw him but I asked him in and we had a lively conversation. He and his wife Amalie, also a notable painter, were holidaying in the resort.

The sun came out as we left Lorne and rode along the magnificent Great Ocean Road which wound in and out of folds of hills. At each turn we caught glimpses of ultramarine Southern Ocean. Flecked with snowy white horses or with long rollers of surf in the bays, it always reminded me of the Reckitt's Blue slogan, 'Out of the blue comes the whitest wash.'

Passing through pretty Airey's Inlet we came to Anglesea where one can see the most astonishing and unique sight. On the smooth rolling fairways of the golf course there are hundreds of kangaroos which do a good job keeping

the grass cropped. As golf balls whistle past them they don't bat an eyelid.
Those slumbering on the greens have to be gently eased out of the way!

Now I was on familiar ground. As a child I had lived for several
years in Geelong, the rich wool town on Port Phillip Bay. I excitedly rode
into the city and found I could remember the layout of the streets. I revisited

the house where I used to live and found some of our erstwhile neighbours.
From there it was but forty-five miles to Melbourne but we stayed in
Werribee the night before our arrival so that we could wash and iron our
clothes and wash our hair ready for the triumphant return to Melbourne.

Almost three years to the day since we set off to Tasmania, we left
Werribee on the last 27 miles. It was quite hot and windy so when we heard
the familiar roar of an approaching truck we hailed it from force of habit. We
climbed up on the back with our gear and set off, the refreshing wind
blowing our hair. Idly I watched an approaching truck coming from
Melbourne and as we passed saw an elderly man with a bike on the back.

'It's Ernie Old!' I yelled and hammered on the roof of the cabin. 'He
must have come out to meet us!'

Ernie's truck had also stopped and was backing up. He and his bike transferred to our truck and together we travelled up the long uninteresting road to Flemington on the outskirts of Melbourne. We all climbed down, Shirl and I strapped on our haversacks and rode into the city accompanied by Ernie. We reached Elizabeth Street, full of excitement at the prospect of the grand reception awaiting us. Shirl had to ride carefully with Pete on the back but I impatiently increased my speed down to Bourke Street. There, at the beautiful old General Post Office with its clock tower, was a large crowd spilling over the footpath onto the road. Our mothers were there and amidst hugs and tears I was pestered by numerous reporters. Shirl and Pete arrived, causing a sensation, and Ernie Old joined the group. Photographers too and a Cinesound newsreel cameraman, one we had met at Kuranda in Queensland, added to the noise and confusion. Stan Hughes from my radio station 3KZ was describing the scene.

'And what are you going to do next?' he asked.

'Have a bath!' I said. Everyone laughed.

What *were* we going to do next? Shirl already had a passage booked on a ship to England. I wanted to go to Borneo to visit my brother Pete on the oilfields in Brunei. First, though, I wanted to have a good dose of home comforts in a family environment and I wanted to spend a lot of time with Keith.

Little Pete now had to divide his time between the Duncans and my family. He was ceremoniously made a member of the Tailwaggers' Club and for a while was the most famous dog in Australia. He had to get used to other food now as no longer did icecream appear on his menu.

I loved being back in beautiful Melbourne. Fêted by friends and family, enticed by a soft bed and three meals a day, I relaxed into a lotus-eating life style.

In March Keith proposed, we became engaged and Borneo dwindled to a speck on the horizon. I wrote to Pete and said I was enjoying being at home after three years of travelling and perhaps I'd come and see him next year. Back came a furious letter. He said that everything was arranged for my visit, accommodation organized and he'd never forgive me if I didn't come. My family added its weight to his persuasion (they didn't think I was really sure about Keith) and so, on the 28th May I left Melbourne and crossed the continent on the Transcontinental train to Perth, the longest stretch of straight railway in the world, which crossed the treeless gibber plain we had missed by following the coastal road.

At Perth, I found my ship, the S.S. *Charon*, which was to take me to Singapore. In Borneo my life was to change dramatically and my horizons extend far wider than anyone could have foreseen.

For the next four years Wendy lived in Brunei and the Crown Colony of North Borneo (now Sabah, East Malaysia). She has written about her exotic experiences in *The Lingering Eye – Recollections of North Borneo.*

Her subsequent life in countries around the world (Hong Kong, Bahrain, Jamaica) is described in the fascinating *A Mem's Memoirs – Colonial Swan Songs.*

Shirley never lost her wanderlust and although she eventually settled in Washington D.C., she continued to travel the world.

Peter had to forgo the delights of the open road and became a suburban dog in Melbourne.

GLOSSARY

BILLY	A tin can in which water is boiled over a camp fire or in which cooking is done. Also billy-can.
BRUMBY	A wild horse.
DAMPER	Bread baked in the ashes of a fire.
DIGGER	Originally a gold miner. An Australian soldier in World War 1.
DILLY BAG	A small bag used to carry things. Originally an aborigine's string bag.
DINK	To give a person a lift on a bicycle.
DUNNY	Lavatory.
GIBBER	A stone. Gibber plain or desert - an inland area covered with stones.
GIN	An aboriginal woman.
GOOD ON YOU!	A term of approval.
JACKEROO	A station hand.
LARRIKIN	A boisterous youth or hoodlum.
LUBRA	A young aboriginal woman.
NEVER NEVER	Remote areas in the far outback.
OUTBACK	The back-country. The bush in general.
SPRUIKER	Someone who calls out to attract customers to a sideshow.
SQUATTER	A large land-holder in the outback.
STATION	A squatter's property, sometimes vast in size.
STOCKMAN	A station worker who cares for animals, especially cattle.
SWAG	A rolled blanket which contains the swagman's personal effects.
THE WET	The rainy season in Australia's north from December to March.
TUCKER	Food. Also tuckerbag, tuckerbox.
TWO-UP	A gambling game in which two pennies are tossed.